THE OTHER FRIARS

THE CARMELITE, AUGUSTINIAN,
SACK AND PIED FRIARS
IN THE MIDDLE AGES

Monastic Orders

ISSN 1749-4974

Monastic houses – houses of monks, regular canons, nuns, and friars – were a familiar part of the medieval landscape in both urban and rural areas, and members of the religious orders played an important role in many aspects of medieval life. The volumes in this new series provide authoritative and accessible guides to the origins of each of these orders, to their expansion, and to their main characteristics.

Already Published

The Franciscans in the Middle Ages
Michael Robson

Forthcoming Volumes

The Benedictines
James Clark

The Canons Regular
Janet Burton

The Carthusians
Julian Luxford

The Other Friars

The Carmelite, Augustinian, Sack and Pied Friars in the Middle Ages

Frances Andrews

THE BOYDELL PRESS

First published 2006
The Boydell Press, Woodbridge

ISBN 1 84383 258 5

The Boydell Press is an imprint of Boydell & Brewer Ltd
PO Box 9, Woodbridge, Suffolk IP12 3DF, UK
and of Boydell & Brewer Inc.
Mt Hope Avenue, Rochester, NY 14620, USA
website: www.boydellandbrewer.com

A catalogue record for this book is available
from the British Library

This publication is printed on acid-free paper

Typeset in Garamond Premier Pro by Word and Page, Chester

Printed in Great Britain by
Athenaeum Press Ltd., Gateshead, Tyne & Wear

CONTENTS

ACKNOWLEDGEMENTS

I should like to begin by acknowledging the help of all those individuals who have been generous with time and information during the preparation of this volume. Particular thanks belong to Janet Burton, who first suggested that I contribute to this series and has been encouraging throughout the process of writing and production. I would also like to thank all those who read and commented on one or other section of the text: Cristina Andenna, Brenda Bolton, Christa Gardner von Teuffel, Machtelt Israëls, Andrew Jotischky and Kathryn Windslow. Others supplied essential references or specific expertise: Andrew Brown, Michael Brown, Giovanna Casagrande, Sally Dixon-Smith, Anthony Goodman, Bridget Heal, Ian Johnson, Julie Kerr, Rhiannon Purdie and Clive Sneddon. Some of these same people were kind enough to allow me to read their work ahead of publication, as were Louise Bourdua and Anne Dunlop. Information about seals was kindly provided by Irene Blasczyk and her colleagues, of the Gelders Archief in Arnhem, Dr Roger Lovatt, Archivist of Peterhouse, Cambridge, Dr Kaj van Vliet of the Utrecht Archief and Dr Josef Zwicker, Staatsarchivar Basel. I must also thank Patrick Zutshi for providing a very pleasant place to stay, sometimes at very short notice, to allow me to work in the Cambridge University Library. The University of St Andrews, the Humboldt Stiftung and The Harvard University Center for Italian Renaissance Studies at Villa i Tatti in Florence have also all provided me with the time and resources to complete this book. The library of Villa i Tatti in particular is a wonderful place to finish footnotes. Finally, I am enormously indebted to all those whose work is cited below. Without it this book could not have been written. I dedicate it to Louise, who long ago engaged my interest in friars of all sorts, and to the many students who have passed through my special subject course in St Andrews, asking interesting questions.

ABBREVIATIONS

AA	*Analecta Augustiniana* (Rome, 1905–)
Alonso	*Bullarium ordinis sancti Augustini, Regesta*, ed. C. Alonso, vols 1–4 (Rome, 1997–99)
Auvray	*Les Registres de Grégoire IX*, ed. L. Auvray, 3 vols (Paris, 1896–1910)
BC	*Bullarium Carmelitanum*, ed. E. Monsignani and J. A. Ximénez, 4 vols (Rome, 1715–68)
Berger	*Les Registres d'Innocent IV*, ed. E. Berger, 4 vols (Paris, 1884–1919)
Bourel	*Les Registres d'Alexandre IV*, ed. C. Bourel de la Roncière, 2 vols (Paris, 1902–59)
Digard	*Les Registres de Boniface VIII*, ed. G. Digard *et al.*, 4 vols (Paris, 1884–1939)
DIP	*Dizionario degli Istituti di Perfezione*, ed. G. Pelliccia and G. Rocca, 10 vols (Rome, 1962–2003)
Empoli	*Bullarium ordinis eremitarum sancti Augustini*, ed. L. Empoli (Rome, 1628)
Gay	*Les Registres de Nicolas III (1277–1280)*, ed. J. Gay (Paris, 1898–1904)
Jordan	*Les Registres de Clément IV (1265–1268)*, ed. É. Jordan (Paris, 1893–1912)
Langlois	*Les Registres de Nicolas IV*, ed. E. Langlois, 2 vols (Paris, 1886–93)
Potthast	A. Potthast, *Regesta pontificum Romanorum*, 2 vols (Graz, 1957)
Pressutti	*Regesta Honorii papae III*, ed. P. Pressutti, 2 vols (Rome, 1888–95)
Prou	*Les Registres d'Honorius IV*, ed. M. Prou (Paris, 1888)
Van Luijk, *Bullarium*	*Bullarium ordinis eremitarum sancti Augustini. Periodus formationis (1187–1256)*, comp. B. van Luijk (Würzburg, 1964)
VCH	*Victoria Histories of the Counties of England* (London, 1899–)

INTRODUCTION

Walking west from the Ponte Vecchio in Florence along the River Arno, several churches come into view on the left bank, in the Oltrarno. The first, its cupola just visible behind more modern buildings, is the great Renaissance temple and convent of Santo Spirito, still occupied by the Augustinian (Austin) friars. Beyond it is the complex of Santa Maria del Carmine, its Brancacci chapel housing luminous frescoes of St Peter. Behind Santo Spirito and invisible from the river stands the now deconsecrated church of Santa Monaca, a convent of Augustinian nuns founded in 1443. These churches were built to house communities of religious from some of the orders described in this book. Their disposition in Florence today, in the medieval suburb of the Oltrarno, serves as a visual reminder of the role of their communities in the life of the city. Their proximity mimics the similarities in their histories; it places them outside the central axis of urban life to the north of the river, marked at one end by the Dominicans (the Friars Preacher) at Santa Maria Novella and at the other by the Franciscans (or Friars Minor) at Santa Croce. To some extent this topography is a neat coincidence, the product of opportunism and accident, but it also underlines the secondary status of the first two orders to be examined in this book: the Carmelites and Augustinians. Historians of the Latin Church or of late-medieval religiosity, let alone those concerned with politics or war or economics, generally restrict references to the mendicants to the followers of Francis and Dominic, ignoring the other orders. My title, 'The Other Friars', reflects this reality. They were to be enormously successful, but throughout the period discussed here were always in the shadow of the original mendicants, the Franciscan and Dominican friars. Rarely did they acquire quite so many legacies from the faithful or send quite as many students to the universities. Yet the origins and particular identities of those discussed here are essential to the history of late-medieval religious practice. They demonstrate the power and flexibility of the mendicant ideal, as also its limitations; and by comparison with the orders discussed in part three of this book, this secondary status still counts as success. A General Council of the Latin Church, assembled at Lyons in the spring and early summer of 1274, decreed the end of the numerous mendicant orders that had appeared since 1215. The Franciscans and Dominicans were explicitly exempted. As we shall see, the Carmelites and Augustinians were able to obtain a stay of execution at the time and later won permanent immunity

1

from the effect of the decree. But the Friars of the Sack and the Pied Friars were subjected to its full force, destined to wither away over the following decades. The first of these, the Friars of the Sack, were flourishing in the years leading up to 1274, both numerically and in their involvement in the world of the universities. Why they were unable to withstand the effect of Lyons, unlike the smaller orders of Augustinian and Carmelite friars, is one of the issues to be explored in what follows.

Florence is a city of remarkable art, but the pattern of religious houses crowded on the periphery of urban space hinted at above is typical of the friars. By the end of the thirteenth century innumerable European cities had similar mendicant settlements on their fringes or edging towards their centres. What brought them was the availability of land and proximity to growing urban populations, providing not only an audience for their pastoral message but also alms and pious donations to support their material needs. In London, the convent of Austin Friars with extensive gardens stood at the northern edge of the city on Bradstreet, not far from the Sack Friars in Coleman Street, east of the Guildhall, while the Carmelites or Whitefriars were located outside the city walls, on the river south of Fleet Street, adding to the ring of major religious foundations outside the walls.[1] At the other end of Europe, in Barcelona, the Carmelites settled in the suburbs to the west of the city centre and the cathedral, while the Augustinians established themselves away to the north-east, close to the Friars of the Sack.[2]

All the orders discussed here emerged in a period of experimentation with forms of the religious life and in response to a more complex and articulated society, centred on the urban world.[3] What follows deals with orders which began as 'mendicants', living by begging, not those whose members were (and are) often referred to as 'friars' (from *fratres*, 'brothers') such as the Trinitarians and Servites, but who did not beg.[4] The Pied Friars are included despite a lack or records because from what we can tell of their style of life and reputation for poverty, they appear to have been mendicants. New evidence may yet show this to be a false assumption. As with many institutions, new and old, a combination of enthusiasm, controversy and change marked the histories

[1] See C. Barron, 'The Later Middle Ages 1270–1520', along with the excellent maps, in *The City of London from Prehistoric Times to c. 1520*, ed. M. Lobel, The British Atlas of Historic Towns, III (Oxford, 1989), pp. 42–56.

[2] A convenient map of the religious houses in medieval Barcelona is provided by N. Jaspert, *Stift und Stadt. Das Heiliggrabpriorat von Santa Anna und das Regularkanonikerstift Santa Eulalia del Camp im mittelalterlichen Barcelona (1145–1423)* (Berlin, 1996), p. 383.

[3] D. Knowles, *From Pachomius to Ignatius: A Study in the Constitutional History of the Religious Orders* (Oxford, 1966), p. 16.

[4] Franco dal Pino has provided numerous comprehensive studies of the Servites, most importantly, *I frati Servi di S. Maria: dalle origini all'approvazione (1233 ca. – 1304)*, 2 vols (Louvain, 1972). On the Trinitarians, see *Tolleranza e convivenza tra Cristianità ed Islam. L'Ordine dei Trinitari (1198 –1998)*, Atti del Convegno di Studi per gli ottocento anni di fondazione, Lecce 1998, ed. M. Forcina and N. Rocca (Lecce, 1999).

of the orders under consideration. They encountered similar problems and opportunities and faced the same predictable comparison with the larger mendicant orders, whose paradigm inevitably lies behind this book, as it did the orders it describes. Unlike the Dominicans and Franciscans, however, they mostly lacked compelling (or at least compelling documentation for) saintly founders or leaders of the first generation. It was a deficiency which undoubtedly influenced their early development and later sense of identity.

The Carmelites first appeared in the Holy Land as an informal gathering of hermits living on Mount Carmel, near the important northern port city of Acre (Akko) and modern-day Haifa. While their association with a site of special holiness in the East initially provided easy definition, by the mid-thirteenth century they had established themselves in the Latin West as an order of itinerant mendicant friars. The Austin Friars also grew out of communities of hermits, in this case those to be found in the hills of central and northern Italy, and were formed into a centralised mendicant order over two decades in the mid-thirteenth century. Both followed the Franciscans and Dominicans into the urban context. The origins of the Sack and Pied Friars are less easy to determine, but may equally have lain in withdrawal and solitude, before turning to the cities. Despite these disparate roots, their organisation, membership and emphasis on the apostolate developed as if in symphony, guided by the papal Curia and by similar economic and political pressures and dilemmas. All faced both support and hostility from the secular clergy as they began to provide pastoral care and to share in the oblations and legacies of the laity. They were also deeply involved in the world of learning. Augustinians were perhaps second only to the Dominicans in their importance to the late-medieval universities. Both Augustinian and Carmelite friars contributed to the pressing theological debates of the era. The fragmentary evidence for the Sack Friars suggests that they too soon engaged in study; too little is now known to be able to say anything about the learning of the Pied Friars.

During the fourteenth and fifteenth centuries, when the Pied and Sack Friars had become no more than memory, the two surviving orders saw substantial modifications in direction and purpose. They witnessed the formation of new gatherings of 'observant' religious, and the increased inclusion of women. Then in the sixteenth century both underwent more dramatic change. They lost houses in areas which took up the Protestant reform but also saw the multiplication of new congregations; indeed for both Carmelites and Augustinians the sixteenth century was a period of renewal almost as creative as the expansion of the 1200s. This placed them in the forefront of spiritual developments in the Tridentine world, a subject deserving detailed exploration, but one for another book.

What follows is an attempt to explain how and why these orders assumed the forms they did in the course of the late Middle Ages, how these related to other religious orders and to the wider society in which they emerged. Wherever possible the British Isles play a central role in the discussion, but the Augustinian provinces in Britain did not achieve prominence in the history of their order. As the seat of the papacy and the land where the Augustinians originated, Italy will inevitably play a prominent role. So will Provence, where both the Sack and Pied Friars first took hold. The geographical scope and detail of this analysis are guided by the focus of the orders themselves, the survival of archives and the work of previous scholars: thus the English Carmelites are relatively well documented, while the German Augustinians are more extensively accessible than their Carmelite brothers, but to detail the history of individual friaries in Italy, France and much of Spain beyond Catalonia presents a more problematic picture, awaiting fuller analysis and investigation of the archives. No book of this length can do justice to the vast scholarship produced by and about the religious orders of late-medieval Europe, but wherever and whenever possible I have tried to present examples from across Latin Christendom. This sometimes means the reader has to follow as the text leaps and bounds across the physical and political borders of the medieval continent. I make no excuse, however, since in many cases the common experience of these groups (the object of this analysis) far outweighs the differences, and the friars themselves often made the journey.

By their nature, the surviving normative sources for these orders are prescriptive and generic. Where possible other evidence is invoked, but uncomfortably often the text which follows is a description of the theory, without being able to ascertain the practice: not all novice masters, for example, can have been of proven virtue, but that is what the Augustinian constitutions required and therefore it is mentioned here. I hope the reader will go away with a better idea of what these friars were trying to achieve and why, as well as the parameters within which they operated.

Chronological considerations as well as the parallels discussed above make it appropriate that the Carmelites and Augustinians should be treated together with the orders that failed after 1274. Since the primary aim of this series is, however, to produce accessible introductions to the medieval monastic and religious orders, each is dealt with in a separate section for ease of reference. Footnotes have been kept to a minimum, particularly for the two better-known orders, but guidelines for further reading are provided at the end of the volume. This structure means that some themes, such as the Council of Lyons, return to haunt the reader at several points: viewing it from the different perspectives of those who survived and those who succumbed may nonetheless help to explain what made the difference between success and failure in the late-medieval Church.

A note on spellings and money

I have used the simplest form of Latin spellings wherever possible, since the diphthong was only reintroduced in the Renaissance, and was not used by most of the authors cited here, even if inserted by their modern editors.

There is no attempt to compare monetary values: the shillings/*solidi*/*sous*, £ (i.e. pounds)/*lire*/*livres* of various cities and kingdoms are referred to in the currency of the original documents and secondary sources. What matters is a sense of scale, not the financial details.

PART ONE

The Carmelites

The Carmelites are best known as one of the mendicant orders which rose to prominence in the thirteenth century. By the 1290s contemporaries listed them alongside the Franciscans, Dominicans and Augustinians as one of the orders of friars whose mission lay in the urban world of the Latin West. Yet their origins were far removed from Europe. They took their name not from a charismatic leader, as did the followers of Francis or Dominic, but from Mount Carmel, a holy site overlooking the Mediterranean coast in the Latin Kingdom of Jerusalem, next to Haifa in modern Israel. From the fourth century, it had been identified as the mountain from which the prophet Elijah brought down fire on the men of King Ahaziah (II Kings 1). Defined by their attachment to this holy place, the first Carmelites were not itinerant like the friars, but instead were hermits pursuing lives of solitary contemplation. They never entirely forgot their eremitical roots, yet within decades of the approval of their first community, they were living in houses on the fringes of the great cities of the Latin West, preaching and sharing in the pastoral care of lay women and men. It was a transition which requires explanation.

CHAPTER ONE

Origins and Early History

The hermits on Mount Carmel

The origins of the Carmelites, as with so many medieval religious movements, are now obscure. The first western hermits on Mount Carmel wrote nothing that has survived, and the earliest document to name them can be dated only to the early thirteenth century. This records the request for a rule of life from a group of hermits which marks an already advanced stage in the development of their community. How long they had been together on the mountain is impossible to say. Earlier sources do, however, allow us to gain some idea of the life of twelfth-century Frankish hermits in the East. One such is the *De conversatione servorum Dei* of Gerard of Nazareth, bishop of Laodicea (Goncali, near Denizli in Turkey), *c.* 1140, which gives thumbnail sketches of men of standing who abandoned wealth and status to take up penitential lives of extreme deprivation in the places associated with the birth of Christianity. Eating irregularly, avoiding meat, practising self-flagellation and other bodily torments, they sought a personal experience of God. A Hungarian priest named Cosmas, whose existence is confirmed by other sources, lived as a hermit in a narrow cell on the walls of Jerusalem.[1] Others built themselves shelters as remote as possible from human contact. One man, named Henry, erected a hut on the Black Mountain near Antioch, went bare foot, or sometimes totally naked, and ate nothing that had been killed. Another prophetic fragment refers to 'those who, following the example of Elijah, chose the silence of solitude over the tumult of cities'.[2] Some adopted highly individualistic interpretations of the ascetic life, while others chose to pursue the eremitical life together with other men, as in the small cells on the Black Mountain or at Jubin or Machanath, which later developed into monasteries.

A contemporary of Gerard of Nazareth provides us with a fuller explanation of the ascetic life of hermits from a western perspective in the *Libellus*

[1] Cosmas is documented as witness to a charter in 1135. See B. Z. Kedar, 'Gerard of Nazareth: A Neglected Twelfth-Century Writer in the Latin East. A Contribution to the Intellectual and Monastic History of the Crusader States', *Dumbarton Oaks Papers* 37 (1983), 55–77 with an edition of the surviving excerpts. Addenda 2. Reprinted in B. Z. Kedar, *The Franks in the Levant, 11th to 14th Centuries* (Aldershot, 1993).

[2] Cited in A. Jotischky, *The Carmelites and Antiquity. Mendicants and Their Pasts in the Middle Ages* (Oxford, 2002), p. 142.

de diversis ordinibus qui sunt in Aecclesia, or 'Little Book on the different orders and professions in the Church', written *c.* 1140 in north-east France or the Low Countries.[3] Its anonymous author identifies hermits, 'who usually live alone or with few others', with the first men, who existed before Cain murdered Abel and built the first city. In this pre-urban world, he writes, they lived 'very innocently, having as yet no need to worry about food and drink as much as is done now, nor about the vanity of clothing . . .'. He also notes that they probably 'stayed in the same place, and even if men sometimes came to see them, they nevertheless gave little thought to buildings or clothes, food or money'. Adopting 'coarse clothing, rougher food and little drink', they attained glory through 'bodily exercise, fasts and vigils'. Remaining celibate and unencumbered by secular responsibilities, their time was instead spent 'meditating on the things which are of God'. In addition to this link with the lives of the first men, the models cited indicate the high status accorded the hermit life: Moses, Elijah, the hermits of the Egyptian desert, even Jesus, who withdrew 'alone into the mountain' and 'consecrated [the life of hermits] in Himself'. Like eremitically inspired monastic reforms of the Latin West at La Grande Chartreuse or Grandmont, western hermits in the Holy Land sought to relive the earliest forms of Old Testament asceticism within a community, receiving occasional visitors, but mostly lost in contemplation and devotion to God.

Apart from Gerard of Nazareth's text, the first external evidence for Christians who may have been hermits on Mount Carmel itself comes from the account of a Jewish writer known to historians as Benjamin of Tudela, who travelled in the area in the 1160s. He records that near the summit 'two Christians have built a place of worship near this site which they call saint Elijah. Christian monks inhabit some of the Carmel caves.'[4] Whether these were Latin or Greek Christians did not interest Benjamin and a second report by a Greek pilgrim also leaves us with problems of identification. In his account of the Holy Land (*c.* 1185), John Phokas describes the cave of Elijah and a long-lost monastery on the site:

> Some time ago a monk, a priest in rank, grey-haired, who came from Calabria, lived in this place after having a vision of the Prophet. He erected a wall around the conventual ruins, built a tower and a small church, and gathered about ten brothers. He still lives in that holy place.[5]

Both the Greek and Latin Churches flourished in Calabria in southern Italy and this monk-priest may have belonged to either tradition. By the

---

[3] *Libellus de diversis ordinibus qui sunt in Aecclesia*, ed. and trans. G. Constable and B. Smith (Oxford, 1972), pp. 5–17.

[4] S. Benjamin, *The World of Benjamin of Tudela. A Medieval Travelogue* (Madison, 1995), p. 161.

[5] John Phokas, 'Descriptio Terrae Sanctae', trans. A. Jotischky, *The Perfection of Solitude. Hermits and Monks in the Crusader States* (University Park, Pa., 1995), p. 120.

1160s there was an Orthodox monastery on the summit of Mount Carmel and their most recent modern historian, Andrew Jotischky, hypothesises the existence there of hybrid communities of Orthodox and Latin hermits, as were to be found elsewhere in the Holy Land.[6] Whatever the confessional identity of these hermits, they are as close as we shall come to a pre-Carmelite community on the Mountain itself.

These proto-Carmelites lived without any direct ecclesiastical supervision, following a vaguely regulated way of life based on the long-established practices of Christian ascetics going back to St Anthony and St Paul, the first hermit, in the deserts of Egypt. The formation of a monastic community, however, crystallised only in the early thirteenth century. Hermits identified as living at the 'spring of Elijah' on Mount Carmel petitioned Albert of Vercelli, the Latin patriarch of Jerusalem (1205–14), whose see, after the battle of Hattin in 1187 and the loss of the city, had transferred to the port of Acre and the strip of coast still remaining in Christian hands. From Albert they received a *vite formula* or simple rule for the religious life. The reasons for this petition are not given, but the community may have expanded following the fall of Jerusalem when hermits and other religious fled to the relative safety of the area around Acre.[7] It has recently been argued that the lack of evidence from Albert's patriarchate for any link with Mount Carmel may mean that the early rule was drawn from precepts ascribed to him after his death.[8] If so, the attribution was certainly apt. Albert's experience as an ecclesiastical legislator in the West, providing a rule for the canons of Biella in northern Italy and helping to negotiate a new rule for the Humiliati, was highly appropriate.[9] It was likely to encourage him to push the growing community of hermits on his doorstep to formalise their existence.

The first Rule

The first *vite formula* or outline of the Carmelite way of life does not survive, but has been reconstructed from later texts. It was addressed to 'B. and the other hermits who live under his obedience near the spring on Mount Carmel'.[10] This 'B.' is otherwise undocumented. Carmelite tradition, based on a history of the order written in the late fourteenth century by the Catalan

6   Jotischky, *The Perfection of Solitude*, p. 131.
7   Jotischky, *Carmelites and Antiquity*, p. 10.
8   Ibid., p. 124.
9   See F. Andrews, *The Early Humiliati* (Cambridge, 1999), pp. 83–92.
10 V. Mosca, *Alberto Patriarca di Gerusalemme. Tempo – Vita – Opera* (Rome, 1996), gives parallel transcripts of the *Vite formula* taken from F. Ribot, 'Libri decem de institutione et peculiaribus gestis religiosorum Carmelitarum', Paris, Bibliothèque de l'Arsenal, MS 779, fols 57v–59r, and of the *Regula bullata* from the *Constitutiones ordinis fratrum Beatissimae Virginis Mariae de Monte Carmelo* (Rome, 1971) which is in turn based on a transcription of Bibliotheca Apostolica Vaticana, Reg. Vat. 21, fols 465v–466r.

Felip Ribot (†1391), identified 'B.' as Brocardus, second prior general of the order, who succeeded a certain Prior Bertholdus in 1199. He may of course be the grey-haired priest referred to by John Phokas, but there is no way of substantiating this point.

The *vite formula* was issued in response to a request from the hermits themselves and explicitly conforms to their own proposal for a way of life. Although other rules are not overtly cited, their proposal reflects a combination of eremitical and communal or 'cenobitic' elements also found in the rules of other 'mixed' orders. Like the Carthusians, the brothers were to live in separate cells under the authority of a prior, not an abbot. They were to come together each day for Mass in an oratory built in the midst of the cells and each week for chapter meetings. The prior was to be chosen either by unanimous agreement or by the majority, the traditional 'greater and wiser part' familiar from the rule of Benedict. His cell was to stand next to the entrance so that he would be the first to encounter visitors. The brothers were to fill their time with solitary prayer and contemplation in or near their cells, both day and night. These first hermits numbered among them both clerics and laymen, the latter probably the majority. Those who could not read were instructed to say a prescribed number of *Pater nosters* (Our Fathers), allocated according to the Office and varying on feast days, a practice which echoes earlier Cistercian observance and, incidentally, also recalls arrangements agreed by Albert in 1201 for the lay third order of the Humiliati.[11]

In this initial rule, the Carmelite hermits were to have no personal possessions but were to share all property in common, following a long-established practice for the support of monasteries. Goods would be distributed by the prior or by his deputy according to the age and needs of individuals. The hermits were expected to fast from the feast of the Exaltation of the Cross (14 September) until Easter, except on Sundays, unless sickness persuaded them otherwise, 'because need has no law'. Meat was always to be avoided unless required for convalescence.

The attitudes to work and silence again reflect a combination of earlier monastic rules and what would have been familiar from biblical guidance. Invoked by the instruction of St Paul, 'He who will not work, neither shall he eat' (II Thessalonians 3:10), work was probably also intended (as ordained by the Benedictine rule) to forestall the dangers of idleness, so that 'the devil would always find them busy'. Similarly, the justification for silence based on biblical precept and twice repeated, 'the effect of righteousness is quietness' (Isaiah 32:17), was also found in the rule of the Humiliati. In practice silence was imposed from vespers in the evening to terce on the following day, unless interrupted by the prior for good reason. At all other times the brethren were to avoid talking too much because of the associated dangers of sin.

[11] Andrews, *The Early Humiliati*, pp. 104–5, 125.

This contemplative and penitential life focused on prayer, work and silence would not be easy to sustain. Yet the last instruction, perhaps taken from John Cassian's *Institutes*, 'use discretion, which is the guide of virtues', was both reassuring and a typical monastic proviso, allowing the superior to provide dispensations according to need. It is probably what made most monastic communities viable.

The hermits in the early thirteenth century

Jacques de Vitry, bishop of Acre (1216–27) and himself a close neighbour to Mount Carmel, included an enthusiastic mention of these hermits in his *Historia orientalis*, which points to a thriving community:

> After the example of that holy man and solitary the prophet Elijah, [they] led the hermit life on Mount Carmel, and especially on that part which is above the city of Porphyry, today called Haifa, near the spring called Elijah's Spring, not far from the monastery of the blessed virgin Margaret, in little cells like so many hives where, as bees of the Lord, they produced the honey of spiritual sweetness.[12]

There are very few other mentions of the Carmelites in the early thirteenth century and no named individuals can be identified before the 1240s, but a sequence of papal letters allows us to trace the evolution of the order over the intervening decades. Papal approval of the first *vite formula* came in 1226 from Pope Honorius III (1216–27).[13] In the interim, the Fourth Lateran Council, a general council of the Church, presided over in November 1215 by Pope Innocent III (1198–1216), had prohibited new rules. Concern about the proliferation of different forms of religious life resulted in *Ne nimia religionum diversitas,* constitution 13 of the council, which instructed all new petitioners to choose an existing text, lest diversity of religions 'should lead to serious confusion in the Church of God'. This decision was to encourage the Dominicans to turn to the rule of Augustine. For the Carmelites, it made the previous intervention of Albert of Jerusalem critical to their status when they came under attack together with other new orders in the later thirteenth century.

In 1229 Gregory IX granted the Carmelites the traditional monastic privilege of papal protection and allowed them to celebrate the Office during interdicts, when religious rites were forbidden to others.[14] In the same month

---

[12] Cited in *The Rule of St Albert: Latin Text Edited with an Introduction and English Translation*, H. Clarke and B. Edwards (Aylesford, 1973), p. 11. There has been no modern edition of the *Historia orientalis* since that of F. Moschus (Douai, 1597), but Jessalyn Bird is preparing one. See J. Bird, 'The *Historia Orientalis* of Jacques de Vitry: Visual and Written Commentaries as Evidence of a Text's Audience, Reception and Utilization', *Essays in Medieval Studies* 20 (2003), pp. 56–74, n. 1.

[13] *Ut vivendi normam*, 30 January 1226 (*BC* I, 1, Pressutti 5811).

[14] *Religionis vestrae*, 9 April 1229 (*BC* I, 4); on all these bulls see S. Teuws, 'De evolutione privilegiorum ordinis carmelitarum usque ad concilium tridentinum', *Carmelus* 6 (1959), pp. 153–223.

he reconfirmed their rule and also prohibited the ownership of any land or possessions save for a small quantity of livestock or poultry.[15] He insisted on absolute poverty on the basis that property ownership would entangle the brothers in the secular world: 'those who have washed their feet when they ascended the mountain to pray with the Lord', should not 'soil them again by descending from the observation post of contemplation'.

Gregory's interventions were designed to protect the contemplative solitude of the hermits. By contrast, a series of letters, issued in the 1240s by Pope Innocent IV (1243–54), documents a second substantial shift in their status, which also sowed the seeds of a new religious identity.

The move to the west and a new 'mendicant' role

In June 1245 Innocent issued *Quoniam ut ait*, urging all Christian faithful to assist the prior and hermits of Mount Carmel. Since, the letter reports, they had chosen to possess nothing in order to 'free body and soul for the service of the Lord', the brothers were dependent on alms, subsidies and subventions.[16] Uncertainty about their future in the Latin kingdom of Jerusalem, brought on by attacks which would eventually lead to the retaking of the Holy Land by the Mamluks, had encouraged some of the hermits to seek alternatives. A second papal letter, *Cum dilecti filii* records that 'frequent pagan incursions' had forced some to leave for 'various and remote regions' and the pope appealed to the Christian faithful to receive them kindly and provide them with appropriate places where they might safely render service to God.[17] What these letters reveal is the papal response to the first exodus of Carmelites from the East, as the security of the Holy Land became increasingly doubtful. An initial move to Cyprus in 1238, recorded by the Dominican Vincent de Beauvais,[18] had been followed by Carmelite settlements in Sicily (1240/42) and England (1242). Papal backing was indispensable to the establishment of communities in the West. Indeed a letter of July 1246, undoubtedly prompted by Carmelites petitioning the Curia, further underlines the problems of 'pagan incursions', forcing the hermits to travel beyond the seas, 'not without great affliction of spirit' and loss of 'the sweet-

---

[15] *Ex officii nostri*, 6 April 1229 (*BC* I, 3). Reissued by Innocent IV, 8 June 1245 (Berger 1311).

[16] *BC* I, 7; the bulls concerning this period are now re-edited in A. Staring, 'Four Bulls of Innocent IV: A Critical Edition', *Carmelus* 27 (1980), pp. 273–9, whose edition and dates are to be preferred. It should, however, be noted that bulls were frequently issued a number of times and also inserted in papal registers on different dates, so that the precise dating of papal correspondence is not consistent.

[17] 20 June 1245 (Staring, 'Four Bulls of Innocent IV', pp. 279–81; different dates in *BC* I, 11, Berger 3287).

[18] *Medieval Carmelite Heritage. Early Reflections on the Nature of the Order*, ed. A. Staring (Rome, 1989), p. 10. Vincent de Beauvais's *Speculum historiale* was written before 1247.

ness of contemplation'.[19] Innocent directs his bishops to be sympathetic to these new arrivals, allowing them to celebrate the Office and bury their dead, since their purpose was 'through apostolic favour to reach a state in which, with the help of God, they might have the joy of contributing to their own and their neighbours' salvation'. This letter already hints at a new outward-looking interest among the Carmelites. The same concern is reflected in modifications to their rule, opening the way to a more itinerant form of life focused on the mendicant ideals of the active life, the *vita activa*, in contrast to their by now long-standing *vita contemplativa*. Carmelite tradition dating from the late fourteenth century holds that these revisions were prompted by Simon Stock, an Englishman elected prior general at the first recorded general chapter, held in Aylesford (Kent) in 1247.[20] There is no external evidence for the existence of Simon as prior general and the Curial response, *Que honorem conditoris*, makes no mention of him.[21] The letter reveals a community now organised on contemporary lines. Two clerical proctors, the brothers Reynald and Peter, had been sent to the Curia, where amendment of the rule issued by Albert was entrusted to two Dominicans, Cardinal Hugh of Saint-Cher and William, bishop of Tartus on the Syrian coast. Presumably prompted by the Carmelite proctors themselves, these two friars instigated several apparently small changes to the rule, whose cumulative effect was substantial. The *vite formula* had made no reference to the location of any communities beyond the hermits living near Elijah's spring on Mount Carmel. By contrast the revised rule now envisaged both hermitages and other property, if this is what they were given. Without explicitly saying so, this sanctioned houses in less remote locations, including urban and suburban settlements and an important change in the understanding of the Carmelites' role.

Further innovations at this date strengthened the cenobitic character of the order and brought the Carmelites much closer to the practices of the most successful mendicant orders, the Franciscans and Dominicans. These included the introduction of a common refectory for meals, recitation of the Office in common by all those who could read (clerical and lay)[22] and, echoing Gregory IX's intervention of 1229, explicit mention of chastity and renunciation of ownership in their vows. Other modifications suggest dispensations to accommodate a more mobile community: a reduction in the overnight silence (now broken at prime, not terce), the use of donkeys or

---

[19] *Paganorum incursus*, 27 July 1246 (Staring, 'Four Bulls of Innocent IV', pp. 281–2; *BC* I, 9; Berger 3279).

[20] The Carmelites received a royal grant of 2 marks *ad pitantium* on the day of their chapter at Aylesford, *Medieval Carmelite Heritage*, pp. 289–90.

[21] 1 October 1247 (*BC* I, 10, pp. 8–11; Berger 3288) which confirms the letter from the two prelates of September 1247. See also M. H. Laurent, 'La Lettre "Quae honorem conditoris" (1ᵉʳ Octobre 1247). Note de diplomatique pontificale', *Ephemerides Carmeliticae* 2 (1948), pp. 5–16.

[22] Those who could not read were to say prescribed numbers of the Lord's Prayer (*Pater noster*).

mules as needed and the food allowed when travelling 'lest they be onerous guests'. This 'Innocentian' rule, the earliest now extant, was to remain largely unchanged until the 1430s.

In 1252 the pope strengthened his support for the Carmelites still further. The wariness of bishops about new and independent religious groups within their dioceses was a potential obstacle for many new orders. In *Ex parte dilectorum* Innocent instructed his bishops to protect the Carmelites and to allow them to build cells and churches in their cities and dioceses and to have cemeteries and bells for their own use.[23] This was the first papal document to use the juridical term *ordo* to describe the Carmelites and the rights it instituted were designed to establish the new arrivals as self-sufficient in both spiritual and administrative terms. A first reference to cities also suggests that the move from remote mountain seclusion to an urban context, and from the ideal of eremitic contemplation to emphasis on love of neighbour implicit in the mendicant ideal, was already well advanced. The Franciscans and Dominicans had mapped the route to this novel form of religious life, by physically living in the world rather than seeking escape from it. The scale of this transformation for the Carmelites, however, is perhaps most easily understood by reference once again to the twelfth-century *Libellus de diversis ordinibus*. This work describes the orders and professions of the Church in a continuum beginning, as we have seen, with the life of hermits. It ends at the opposite pole, with those 'who live among men of the world'. By the 1240s the Carmelites, whose origins lay in the solitude of the hermitage, were beginning to live within secular society, imitating their mendicant colleagues. The hermit ideal was to remain important (as it was to the Franciscans), but the emerging paradigm could hardly have been more different from its eastern origins.

Modern historians have not found it easy to agree on the reasons for, or the timing of, this shift. Andrew Jotischky sees *Que honorem conditoris* as simply turning the Carmelite hermits into mendicants.[24] Others consider that they became fully mendicant only in the 1320s once they shared in all the rights and privileges accorded to the Franciscans and Dominicans. Joachim Smet suggests that changes in the rule in 1247 were not premeditated, but that the hermits had simply found it impracticable to pursue their original way of life. Mendicancy according to this view was an accident, the result of their dependency on the faithful for support – and a problem that was later to lead to division.[25] Our sources do not allow for certainty about the Carmelites' intentions in the 1240s. Yet, as Jotischky points out, they had petitioned the Curia for modifications to their rule and must have been involved in the outcome. It is in any case likely that the Dominicans entrusted with revising

[23] 13 January 1252 (Staring, 'Four Bulls of Innocent IV', pp. 282–5; Berger 5563).

[24] Jotischky, *Carmelites and Antiquity*, p. 15.

[25] J. Smet, *The Carmelites: A History of the Brothers of Our Lady of Mount Carmel*, 2 vols (Barrington, Illinois, and Rome, 1975–6), I, pp. 11–12.

the rule saw a pastoral role close to their own as the most appropriate and most promising way forward.

The rights necessary to fulfil this pastoral role were quickly obtained over the following decade. In 1253 Innocent gave permission for the brothers to preach and hear confession.[26] Their reliance on the generosity of benefactors great and small was further acknowledged in a letter exempting them from the payment of tithes on their gardens and fields, because they had no possessions and lived on the alms of the faithful.[27] Finally, in 1261 they were permitted to allow the laity to frequent their churches, an essential element in pastoral care.[28]

The struggle for survival

The order expanded quickly between the 1240s and the 1270s but these modifications were not adopted without opposition. Some brethren escaped to the more traditional monastic life of the Cistercians, while others, presumably frustrated by the gradual pace of change, transferred to the Friars Minor. In 1270 Nicholas of Narbonne (1266–71), prior general of the Carmelites, wrote *Ignea sagitta*, the *Flaming Arrow*, an angry and grief-stricken appeal to his brethren to return to the old, pre-1247 rule and the hermit life of solitude and contemplation.[29] His regrets about the path taken by the order are presented in the form of a dialogue between Mother Religion and her son, Brother Nicholas. He contrasts the virtues of the hermitage with the dangers and worldly vanities of the city. Armed with the authority of his own knowledge of the order: 'I who have circulated the provinces and know the people', Nicholas is not afraid to criticise the motives and skill of his brethren in assuming pastoral roles. 'Tell me, where are the preachers among you who know the word of God or wish to preach in the proper way?' His judgement is severe: he considered that very few of the Carmelites were qualified to preach or hear confession or to advise the people as befitted those living in the cities.

The assessment of the prior general may well have been accurate, but *Ignea sagitta* fell on deaf ears, and indeed his work does not appear to have circulated or have been widely known before the modern period.[30] The years following the death of Nicholas saw the Carmelites entangled in disputes about the status of the new orders, which came to a head at the Second Council of

---

[26] *Devotionis augmentum*, 24 August 1253 (*BC* I, 17).

[27] *Sacrosancta Romana*, 24 August 1253 (*BC* I, 16, pp. 12–13).

[28] *Speciali gratia*, 8 March 1261 (*BC* I, 20). See also Teuws, 'De evolutione privilegiorum', pp. 173–5.

[29] 'Nicolai prioris generalis ordinis Carmelitarum Ignea sagitta', ed. A. Staring, *Carmelus* 9 (1962), pp. 237–307.

[30] See R. Copsey, 'The *Ignea sagitta* and Its Readership: A Re-evaluation', *Carmelus* 46 (1999), pp. 166–73, reprinted in *Carmel in Britain, Essays on the English Carmelite Province*, 2 vols, ed. P. Fitzgerald-Lombard (Rome, 1992), III, pp. 17–28, who argues on this basis against later divisions in the order.

Lyons in 1274. In the first decades following their arrival in the West, just as the Carmelites began to acquire a more 'mendicant' identity, criticism of this form of life had exploded at the University of Paris. Galvanised by the refusal of both the Dominican and Franciscan masters to participate in a teaching strike, William of St Amour, a secular master, had composed a polemical treatise (*c.* 1255) denouncing the mendicants as harbingers of the Last Days and accusing them of preaching without mission, since they were neither bishops nor parish priests. Innocent IV had been inclined to back the secular clergy, but his successor Pope Alexander IV (1254–61), formerly cardinal protector of the Franciscans, strongly supported the mendicants against the secular masters.[31] Although William and the other seculars were eventually forced to submit, William's scorn was to have a long afterlife in satire against all the mendicants, including of course the Carmelites.

At Lyons in 1274, criticism was still in the air when the council noted that many new orders, particularly of mendicants, had been established despite the prohibition on new rules issued in 1215. The original prohibition was now reiterated, and in constitution 23 it was decreed that orders of mendicants formed after 1215, even those with papal approval, were to be suppressed.[32] Whereas the Franciscans and Dominicans, undoubtedly aided by the lobbying of their superiors, achieved acceptance because of their 'evident utility to the universal Church', the Carmelites and Augustinian Hermit Friars obtained only temporary relief. The final conciliar statement affirmed that since they predated the prohibition of the Fourth Lateran Council, they might continue to exist in their current state 'until it should be otherwise arranged'. Stephan Kuttner demonstrated that at the time of the council, Pope Gregory X's attitude was still harsher than at the final formulation of this text. In an earlier draft of the decree, the existence of the two orders before the important date, the Fourth Lateran Council of 1215, was acknowledged not as fact but only as an allegation. Presumably the Carmelites and Augustinians had joined forces to counter this view, with at least partial success.[33]

Until this point the Carmelites had been expanding rapidly and had enjoyed constant papal support. Alexander IV had confirmed the 'Innocentian' rule (1256) and the order had accrued numerous privileges.[34] The opposition of members of the secular clergy to the mendicants and their privileged status must have stimulated the change of tack represented by the

---

[31] For more details, see below, pp. 90, 180.

[32] For the details, see below, pp. 207–8.

[33] S. Kuttner, 'Conciliar Law in the Making. The Lyonese Constitutions (1274) of Gregory X in a Manuscript at Washington', in *Miscellanea Pio Paschini. Studi di storia ecclesiastica*, Lateranum ns 15, 2 vols (Rome, 1949), II, pp. 39–47. Another version of events states that the Dominicans, Franciscans and Augustinians were to be preserved but does not name the Carmelites. See B. Roberg, *Das zweite Konzil von Lyon [1274]*, Konziliengeschichte, ed. W. Brandmüller (Paderborn, 1990), pp. 334–7.

[34] *Cum a nobis*, 3 February 1256 and 22 May 1262 (*BC* I, 22 and 45; Bourel 1091).

conciliar decree of 1274. Perhaps the pope's plans for the union of religious and military orders in general served to influence his views. Members of the more successful orders of mendicants feared competition, or considered that excessive numbers of friars would provoke still greater hostility from the secular Church. Richard Emery noted that it was the former Dominican master general Humbert of Romans (†1274) who first wrote of the 'multiplication of mendicants as an evil requiring correction'.[35] In preparation for the council Gregory X had asked senior churchmen to submit reports on the state of the Church with proposals for action. Humbert's reply baldly suggested that the mendicant orders should be reduced 'to the number that the world could comfortably support' (*tantum quantum potest mundus commode portare*). Bruno, bishop of Olmütz, who provided details on the Church in the German kingdom, complained that the pastoral activities of the Franciscans and Dominicans were prejudicial to the secular clergy.[36] Both views were to prove influential.

Other reasons for the vulnerability of the Carmelites had more to do with their own circumstances at this date. While Adrianus Staring has suggested that the Carmelites were left in suspense because they were not sufficiently mendicant,[37] it has more plausibly been argued that it was their lack of interest in education that made them vulnerable. Carmelite houses were already established in university towns by mid-century and there was, briefly, a Carmelite Latin school in Cologne. Until 1281, however, no university-trained members of the order can be documented.[38] Nicholas of Narbonne's assessment of his own order in *Ignea sagitta* would seem to endorse this view, although the Council made no mention of such issues. The simple lack of an authoritative Carmelite voice at the Curia during preparations for the council must have been crucial. By the 1250s both the main mendicant orders had powerful superiors advocating their cause, most notably Humbert himself and the newly appointed cardinal, Bonaventura di Bagnoregio, Franciscan minister general from 1257 to 1273, who died during the council and whose funeral the pope attended just days before the issuing of constitution 23. Both orders held their general chapters in Lyons that year.[39] General proctors were also resident at the Curia to represent their friars in cases referred to the apostolic see. By contrast, Ralph, the Carmelite prior general *c.* 1271–4, is a relatively obscure figure, and a Carmelite general proctor is only documented in 1318, when the general chapter appointed a Brother Raymund Durandi.

[35] R. W. Emery, 'The Second Council of Lyons and the Mendicant Orders', *Catholic Historical Review* 39 (1953), pp. 257–71, 259.

[36] See now Roberg, *Das zweite Konzil von Lyon*, pp. 95–101, 110, 126. For an example of the criticisms, see the text almost certainly by Gilbert of Tournai, 'Collectio de scandalis ecclesiae', ed. A. Stroick, *Archivum Franciscanum historicum* 24 (1931), pp. 33–62.

[37] 'Nicolai prioris generali ordinis carmelitarum Ignea sagitta', ed. Staring, p. 258.

[38] F.-B. Lickteig, *The German Carmelites at the Medieval Universities* (Rome, 1981), p. 26.

[39] Roberg, *Das zweite Konzil von Lyon*, p. 333.

At least two orders were indeed discontinued after 1274, the Pied Friars and the Sack Friars, despite the latter's large numbers.[40] The newly approved Servites and the Williamites were also threatened, though the former were later able successfully to argue that they were not strictly mendicants since they were not obliged to beg; both orders later acquired reconfirmation.[41] The threat of extinction must have felt very real. It is not easy to assess the immediate impact of this uncertainty on the daily lives of members of the Carmelite order or their recruitment of new brothers, but it spurred the superiors of the order into a campaign that probably began at the council but really took off in the following decades. Several elements can be identified. Lickteig has argued that the threat to their existence pushed them towards academic study as preparation for the apostolic life.[42] Lobbying for support was probably widespread. Pierre de Millau, prior general 1277–94, wrote to the king of England, Edward I, in 1282, requesting that he appeal to the pope on behalf of the order. The king instead ordered letters to be sent to several cardinals.[43] Pierre probably also convinced bishops in the Holy Land and the grand masters of the Hospitallers and Templars to write to the pope in 1282 and 1283, arguing that the Holy Land desperately needed the alms the order supplied. At much the same time there began to appear histories of the order, asserting its antiquity, perhaps the simplest way to avoid the full impact of the decree.[44]

The problems faced by the order may also have encouraged more rapid clericalisation. In common with the Franciscans, most of the early Carmelite hermits had probably been laymen. Again like the Franciscans, this situation changed as the order expanded. It is no longer possible to give any sense of the numbers involved, but by 1281 the constitutions of the general chapter required that no layman be received unless suitably qualified in a technical skill (*ars mechanica*) of value to the order. In the same year laymen were also excluded from provincial and general chapters, while in 1294 clerical brethren were instructed to speak in Latin to help them to become more fluent – a move which can only have amplified the gulf between clerical and lay brothers.

Another important change intended to promote the order was a simplification of the habit. The early Carmelites wore a tunic and scapular (a sleeveless outer garment) with a grey capuce or hood attached. Over this they wore a striped mantle alternating light and dark, woven from one piece of cloth, so

[40] See below, pp. 181–5.

[41] Dal Pino, *I frati Servi*, II, pp. 1076–81; K. Elm, 'Ausbreitung, Wirksamkeit und Ende der provençalischen Sackbrüder (Fratres de Poenitentia Jesu Christi) in Deutschland und den Niederlanden. Ein Beitrag zur kurialen und konziliaren Ordenspolitik des 13. Jahrhunderts', *Francia. Forschungen zur westeuropäischen Geschichte* 1 (1973), pp. 257–324, 259, 317.

[42] Lickteig, *The German Carmelites*, p. 413.

[43] *Medieval Carmelite Heritage*, pp. 44–48.

[44] See below, p. 57.

that in Paris they were know as *barrés* (see jacket).[45] This habit was the symbol of their affiliation, identifying the wearer as a Carmelite: the 1281 constitutions called it the 'sign of our *religio*'. But the general chapter of Pavia in 1284 appointed proctors to petition the Curia for permission to change. The pope, approached through the offices of the order's cardinal protector, Gervasio Giancoleto, gave permission for a mantle of one colour.[46] Gervasio's letter identifies some of the reasons for the change: it was expensive and difficult to get hold of the striped cloth needed and it was anyway inappropriate and a cause of scandal. The record of the general chapter held at Montpellier in 1287 adds another, possibly more important reason. As well as provoking derision, the habit was preventing recruitment. It was claimed that men who would otherwise have wished to join the order had changed their minds and held back on account of the habit, which they despised. The chapter also claimed that the striped mantles prevented the brothers from becoming university masters since they were assumed to be lay brothers. While perhaps over-stating the case, such complaints underline the importance of the habit, particularly for regular religious living in the world. They also betray the eagerness of the order to progress in the universities by this date. The new colour chosen was white, allegedly to avoid prejudice to any other order. In practice this prompted complaints from the Premonstratensians or 'White Canons', but at the general chapter in 1294 the white cloak was already acknowledged as the new 'sign' of their *religio* and Pope Boniface VIII (1294–1303) confirmed its adoption in 1295.[47] This is the origin of the popular name, Whitefriars, by which the Carmelites became known in England.

If these changes were designed to strengthen the case for Carmelite survival, then they were successful: in the 1280s bishops and prelates were instructed to protect the friars and the rule was given papal approval.[48] Finally, in May 1298, Boniface VIII removed the remaining uncertainty hanging over the Carmelites, as over the Augustinians, by confirming their right to exist on the basis that they had been instituted before the ban of the Fourth Lateran Council in 1215.[49]

---

[45] See below, p. 228.

[46] See *Medieval Carmelite Heritage*, pp. 54–70, for the relevant documents.

[47] *Justis petentium desideriis*, 25 November 1295 (*BC* I, 70; Digard 908).

[48] *Olim ad aures*, 6 March 1286 (*BC* I, 524; Potthast 22387); *Cum a nobis*, 1 July 1289 (*BC* I, 61; Langlois 1042); *Inundans malitia perversorum*, 1 July 1289 (*BC* I, 63; Langlois 7496).

[49] *Tenorem cujusdam*, 5 May 1298 (*BC* I, 74; Empoli, *Bullarium*, 46–7).

CHAPTER TWO

The Geographical Dispersal of the Order

Structures of authority

Like all organisations spread over a vast geographical area, the Carmelites quickly found it necessary to subdivide for administrative purposes. This process was encouraged by *In singulis regnis*, the constitution issued by the Fourth Lateran Council requiring that exempt abbeys hold chapters in each kingdom or province (ecclesiastical or political). The model for the Carmelites was once again that of the Franciscans and Dominicans. A provincial prior headed each province and the body binding these provinces together was the general chapter, attended by these priors. The general chapter enjoyed both legislative and administrative authority and as far as we can tell, was to meet every three years, though by the fifteenth century it was often held at four- or five-year intervals and sometimes longer. The general chapter elected the prior general and his companions or *socii*.

As well as approving the Carmelite rule, papal pronouncements provided backing for these emerging authorities within the order: in 1256 Alexander IV ordained that the prior general and provincial priors should exercise the office of visitation, might move the brothers and receive novices.[1] Following standard monastic procedures, they were entirely responsible for the spiritual lives of their brethren. The general chapter also appointed the general proctor and allotted taxes for the administration of the order and for the house of studies set up in Paris, choosing the students who were to attend. Most importantly, it was empowered to draft new constitutions, which were binding decrees designed to complement or clarify the rule, to resolve disputes and to strengthen the observance within the order. The earliest recorded general chapter took place in 1247 and while constitutions are mentioned in a papal letter of 1256, the London chapter of 1281 appears to be the first from which they survive. From 1318, when the Catalan Guiu Terrena was appointed prior general, the decisions of the general chapter were recorded in the *Liber ordinis*. Excerpts were copied as needed by those attending the chapter and the *Liber* was then taken to the house in which the next meeting would take place. In the absence, however, of a 'mother house', comparable to the convent of San Francesco in Assisi for the Friars Minor, each general was

[1]   *Religionis vestre meretur*, 15 January 1256 (*BC* I, 20; Bourel 1090).

based in his own province and the archive for each term of office remained there. This meant that there was no continuous record keeping and, apart from the *Liber ordinis*, much was lost. It also meant that there was no living paradigm for a Carmelite house.

Provincial priors were appointed by the prior general with the consent of the priors of the province. By 1281, provincials were entrusted with various responsibilities, including visitation of houses, scrutiny of their priors, the concession of letters of confraternity to laymen seeking association with the order, the reception of novices, profession of new brethren, and absolution from certain crimes. They also held a yearly provincial chapter attended by all the priors, who were required to provide a written report on their houses, including their economic condition and debts. According to the Carmelite constitutions of 1294, during a vacancy the prior of the Holy Land was to act as vicar general and to preside whenever the prior general was absent, 'out of reverence for the sweetness of Carmel which is the principal *locus* (place) of our religion'. It seems that associations with the Holy Land were still powerful and perhaps even magnified, so soon after the fall of Acre in 1291.

Geographical spread

The original hermitage on Mount Carmel was the centre of the province of the Holy Land in the thirteenth century. Later catalogues of the order register ten houses there and five in Cyprus, but much of this was wishful thinking. Carmelite houses are known to have existed only on Mount Carmel itself and at Acre and Tyre. These survived the departure of many brethren for the West and in 1262 were granted exemption from episcopal jurisdiction, being subject only to the patriarch, but recruitment must have been increasingly difficult. The 1281 constitutions encouraged provincial priors to be on the look-out for clerical novices for the Holy Land. They also stipulated rather optimistically that the books of the province at that time dispersed throughout the order should be gathered together, so that they could be returned once the Holy Land was again in Christian hands. As it turned out, the fall of Acre in 1291 saw the destruction of the remaining house on Mount Carmel. Those brothers who survived moved to Cyprus, where Carmelites continued to live until 1571.

The first Carmelite houses in the West were established as archetypal hermitages, remote from centres of population.[2] Hulne in Northumberland (1242) recreated the desert in the forests of Alnwick. Founded by John de Vesci for hermits whom he had brought to England, the house seems first to have been intended for as many as twenty-four brothers and by 1301 there

---

[2] The suggestion that Peter of Corbie may have brought one of the earliest groups to Valenciennes in France in 1235 (Smet, *The Carmelites: A History*, I, p. 11) does not seem to be well founded.

were twenty-eight. At Aylesford, also founded in 1242, the community seems once again to have been initiated by a patron bringing refugees from the Holy Land. According to the Franciscan Thomas of Eccleston (writing *c.* 1258), their patron, Richard de Grey, lord of Cudnor had been on crusade with Richard of Cornwall. The hermits almost certainly came to England directly from the Holy Land.[3] They quickly obtained the support of the local bishop who granted an indulgence to contributors towards the erection of their chapel. Building was presumably soon under way, since the general chapter of the order met there in 1247 and in the following year the friars stipulated an agreement compensating the parish church of Aylesford for loss of revenue, an indication that local people were expected at the Carmelite church. In 1247 Richard de Grey also gave the Carmelites land in London, but this time the setting was very different. The house – the first following modification of the rule – stood near Fleet Street, outside the walls but only a short walk from St Paul's Cathedral. Its site underscores the new urban and pastoral concerns of the order.

Other early settlements in England include Lossenham in Kent (1242), Burnham Norton on the north coast of Norfolk (before 1247) and Cambridge. In the university town the friars appear to have arrived independently and subsequently obtained support. They settled first at Chesterton, north of the river, where King Henry III gave permission for the building of a house in November 1247, two years later granting them six oaks for the construction of their church. In 1249, however, Michael Malherbe gave them a house at Newnham to the south-west of the city. The new house was in the parish of St Peter-outside-the-gate at Trumpington, which belonged to the hospital of St John the Evangelist. The Carmelites agreed to pay 20 shillings to the hospital. They further undertook not to enlarge their property without the hospital's consent and to administer sacraments to the parishioners of St Peter's only in urgent need or with special licence. Numerous cells, a cloister and church were built in Newnham, but in the early 1290s the friars moved again, this time to St John Milne Street on a site later occupied by Queen's College. This they justified on account of frequent flooding and the inability of friar students to get to lectures. Nor, they claimed, could the friars reach the town to obtain food supplies. Once again they obtained royal permission for the move and agreed to indemnify the new parish for any loss incurred.

Further foundations were made at Bristol, King's Lynn, Lincoln, Norwich and Oxford in the 1250s, and despite the crisis of 1274, by 1293 the Carmelites had twenty-eight foundations in England and five in Scotland. Expansion continued apace in the fourteenth century. Royal permission for grants of land and gifts of wood for building remained important. A typical example is

[3] Thomas de Eccleston, 'De adventu minorum in Angliam', in *Monumenta Franciscana*, I, ed. J. S. Brewer, Rerum Britannicarum medii aevi scriptores IV, 1 (London, 1858), p. 71.

the house at Ludlow, where in November 1349 a royal inquisition was ordered to establish whether a friary could be founded. Four months later Laurence of Ludlow was licensed to alienate a messuage (house and land) to the Carmelites on which to build, and by 1353 they had erected their first church.

In 1271 the Carmelites arrived at Leighlinbridge in Ireland, settling on land provided by the Carew family. They were supported and protected by the English Crown, in part because the friary stood close to an important bridge, for which the brothers held some responsibility. By the early fourteenth century they were popular beneficiaries in the area, so that by the 1540s, at the Dissolution, they possessed an acre of garden, twenty-four acres of arable land and an eel-weir. The order had spread quickly in Ireland: to Dublin (1274), Ardee (*c.* 1280), Ballinasmale in county Mayo (*c.* 1288), Kildare (1290), Drogheda (*c.* 1297), Burriscarra in county Mayo (1298) and Loughrea and Thurles by *c.* 1300.

Yet faster growth was to be seen in France and in Provence. According to his biographer, Joinville, Louis IX built and endowed a Carmelite house on the Seine near Charenton[4] and his name is linked with the foundations at Paris (1258) and Valenciennes (1259).[5] Still earlier documentary evidence for the friars comes in 1248 from Aygalades near Marseilles in Provence, where again they probably arrived directly from Palestine. Louis IX's younger brother Alphonse, count of Poitiers, was an important patron of the Provençal Carmelites (as indeed of all the mendicant orders) and by 1275 there were twenty-one houses in France, most of which were in the south. By the end of the fifteenth century this number had expanded to eighty-seven houses in the French province, making it the most substantial of the order.

Arriving in the Empire the Carmelites settled first at Cologne, perhaps attracted by its reputation as a centre for theological study. They must have enjoyed some success, since in 1260 the Archbishop, Conrad von Hostaden, banned a Carmelite Latin school, presumably so as to protect the cathedral school. The friars also established a house at Würzburg in that year and by 1291 there were some fifteen houses in the upper Rhineland. In the 1300s the German settlements expanded both north into Denmark and eastwards, including Magdeburg (1337) and Prague (1347). The Low Countries, despite, or perhaps because of their high population density, had relatively few houses in the thirteenth century: Brussels, Bruges, Mechelen and Haarlem, but again new foundations continued throughout the 1300s and 1400s.

---

[4] Jean de Joinville, 'The Life of Saint Louis', chapter 18, most easily available in Joinville and Villehardouin, *Chronicles of the Crusades*, trans. M. R. B. Shaw (Harmondsworth, 1963), p. 344. In 1310 they described the site as miserable and subject to flooding. See Y. Dossat, 'Opposition des anciens ordres à l'installation des mendiants', in *Les Mendiants en Pays d'Oc au 13e siècle*, Cahiers de Fanjeaux 8 (1973), pp. 263–306, 264.

[5] For a general account of Louis's relations with the mendicants see L. K. Little, 'Saint Louis's Involvement with the Friars', *Church History* 33 (1964), pp. 125–48, though, as is typical of much mendicant historiography, he discusses only Franciscans and Dominicans.

In southern Europe, expansion was slower. The decision to extend into the Iberian Peninsula was apparently taken at a general chapter held in London in 1254 but it was more than twenty years before the order took hold. As in France and England, royal backing was invaluable. Thus in 1277 King Phillip III of France and Navarre instructed his representative in Navarre to allow the Carmelites to build a house in Sangüesa and in the following year King Pere III of Aragon permitted the order to acquire land for a monastery with a garden in Lleida. In Italy, after the first foundation at Messina in Sicily, houses were established in Pisa (*c.* 1249), Milan (*c.* 1250), Bologna (*c.* 1260), Siena (before 1261) and Florence (1268). They had reached Parma by 1273 and Lucca by 1284, where the house initially stood outside Porta San Donato and later moved into the city. In 1291 the Carmelites arrived in Pistoia and in 1295 they acquired from the bishop the parish of San Paolo in Ferrara formerly held by the Sack Friars. By 1333 there were twelve houses in central Italy (Arezzo, Civitavecchia, Florence, Lucca, Montecatini, Perugia, Pisa, Pistoia, Prato, Rome, Siena and Viterbo). In the first half of the fourteenth century new houses were founded at Modena (*c.* 1313), Verona (before 1316), Mantua (before 1316), Le Selve near Florence (1344) and Brescia (1346). By the end of the century, most of the major cities of northern and central Italy housed a Carmelite friary, the object of substantial support from city governments and individual donors, as were the friaries of the other mendicant orders.

The English foundations at Hulne, Aylesford and Cambridge, which demonstrate the importance of lay patrons, the need for agreements with the established parish clergy and the support of bishops, are characteristic of Carmelite settlements all over the West. In 1265 in Ypres, the prior provincial of France himself had to arrange terms accepting that, should they wish to move to a new site, the Carmelites would first require the permission of the provost and convent of St Martin as well as confirmation from the bishop, the prior general and even the pope before starting to build within the parish. Such hurdles were not unusual. Three years later the pope wrote to the bishop and chapter of Salisbury instructing them to stop obstructing the Carmelites of Bridport who wanted to celebrate the Office in their oratory. At Esslingen am Neckar, near Stuttgart in Baden Württemburg, the Carmelites seem to have arrived in the town in the 1270s but faced fierce opposition from the secular clergy and other mendicant orders who had been resident for several decades. The attempts to have the order suppressed at the Council of Lyons in 1274 may well have had some bearing on their position. They acquired permission to build a friary only in 1281 on a partially inhabited though marshy site on the edge of the town and with strict conditions attached, similar to those imposed twenty years earlier in Cambridge. The friars were not to perform burials, hear confessions or participate in the making of wills without the express permission of the parish priest. Such terms parallel those imposed on many other new communities including the other friars and the

Humiliati and underline the concern of established clergy, both secular and regular, to protect their pastoral role and revenues.[6]

Numerous other instances demonstrate analogous problems and equivalent solutions: the new arrivals compromised their own freedom of action to satisfy their ecclesiastical neighbours and agreed to pay compensation to local parishes. Careful preparation was thus increasingly decisive to the foundation of a new house. In 1307 Domingo de Olite, prior provincial of Spain, attended a meeting of the city council in Manresa to discuss the construction of a new priory. The council assigned them a site and promised a payment of 100 gold florins towards building expenses. By 1311 Carmelites were already living in the new building. In the same year the order obtained papal backing for houses in twenty dioceses, from Benevento to Salisbury, on the basis that they needed particular help because their origins in the Holy Land meant that they had come later than others to receive houses in the West. Such papal letters were increasingly common, and the Carmelites did indeed arrive in the West after the approval of the Franciscans or Dominicans, but in a competitive atmosphere even planned houses were not always successful. In 1287 Archbishop Peckham had prevented the creation of a new house in Coventry because it would have stood less than 140 rods or *canne* from the Franciscan friary, the minimum distance laid down by the pope.[7] Active opposition from the secular clergy, such as that encountered by the Carmelites at Esslingen, also delayed the building of convents elsewhere: in Mallorca royal intervention was necessary to overcome clerical hostility. In Barcelona it took fifty-four years before the friars had gathered sufficient resources to acquire neighbouring plots for the construction of a large church and conventual buildings and the Barcelona clergy remained hostile. A particularly well-documented dispute occurred in Nantes where the generosity of the governor, Thibaut de Rochefort, both brought them to the city (1318) and enabled them to find a new house after the Franciscans complained about the proximity of their original settlement, but the bishop subsequently objected and excommunicated the friars for moving without papal authorisation, threatening the faithful with a fine should they attend a Mass or sermon in their church. In 1328 John XXII ordered the bishop of Angers to confirm Thibaut's foundation, but Thibaut was still forced to accord the secular clergy financial compensation. Meanwhile, the Franciscans and Dominicans, supported by the secular clergy, prevented the Carmelites from having a

---

[6]   See also pp. 109–10 and 202–5.

[7]   Privileges issued to the Dominicans in Bologna, reserving an area around their house for preaching and alms-collecting, provided the basis for this rule, later extended to the Franciscans. In 1268 Clement IV reduced the impractical original distance of 300 *canne* to 140. Disputes frequently arose over the correct length of a *canna* and whether the distance should be measured in a straight line or around buildings. The Carmelites first received this privilege themselves under Clement V: *Statum religionis*, 5 November 1309 (*BC* I, 54).

cemetery. Thibaut was therefore buried in a Cistercian house and the friars themselves had to be buried outside their community. According to a later account, the Franciscans of Nantes next re-measured the distance between their own convent and the new house of the Carmelites, accusing them of being within the restricted distance. Rods (*canne*) guaranteed with the papal seal were sent for from Rome and the distance was re-measured, establishing that the Carmelite house in fact lay outside the limits set by the privilege. Only in the 1340s were the brothers finally able to settle in their house.

By 1247 there were perhaps three provinces in the West: Sicily, England and Provence, all of which included brethren who had arrived directly from Palestine. Later developments probably mostly reflect recruitment in the West rather than further emigration from the Holy Land. The number of provinces is an indication of just how fast the order was expanding. By 1294 they already numbered twelve: the Holy Land, Sicily, England, Provence, Tuscany-Rome, France, Lower and Upper Germany, Lombardy, Aquitaine, Spain and Scotland-Ireland. The English houses were further divided for administrative purposes into four *distinctiones*: London, Oxford, Norwich and York. Until the 1290s the Scottish houses had been included with the English, but in 1294 they joined with Ireland to form a separate province. Objections from the English provincial forced the prior general Gerardo da Bologna to seek both royal and papal backing for this change and at the provincial chapter held in 1305 the English provincial William Lidlington was removed from office and sent abroad with other senior members of the province. In practice the Irish houses alone were separated at this point and given the status of an independent province. Only in 1324 did Scotland, with six houses, become an autonomous province, a year after the pope officially recognised Robert the Bruce as king of Scotland.[8]

The determinations in the *Liber ordinis* for the general chapter held in 1348 record the taxes due from the various provinces. The highest sum, 35 florins, was to be paid by the province of France, followed by England, which owed thirty. The smallest figure, 12 florins, was required from the provinces of Mallorca, Provence, Scotland, Toulouse and Upper Germany. Although the rates sometimes varied considerably, France and England frequently paid more than the other provinces, a reflection of their relative size and wealth.

Still the number of provinces continued to grow: to eighteen by 1357, twenty-five by 1462. Much of this expansion was created by the division of larger provinces into vicariates which in time gave rise to new provinces and, as in the case of Scotland, reflected the vagaries of political change. Toulouse

---

[8] For parallel difficulties for the Franciscans in Scotland, who first obtained a separate province in 1278, lost their autonomy in the 1290s and regained it in 1329, with the strong support of the Scottish kings, see W. M. Mackenzie, 'A Prelude to the War of Independence', *Scottish Historical Review* 27 (1948), pp. 105–13.

lay within the lands of the king of France but belonged to the Carmelite province of Aquitaine, which was in the hands of the English. At the outbreak of the Hundred Years' War in the fourteenth century the house preferred to become independent and in 1336 the vicariate of Toulouse appears in the records. In 1342 it was formed into a new province with the houses of Castelnaudary, Castelsarrasin and Pamiers. This reflects the normal size for a new province, which seems to have been four friaries, while six was the minimum for representation among the diffinitors of the general chapter.

Beyond the cloister: lay patronage and support

The expansion of the order and multiplication of provinces depended very substantially on lay patrons, but together with patronage came close ties with seculars. The constitutions of 1281 tried to restrict the presence of the laity in the cloister and ordained that no woman was to be allowed to stay in Carmelite houses, if this could be avoided without causing a scandal. The constitutions of 1294 followed this with an explicit ban on friars acting as ambassadors or bearers of the letters of magnates when this might lead to scandal. In practice, as both regulations imply, such links could not be avoided. The foundation and survival of houses of the order depended on lay resources and in return the Carmelites often provided a variety of services. Like other orders, their relatively secure buildings meant that they were entrusted with valuables by outsiders: the early constitutions warn that anything received in custody must be checked on receipt by three brethren and either counted, weighed or measured. Their houses were used for signing treaties – a convention between war captains in 1371 was signed in the Bergerac house – and their churches were, like others, places of sanctuary. Carmelite friars were also frequently present in noble and royal entourages, often to the direct benefit of the order. Robert Baston, prior of the convent at Scarborough, accompanied Edward II to the Battle of Bannockburn (1314). Edward's unexpected defeat led the king to vow that he would found a Carmelite house of theology for twenty-four friars if his life were spared, and he did eventually give them Beaumont Palace outside Oxford.

The Lancastrians particularly admired the Carmelite house near Fleet Street. Before he came to the throne, Henry IV (1399–1413) dined there in the *hospitium* with the king and queen and purchased rich hangings to adorn the canopies of the chairs provided for the royal couple. His father, John of Gaunt (†1399), duke of Lancaster, was a generous patron of all the mendicants and seems to have been particularly well disposed towards the Carmelites.[9] They may indeed have helped dissuade him from his support for

---

[9]   See A. Goodman, *John of Gaunt: The Exercise of Princely Power in Fourteenth-Century Europe* (Harlow, 1992).

Wyclif (†1384), an Oxford master whose criticisms of ecclesiastical practice were condemned in 1382 but taken up by his followers, known in England as Lollards. Gaunt had a series of Carmelite confessors, who lived in his household in close association with him: from 1372 William Badby (†1380/1), a famous preacher to whose sermons people flocked 'as to a show', received an annuity of £10. In 1375 Walter Disse was granted £10 per year, raised to £20 in 1380. In 1392–3 and 1397–8 Gaunt's confessor was John Kyningham (†1399), who had earlier written *Three Determinations* against Wyclif (1370) and was briefly prior provincial.

Gaunt also patronised Nicholas of Lynn, an Oxford Carmelite who lectured on theology, was famous for his mathematical and astronomical learning, and dedicated to the duke his *Kalendarium* for the period 1386–1462 (referred to by Chaucer in his treatise on the astrolabe). The theologian Stephen Patrington, provincial from 1399–1414, also received an annuity from Gaunt in 1397, being later consecrated bishop of St David's and finally bishop of Chichester. Gaunt gave equally to communities: he provided oaks for the houses in Nottingham and Doncaster, while the Carmelites of Sandwich received 40 shillings just before he departed on a naval expedition from the port. In 1374 in London he granted the same sum in aid of the chapter and in alms. In 1382 the provincial chapter of the English Carmelites asked Gaunt to assume the position of founder of the Doncaster friary, which he did, 'to the honour of God and Our Lady and of holy religion and at the same time for the great and special affection which we have for the said order'.[10] In 1398 Gaunt requested that should he die outside London his body be taken to Whitefriars overnight before burial in St Paul's and, as Anthony Goodman suggests, he probably planned to wear the scapular on his deathbed and to be buried in it, perhaps a sign that he was a Carmelite *confrater*.[11]

As well as annuities, powerful figures such as Gaunt could provide political assistance. Edward II was a substantial backer of the order and Gaunt supported the order's claims to an exceptional bond with the Virgin Mary.[12] He petitioned Pope Urban VI to condemn 'slanderous and malicious insinuations' against the spiritual and historical claims of the order and asked him to confirm the assertion of a special relationship with the Virgin.

The tradition of royal ties in England continued in the fifteenth century. The London Carmelite Thomas Netter of Walden, prior provincial (1414–30) and Inquisitor in England, was also English ambassador to King Władysław Jagiełło of Poland (1386–1434) and travelled to France with Henry V. John Stanbury (later bishop of Hereford) was confessor to King Henry VI and was with him when he was wounded at the battle of Northampton (1460).

Carmelites elsewhere in Europe also acted as royal chaplains. In 1382,

[10] Cited ibid., p. 245.
[11] Ibid., pp. 245, 247. On the scapular, see below, pp. 53–4.
[12] On this see again below, p. 53–4.

Francesc Martí, a scholar and master, was mentioned as chaplain to Prince Joan, the heir to the throne of Aragon. Employment in the royal household, however, meant that friction between secular rulers might occasionally re-echo within the community. Tensions between Jaume III of Mallorca and Pere III of Aragon in the 1340s may explain the imprisonment of the prior of Mallorca by his confreres in Peralada (Aragon). Nonetheless royal support can again be traced in numerous ways: the Aragonese Crown paid large sums to Carmelite scholars, both in response to requests from the men involved and at times when the king sought individuals to send to study in Paris. The Crown also allowed tax exemptions for particular houses, such as for purchases made by the Carmelites of Valencia in 1298. As in England, support often came with more or less explicit expectations attached. In 1323 Jaume II paid 100 *sous* to the prior of Barcelona to cover the costs of work undertaken in preparation for a royal visit. In 1324 he employed a Carmelite friar who was attending the Barcelona chapter meeting to deliver a letter to his daughter and to the papal Curia. In 1399 King Martí wrote to Pope Benedict XIII (also Aragonese) appointing four Carmelites who would be paid to obtain their university qualifications – but thereafter might be employed as royal messengers.

Relations with other secular authorities could also cause tensions, most frequently over taxes, jurisdiction or land. In 1409 in Bergerac a man called Vignonet and his wife had 'given themselves' to the Carmelite house. They were presumably 'corrodians', receiving accommodation and support (both spiritual and material) in later life in return for a gift of their property. They refused to observe what the consuls claimed as city custom: that all religious who had property in the town must serve as watchmen and pay tax.[13] We do not know the outcome of Vignonet's dispute, but such struggles over the separate and tax-exempt status of religious, often presented in terms of the *libertas ecclesie* (the freedom or autonomy of the Church), were commonplace throughout the late Middle Ages. Certainly cities needed to watch over their jurisdiction: in Bergerac the Carmelites tried to extend their property by closing a public road near to their house and planting fruit trees on it. The city consuls dispatched a gang armed with pickaxes to the convent, intending to reopen the road, but the Carmelites acknowledged their wrongdoing in time and promised to keep the road open in future.

Cities and other secular authorities often agreed payments to the Carmelites, in return expecting them to participate in public devotions and to help in maintaining both social order and health. In Bergerac, annual processions were held in July on the three Sundays following the renewal of the consulate. In 1424 the Carmelites of the city, together with the Dominicans

---

[13] J. C. Ignace, 'Le Couvent des Carmes de Bergerac des origines a 1790', *Carmelus* 41 (1994), pp. 165–78, 171.

and Franciscans, were required to say a hundred masses to protect against war and epidemic. In Manresa in 1422 the Carmelites held a procession for relief from the plague. The sums involved might be very substantial and sometimes indicate the relative importance of the different mendicant communities. In Siena regular alms were paid to all the mendicants from the late thirteenth century onwards. The Dominicans, Franciscans and Augustinians regularly received 50 *lire*, while the Sack Friars received twenty-five and the Carmelites just fifteen, an indication of their comparatively smaller size in the city.

Confraternities

As well as letters of confraternity issued to individuals, the success of the mendicant friars led to a great flood of brother- and sisterhoods or confraternities linked to their churches. Membership allowed lay men and women to perform pious acts in honour of a patron saint (or saints) and thereby to earn both spiritual guarantees for the next life and more immediate social advantages in this. Confraternities frequently provided both charity to the poor and a forum for the development of social networks through regular meetings. Their activities ranged from participation in spectacular processions to arranging the funerals of poor members or private self-flagellation. Confraternities of the Virgin of Mount Carmel were quick to develop. At Toulouse, where miracles were associated with the foundation of the house, the Marian confraternity apparently already numbered in the thousands by the 1260s.[14] Membership of such confraternities was usually a long-term commitment. The surviving statutes of the Confraternity of Our Lady of Perpignan (1399–1401) are unusual in that they allowed members to join and resign as often as they chose. Each member paid 12 pence and a further 8 on the feast of the Conception.

In Florence, studied by John Henderson, a series of different confraternities were linked to the Carmelites over the course of the later Middle Ages and give a sense of the possible range: the Compagnia of Santa Maria delle Laude and Sant'Agnese, dedicated to praise of the Virgin and Agnes (before 1280), St Nicholas of Bari (1334, flagellants), St Albert (1411 flagellants, 1419 for boys), St Catherine (*c.* 1435, for German artisans), the Crucifix (1453, flagellants), San Bastiano (*c.* 1456, for boys), Santa Maria del Popolo (1460, a devotional fraternity for women linked with the Madonna del Popolo panel in the Brancacci chapel) and Santa Concordia (1495).[15] Such confraternities usually had an altar or chapel in the church and were frequently responsible for the commissioning of furnishings such as hangings, retables or other

---

[14] This seems to have particularly provoked the irritation of the canons of the chapter of Saint-Étienne and despite a compromise, their hostility to the Carmelites led to the intervention of Alphonse of Poitiers. See Dossat, 'Opposition des anciens ordres à l'installation des mendiants', p. 293.

[15] See J. Henderson, *Piety and Charity in Late Medieval Florence* (Oxford, 1994).

liturgical equipment. The most important in Florence was the Compagnia of Santa Maria delle Laude and Sant'Agnese, which staged grand spectacles in the Carmine. As well as fulfilling their statutory obligation to sing lauds and do good works, they organised an Ascension play at least from the 1390s, which continued throughout the fifteenth century until finally closed down in 1497 under Friar Savonarola's influence. The theme of the Ascension may have been chosen because of the typological associations between the ascent of Christ and the fiery chariot of Elijah, the Old Testament figure whom the order claimed as its patron. The performance was a major undertaking supported by government subsidies and became a vehicle for Medici propaganda, reflected in the giant fleur-de-lis placed on the façade of the church during the *festa*. The actors were men and young boys dressed up in brightly coloured costumes; garlands of flowers, lanterns and music filled the church. Christ, surrounded by *papier mâché* angels, was drawn up to a heaven constructed above the high altar using complex platforms, pulleys and winches with a wooden 'cloud' or frame which, in the early fifteenth century, was painted by Masolino. As reported by a Russian bishop visiting Florence in 1439, it was a 'wonderful performance' and deservedly famous, occasionally being repeated out of season for honoured guests of the city.[16]

Confraternities were also commonly linked to indulgences. In 1397 Bishop Ramon of Barcelona (1386–98), gave an indulgence of forty days to donors to the Carmelite confraternity of Mary Magdalene and to those who cared for the sick or did other good works in their support. Indulgences were also often used to encourage visitors to Carmelite churches, as from 1290, when an indulgence of one year and forty days was issued for any faithful attending about twenty of their churches on the feasts or octave of the Virgin.[17] By the fifteenth century a general indulgence was widely accepted for members of the order and of its confraternities. John XXII allegedly issued the so-called *bulla sabbatina* in 1322 and it was re-issued by Alexander V. In practice Ludovico Saggi has demonstrated that the bull was concocted in Sicily *c.* 1430, in imitation of the Franciscan plenary indulgence attached to the Porziuncola, but this did not prevent it achieving enormous success.[18] To acquire its benefits, those who could read were to say the Office; those who

---

[16] See C. Barr, 'Music and Spectacle in Confraternity Drama of Fifteenth-Century Florence. The Reconstruction of a Theatrical Event', in *Christianity and the Renaissance. Image and Religious Imagination in the Quattrocento*, ed. T. Verdon and J. Henderson (Syracuse, NY, 1990), pp. 376–404 and N. Newbigin, *Feste d'Oltrarno, Plays in Churches in Fifteenth-Century Florence*, 2 vols (Florence, 1996).

[17] In 1290–1 indulgences of a year and forty days were issued for their churches in Bordeaux, Langon (diocese of Bazas), London, Cologne, Siena, Toulouse, Agen, Millau, Condom (diocese of Agen), Montpellier, Pisa, Florence, Lucca, Viterbo, Bologna, Milan, Trapani, Alessandria, Venice and Figeac (Langlois 1960, 2522, 2558–65, 2641–6, 3207, 3289, 3892, 4142).

[18] L. Saggi, *La 'Bolla Sabatina': ambiente, testo, tempo* (Rome, 1967). The Dominicans also produced a plenary indulgence in imitation of the Franciscans, see *Indulgenza, città, pellegrini. Il caso della perdonanza di S. Stefano a S. Domenico di Perugia* (Perugia, 2001).

could not were to fast on the set days and abstain from meat on Wednesdays and Saturdays. On the Saturday following their death, the Virgin Mary would free their souls from the suffering of purgatory and accompany them personally to paradise (thus a *sabbatine* indulgence). This specific indulgence was not included in a great confirmation of the order's privileges issued by Sixtus IV in 1476, so the general chapter sought to remove the lacuna. Nicholas Audet, the prior general (1524–62), was to tax the order for the expenses of obtaining this and other indulgences. In 1528 Clement VII reconfirmed all the indulgences of the order including the choice of a confessor for members of confraternities of either sex, participation in the spiritual benefits of the Church for those who assisted the brethren or their churches and houses, remission of one third of all sins for members of the confraternity of Mount Carmel who observed its rules, wore the habit of the order, called themselves 'brothers' or 'sisters' and observed chastity. The sabbatine indulgence was not, however, confirmed by Clement; instead he affirmed only that the Virgin would provide special protection and intercession and no mention was made of the Saturday, though this was reintroduced in 1577 by Gregory XIII. The sabbatine indulgence merged with a tradition linking the giving of the Carmelite scapular to the Virgin and stimulated great devotion to the Carmine.[19] In the 1560s in Seville and Salamanca, butchers complained about the loss of business caused by the Wednesday and Saturday abstinences. In the early seventeenth century, however, these were withdrawn.

Women

The original Carmelite houses were exclusively male, and in 1261 the order obtained papal permission to refuse responsibility for the pastoral care of women religious, the *cura monialium*. This did not prevent women wishing to be attached to the order, whether through confraternities or more exacting ties. In 1284 a group of laywomen was associated with the priory in Lucca and in 1300 some women in Venice were admitted to the order as a distinct congregation. Carmelite friars also occasionally developed links with individual devout women: in the early fifteenth century in Lynn a learned Carmelite friar, Master Aleyn, particularly sympathised with Margery Kempe (1378–c. 1434), a famously intense lay woman whose religious enthusiasm, expressed by visions and loud weeping, raised eyebrows among her neighbours and other churchmen. The formal incorporation of women within the Carmelite order, however, took place only in the mid-fifteenth century. The trigger came from the Low Countries, where the Carmelites held the parish of Guelders and therefore had responsibility for the beguinage of 'Ten Elsen founded in the late fourteenth century from the union of three previous

[19] See below, pp. 53–4.

communities.[20] The women who lived there took no vows but promised to observe chastity and to live according to the statutes of the beguinage under the authority of a superior. They lived in houses around an oratory or church, where they attended daily Mass provided by Carmelite clergy. In 1452 at the provincial chapter of Lower Germany, the prior general Jean Soreth (1451–71) accepted a petition from the sisters of Guelders, allowing the local prior to admit them to the order. They were to live *regulariter* under the prioress, called 'Mother', and under the authority of the prior. A year later Soreth provided them with statutes. These do not survive, but the first extant constitutions for Carmelite nuns were drawn up by Soreth for Nieuwkerk in Holland three years later. In these Soreth reveals that these enclosed women had already lived under the title of the order for a long time, but had not previously enjoyed papal approval. The statutes laid down clear provisions for their new status in the order. There was no question of the women following the mendicant preaching life of the male Carmelites. As was the norm at this date for women religious, the statutes emphasised enclosure, together with strict poverty, a common life of work, prayer and the liturgy. Soreth appointed a vicar, Peter, to translate the rule and the constitutions of the order as appropriate for the women and to supervise the community. This included both *incluse* or cloistered sisters and *non incluse* who might go out on errands. The *non incluse* were to be distinguished in their dress from their enclosed sisters. The constitutions reveal that a new *inclusorium* had been built and the sisters were to move there. By 1574 there were twenty-eight women at Nieuwkerk and acceptance of the beguinage at Guelders in 1452–3 was matched by houses at Dinant (1455), Liège (1457), Haarlem (1466), Vilvoorde (1469), Rotterdam (1482) and Bruges (1487).[21]

The first French houses for women were the initiative of Françoise d'Amboise (1427–85), widow of Pierre II, duke of Brittany (†1457). Despite the opposition of her entourage and of the French king, Françoise professed at Soreth's hands (1468) and entered the Carmelite house which she had founded five years earlier at Bondon near Vannes. Staring has shown that these houses belonged to the 'regular observance'. In other words, the sisters did not have the management of their dowry or any personal revenues, nor did they cook for themselves but instead ate in a common refectory. Sisters of noble birth had no servants or special precedence.[22] In Florence meanwhile, prior Bartolomeo di Maso Soderini obtained papal approval in *Cum nulla* for the creation of a house of 'white ladies' and their exemption from the parish of San Frediano. These *donne mantellate* had lived in Florence

---

[20] Beguine is the term frequently used for religious women often only loosely associated with a regular house or church, but sometimes living in communities following a rule.

[21] V. Wilderink, 'Les Premiers Monastères de Carmélites en France', *Carmelus* 10 (1963), pp. 93–148. See also A. Staring, 'The Carmelite Sisters in the Netherlands', ibid., pp. 56–92.

[22] Staring, 'Carmelite Sisters', p. 91.

under the guidance of the Carmelites, and *Cum nulla,* issued in October 1452, allowed the order to receive convents of virgins, widows and beguines as well as *mantellate* taking the habit and the order of the Carmelites. Thus the order was allowed to institute both a 'second' order of enclosed nuns and regular tertiaries (a lay third order), though this distinction was made clear only in 1517.[23]

In Spain Écija was the first house of Carmelite women, *c.* 1457, and in the following century five further convents were founded in Andalusia, three in Castile and one in Valencia. Unlike those founded under Soreth's supervision in the north, the Spanish houses were subject to annual visitation, but were otherwise autonomous, lacking uniform legislation. However, surviving constitutions observed in Seville and perhaps elsewhere suggest that these women were also strictly enclosed and that their practices were based on a modified version of the constitutions for male houses. They were to live in simple buildings, surrounded by a high wall with just one entrance. The constitutions mention servants (*familiares*) but the sisters were to have no property of their own. Novices were to be taught how to behave in the community, and how to pray and how to dress, but, although the books of the convent are referred to more than once, no mention is made of any other education.

---

[23] On the tertiaries in the order see T. Motta Navarro, *Tertii Carmelitici saecularis ordinis historico-iuridica evolutio* (Rome, 1960).

CHAPTER THREE

Daily Life

Houses of the order (size, topography and architecture)

The size of male Carmelite houses fluctuated substantially between communities and over time: individuals belonged to the order rather than to a particular friary and might move quite often to study or to fulfil the needs of their pastoral mission. In 1315, numbers in the London house varied from thirty-six to eighty over the course of just twelve months, though the average in the first quarter of the fourteenth century seems to have been somewhere around fifty – no small number. In most cases discontinuous records make generalisations difficult and unlikely to be helpful. Nonetheless a striking indication of the comparative size and success of the different orders is provided by information about ordinations in London in the second half of the fourteenth century. Virginia Davis has demonstrated that more than 220 recorded Carmelite ordinations took place in the city in the period 1361–99, compared to 193 for the Dominicans and fewer for the other mendicants; the difference was particularly marked in the 1390s.[1] By a small margin, then, the Carmelites appear to have been the most successful of the city's mendicant houses in those years. This is not, however, a pattern that can be extrapolated to the rest of England nor indeed to the remainder of the Middle Ages. London was probably the largest friary in England and housed the English Carmelite *studium generale*. Moreover, in the 1390s the Carmelites may have been in particular favour because of their keen opposition to the Wyclifites. Earlier figures for the English university towns of Oxford and Cambridge (where the other mendicant orders had their *studia generalia*) present a different order of magnitude:[2]

		Carmelites	Augustinians	Dominicans	Franciscans
Oxford	1305	54	52	96	84
	1377	57	49	70	103

[1] V. Davis, 'Mendicants in London in the Reign of Richard II', *The London Journal* 25/2 (2000), pp. 1–12.

[2] This table is based on B. Flood, 'The Carmelite Friars in Medieval English Universities and Society 1299–1430', *Recherches de théologie ancienne et médiévale* 55 (1988), pp. 154–83, 161, and K. J. Egan, 'The Carmelites turn to Cambridge', in *The Land of Carmel: Essays in Honor of Joachim Smet, O. Carm*, ed. P. Chandler, K. J. Egan (Rome, 1991), pp. 155–70, who gives fifty-five Dominicans; his other figures are identical.

	Carmelites	Augustinians	Dominicans	Franciscans
Cambridge 1297	35	36	59	55
1326	50	70	54	70

If this is typical, and it probably is, the Carmelites are confirmed as one of the smaller mendicant orders, generally overshadowed by the Dominicans and Franciscans, with less substantial communities on the whole than either order. They certainly had far fewer houses than the Friars Minor. Nonetheless the London ordination figures suggest that they were sufficiently close to enable them on occasion to make more recruits than either of the main mendicant orders (just as Humbert de Romans had feared). The white habit of the order must have been a familiar sight in many university towns, as in many other centres of population.[3]

In common with the houses of other mendicants, the Carmelites usually settled at first on the edge of towns. In Avignon in the early fourteenth century, their house stood to the east of the city, near the Austin Friars, whereas those of the Dominicans and Franciscans were to the south. In Lynn (Norfolk) the friary was situated 'damply at the town's edge', near the confluence of the rivers Ouse and Nar.[4] This was in part because the Carmelites were late arrivals on the scene and more central locations were both densely occupied and expensive; in part it was a reflection of their pastoral concerns with populations beyond the parish boundaries of communities, as it was for the other mendicants. In the same way as at Cambridge, they frequently moved later into more central locations, either to escape danger or to improve access and the quality of their site. At Peralada in Catalonia, the Carmelites resided outside the walls until 1293 when they were given a house previously occupied by the Sack Friars. In Rome in 1299 they successfully petitioned Boniface VIII for San Martino al Monte, his former titular church, because, according to their request, their previous site was remote from human habitation, was in ruinous condition and lacked a convenient water supply. In Huesca the friars settled right next to the city walls, in which they obtained permission to make a gate for public use in 1286. In Montpellier, on the other hand, they were forced to pull down their house in the mid-fourteenth century on the grounds that it stood too close to the town walls and put the whole defensive system at risk. Similarly, in Newcastle, the friars had to move from their original site because of the building of a tower and extension of the town wall on the site of their church. As in Peralada they were given a house formerly occupied by the Sack Friars. In numerous other cases, having started by settling outside the town walls, the friars later found themselves incorporated inside the new circuits of walls built to protect expanding suburbs.

---

[3] Comparative figures for friars in England are provided by D. Knowles and R. N. Hadcock, *Medieval Religious Houses. England and Wales* (2nd edn, London, 1971), p. 492.

[4] A. Goodman, *Margery Kempe and Her World* (London, 2002), p. 85.

The vulnerability of a particular community may even have prompted some building works. The friary at Valls in Catalonia was in an exposed position outside the walls and in 1388 King Joan I wrote to renew his father's instruction that new walls should be built so as to enclose the house.

An informative site for the houses of late-medieval Carmelites is the recently excavated friary at Esslingen, south of Stuttgart, where two clear phases can be identified in its construction. In the late thirteenth century, previous agricultural buildings on the land were flattened and replaced by a stone church and four timber-frame houses for perhaps twenty to twenty-five brothers. Like many other religious communities they set up house next to a stream and soon had a mill for grinding cereal. In general the Carmelites seem to have kept livestock only for their own consumption, but most houses probably had chickens and goats as well as mules for transport. They also had gardens, looked after by lay brothers.

The Esslingen church, modelled on the contemporary Franciscan church in the neighbourhood, was initially limited to the choir. This was by no means unusual in church building, where the choir frequently long pre-dated the nave. The precedence given to its construction reflects the importance of having a spiritual focus for the friary. In Esslingen, the lack of a nave may also derive from early restrictions on the Carmelites' involvement with the laity in the city, for whom a nave would have been intended, but above all it must point towards restricted resources. In other cases, as at Linlithgow in Scotland (founded 1401), a smaller chapel given to the new community came to form part of a larger church. The original Lady chapel granted to the friars became the nave of their new church and therefore dictated the proportions of their construction. Linlithgow is also typical of another pattern, that of starting off in a previously established building. Thus in Siena the Carmelites first stayed at San Niccolò and perhaps at the neighbouring church of San Marco, before commencing work on their own church, for which they received yearly gifts of building materials from the city.[5]

In Sandwich the friars arrived in 1268 and settled on a small plot of marshy land. Their church was constructed of flint and brick with pillars of Purbeck and Caen stone, stained-glass windows and floor slabs of Purbeck marble and decorated tiles. Even the early complex of timber-frame houses in Esslingen had tiled floors, while finds such as 'Swabian' red fineware pots and glazed stove tiles suggest that the friars lived in some comfort. The existence of large numbers of small, unglazed bowls in coarse grey ware may even indicate that distributions of food were made to the poor. Nonetheless, this relatively simple group of houses did not reflect the standard monastic layout. Whether through poverty or by design, it was much humbler than

[5] A brief stay at San Marco may explain the reference to the Carmelites there in *Il constituto del comune di Siena dell'anno 1262*, ed. L. Zdekauer (Milan, 1897, reprinted 1983), p. 46.

usual until, as the second phase of excavations reveals, a disastrous fire in the mid-fifteenth century prompted the building of a more traditional stone structure centred on a cloister. By this date the priory had also become the focus of a suburb, first enclosed by walls in the mid-fourteenth century.

The friars of Newcastle were also building in stone: their choir was probably 20m long – corresponding closely to the choirs of the Carmelites at Hulne, Sandwich and Aylesford. The cloister was again similar in size to these houses. An inventory of its contents drawn up when the house was suppressed in 1539 illustrates the accretion of buildings typical of a monastic or mendicant community and suggests again that the friars were enjoying some degree of comfort. It includes the choir with four altars, two lecterns and stalls, a vestry, kitchen, cloister with a *lavatorium* of tin and lead, frater, brewhouse, buttery, dorter (with partitions replacing the original hermit cells), a Lady chapel, rood chapel and a chapel 'next the dore'.

As with the 'Franciscan'-type church at Esslingen, building styles most frequently imitated those of the region, a corollary of the men entrusted with the task. Thus an architect also responsible for other ecclesiastical buildings in the area built the church of the Carmelites in Barcelona. It had a single nave with lateral chapels and two cloisters, a feature typical of fourteenth-century Catalan gothic. By the same token the Carmelite church at Pavia in northern Italy was built at the end of the fourteenth century by the architect responsible for the signorial castle in the town and shares with it various decorative features.

Other churches reflect a combination of 'Carmelite' and local characteristics. The extant choir and crossing of their church at South Queensferry on the Forth near Edinburgh is the only building of the order still standing in Scotland. Its long narrow church seems to follow the pattern of the English Carmelite house at Hulne, but is also typical of rural churches in medieval Scotland. At Linlithgow, a passageway between the nave and the chancel connecting the cloister with the cemetery and the 'outside world' was similar to the English Carmelite houses of Aylesford and Hulne. The church at Denbigh in Wales was also a long narrow building, and had a wooden steeple destroyed by fire in 1898. By contrast, at Coventry in the Midlands a large preaching nave (around 49m) was built in the mid-fourteenth century.

The hostility of other clergy, financial constraints and war frequently disrupted or delayed the building campaigns of the order. The archaeological record for Aberdeen in north-east Scotland, although fragmentary, suggests that construction was a slow process extending over much of the thirteenth to fifteenth centuries. Edward III's raid on the city in 1336 may have made matters still worse: although any damage done cannot be precisely measured, grants to the Carmelites in the 1340s included payments for the refurbishing of the friary church and its roof.

On the other hand the Hundred Years' War and plague in some cases benefited houses in the longer term. As well as large naves, mendicants of all orders sought to have open space for preaching near or in front of their churches. At Bergerac, where the city was sacked in 1345, the effect of the disastrous plague was to leave empty plots of land to which the Carmelites moved in the second half of the fourteenth century. Near the gate on the main royal road, their new site had sufficient space for a large church and friary with a garden, fishpond and a square in front.[6] The large number of legacies following the Black Death also allowed the friars to consider new foundations; the Carmelites of Catalonia, for example, enjoyed a period of unusual splendour and achievement, marked by the building of new houses. Nonetheless, plague remained a constant threat: in a letter written in 1421 Thomas Netter of Walden, the English prior provincial (1414–30) referred to twenty-four friars of the London house who had died as a result of infection.

THE LIFE OF A FRIAR

Novices

The constitutions of 1281 provide the first guidelines for the reception of novices. The opening principle was caution – a touchstone of monastic and mendicant life, and comprehensible in view of the extent of the commitment on both sides. A postulant must not be received should he be married, financially indebted, professed in the Cistercian order, or in any other religion 'of our condition' (presumably an indication of their identification with the mendicants by this date). Further vetoes covered doubts about orthodoxy, expulsion from any order for vice, a concealed infirmity or any bodily deformity. Sick laymen were not to be admitted unless 'determined to persevere' or unless refusal would damage the order. Nor was any layman to be welcomed unless suitably qualified in a technical capacity needed by the friars. The only clerics admitted were those who were 'probably literate or at least sufficiently instructed in the Office, and capable of chanting and reading'.

If he overcame these hurdles, the postulant was to be led to the chapter to petition for admission, lying prostrate before the brothers. The prior was then to explain the harshness and poverty of the life (*religio*) and outline the vows of chastity, poverty and obedience. Before entering, the novice must give up all property. If he wished to make a gift to the order, this could not be accepted directly: he was to be asked to pay it to one of the order's creditors. His secular clothes were usually to be kept until profession was complete. Any postulant buying his own habit must renounce his rights to his clothing and if he later left the order would not be allowed to take the habit with him, a reflection of its symbolic importance to the friars. The novice would then be

---

[6] Ignace, 'Le Couvent des Carmes de Bergerac', p. 168.

received with the kiss of peace and given his place. Following both monastic custom and papal edict, the noviciate lasted a year, to allow understanding of the austerity of the *religio* and the customs of the brethren. During that time he was enjoined to wear distinctive clothing, could not attend the chapter, was not to be entrusted with any office unless there were desperate need and was to be subject to the novice master assigned to introduce the new recruits to the order and its customs. The rule was to be explained to the novices, as to the professed brethren, four times a year (by 1294 this had been restricted to just the novices and lay brethren). Any novice leaving and then choosing to return would have to start all over again at the beginning. With the licence of either the prior general or provincial, at the end of twelve months he could make profession, promising obedience to God, to the Virgin Mary, to the prior general and his successors and to the constitutions of the order. The habit would then be blessed and given by the prior to the novice, who would be asperged (sprinkled) with holy water and accompanied to the choir to lie prostrate before the altar while the community prayed for him. Finally the novice was to kiss the altar, give the kiss of peace to his brethren and be led to his place.

Education

By the last decades of the thirteenth century, a key element in any new clerical Carmelite's life was an emphasis on learning as a preparation for preaching. As in so many other activities, the order imitated the Dominicans and Franciscans in their scholastic organisation. The 1281 constitutions provide for a Carmelite *studium generale*, a house of advanced studies located near the university in Paris. Those with the ability to become lectors were to be sent to study at the theology faculty of the university itself. As we have seen, this was a logical but by no means an inevitable development. Most of the early brethren appear to have been laymen. Their contemplative eremitic life did not encompass an emphasis on theology or learning. Whereas St Dominic had rapidly identified the universities as places of recruitment, and the training of preachers as essential to effective pastoral mission, the Carmelites, like the Franciscans, encountered more difficulties in entering the university world. The prior general Nicholas of Narbonne and perhaps his English successor Ralph (buried at Hulne) preferred the eremitical contemplative life. The first member of the order to have had university training appears to date only from the year of the earliest constitutions, 1281. The need for professional schooling to develop an effective apostolate was acknowledged during the priorate of Pierre de Millau (1277–94). Students from every province were to attend the Paris *studium generale* and the provinces were initially to pay 10 Paris *livres* per student, to cover their books, clothing and housing (16 *livres tournois* in 1294). In common with the Dominicans, there were also to be *studia particularia* in each province, for the study of the fundamental skills of grammar, logic and philosophy, and centred on Peter the Lombard's *Sentences*. Each student was to be supported with 40 *solidi* in money of Tours and the whole network of *studia* was further sustained by a tithe on all the provinces.

In 1294 this skeletal framework was expanded. The Paris convent undertook the teaching of logic and philosophy as well as theology, and four other *studia generalia* were established in Toulouse, Montpellier, London and Cologne. Cologne had been the headquarters of the German provincial Heinrich Jonghen de Bacheim since *c.* 1279 and it was Jonghen who fostered the development of a *studium* for logic and philosophy in the city, the intellectual hub of the Rhineland and already a centre of learning for the Franciscan and Dominican friars. Oxford and Cambridge were never officially *studia generalia* but Carmelite houses in both towns had students at the university. The first Carmelites to incept for the *magisterium* in theology in Oxford and Cambridge are recorded in the 1290s.

Any uncertainty about their dedication to the universities and learning came to an end with Gerardo da Bologna, who became a master in Paris in 1295 and in 1297 was elected prior general. His generalate heralded the tradition of a master of theology as superior of the order and also its strong papalism. He represented the Carmelites at the Council of Vienne (1311–12) and defended the papal position against the criticisms of the Franciscan spirituals who advocated a return to absolute poverty. A letter from Cardinal Berenger Fredol to the general chapter held in London in 1312 praises Gerardo's great learning, candour and maturity of counsel. Significantly, the cardinal also identified the 'utility' of the order (the quality essential to its confirmation a decade or so earlier) as its assiduous prayer life and preaching based on training in theology.[7]

Lickteig's study of German Carmelites demonstrates the enormous commitment of the order to university studies, both financial and numerical.[8] This is confirmed by Copsey's provisional list of English Carmelites attending university between 1350 and 1450, which indicates that of some three thousand brethren, including lay brothers, about 230 attended university, a figure comparable to the Dominicans.[9] The vast majority of these went to Oxford or Cambridge, but a fair number also travelled to Paris. From 1327 there was a *studium generale* in the 'convent' at the Curia, while six years later another was established in Barcelona, which was to become important in the order in the second half of the fourteenth century. By 1379 there were sixteen altogether, including smaller centres such as Valencia or Bruges. In

---

[7] Jotischky, *Carmelites and Antiquity*, p. 31.

[8] Lickteig, *The German Carmelites*, as above p. 19n.

[9] R. Copsey, 'The Formation of the Medieval English Friar: From Dominican Model to Carmelite Practice', in *Omnia disce: Medieval Studies in Memory of Leonard Boyle, O.P.*, ed. A. J. Duggan, J. Greatrex, B. Bolton (Aldershot, 2005), pp. 245–62.

the German province, further *studia generalia* were established in Prague, Vienna, Trier and Mainz, and by the end of the fifteenth century the network of *studia* extended across the west, from Lleida to Krakow, Dublin to Rome. Indeed, by this date, the value of study in the activities of the order is underlined by the prominence given in the records of general chapters to the lists of masters and lectors appointed to each *studium*.

Preaching

The importance of learning was further underlined by the status acquired by the qualified lector: once appointed to a house he was not to undertake any other office but was to have first voice and place after the prior in the choir, refectory and chapter. However, the primary purpose of study was to prepare for preaching. Most ordinary Carmelites divided their lives between contemplation, study, pastoral care and preaching. Some idea of their approach to the latter may be garnered from surviving sermon collections. The Carmelite scholar, Master John Paschal (†1361), who studied at Cambridge before becoming bishop of Llandaff and then Rochester, produced a cycle of seventy model sermons.[10] These were probably written with religious of the order in mind and allow us some inkling of the devotional and spiritual life of a Carmelite community. Thus John the Baptist, who withdrew into the desert, is assimilated to Elijah and presented as a model of virginity and modesty but also as a paradigm for the ministry of preaching. Mary Magdalene, who was particularly venerated by the Carmelites, is commended both as an ideal of abstinence and self-mortification and as a paradigm for the contemplative life. Such models predictably emphasise the virtues of a life that was both contemplative (hermits) and active (friars).

The Virgin Mary is celebrated in various ways: for her purity, as a means of redemption, as a feudal lady and powerful patron, as an example of discipleship and as a powerful intercessor. In the choice of other feasts, the sermons give some idea of the patterns of devotion in the order by this period. The inclusion of mendicant saints such as Dominic, Francis, Clare of Assisi and Louis of Toulouse is particularly interesting since Paschal omits all the eastern saints of the Carmelite calendar. Valerie Edden rightly sees the sermons as elucidating the compromise at the heart of Carmelite life by this date, combining pastoral care in the cities with prayer and silent contemplation.[11]

Another more widely dispersed collection of sermons is that of the prior general Michele Aiguani of Bologna (†1400), a prominent biblical scholar and prior general of the Roman obedience (1381–6).[12] His *Planctus Marie*

[10] V. Edden, 'A Carmelite Sermon Cycle British Library Royal 7.B.I', *Carmelus* 43 (1996), pp. 99–122, 116.

[11] Ibid.

[12] P. Chandler, 'The Lamentation of the Virgin. A *Planctus Mariae* Sermon by Michael Aiguani of

or Lamentation of the Virgin over the sufferings of her son, typical of the genre, gives a sense of the emotional and dramatic potential of a professional preacher. Using a dialogue structure it evokes the conversations of Mary with the women of Jerusalem and with some of the Apostles as she searches for her son, asking each of them where she might find him and weeping throughout. The dramatic highpoint is when Jesus himself calls her to the Cross. Her grief knows no bounds: she cannot go on living, she says, but neither can she die. She reproaches her son for leaving her and contrasts the glory of his birth with his death. In the end she returns to the house of John and rests, weak and ill, as John tries to console her. Though prostrate with grief, after the crucifixion she alone preserves faith in Christ's promise of resurrection. The sermon ends with a reminder of the Virgin's traditional role as intercessor. As Paul Chandler notes, it expresses Mary's suffering with pathos and invites all Christians to share in her suffering. Such sermons were intended to prompt the faithful to a more holy life and Carmelites, like other mendicants, often attracted great crowds to their sermons. This, together with other more regular contact with the laity in their churches, meant that Carmelite priests often found themselves hearing confessions. In 1378 Thomas Hatfield, bishop of Durham (1345–81), who was cautious in the issuing of licences to friars, authorised a Carmelite of Hulne, A. de Clyffe, to hear the confessions of a hundred persons in a year.[13] De Clyffe was certainly not unusual.

It is difficult to say much about individual friars, beyond recording their office-holding or academic careers, but the exceptional career of the Occitan Pierre Thomas (d.1365), who was beatified in the seventeenth century, allows an idea of the kind of career available to high-flying members of the order.[14] Professed in the house at Bergerac, he became a prominent university figure and was used by the popes as a diplomat and legate. Two *vite*, one written by a close associate, Philippe de Mézières, chancellor of the king of Cyprus during 1366 and the other by the Franciscan, John Carmesson, prior of the province of the Holy Land, who preached at his funeral, bear witness to his career as well as to his saintly reputation. According to Philippe, he came from a poor family, but showed early enthusiasm for learning, maintaining himself by his own manual labour and by begging. Once he had joined the order, he trained at various *studia* before finally completing the *magisterium* in record time at Paris. He became Carmelite proctor general at the papal Curia but spent most of his later life promoting crusades in the eastern Mediterranean. He died shortly after the capture of Alexandria in 1365, at which he was present. Both in life and in death Pierre Thomas was credited with miracles. Even without such saintly qualities, he was of course an outstanding member of the order, picked out early on for a career beyond the cloister. He was, however,

---

Bologna, O.Carm.,' *The Land of Carmel*, pp. 209–29.

[13] Durham, Dean and Chapter muniments DPK (no class reference), fol. 133r.

[14] *The Life of St Peter Thomas by Philippe de Mézières*, ed. J. Smet (Rome, 1954).

typical of many friars in that he fulfilled his vocation by study, preaching and itineracy. There is little trace of the hermit life in his experience.

Discipline

Once professed, a brother remained subject to the order for life. Inevitably, not all recruits were ready to keep the observance or happy to remain, but any departure from the rule was subject to harsh discipline. Already in 1227 Gregory IX allowed the prior to deal with apostates (runaways) from the order and by 1269 the prior general was authorised to excommunicate and imprison both apostates and the disobedient.

The range of crimes envisaged in the legislation of the order is revealing: many minor misdemeanours were concerned with maintaining the observance, such as the overnight silence. Others reflect fears common to those both inside and outside the cloister. Any brother found guilty of the 'unspeakable crime' of sexual acts with another man was to spend a long period in prison and then be expelled from the order. By 1294 anyone defaming a brother by accusing them of leprosy or any other 'enormous vice' without being able to prove it, was to be subject to forty days' punishment. Necromancers or alchemists were subject to similar penalty.

In 1281 the London general chapter required that apostates be imprisoned for forty days. In the fourteenth century this was modified according to the length of the period away: longer absences merited longer imprisonment. In 1357 the order adopted a broad definition of apostasy to include any friar who left his convent without permission for however short a period, or any friar who left with permission but failed to return at the designated time. Such regulations required the building of prisons: by the late thirteenth century each province was to have a prison for the insolent and rebels; by 1342, every house was to have its own.

In England as elsewhere, the order also sought the support of the secular arm in maintaining discipline. In 1255, Henry III instructed his officials to assist both Carmelites and Dominicans by arresting apostates of their orders and delivering them to their priors.[15] He wished to 'suppress their insolence' and to come to the assistance of the friars. Such concessions gave the orders immediate access to royal officials without having to proceed by requests to chancery for writs in individual cases. The grant for the Carmelites was renewed in 1265 and 1267 and five times in the fourteenth century.[16] Other rulers and their officials provided similar guarantees. Antoni de Pons of Zaragoza in Aragon is typical of the type of individual targeted. He transferred to the Carmelites from the Franciscans in 1321, but did not stay long

---

[15] On English apostates see D. Logan, *Runaway Religious in Medieval England c. 1240–1540* (Cambridge, 1996).
[16] Ibid., pp. 180–1.

with the Carmelites either and left to get married. The records of the Aragon royal chancery show, however, that he was required to divorce and to return the books he had stolen from the Franciscans.

On occasion secular authorities intervened more generally in the disciplinary affairs of the order. In 1373 the king of Aragon wrote to the Perpignan house admonishing the friars for not obeying the established laws and urging them to submit to the prior's judgement in accordance with the requisites of their Rule. Other secular patrons issued similar warnings.

The order was regularly active against individuals, campaigning for the arrest of apostates. In practice, however, there do not seem to have been many: in his study of runaway religious in medieval England based on the Patent Rolls and on writs against individual friars, Donald Logan lists only thirty-seven Carmelites between the 1290s and 1453. From the 1380s down to 1415 some of these became papal chaplains as a legal alternative exempting them from the regular life and obedience to their superiors. In 1386, according to Thomas Walsingham, monk of St Albans and author of the *Gesta abbatum*, Walter Disse, a Carmelite friar, was empowered by papal mandate to create fifty honorary papal chaplains to support the Lancastrian crusade in Spain. Walsingham reports that monks and friars of all orders took advantage of this opportunity to pay Rome for release.[17] But in 1395 the Carmelites obtained papal authority to correct errant friars and in 1399 the help of the secular arm to bring papal chaplains and apostates back to obedience; they also again sued writs against individual friars. In 1415 the practice of appointing honorary papal chaplains ceased.

The Carmelites, like other religious, were also at times accused of accepting boys who were too young. In 1358 John de Thornton, citizen and spicer of York, claimed that the Carmelites of the city had ensnared his son Richard, who had taken his profession before he reached fourteen. Although Richard had departed before this age, the friars called him an apostate and sought his arrest. The king took Richard under royal protection pending further investigation. In 1443 the London Carmelites were involved in a similar dispute when John Hawteyn claimed that he had been placed in the London priory at the age of eight. He had run away but had been returned by his mother and imprisoned by order of Thomas Netter of Walden, the prior provincial (1414–30). He was later held in prison in Oxford but in 1447 the sentence went against the Carmelites and Hawteyn was released from the order.

Death

Even for the most reluctant friars, membership of the order offered the potential of solidarity in life and also in death. The passing of a brother was

---

[17] Cited ibid., p. 51. On papal chaplains, see also below, p. 164.

to be reported to the prior provincial and by him to all priors in the province without delay. The body was to be buried in the cemetery of the house, at a distance from any secular tombs. The right to have a separate cemetery was implicit in early papal letters supporting the order and made explicit by Urban IV already in 1262.[18] Masses were to be said for the dead friar's soul, as for the servants and the benefactors of the order, both living and dead. Any books belonging to the dead were to be returned to the province of origin: some might be sold, others given for the use of other brothers.

[18] *Speciali gratia*, 17 May 1262 (*BC* I, 25).

CHAPTER FOUR

Later History and the Development of a Historiographical Tradition

Institutional change and growth in the fourteenth century

In an attempt to put an end to disputes with the secular clergy, in 1300 Boniface VIII defined limits for the pastoral activities of Franciscans and Dominicans which were later applied to the Carmelites. In *Super cathedram* (18 February 1300) he stated that the care of souls was fundamentally the duty of bishops and parish clergy.[1] The activities of the mendicant friars were therefore only supplementary to the work of seculars. The friars might preach in their own churches and public squares, but must avoid times when local churchmen were accustomed to preach. Friars were not to preach in parish churches, hear confessions or perform burials without the permission of the bishop. Once so authorised, they were nonetheless to share any revenues, paying the canonically defined portion to the parish clergy. Benedict XI (a Dominican) revoked Boniface's bull, but the restriction was renewed by Clement V at the Council of Vienne (1311–12) and remained in force until the Council of Trent (1545).[2] Originally *Super cathedram* named only the Franciscans and Dominicans, but in 1326 John XXII added the Carmelites.[3] This was also an admission of the full 'mendicant' status of the order. The eremitical element was not lost in the fourteenth and fifteenth centuries, but from this date the Carmelites enjoyed both the range and the limitations of mendicant privileges.

Conflict over exemptions between seculars and regulars also reached a peak at Vienne. Being exempt placed an institution or order in a privileged position subject only to the pope and beyond the authority of bishops, who frequently objected. James de Thermis, abbot of the Cistercian monastery of Charlieu (and later of Pontigny) defended the exempt status of his own order and that of the Cluniacs, incorporating in his account the four mendicant orders: the Dominicans, Franciscans, Augustinians and Carmelites. The grounds for his inclusion of the Carmelites here are not obvious since their

---

[1] Digard, 3473.
[2] Constitution 10 of the Council of Vienne, *Conciliorum oecumenicorum decreta*, ed. J. Alberigo *et al.* (Bologna, 1973), pp. 365–9.
[3] *Inter ceteros ordines*, 21 November 1326 (*BC* I, 66).

exempt status is not previously documented. However, in 1317 John XXII finally made them fully exempt, releasing the brothers and their property from either the spiritual or temporal jurisdiction of diocesan bishops or any other authority 'by special grace'.[4]

The fourteenth century might be considered a golden age for the Carmelite order. They had acquired all the privileges of their mendicant status, were established and expanding in the universities and enjoyed substantial lay patronage. In England this included considerable support from the Crown. There were, however, changes in the observance, tellingly illustrated in the extant constitutions on property. Whereas the original ideal had been one of individual poverty, by 1362 provisions proved necessary concerning any buildings constructed by the brethren themselves. If any friar bought or built a room or other accommodation in a convent, he was not to be allowed to sell or bequeath it. Rather, on his death it must automatically belong to the convent. The friars were evidently maintaining property of their own. Regular assistance from the laity was essential to the survival of the order and its houses, and Jens Röhrkasten has shown that London mendicants were openly receiving gifts for their own personal use.[5] London was certainly not unique. The principle of begging and the use of *questors* sent out to collect alms survived, but the early emphasis on personal poverty and communal austerity was lost.[6] Donors' gifts in return for masses often reflected the hierarchy of a community in economic terms, distinguishing between small gifts for ordinary friars who said prayers and larger donations for the celebrant or prior. Attempts were repeatedly made to restrict ownership: the general chapter of 1372, amongst others, specifically prohibited the purchase of land, houses, animals or other property by any individual friar and instructed those who had property to dispose of it within six months. The pattern of property ownership had, however, been firmly established, though extant records for the province of Lower Germany, where the largest house by far was Cologne (ninety-two brothers in 1433), show that income (including in grain) varied substantially from year to year and was closely dependent on offerings for Masses, preaching and begging. Deficits were not unknown.[7]

During the papal schism (1378–1417) the friars, so closely dependent on lay patronage, identified with the policy of the secular authorities in the lands in which they resided. Thus, as Catalans living in the Crown of Aragon, the prior general Bernat Oller and the provincial Felip Ribot were supporters

---

[4] *Sacer ordo vester*, 13 March 1317 (*BC* I, 57).

[5] J. Röhrkasten, 'Mendikantische Armut in der Praxis – das Beispiel London', in *Proposito paupertatis. Studien zum Armutsverständnis bei den mittelalterlichen Bettelorden*, ed. G. Melville and A. Kehnel (Münster, 2001), pp. 135–67, 154.

[6] On *questors*, used by all the mendicant orders, see pp. 140, 198.

[7] H.-J. Schmidt, 'Die Wirtschaftsführung der Bettelorden in Deutschland (XIII.–XIV. Jahrhundert)', in *L'economia dei conventi dei frati minori e predicatori fino alla metà del trecento*, Atti del XXXI convegno internazionale, Assisi 2003 (Spoleto, 2004), pp. 263–94, 285–93.

of Clement VII (1378–94). In April 1380 schism was introduced directly into the order when Oller was deprived of his office by Clement's opponent, Urban VI, and replaced by Michele Aiguani of Bologna. The 'pro-Urban' provinces in Italy, Germany, Ireland, England and those areas of France under English influence supported the move. Oller's deposition was not, however, recognised in the lands of the Clementine obedience (France, Scotland, Sicily, Cyprus, and Corfu) and he remained at the head of the schismatic wing of the order until his death (1383). In 1381 Moreto, a Venetian loyal to Urban VI, was in turn appointed to replace Ribot as prior provincial, but Ribot continued to perform the duties of the office and was confirmed in position along with all the 'schismatic' provincials by the Carmelite general of the Clementine (Avignon) party in 1385.

These divisions no doubt prompted spiritual difficulties. As Jill Webster has noted, the Rome and Avignon popes sought support among the clergy by issuing special privileges and dispensations; the beneficiaries included the Carmelites.[8] Disagreement was almost inevitable and division also affected the students of the order. German Carmelites could no longer attend the French universities, which led them to move to Italy and to other universities of the Empire. Only in 1409, when the Council of Pisa deposed the schismatic popes, were the two sides brought back together. The order was finally reunited at a general chapter in Bologna in 1411 under Jean Grossi, prior general of the Avignon obedience since 1389 and of the united order until 1430.

Liturgy

As they developed an increasingly mendicant way of life the Carmelites replaced individual recitation of the Office in the hermit's cell with communal recitation in choir. This required the development of a tradition for the Office: like their mendicant predecessors, they adopted the shorter observance based on the practice of cathedral canons rather than the longer monastic *cursus* (order of the Office). The reduction allowed time for pastoral concerns while still maintaining communal recitation. At this early date the Carmelites still had houses in the East and they adopted the rite of the church of the Holy Sepulchre, Jerusalem, developed from French origins by the Austin canons who served there. Thus the early Carmelite rite replicated that of the diocese in which they found themselves. It was to include both eastern and western elements: saints of French derivation alongside new feasts for biblical figures such as Abraham, Isaac and Jacob.[9]

---

[8] J. Webster, *Carmel in Medieval Catalonia* (Leiden, 1999), p. 114, identifies this as a cause of loss of discipline.

[9] J. Boyce, 'The Liturgy of the Carmelites', *Carmelus* 43 (1996), pp. 5–41; C. Dondi, *The Liturgy of the Canons Regular of the Holy Sepulchre of Jerusalem. A Study and a Catalogue of the Manuscript Sources* (Turnhout, 2004).

Sibert de Beka, provincial of Lower Germany and a master in Paris (†1332), compiled an ordinal adopted for use by the whole order in 1312. This prescribed the texts of chants, prayers and readings to be used each day, proposed the feasts to be celebrated and the appropriate degree of solemnity. In constructing the new Ordinal, Sibert relied closely on the rite of the Holy Sepulchre; he was also probably familiar with an earlier English ordinal. Surviving manuscripts, such as the Office books of the Carmine in Pisa (before 1342) and Florence (late fourteenth century) or a set used in Mainz (fifteenth century), suggest that the result was widely observed. The new ordinal gave the Carmelites a single liturgical identity. A visitor to a Carmelite church would have experienced a rite different from local diocesan practice, but similar to that in other churches of the order. The distinctive features were the cycle of saints and specific chants. The order claimed the Virgin Mary as its special patron so the *Ave stella matutina* antiphon honouring her was used daily and the feasts of the Purification and Annunciation were placed on successive days in order to create a Marian festival. In 1342 Marian devotions were extended to include a daily Mass to the Virgin and the *Salve regina* after each Office. By 1369 a special Carmelite hymn to the Virgin known as the *Flos Carmeli* ('Flower of Carmel') had been composed and was later to be linked to the name of Simon Stock:

> Flower of Carmel,
> blossoming vine,
> splendour of heaven,
> child-bearing Virgin
> unequalled.
> Tender Mother
> whom no man didst know,
> to the Carmelites
> give privileges,
> Star of the Sea.[10]

Whereas the liturgy developed uniformly, Carmelite music was not standardised. Unlike the Dominicans or Augustinians, no prototype of liturgical books was ever produced and the Carmelites did not immediately adopt a single musical tradition. The careful preservation and transmission of chants from one house to another implies particular prestige amongst the Carmelites but individual convents were often left to devise the details of their own musical settings. Just four Carmelite musicians from the medieval period have been identified: Bartolino da Padova, 'Frater Carmelitus' (fl. 1381–1410), an Englishman, John Hotby (†1486), and Giovanni Bonadies (fl. 1450–1500).[11]

---

[10] On the links with Stock see R. Copsey, 'Simon Stock and the Scapular Vision', *Journal of Ecclesiastical History* 50 (1999), pp. 652–83, reprinted in *Carmel in Britain*, III, pp. 75–112, from whom this translation is taken.

[11] P. Mirck, 'Biblioteca Carmelitana musices', *Carmelus* 5 (1958), pp. 100–31.

Saints

Devotion to the Virgin was to become the focus of the spirituality of the order, which was named the Hermits of the Blessed Virgin of Mount Carmel in her honour. Already in 1252 Innocent IV was using the Marian title, but the first text to express the idea that the order was especially founded to honour the Virgin Mary is a letter of Pierre de Millau, prior general 1277–94, addressed to King Edward I of England some time before October 1282. The same idea is repeated in the acts of the general chapter of 1287.

Following Dominican and, more recently, Franciscan practice, in 1306 the Carmelites adopted the feast of the Conception of the Virgin on 8 December. The doctrine that the Virgin was conceived without sin was much disputed in these years. It was not generally accepted by the Dominicans or by the Carmelite priors general, Gerardo da Bologna and his successor Guiu Terreni (1318–21, †1342). Indeed Sibert's ordinal entitles the feast only 'Conception of Saint Mary or rather veneration of the sanctification of Saint Mary'. Not until the work of the Carmelite theologian John Baconthorpe (†1348), who argued in 1340 that Mary bore the necessity of contracting original sin but that God removed this as a special privilege, did the Carmelite position on the Immaculate Conception become clear. Two years thereafter, Richard FitzRalph, later Archbishop of Armagh, was invited to preach on the feast of the Conception in the Carmelite church in Avignon and in his sermon laid out the reasons why the feast should be celebrated.[12] A manuscript version of the sermon was to achieve wide circulation, a marker of the interest aroused by the issue.

The order's claim to a special relationship with Mary acquired other new features in the following decades. In 1393 the order was one of the first to recognise the feast of the Visitation, celebrated on 2 July, and Mary's mother, St Ann, was to acquire particular prominence in the west through the efforts of the Carmelites. Catalogues of the order's saints from the end of the 1300s, begin to record a singular privilege: in a vision attributed to Simon Stock in 1251, the Virgin herself gave the Carmelites their scapular. As she handed this garment to Simon she said 'this will be your and your brethren's privilege, that whoever dies wearing it will be saved'.[13] The parallels with the Dominican tradition of the giving of the habit to Brother Reginald by the Virgin would not have been lost on contemporary churchmen. Northern European Carmelites may originally have promoted the story. A catalogue of saints written in the early fifteenth century, probably by an English Carmelite, claimed that Louis IX, Edward II and Henry, duke of Lancaster, all wore the

---

[12] Ricardi archiepiscopi Armacani, 'Bini sermones de immaculate conceptione B. V. Mariae,' ed. B. Zimmerman, *Analecta ordinis Carmelitarum discalceatorum* 3 (1931). On FitzRalph's later criticisms of the mendicants see below, pp. 154–6.

[13] See Copsey, 'Simon Stock and the Scapular Vision', pp. 652–83.

scapular secretly in life and died clothed in it. The theme of the protective power of the scapular achieved wide acceptance in the order and continued as an important feature of Carmelite devotion in the modern period; thus in the 1740s Tiepolo portrayed the giving of the scapular on the ceiling of the chapter hall of the Venetian Carmelites.

The order's Marian patronage was to be contested by opponents of the Carmelites in the universities but it also led the Carmelites themselves to explore it. The Catalan provincial Felip Ribot attempted to make sense of it by attributing to Elijah the prophesy of the role of Mary as the Mother of God and thus the dedication of the order to the Virgin.[14] His Catalan colleague Bernat Oller also laid emphasis on the Marian associations of the order. In a work on the conception of the Virgin he identified Mary as both the patron and the 'mother' of the Carmelites, *mater Carmeli*, an idea which had first been recorded in the acts of the provincial chapter of Lombardy in 1333.[15]

The Carmelite sanctoral year reflects the development of the order, incorporating both eastern and western elements. Alongside the feast of the patriarchs Abraham, Isaac and Jacob adapted from the rite of the Holy Sepulchre with a full Proper Office and Mass, other feasts for bishops and martyrs linked with Jerusalem included Sts Quiriacus, Simeon and Narcissus. James Boyce has shown that the Carmelites were willing to accept feasts into their liturgy from a variety of sources. Thus Sibert's ordinal reveals that the order was early to celebrate the feast of the Transfiguration (6 August). Additionally, in the mid-fourteenth century they adopted the feast of the Three Marys. According to Provençal tradition, Lazarus, Mary Magdalene and two sisters of the Virgin Mary were set adrift in an oarless boat, which carried them to the coast of Provence, near what is now known as Les Saintes-Maries-de-la-Mer. Devotion to the Three Marys rapidly developed in the region and at the general chapter of Lyons in 1342, hosted by the Provençal brethren, the Carmelites added the feast to their rite. Carmelite devotion was encouraged by a poem by the Carmelite chronicler Jean de Venette, *Histoire des trois Maries*, in 1357. The two surviving complete sets of early Carmelite antiphoners each contain a complete rhymed Office for the feast but, as we might expect, the musical settings are quite different.[16]

In the late fourteenth and early fifteenth century, other saints and *beati* were added to the musical and visual language of the order. In addition to Simon Stock and Bertholdus, two other Carmelite friars began to be venerated: in 1457 an office was established both for Angelo of Licata (†1225), who was supposed to have lived on Mount Carmel for many years before travelling

---

[14] See Webster, *Carmel in Medieval Catalonia*, pp. 3–4.

[15] Ibid., pp. 91, 108.

[16] J. J. Boyce, 'The Office of the Three Marys in the Carmelite Liturgy, after the Manuscripts Mainz, Dom- und Diozesanmuseum, Codex E and Florence, Carmine, Ms. o', *Journal of the Plainsong and Mediaeval Music Society* 12 (1989), pp. 1–38.

to Sicily and Rome and meeting Sts Francis and Dominic, and for Alberto of Trapani (†1306), a model for cenobitic monasticism, who had lived a life of prayer and study, ministering to the laity of Messina.

Marian themes also played an important role in Carmelite iconography. In the thirteenth century, in Italy at least, the brothers often placed on their high altars venerated images of the Virgin Mary believed to have been brought from the Holy Land.[17] As we might anticipate of an order dedicated to poverty, few of these panels were artistically conspicuous. In 1329, however, perhaps emboldened by the final approval of their privileges by Pope John XXII in 1326, the Carmelites of Siena acquired a polyptych in the latest style: Pietro Lorenzetti was commissioned to produce the most spectacular altarpiece for the Carmelites anywhere in the 1300s. It was placed on the main altar of their church. St Elijah (wearing the white Carmelite mantle) and St Nicholas (to whom the church was dedicated), flank the enthroned Virgin and Child in the main panel. Elijah presents to the Child a text from the Book of Kings referring to his victory over false prophets. Side panels show Elijah's disciple and successor Elisha, John the Baptist (the new Elijah and a prototypical hermit), Catherine of Alexandria and Agnes.[18] These main panels were supported by a predella with five historical scenes and topped with further panels with pairs of apostles and busts of prophets. The heavy cost of 150 *lire* was such that the Carmelites successfully petitioned the city for a subsidy towards this 'renowned and very beautiful panel'.

Lorenzetti set a model for subsequent Carmelite altarpieces and especially for the inclusion of Elijah, the proclaimed founder of the order, repeated for example in the polyptych attributed to Andrea di Bonaiuto, painted in the 1360s for the Florentine Carmine. In this, the figure of Elijah is holding a scroll with a text from the Book of James which, as Megan Holmes has argued, identifies Elijah as a Carmelite and as a model for deeply felt prayer: 'Elijah was a man of like passions with us and he prayed fervently'.[19] Similar commissions were soon undertaken elsewhere, so that alongside small-scale panels of the Virgin Mary numerous fourteenth- and fifteenth-century Carmelite altarpieces survive in Italy, Sicily and beyond. The production of images was encouraged by the superiors of the order: in 1420, the general chapter ordained, for example, that there was to be an image of Beato Alberto of Trapani in every convent.

[17] C. Gardner von Teuffel, 'Masaccio and the Pisa Altarpiece: A New Approach', *Jahrbuch der Berliner Museen* 19 (1977), p. 37.

[18] J. Cannon, 'Pietro Lorenzetti and the History of the Carmelite Order', *Journal of the Warburg and Courtauld Institutes* 50 (1987), pp. 18–28; M. Israëls, 'Sassetta's Arte della Lana Altarpiece and the Cult of Corpus Domini in Siena', *The Burlington Magazine* 143 (2001), pp. 532–43; M. Israëls, 'Altars on the Street. The Wool Guild, the Carmelites and the Feast of Corpus Domini in Siena, 1356–1456', in *Ritual in Renaissance Siena. Comparative Disciplinary Approaches*, ed. P. Jackson and F. Nevola, special issue of *Renaissance Studies*, forthcoming 2006.

[19] M. Holmes, *Fra Filippo Lippi the Carmelite Painter* (Newhaven, 1999), p. 31.

By the late fourteenth century many of these panels were placed within larger decorative schemes, including monumental fresco cycles underlining both the importance of Carmelite saints and their history. Major Carmelite churches often had a large number of decorated chapels each with altarpiece, frescoes and other furnishings provided by lay patrons. Perhaps the most famous is the Brancacci chapel in Florence, which came to house a miraculous thirteenth-century image of the Madonna del Popolo at the centre of a popular local cult. In the 1420s the painters Masaccio and Masolino began work on a cycle of frescoes for the chapel focusing on St Peter, which was to become famous as one of the key works of the Florentine Renaissance. Watching these masters at work on the Brancacci frescoes may also have been formative in the unusual career of a Carmelite painter, Fra Filippo Lippi (1406–69). The son of a butcher, Lippi joined the order as a boy and professed in 1421: ten years later he was referred to as a *dipintore*. In 1430–4, he in turn completed a monumental fresco portraying the confirmation of the rule of the order for the cloister of his own friary, before being expelled for a scandalous love affair.

For the Carmelites as for others, Marian iconography was also often combined with representations of the Trinity. The eminent theologian and chancellor of the University of Paris, Jean Gerson (1363–1429), complained in a sermon about a statuette of the Virgin that he had seen at the Carmelite church in Paris. Her body opened to show the Holy Trinity, conveying the mistaken notion that the entire Trinity took flesh in the Virgin Mary, rather than just her son.[20] What Gerson saw may have been similar to a statuette of unknown provenance now in the Musée de Cluny in Paris.

History and conflict

In the twelfth century Gerard of Nazareth's *De conversatione servorum Dei* had underlined the importance of a hermit's dedication to the solitary life as adopted by the Old Testament exemplars of Elijah and Moses. In the absence of a charismatic founding figure, fourteenth-century historians of the order claimed this same prophet Elijah as their originator and contended that there had been eremitical monasticism on Mount Carmel continuously from the time of Elijah down to the fall of Acre in 1291. This tells us little about the origins of the order but a great deal about narrative competition between religious in the late-fourteenth-century West. In the face of their critics the friars urgently needed reassurance about their origins, a common concern of the new religious orders of the thirteenth and fourteenth centuries. The

---

[20] J. C. Schmitt, 'Liberté et normes des images occidentales', in J. C. Schmitt, *Le Corps des images* (Paris, 2002), pp. 135–64, 161, originally published as 'Normen für die Produktion und Verwendung von Bildern im Mittelalter', in *Prozesse der Normbildung und Normveränderung im mittelalterlichen Europa*, ed. D. Ruhe and K.-H. Spieß (Stuttgart, 2000), pp. 1–25.

constitutions of the order surviving from 1281, but certainly based on earlier texts, reflect this anxiety and the self-doubt it may have engendered. The opening rubric is a model answer addressed to those, including younger friars as well as outside sceptics, who asked about their beginnings. The answer is apparently straightforward: since the time of Elijah and Elisha, there had been a succession of holy fathers of both the Old and the New Testament living in the solitude of Mount Carmel as true lovers of heavenly contemplation, in holy penitence next to the spring of Elijah. In the time of Pope Innocent III, Albert of Jerusalem brought their successors together in one community (*collegium*) and wrote a rule for them. Pope Honorius III and his successors later approved it. Ancient tradition was thus neatly wedded to contemporary juridical propriety.

Later versions of the constitutions add details to this account, betraying the current concerns of the compilers. In 1294 they affirm that Albert wrote the rule '*before* the Lateran council'. *Ne nimia religionum diversitas*, constitution 13 of the Fourth Lateran Council (1215), had prohibited new orders (new rules or *religiones*) or the adoption of new habits. As we have seen, this test had been applied at the Second Council of Lyons in 1274 and it was therefore essential to underline that the Carmelite rule and order predated 1215. Some time between 1294 and the 1320s the compilers of the constitutions also added an explanation of the Marian association of the full name they had adopted. Following Christ's incarnation, the successors of the first fathers built a church in honour of Mary, and henceforth they became known by apostolic privilege as the Brothers of the Blessed Mary of Mount Carmel (*fratres beate Marie de monte Carmeli*). Later constitutions add further revealing details: by the second half of the fourteenth century it was even deemed necessary to explain the location of Mount Carmel, 'not far from Acre'. Since the loss of the city in 1291, knowledge of the Holy Land could no longer be taken for granted.

From the end of the thirteenth century onwards, as Andrew Jotischky has shown, the Carmelites produced a remarkable series of short historical treatises filling in the details in the history of the order and bridging the two-thousand year gap between the prophet Elijah and the interventions of Albert in the early 1200s. Their purpose was to provide an ancient origin for their order and above all to counter sceptics by proving that there had been a continuous monastic presence on Mount Carmel since Elijah. The first rubric was a foundational text, as was a late-thirteenth-century text known as the *Universis christifidelibus* which may have been written by Sibert de Beka. Non-Carmelite authors were also important, such as the Dominicans Vincent de Beauvais or Stephen of Salagnac, whose *De quatuor in quibus Deus Predicatorum Ordinem insignivit* (1277–8) replaced Albert of Jerusalem with Aymericus Malafayda, patriarch of Antioch (1140–93). According to Stephen, Aymericus wrote the Carmelite rule, brought them together and obtained papal confirmation.[21] Allegedly a native of Salagnac like Stephen, Aymericus's role was to be accepted by later writers such as the English theologian John Baconthorpe, who wrote four treatises on the order and emphasised the Marian devotion of the first Carmelites, or his contemporary Jean de Cheminot, whose treatise written in 1337 was used by Richard FitzRalph in his sermon of 1342 on the Immaculate Conception.[22] Later Carmelites also dedicated energy and resources to developing the narrative of their order, taking the accounts of Baconthorpe and Cheminot and producing regional perspectives. Jean de Venette, prior provincial of France (1342–66), like Cheminot, furnished a Franco-centric slant, while William of Coventry provided an 'English' version which was to influence numerous later writers. In the late fourteenth century Felip Ribot provided a new version which was widely accepted, but over the course of the fourteenth to sixteenth centuries numerous derivative and ever more embellished and mythical accounts of the history of the order were produced by men such as Thomas Scrope, an English Carmelite writing in the mid-fifteenth century, or John Paleonydorus who wrote three historical works at the very end of the 1400s. John Bale, an English Carmelite, in turn used these texts in the 1520s to 1540s, his antiquarian interests leading him to transcribe and compile vast numbers of Carmelite works, many of which would otherwise now be lost. By an odd coincidence, therefore, much of our knowledge of one of the key mendicant orders of the Middle Ages depends on the work of a man who was to abandon the Catholic Church for Protestantism.

Images played a key role in the interpretation and communication of the history of the order, perhaps best demonstrated in the altarpiece painted for the Carmelites of Siena by Pietro Lorenzetti. Beneath the main panels with Mary and standing saints already mentioned, the five narrative scenes of the predella pick out key moments in the formation of the order, beginning with an angel appearing to Sobac, Elijah's legendary father, and prophesying his son's destiny as the originator of an order of white robed men. In two scenes the predella then shows the hermits at Elijah's well on Mount Carmel and Albert giving the rule to a kneeling group in striped robes next to the same fountain. The final pair of panels portrays papal approval of the rule, and the giving of the new white habit, in fulfilment of the angel's prophecy. The whole history of the order from Elijah to the thirteenth century was thereby succinctly encapsulated.

Artists also explored the implications of this Old Testament identity in less direct but no less engaging ways. A century after Lorenzetti, Masolino's and Masaccio's fresco cycle of the apostle Peter in the Florentine Carmine, and included Carmelites standing behind the saint, a logical projection of

---

[21] *Medieval Carmelite Heritage*, p. 93.
[22] Ibid., p. 114.

the Carmelites' claim to date from the time of Elijah. As Jotischky has noted, 'other mendicants might try to prove that they were *like* the Apostles; the Carmelites could show that they had been *among* the Apostles'.[23]

These and numerous other accounts of the history of the order were both provocative to their critics and an important weapon in its defence. Sceptics, in particular the Dominicans, were quick to spot the implausibility of the Carmelite claim to continuity from Elijah to the present, with its implicit need for a transition from Judaism to Christianity. In the 1370s, conflict flared up with an attack on the Carmelites by John Stokes, a Dominican at the University of Cambridge.[24] Stokes challenged the order on several counts, symptomatic of the problems it was facing. He questioned not only the descent of the Carmelites from Elijah and Elisha, but equally their claim to the Marian title, the change of habit from a striped mantle to white and even the confirmation of the order and Rule. In the face of such public denunciation, John Hornby, regent of the Carmelite *studium* in Cambridge, was chosen to come to the defence of his order. He appeared armed with documentary evidence at an assembly of university figures, including Franciscans and Augustinians, probably held in Little St Mary's, which was commonly used for consistory courts. As well as the privileges granted by a succession of popes and the papally approved rule, Hornby produced the chronicles of the order to show that it legitimately bore the title of Our Lady of Mount Carmel, with special dedication to the Mother of God, and could rightly be considered to imitate and follow Elijah and Elisha.

Hornby was at least formally victorious. In February 1375, John of Dunwich, chancellor of the university, issued a decree vindicating the Carmelites. A copy was kept at the London Carmelite convent. Stokes was, however, by no means unique: John of Hildesheim's *Dialogus inter directorem et detractorem de ordine Carmelitarum* (*c.* 1370–4) also stemmed from a defence of the order against an opponent who was probably another Dominican. Some time later, Richard of Maidstone (†1396) wrote the *Protectorium pauperis* in reply to the Lollard John Ashwardby, vicar of St Mary's, Oxford. Ashwardby preached against the mendicants in his church, following arguments adopted by Richard FitzRalph of Armagh who, in his Avignon sermon in 1342, seems to have accepted the Carmelites as monastic ascetics and therefore their accounts of their origins, but who had later become a harsh critic of the very idea of mendicancy.[25]

---

[23] Jotischky, *Carmelites and Antiquity*, p. 333.

[24] Discussed by J. P. H. Clark, 'A Defense of the Carmelite Order by John Hornby, O.Carm., A.D. 1374', *Carmelus* 32 (1985), pp. 73–106.

[25] "'Protectorium pauperis", a Defense of the Begging Friars by Richard of Maidstone, O.Carm. (†1396)', ed. A. Williams, *Carmelus* 5 (1958), pp. 132–80; discussed by V. Edden, 'The Debate between Richard Maidstone and the Lollard Ashwardby (ca. 1390)', *Carmelus* 34 (1987), pp. 113–34. See also K. Walsh, *A Fourteenth-Century Scholar and Primate: Richard FitzRalph in Oxford, Avignon and Armagh* (Oxford, 1981) and below, pp. 154–6.

Hornby, Hildesheim and Maidstone are typical of the defenders of the order: they responded to their detractors with creative flair, remedying the gaps and problems in the early accounts and invoking both history and papal authority. Such rewriting of the Carmelite past continued throughout the later Middle Ages, as did the criticisms of Dominicans, Wyclifites and their successors. By the early sixteenth century, therefore, when Bale began to investigate the details, Carmelite historical tradition was both widely known and, it must be admitted, probably as widely disbelieved.

Learning

One of the best guides to the spiritual and intellectual life of any order is the collection of books owned and used by its friars. Individual Carmelites were supposed neither to keep nor to bequeath books without licence. However, in Italy from the 1320s if not before, at the end of the noviciate a friar was provided with money to acquire a breviary and, should there be any left over, to buy other books. These remained his property until death, when they were to be returned to the convent where he had said his first Mass. Most books therefore belonged to convents rather than individuals. By 1324 collections of books were to be found in most houses and in 1330 the provincial chapter in Lombardy found it necessary to decree that books were not to be loaned out from any library to anyone, of whatever status, whether for making copies or for any other purpose. By the 1370s, however, the libraries were well enough supplied for the general chapter to allow the sale of library books which were useless or duplicates, as long as the money was used for the convent, either to pay off loans or for building works.

The best-documented Carmelite library before 1400 is certainly that in Florence.[26] An extant account book shows the gradual development of the collection over the course of the 1300s, including the sale of books to pay for new texts or for the repair of old ones. An inventory from the end of the century shows that there were separate collections of service books (forty-seven items, one of which is fourteen volumes of antiphonaries), a 'reference collection' (113 items) and books available to the friars on long or short loan (655 books), for which some may have paid a 'fee'.[27] The reference collection, kept on fourteen shelves in close proximity to the church, included a few canon-law texts, biblical commentaries, Peter the Lombard's *Sentences* with commentaries, Aquinas's *Summa theologica* and similar texts. Philosophical works included Aristotle and Aquinas; moral theology was

---

[26] See K. W. Humphreys, *The Library of the Carmelites at Florence at the End of the Fourteenth Century* (Amsterdam, 1964).

[27] See L. Pellegrini, 'Libri e biblioteche nella vita economica dei mendicanti', in *L'economia dei conventi dei frati minori e predicatori fino alla metà del Trecento*, Convegno del Centro interuniversitario di studi francescani, Ottobre 2003 (Spoleto, 2005), pp. 187–214, 202.

encompassed by a variety of authors including Richard of Middleton, the Augustinian Richard Kylington and the Dominican Guillaume de Peyraut. Much of the remainder consisted of collections of sermons (including those of the Carmelite Gerardo da Bologna) and lives of saints by writers such as Jacopo da Voragine (author of the Golden Legend) or Luca da Bitonto. The loan collection included second copies of some of the reference collection necessary for study, liturgical books and preaching aids such as Alan of Lille's *Summa*, Voragine, Caesarius of Heisterbach's *Liber miraculorum*, works of the fathers, more recent theologians and the very popular writings of Albertanus of Brescia, a thirteenth-century lay preacher. As Humphreys has noted, the Florence friary had relatively few books for the non-theological elements of the later-medieval curriculum. There were a few medical texts (Constantinus Africanus, Isaac and Godfrey of Viterbo), some historical works, appropriately including Jacques de Vitry's *Historia orientalis* with its reference to Mount Carmel, and just a couple of what might be called 'recreational' works, Dante's *Divina commedia* and Albertanus of Brescia's edifying *Tale of Melibee* in the vernacular. The works of Carmelites are included: alongside Gerardo da Bologna and Michele Aiguani they had the writings of John Baconthorpe and Guiu Terreni, but the largest section, as we might expect, concerned preaching aids: collections of *exempla* and sermons.

Such library collections were built up by gifts from patrons, friends and relatives of the friars and by the friars themselves: for exmple, the Carmelite Office books surviving from Mainz were commissioned in memory of his parents by Friar Johannes Fabri and completed in 1432.[28] Among the donors in Florence there were lay brethren: Friar Ludovico Pieri who died in 1394 left 'a book with a commendation of his soul and many other offices', but many more had belonged to learned brothers such as Friar Zanobi Tinghi, a lector and provincial prior (†1369), who bequeathed a number of volumes, including commentaries on the *Sentences* by Michele Aiguani and by the Franciscan Bonaventura, the *Summa* of another Franciscan, Monaldus Justinopolitanus, and a volume on metaphysics. In some cases the collections given by the brothers were extensive: in 1368 friar Andrea Corsini (bishop of Fiesole 1349–73, canonised 1629) gave twenty-one books to the library, while a less distinguished friar, Simone Petrus, who died in 1388, left twenty-seven volumes, including sermon collections, volumes of glossed books of the Bible and Alan of Lille's *Summa* on preaching.

The Florentines had a substantial library by Carmelite standards: a surviving book list from Hulne in 1365 records a number probably more typical of the average house: some sixty library books and twenty others for the church. These included nine volumes of the Bible and glosses, Bernard, Augustine, Gregory, John Chrysostom, Lombard, Aquinas, Fishacre, nine collections

---

[28] See Boyce, 'Liturgy of the Carmelites', p. 19.

of Sermons, thirteen works on law and eight volumes of historical and hagi-ographical works. It also included penitential and preaching sections and lists those loaned to individual friars and, despite legislation to the contrary, occasionally to outsiders: a Bible was lent for life to Lord Percy.[29]

As their book collections demonstrate, both the outstanding writers of the order and the more humble brethren took relatively little interest in secu-lar sciences such as civil law or medicine or grammar. Men such as Gerardo da Bologna, Sibert de Beka, John Baconthorpe, Guiu Terrena or, from a later generation, Felip Ribot, Bernat Oller and Michele Aiguani wrote mainly about biblical, pastoral or theological issues or about the history of their own order.[30]

As they took an increasing role in the universities, so the Carmelites participated in key theological disputes, sometimes with violent results. In the 1330s a riot in the house in Avignon may have been provoked by debates over the beatific vision. Later in the century in England the Carmelites were particularly involved in anti-Wyclifite polemic, which cost them some hostil-ity. In 1370 John Kyningham, later prior provincial of the order, opposed John Wyclif in Oxford, and another Carmelite, Peter Stokes, described him as a 'rabid wolf'. In 1381 both orthodox clergy and Wyclifites accused the Carmelites and the other mendicants of stirring up the Peasants' Revolt. On 16 June 1381 rioters broke into the Carmelite house in Cambridge and stole manuscripts, which were burned in the market square. The strongest critic was the Wyclifite Nicholas of Hereford, who charged the Carmelites with sedition and with having impoverished the people for their own gain. Fol-lowing well-established arguments, Hereford accused them of using men-dicancy to avoid manual work and of setting a bad example by encouraging men to go wandering and to seek wealth by force. The four mendicant houses at Oxford responded in February 1382 with a petition to John of Gaunt in which they defended themselves. Stephen Patrington, Carmelite prior pro-vincial (1399–1414), drew up the petition accusing Hereford himself of insti-gating the riots. Gaunt supported the mendicants.

In 1382 Disse, Gaunt's confessor, and Kyningham attended the Blackfriars council, which condemned twenty-four of Wyclif's teachings. Stokes dic-tated the heresies of Nicholas of Hereford, who was also condemned. The *Fasciculi Zizaniorum* (a collection of anti-Wyclifite and pro-mendicant tracts) were collected, probably by Stephen Patrington and his successors, written up by Thomas Netter of Walden, later also English prior provincial (1414–30), and most likely kept in the Carmelite house in Fleet Street, Lon-don. These include the record of a royal council held in the Stamford house

[29] *Catalogues of the Library of Durham Cathedral at Various Periods, from the Conquest to the Dissolution including Catalogues of the Library of the Abbey of Hulne*, Surtees Society 8 (Durham, 1838), pp. 128, 131.

[30] Humphreys, *The Library of the Carmelites at Florence*, p. 17.

of the Carmelites in 1392 at which a group of bishops and masters, led by the archbishops of Canterbury, York and Dublin, together with seven other bishops, twelve masters from the mendicant orders (three from each), four lawyers and four bachelors in theology, examined Henry Crompe, a Cistercian monk, and forced him to abjure his previous teachings. Henry was discovered to have been condemned previously and in 1393 the king issued a letter to the University of Oxford instructing them to suspend him from all scholarly activity.[31]

Perhaps the most vigorous Carmelite anti-Wyclifite was Thomas Netter. The *Fasciculi Zizaniorum* include the examination of a priest, William Whyte, at a diocesan synod held in Norwich in 1428 and attended by Netter and four other Carmelite masters, as well as members of the other mendicant orders. Amongst the charges against Whyte is the following attack on the mendicants, which, whether accurately reported or not, gives a sense of the heat of the dispute:

> We object and argue that you held, wrote, taught and preached ... that the brothers of the four mendicant orders are pseudo-prophets, mendacious masters, deceiving the people, introducing sects of perdition and blaspheming the way of truth; which lies are nowhere founded in Scripture but absolutely repugnant to evangelical perfection.[32]

Such accusations were radical, but criticism of the Carmelites, as of other friars, was not restricted to the world of the universities and learned clergy. One of the most widely read and heard poets of late-medieval England was Jean de Meun, who used William of St Amour's critique of the mendicants to attack the friars in his *Romaunt de la Rose*, written 1270–80. The anti-fraternal ideas of St Amour thus became common currency among English poets and the Carmelites were easily incorporated into this criticism: the Middle English translation lists them with other friars as not to be trusted for the way they look:

> But sothly, what so men hym calle,
> Freres Preachours ben good men alle;
> Her order wickedly they beren,
> Suche mynstrelles if they weren.
> So ben Augustyns and Cordyleres,
> And Carmes, and eke Sacked Freeres
> And alle freres shodde and bare
> (Though some of hem ben great and square),
> Ful hooly men, as I hem deme;
> Everych of hem wolde good man seme.

---

[31] *Fasciculi Zizaniorum Magistri Johannis Wyclif cum tritico; ascribed to Thomas Netter of Walden*, ed. W. Waddington Shirley, Rerum Britannicarum medii aevi scriptores V (London, 1858), pp. 343–59.

[32] Ibid., p. 419.

But shalt thou never of apparence
Sen conclude good consequence[33]

Piers the Plowman's Crede, written in a similar vein at the end of the four-teenth century, concerns a poor man's quest for spiritual truth. He sets out to learn the Apostles' Creed but at the beginning of the story can find no one to instruct him. He consults friars: a Franciscan, a Dominican, an Austin, and a Carmelite in turn, hoping to learn what he calls the *graith*, the plain truth, but is dismayed that the friars instead each denounce their rival orders or press him for money. The evident implication is that the friars were hardly spiritual in their concerns.

Mitigation and reform

Such criticisms were not aimed exclusively at the Carmelites and should certainly not be taken at face value. They were intended to entertain the reader rather than to explain mendicant life. Nonetheless there were cer-tainly changes in the observance in the later Middle Ages which would have surprised the original hermit friars. The fourteenth century did not see the resolution of the split identity of the order between those who saw the ere-mitical life as their primary aim and those who wished to focus on the active life of pastoral care. The fifteenth century witnessed similar differences of opinion. In 1432, responding to a petition from the order probably debated at the general chapter held in Nantes in 1430, Pope Eugenius IV allowed a mitigation of the rule.[34] The original version had required fasting six days a week and envisaged that the brothers would stay alone in their separate cells day and night in meditation and prayer. They were now instead to fast on just three days each week except during Advent, Lent and the other generally prohibited days. They might also eat meat (a practice in any case often long established), and spend appropriate times freely outside their cells, in their churches, cloisters and their proximity. The focus was more emphatically cenobitic than ever. In 1459 Pius II allowed the prior general to dispense with abstinence and with twice-weekly fasting, and seventeen years later Sixtus IV, who greatly favoured the mendicants, increased their privileges as never before, re-issuing and clarifying previous dispensations and extend-ing those of others to the Carmelites. Known as the *Mare magnum*, Sixtus's

[33] Romaunt of the Rose, in *The Riverside Chaucer*, ed. L. Benson (Oxford, 1987), pp. 685–767, lines 7455–66: 'But truly, whatever men call them/ Friars Preacher are all good men,/ They wear their order wickedly/ As if they were minstrels,/ So do Austin Friars and Cordeliers [Franciscans]/ And Carmelites and Friars of the Sack too,/ And all Friars both shod and bare[foot]/ (although some of them are big and fat),/ Fully holy men, as I them deem,/ Every one of them would like to seem a good man,/ But you should never determine goodness from appearance.'

[34] L. Saggi, 'La mitigazione del 1432 della regola Carmelitana. Tempo e persone', *Carmelus* 5 (1958), pp. 3–29.

intervention in 1476 amounts to an impressive restatement of their privileges and of their autonomy. The compromises with secular clergy and bishops essential to the survival of their friaries in the thirteenth and fourteenth centuries were laid aside. Thus the friars were free from all tithes and other tributes, even when imposed on exempt orders; they were not required to pay the canonical portion on pious legacies; they might live in the lands of excommunicates and if required to travel through them, accept the necessities of life. In their churches they could exercise the care of souls through a chaplain and the bishop might not visit these churches or hold any rights or powers over them. They might celebrate Mass with portable altars anywhere, and for both men and women.[35] Anyone hindering the giving of alms to the brothers of the order would *ipso facto* incur excommunication. The exempt status of the order was declared 'renowned', meaning that the friars could not be required to prove it. They might beg for alms even without having obtained the licence of any local bishop. Bishops were to provide consecration of altars and churches, holy oil and any ecclesiastical sacrament freely. The prior general might regulate fasts and abstinences entirely according to his own conscience. Sixtus also confirmed a decree of John XXII according to which the Carmelites could receive holy orders from any catholic bishop without examination and without any promise or obligation, grounds for understandable opposition from the secular clergy. Finally, the brethren were to be exempt from the jurisdiction of inquisitors, a privilege confirmed by Clement VII in 1530.

These privileges were ratified by Sixtus's successors, but at the Fifth Lateran Council, 1512–17, Leo X mitigated some and revoked others 'in order to preserve mutual charity and good will' between bishops and religious orders and to promote the peace of the universal Church. In a peace-making gesture towards bishops, these were to be allowed to visit Carmelite and other regular churches in some circumstances and to require their presence at solemn processions. Only the diocesan bishop might promote the friars to holy orders, unless he were absent or there were other reasonable cause. The unique right of the bishop to consecrate churches and altars or bless cemeteries and place the first stone of a new church was re-instated, 'unless after two or three requests, made with due reverence, the bishop should refuse without legitimate cause'. Public censures issued by the bishop were to be published and kept in Carmelite churches, as he required. There were also further restrictions on the care of souls. All other privileges were, however, renewed and remained in force until the Council of Trent (1545) in which both the prior general and some forty other members of the order participated.[36]

---

[35] The use of portable altars had been extended to the friars only by Urban V, who, in *Devotionis vestre*, 17 February 1363 (*BC* I, 111), had restricted their use except in response to requests from prelates or magnates.

[36] G. a Virgine Carmeli, 'Die Karmeliten auf dem Konzil vom Trient', *Ephemerides Carmeliticae* 4

As with other contemporary orders, such extensive modifications of the rule led some brethren to wish to return to a stricter observance of what they understood as the original ethos of the Carmelites. Already in 1372 Pope Gregory XI had invited the general chapter meeting at Aix-en-Provence to undertake the reform of the order. In the late fourteenth century, the Catalan provincial Felip Ribot looked back to Elijah as the inspiration and pattern of religious perfection, a reflection of his desire to return the order to the solitary, contemplative way of life of their origins. The steps to the perfect life are outlined in his *Liber de institutione primorum monachorum* (Institution of the First Monks), a mystical work that in Carmelite spirituality was to become second only to the rule in importance and was translated into English, French and Catalan in the fifteenth century.[37] Only through poverty, obedience, chastity, solitude and the achievement of perfect love, he argued, could a pure experience of God be achieved. This continuing interest in the eremitical life led to the decision to establish a hermitage in each province in Catalonia.

The Catalan experiment does not seem to have been very successful but a reformed observance, beginning at Santa Maria delle Selve outside Florence, at Gironda near Sion in Switzerland and above all at Mantua in northern Italy, approved by the provincial chapter of Tuscany in 1413, was to be deeply influential. It developed into the Congregation of Mantua, which obtained papal approval in 1442. Still united to the order, the Observants were to be autonomous, with their own structure under a vicar general. By 1516 and the death of Beato Battista Spagnoli, the best-known member of the congregation, it had thirty-one houses, including San Crisogono in Rome and the *studium* in Bologna. This was eventually to rise to fifteen nunneries founded anew and some fifty male houses, also including numerous new creations. At first the Congregation rejected the 'mitigated rule' and insisted on a more rigid observance of poverty, hermit life in cells and total abstinence from meat. Within a few decades, however, the 1432 rule had largely been accepted, so that despite their separatist tendencies, the Mantuans differed very little from the remainder of the order.

In France, Bishop Louis d'Amboise introduced reform with the assistance of Juan de Standonck, rector of the college of Montaigu and some friars from Mantua. His reform quickly spread to Melun, Ruan, Toulouse and to the college of Place Maubert in Paris.[38] In the German province reform took hold at Mörs (1441) and Enghien (c. 1450), while in France at the very end of the fifteenth century another congregation was established at Albi

(1950), pp. 291–359.

[37] K. Egan, 'The Spirituality of the Carmelites', in *Christian Spirituality. High Middle Ages and Reformation*, ed. J. Raitt (London, 1987), pp. 50–62, 54.

[38] See B. Zimmerman, 'Les Reformes dans l'ordre de Notre-Dame du Mont-Carmel', *Études carmelitaines* 19 (1934), pp. 178–88.

(1499–1584). The result of these reforms, as for the other orders of friars by this date, was a series of new congregations, particularly in Italy.

Jean Soreth, prior general in the 1450s and 1460s, supported the congregations but also encouraged renewal based on the direct action of the general rather than the creation of new and separate entities. His statutes (adopted at the general chapter of Paris in 1456), were approved by Callixtus III in 1457 (hence the later name, the Callixtine observance). The general chapter in Brussels approved new constitutions in 1462. Reformed houses were to remain under the jurisdiction of the provincial prior. The essence of Soreth's reform was a return to the full communal life, without dispensations or special privileges: strict poverty, choir for all without exemptions, common refectory, reduced commitments outside the friary, greater emphasis on early training and on a trial period for postulants, a minimum age of eighteen for profession and twenty-five for the priesthood. The status of the 'mitigated rule' of 1432 was not challenged, but two different types of house were thereby established within the order. Transfers, with permission, were only permitted from a non-reformed to a reformed house, never in the opposite direction.

Soreth carried out direct visitation of numerous houses and sought supporters for the reform to promote his views in his absence. He introduced his strict or 'regular observance' in the Netherlands and in Lower Germany, but there was also resistance. In 1461 the convent in Cologne refused to open their doors to Soreth and in 1462 the general chapter ordained that no convent could be required to live according to the strict observance should the majority dissent, unless the provincial and diffinitors so decided. Soreth never visited Spain but in 1469 he named Bernardo de Montesa as his vicar for the Iberian provinces and he and his successors presumably tried to introduce reforms. In 1480 the provincial chapter in Barcelona forbade priors to allow their brethren to place themselves in the service of temporal lords or parish churches. Soreth's changes were not, however, effective in Spain.

A century after the Congregation of Mantua, Monte Oliveto, founded near Genova by friars from Mantua in 1514 and directly subject to the general, was one of the most important reforms before the great council of the Catholic Reformation at Trent. Nicholas Audet, prior general from 1524 until 1562 was also a keen reformer, introducing reform practices in France, the Low Countries and the Rhineland. The sixteenth century saw perhaps the most significant reform of all, with the foundation in 1562 of the first community of the discalced (barefoot) Carmelites by Teresa of Avila, based on the observance of the primitive, unmitigated rule of Albert of Jerusalem. The sixteenth century also, however, saw the end of several provinces, as the Protestant faith took hold: the English houses were mostly dissolved between 1538 and 1539, the Irish houses were suppressed in 1539–43 and the Scottish houses were dissolved or secularised between 1560 and 1583. Houses were also lost in Protestant lands in Germany, the Low Countries and Switzerland. The order that faced these changes continued to look back to its roots on Mount Carmel: indeed the early modern period saw the beginnings of systematic study of the records of the order which was to lead to the great collection published by Monsignani and Ximénez in the eighteenth century, the *Bullarium Carmelitanum*. These made serious study of the medieval Carmelites possible, but they also mark a new beginning in the history of the community.

PART TWO

The Augustinian or Austin Friars

In the late 1200s the Augustinian Friars were identified as the third of the four main orders of mendicant friars, following the Dominicans and Franciscans in their urban apostolate.[1] By the end of the Middle Ages they were closely linked to the world of the universities and deeply engaged in city life. Yet, like the Carmelites discussed above, their roots lay not in the active life of pastoral care, but in withdrawal to the desert, construed as the forests and caves of central and northern Italy. The early history of the order is thus one of transition and re-invention. It is also perhaps the most disparate of the major medieval religious orders and for that reason numerous aspects of its early history remain problematic for historians, and also of substantial interest.

---

[1] In this they replaced the Carmelites who had earlier been the third order in the 'official' sequence. See D. Gutierrez, *The Augustinians in the Middle Ages 1256–1356* (Villanova, Pa, 1984), p. 52.

CHAPTER ONE

From Hermits to Mendicants

Per plura sacra loca: hermits and hermitages in Italy

From the late tenth century there was a revival of interest across Europe in the reforming ideal of hermit life epitomised by the Desert Fathers of Egypt. The more perfect way of early Christians such as Paul, the first hermit, or Anthony, whose lives seemed closest to the model of the Scriptures, held powerful appeal. In Italy innumerable *ad hoc* settlements of men and (less often) women dedicated to withdrawal (*anachoresis*), asceticism and contemplation set out to recreate the life of the Egyptian Thebaid.[1] What drove them was a desire for salvation through rejection of the world and a penitential life. As Peter Damian, a contemporary enthusiast, famously remarked, 'it seemed as if the whole world would be turned into a hermitage'.[2]

Some of these hermits were true solitaries, living alone in caves or woods for long periods, an ascetic tradition which continued throughout the Middle Ages and was indeed to acquire new life with the urban recluses of late-medieval cities.[3] Many more gathered in groups under the guidance of a charismatic leader or leaders. Men such as Romuald (†1027), founder of a hermitage at Camaldoli in the Appennines (*c.* 1023–6), moved frequently, starting new communities on an experimental basis and then moving on, but always faithful to the idea of the hermit life. In the next generation, Giovanni Gualberto (†1073) stayed at Camaldoli for a while, but then went on to found a community at Vallombrosa (*c.* 1038), high in the wooded hills east of Florence. These foundations were to become the motherhouses of highly

---

[1] The Lower and Upper Thebaid (named from the city of Thebes) were Roman provinces in the upper valley of the Nile. During the third to fifth centuries the region was populated by monks and hermits, led by St Anthony (251–356), whose fame as an ascetic drew disciples imitating his way of life in huts and cells surrounding his own. In 365 one of these, Athanasius, wrote his life, which together with the work of Cassian, was to be an enormously influential text for the development of monasticism. The 'Thebaid' became both a literary and iconographic theme; see A. Malquori: 'La "Tebaide" degli Uffizi – Tradizioni letterarie e figurative per l'interpretazione di un tema iconografico', in *I Tatti Studies: Essays in the Renaissance* IX (Florence, 2001), pp. 119–37.

[2] Petri Damiani, *Vita Beati Romualdi*, ed. G. Tabacco, Fonti per la storia d'Italia 94 (Rome, 1957), p. 78: 'adeo ut putaretur totum mundum in heremum velle converteri et monachico ordini omnem populi multitudinem sotiare. Multos denique illic de seculo abstulit quos per plura sacra loca divisit.'

[3] For the famous case of Umiliana de' Cerchi, who lived as a recluse in her father's house, see, for example, C. Lansing, *The Florentine Magnates* (Princeton, 1991), pp. 115–20.

successful orders of contemplatives, integrating the ideals of the hermit life in the framework of a community cut off from the world.

The *ad hoc*, experimental roots of communities such as Camaldoli and Vallombrosa were echoed in the numerous other groups of hermits that appeared in central and northern Italy throughout the twelfth and early thirteenth centuries. In their efforts to achieve holy perfection, some followed the rule of Benedict, others that of Augustine or simply a form of life based on renunciation and prayer.[4] A few of these may have been involved in a limited form of pastoral care, perhaps assisting a rural priest. But the primary aspiration of such men, implied in the use of names such as *heremita* (hermit), was retreat and solitude, the asceticism of the recluse, the highest level on the ladder of spiritual perfection. It is thus, superficially at least, a paradox that some of these groups were to be united in 1256 into the order of hermit friars of St Augustine, evolving into one of the mendicant orders most engaged in the learned, urban world of late-medieval Europe.

Precursors

The Tuscan Hermits

The bull creating the order of hermit friars issued by Pope Alexander IV in 1256 names five distinct elements: the Hermit Brothers of Tuscany, Williamites, Bonites, Brettini and hermits of Montefavale. Of these the largest were the Tuscan Hermits (*fratres eremitarum tuscie*), an amalgamation of various hermitages spread across central Italy. Two main groups can now be identified: a first in the area of Lucca and Pisa on Monte Pisano and in the Garfagnana (the mountainous area on the River Serchio north of Lucca) and a second in the hills around Siena and down towards the Maremma on the west coast of Italy. By 1223 an initial gathering of four communities was joined in a loose brotherhood which in 1228 increased to thirteen. By their nature, the origins and early history of many of these, as of others to be discussed here, are hard to document. Of those near Lucca, however, Kaspar Elm identifies a hermitage at Santa Maria di Rupecava (or Lupocavo) on Monte Pisano as taking a leading role. An initial community of hermits, centred on a group of caves near Ripafratta, may have come together some time before the mid-twelfth century. They enjoyed the support of the lords of Ripafratta, who donated property, and the bishop of Lucca, who consecrated their church in 1214. Later tradition was to associate the resulting community with St Augustine's

---

[4]   The rule of Benedict, composed in the sixth century, gradually came to dominate the monastic life, replacing most alternatives, so that by the twelfth century it was the standard form of life for regular religious living in enclosed communities in the West and was used by the most successful monks of the twelfth century, the Cistercians. On the rule of Augustine, composed in the fifth century and widely used by regular canons following the reforms of the eleventh century, see below, pp. 93–4.

legendary stay as a hermit in Tuscany.[5] The early thirteenth century also saw a cluster of new or newly documented settlements in the area. To the south of Rupecava stood Santa Maria di Spelonca on Monte Moricone, established before 1198; another hermitage was to be found next to the church of San Giacomo, at Colledonico (1202) while in the same years an *eremo* at Valbuona in the Garfagnana was dedicated to St George and San Galgano, the local hermit saint. Several others could be listed.[6] All were small communities, neither rich nor poor, numbering perhaps no more than ten men. They were frequently subject to a priest, the rector of the church near which they dwelled. Occasionally they shared pastoral responsibilities, leading Elm to suggest that there may have been links with the growing movement of regular canons which emerged as a response to the ideals of reform of the late eleventh century and which frequently turned to the rule of Augustine.[7]

Another cluster of 'Tuscan hermits' emerged during the twelfth and early thirteenth centuries to the west and south of Siena.[8] Some of these survive as little more than names, fleeting references to a hermit or hermitage about which little or nothing can now be said. Others have left sufficient records for us to trace the emergence of community life. One of the earliest was the church of San Leonardo in the Selva del lago (*silve lacus*) a stretch of wooded hills close to the city. The hermitage (*romitorio*), which stood near a small lake, since drained, probably took shape at the end of the eleventh century and, according to a later privilege, was founded in this 'desert place' by Benedetto, a monk-priest.[9] In the second decade of the twelfth century important donations of rights and land from the local lords, the Ardengheschi, began a process of purchases, donations and exchanges which combined to create substantial holdings in the surrounding forest to support the hermits. By

---

[5] A. Ducci, 'L'Eremo di Rupecava nei monti pisani: tracce per una definizione di "storia globale"', in *Augustine in Iconography, History and Legend*, ed. J. C. Schnaubelt and F. Van Fleteren (New York, 1999), pp. 269–331.

[6] A preliminary catalogue is provided in K. Elm, 'Italienische Eremitengemeinschaften des 12. und 13. Jahrhunderts. Studien zur Vorgeschichte des Augustiner-Eremitenordens', in *L'eremitismo in occidente nei secoli xi e xii* (Milan, 1965), pp. 491–559. See also B. van Luijk, *Gli eremiti neri nel dugento con particolare riguardo al territorio pisano e toscano. Origine, sviluppo ed unione* (Pisa, 1968), appendix 8, but note the criticisms of K. Elm, 'Gli eremiti neri nel dugento', *Quellen und Forschungen aus italienischen Archiven und Bibliotheken* 50 (1971), pp. 58–79.

[7] Elm, 'Italienische Eremitengemeinschaften', p. 541. Rupecava was also attractive to religious from slightly further afield. See *Pium est*, 15 December 1243, and *Dilecti filii*, 5 September 1245 (Berger 326, 1535) which record the request to transfer to Rupecava from the prior and brethren of the monastery of San Quirico de Popolania in the diocese of Massa. By 1245 San Quirico was reduced to just the abbot. In 1248 Rupecava seems to have wished to resist inclusion in the 'ordo sancti Augustini', acquiring exemption from visitation and procurations from the latter. *Cum, sicut accepimus*, 16 April 1248 (Berger 3909).

[8] See O. Redon, 'L'eremo, la città e la foresta', in *Lecceto e gli eremi agostiniani in terra di Siena* (Siena, 1990), pp. 9–43.

[9] M. Pellegrini, 'La cattedra e il deserto. L'episcopato di Siena e la chiesa di San Leonardo al Lago (secc. xi–xiii)', in *Santità ed eremitismo nella Toscana medievale*, ed. A. Gianni (Siena, 2000), pp. 29–53.

the 1160s the community had obtained confirmation of its autonomy under episcopal authority, acknowledged by a yearly offering of wax to the cathedral of Siena on the feast of the Assumption. Such links reflect the growing influence of the city, but also perhaps a gradual shift from the seclusion of hermits to the pastoral role of clerics, if not regular canons like those around Rupecava: after the single allusion to the monk-priest Benedetto and his hermitage, later references are mostly to priests or other clergy and their church. The model of a rural canonry with increasingly active ties with the city may also have been encouraged by the acquisition of the forests of the Selva del lago by the commune of Siena over the course of the twelfth and thirteenth centuries. The economic status of San Leonardo gradually came to depend directly on the city.

In the years around 1200 a number of other hermitages were founded in the area of Siena with apparently diverse aspirations. In the hills twenty kilometres to the south, Santa Maria di Montespecchio was established in 1190 by a hermit named Giovanni, again with donations from members of the Ardengheschi family; it was taken into papal protection already in 1193. The original dedication (soon forgotten) was to Notre Dame de Rocamadour, a pilgrimage site in south-west France, leading Odile Redon to suggest that there may have been some tradition of pilgrimage at Montespecchio.[10] If so, it was unique. No such tradition attaches to other hermitages in the area. San Pietro di Camerata was founded in 1239 by a Brother Ildebrando, on the basis of an agreement with the neighbouring village of Monticiano, by which he exchanged the use of land for prayers for the rural commune. Later records show San Pietro never housed more than five to ten men. Nor did most other houses in the region.

Just two kilometres to the west of San Leonardo in the Selva del lago stood the hermitage of San Salvatore di Foltignano, the most important of the new foundations. Later known as Lecceto (from Leccio or *Quercus ilex*, the holm oaks among which it stood), San Salvatore is first documented in 1223. In April 1228 the bishop of Siena, Bonfiglio (1215–52) consecrated its new church, which had been taken into papal protection just two months earlier. Under the astute leadership of the prior, Bandino Balzetti (1227–76) and with the support of the commune of Siena, San Salvatore developed substantial landholdings in the Selva. Indeed, it was eventually to replace San Leonardo as the most significant of the hermitages in the vicinity.

The episcopate of Bonfiglio also saw the reform of the hermit life in his diocese. In 1231, responding to a petition from the hermits of Montespecchio and Selva del lago, Gregory IX (1227–41) charged his bishop to provide them with one of the approved rules.[11] As his privilege, based on the hermits'

[10] Redon, 'L'eremo, la città e la foresta', p. 20.
[11] *Dilecti filii de*, 3 January 1231 (van Luijk, *Bullarium* 16; Empoli 125). On the gradual institutionalisation of the various hermit groups discussed here, see now the important contribution of C. Andenna,

petition, explains, the pope did so because, although they gave up personal property, took vows of chastity and committed themselves to living in obedience following the regular life, they lacked a specific rule to guide them in the Office or in other aspects of their observance. Bonfiglio was to visit the hermits to ensure that their new rule was being observed. Gregory's response is a clear sign that the Curia was already interested in uniting and regulating the hermit movement, a first step on the way to the formation of the Augustinian Hermit order. It was also hardly surprising from a pope who had, as Hugolino, cardinal legate in Tuscany and Lombardy, organised groups of monasteries into a 'Hugolinian' order and encouraged both Francis and Clare of Assisi to do the same.[12]

In 1243 Pope Innocent IV (1243–54) responded to a further petition from these and other groups of Tuscan Hermits led by four men, named as the brothers Stefano, Ugo, Guido and Pietro. As was by now customary for those approaching the papacy for approval, these four presented a *propositum* or proposal for their planned form of life. Their text does not survive, but Innocent's privilege, *Incumbit nobis* of December 1243, assigned them the rule of Augustine subject to their own institutes and instructed them to elect a prior (general). The text refers to the hermits as wandering sheep (*oves errantes*) in need of a shepherd, and directs them to turn to Riccardo Annibaldi, cardinal deacon of S. Angelo in Pescheria, should they encounter any difficulties, identifying him as *corrector ac provisor* of the new order.[13]

In March 1244 Annibaldi accordingly presided at a meeting in the Franciscan house of Santa Maria del Popolo in Rome to which each Tuscan house sent delegates.[14] Two Cistercians, the abbots of Falleri Nova and Fossanova also attended. This was presumably in fulfilment of constitution 12 of the Fourth Lateran Council (1215), which had instituted the Cistercians as experts on the structure and administration of the religious life. As a result of the meeting, the various Tuscan Hermits together adopted the rule of St Augustine.[15] In the same month Innocent gave brothers who were priests the right to preach and hear confessions, as long as this met with the approval of local prelates, another indicator of their pastoral role.[16] Surviving papal letters

---

'*Non est haec vita apostolica, sed confusio babylonica.* L'invenzione di un ordine nel secolo xiii', in *Regulae – consuetudines – statuta. Studi sulle fonti normative degli ordini religiosi nei secoli centrali del medioevo*, ed. C. Andenna and G. Melville, Vita Regularis Abhandlungen 25 (Münster, 2005), pp. 569–632.

12 On the 'Hugolinian order' see M. P. Alberzoni, '"Nequaquam a Christi sequela in perpetuum absolvi desiderio [I will never desire in any way to be absolved from the following of Christ]": Clare between Charism and Institution', *Greyfriars Review* 12 (1998), pp. 81–122.

13 *Incumbit nobis*, 16 December 1243 (van Luijk, *Bullarium* 32; Berger 335; Empoli 164, dated 1244). On Annibaldi, see A. Paravicini Bagliani, *Cardinali di Curia e 'familie' cardinalizie dal 1227 al 1254*, 2 vols (Padua, 1972), I, pp. 141–59.

14 *Presentium vobis auctoritate*, 16 December 1243 (van Luijk, *Bullarium* 33; Berger 336).

15 *Pia desideria devotorum*, 31 March 1244 (van Luijk, *Bullarium* 39; Empoli, 165).

16 *Vestra devotorum ecclesie*, 23 March 1244 (van Luijk, *Bullarium* 34; Berger 572).

from the following years reveal the gradual development of the features necessary to the continuation of an approved order, above all the regulation of annual general chapters.[17] Innocent also asked bishops and other churchmen to allow them to build churches, a necessary condition for success.[18] These letters probably mark a desire on the part of the hermits (and perhaps also of Annibaldi) to see the order expand beyond central Italy, an ambition in which they were certainly successful. By mid-century the Tuscan Hermits had spread to Liguria, Romagna, Rome and the Veneto. They had also reached as far as Germany and probably England. They numbered perhaps sixty houses, enjoyed privileges of exemption from tithes and wore a black belted habit soon to become familiar as the garb of the order of Austin Friars.

The Williamites

A second group, the Guglielmiti or Williamites, at first appear more coherent to the historian because focused around an individual. They claimed as their founder Guglielmo di Malavalle (†1157), even though at his death he had only one disciple and had written no rule. The earliest *Vita* indicates that Guglielmo, a former knight, probably of French origin, had been sent on pilgrimage as a canonical penalty and in 1145 had gone to Rome and the Holy Land. He then attempted various hospital and reform projects before retreating to a hut above Castiglione della Pescaia near Grosseto on the west coast of Italy. In a desolate valley appropriately named Malavalle, Guglielmo adopted a life of extreme asceticism: fasting, silence, prayer and bodily mortification. The aim was pure *anachoresis*: his one companion, Alberto, described in the sources as a *famulus* or servant, joined him only in the last year before his master's death.

The holiness of Guglielmo's life was recognised by Bishop Martino of Grosseto, whose authorisation of a cult limited to his diocese was extended by Popes Alexander III (1159–81) and Innocent III (1198–1216).[19] A first group of hermits living in solitary cells soon gathered close to his tomb and was followed by other hermitages, perhaps led by Alberto, Guglielmo's original companion. They adopted the rule or *ordo* of San Guglielmo, a text possibly composed by Alberto and approved by Bishop Martino. It was confirmed by Innocent III in 1211, but does not survive.[20] The hermits fasted every day

---

[17] *Religiosam vitam eligentibus*, 26 April 1244 (van Luijk, *Bullarium* 46; Empoli 166–9; Berger 658). See also *Quia ex apostolici*, 23 August 1250 (van Luijk, *Bullarium* 75–6; Berger 4807).

[18] *Dilecti filii priores*, 3 August 1252 (van Luijk, *Bullarium* 97; Empoli 181).

[19] K. Elm, *Beiträge zur Geschichte des Wilhelmitenordens*, Münstersche Forschungen 14 (Cologne, 1962), p. 35; K. Elm, 'Der Wilhemitenorden. Eine geistliche Gemeinschaft zwischen Eremitenleben, Mönchtum und Mendikantenarmut', in *Vitasfratrum. Beiträge zur Geschichte der Eremiten- und Mendikantenorden des zwölften und dreizehnten Jahrhunderts. Festgabe vom 65. Geburtstag*, ed. D. Berg, Saxonia Franciscana 5 (Berlin, 1994), pp. 55–66, 57.

[20] On this see Andenna, '*Non est haec vita apostolica*', p. 605.

except Sunday, observed strict silence – interrupted only for the Office – and worked to support themselves, so that the barren valley in which they had settled soon became fertile. In 1232 the strength of their observance was acknowledged when Gregory IX allowed a group of hermits in the diocese of Fermo to abandon the rule of Augustine for the rule of San Guglielmo, identifying it as a stricter form of life.[21] Gregory had personal experience of the order: as cardinal legate in Tuscany he had visited the tomb of Guglielmo and contributed to the expense of building the church. Nonetheless, in 1238 he gave them the Rule of Benedict and institutes of the Cistercians. This was perhaps, as Elm suggests, an attempt to strengthen Benedictine monasticism in Italy, though we cannot now be sure.[22] In practice, Cistercian institutes seem not to have been used.

Despite the links to Guglielmo, the first Williamite hermitages were united only by their shared observance. Their way of life, however, enjoyed extraordinary success, adopted by autonomous houses all across central Italy. To take just one example, south of Siena in 1206 a hermit named Bannerio founded Sant'Antonio d'Ardenghesca, which acquired papal protection in 1211 and continued to enjoy the patronage of the Ardengheschi family until the mid-1300s. Nonetheless, by the late 1240s, a more centralised order was taking shape. In 1248 Innocent IV recognised them as an *ordo monasticus* and ruled that they should have a general chapter.[23] Two years later they acquired the right to preach and hear confession, tasks associated with the *vita apostolica* of the mendicants, though their houses remained remote from towns.[24] Already in 1249 there is a first mention of a prior general and in the following year they acquired permission to correct contradictary instructions in their existing constitutions.[25] This was followed in 1251 by a general chapter meeting at Malavalle which approved new institutions for the order. With papal support, in the 1240s the Williamites had also expanded energetically across the Alps to Brabant, Flanders, France, northern Germany, the Rhineland, Bohemia and Hungary, either introducing their rule into established communities or founding houses from scratch. They wore woollen habits to the ankle with wide and long sleeves and a belt with a knife 'appropriate to religion' (*congruis religioni*). They carried a stick, the symbol of a hermit, and were required to wear shoes. As Elm has demonstrated, however, the new structure lacked administrative unity. Some houses even abandoned the order, which was in practice divided into two groups, north and south of the Alps.[26]

[21] *Dilecti filii fratres*, 5 December 1232 (van Luijk, *Bullarium* 17).
[22] Elm, *Beiträge zur Geschichte des Wilhelmitenordens*, pp. 43–7.
[23] *Religiosam vitam eligentibus*, 1248 (Berger 4430 dates this 31 March 1249).
[24] Elm 'Italienische Eremitengemeinschaften', p. 531.
[25] *Ex parte vestra*, 3 December 1250 (Berger 4937).
[26] Elm, *Beiträge zur Geschichte des Wilhelmitenordens*, pp. 108–9. On the constitutional changes see now Andenna, '*Non est haec vita apostolica*', text at pp. 605–6.

The Bonites

The year 1249 also saw the death of Giovanni Bono, a hermit whose follow-ers were to be known as Zanbonini, Giambonites or Bonites (*fratres eremite Johannis Boni*). According to a fourteenth-century account, he spent perhaps forty years as a jester (*joculator*), a profession disliked by churchmen, but, following an illness, took up a life of penance and retreat. Giovanni began his new life at Bertinoro some time between 1209 and 1211, then, after a year, moved to Budriolo (Budrio) west of Cesena in the Marche. Shortly after his death there was an attempt to have him canonised (1251–4). Although it was unsuccessful, the depositions of the witnesses for the process of enquiry pro-vide us with a unique account of his life.[27] Constructed around set questions, the answers were designed to prove Giovanni's sanctity. Inevitably, they do not resolve all the issues historians would like settled. Yet, almost uniquely for these early hermits, they give us an idea of what his followers wanted him to stand for and an intimate view of the ideals to which they aspired.

As related by the witnesses, Giovanni wore a long beard and a simple, grey, belted tunic to the knee. He either went barefoot or wore wooden clogs, in part for convenience but at other times to add to the suffering of his body. Those who knew him well noted that he wore underwear, but only so that the blood from haemorrhoids would not stain his outer tunic. His cell was a walled-up cave, in which he had a wooden cross, an image of the Virgin and a wooden board on which to sleep when not keeping vigil. Like Guglielmo da Malavalle, the routine of his life was focused around prayer, fasting and bodily mortification, a pattern once again modelled on that of earlier her-mits and ultimately the Desert Fathers. As a layman his prayers were simple. He recited the Creed, *Miserere mei domine* and *Ave Maria*, and repeated the Lord's prayer over and over. According to one witness, Brother Molton-grande, his prayers were so insistent that his cell floor was marked by his toes, knees and hands – an indication that he adopted an extremely awkward stance in prayer. He fasted every day except Sunday and more or less stopped eating during the periods of abstinence of the Church such as Lent. To fight the sin of lust or in periods of particular penance, he forced strips of wood under his nails or lay on a bed of sharp thorns.

To this extreme asceticism Giovanni added anxiety about his spiritual state: he confessed almost daily and always after speaking to outsiders. He received the Eucharist every Sunday – rare for a layman in this period – and also had the gift of tears, in his case a mark of his emotion when receiving or view-ing the Eucharistic host. According to the witnesses he could discern spirits and prophesied both the destiny of his followers and his own death. Like the holy men of Antiquity, he performed healing miracles and extraordinary

[27] *Il processo di canonizzazione di Fra Giovanni Bono (1251–1253/54), fondatore dell'ordine degli eremiti,* ed. M. Mattei (Rome, 2002).

feats such as turning water into wine so as to convince his audience of the truth of the much-debated doctrine of Transubstantiation.[28] His hermitage was not far from the Via Emilia (which led south to Rome) and attracted a regular audience of passers-by, whom he admonished in support of the Church and against the excommunicate King Enzo, the son of Emperor Frederick II, imprisoned in Bologna. What brought the audience was his public *fama* as a miracle worker but also his behaviour as an extraordinary ascetic, a holy man ignoring the normal networks and expectations of lay society, which granted him exceptional personal authority as a peacemaker and counsellor.[29] According to the witnesses he also preached effectively in defence of the sacraments and against heresy, persuading people who had formerly accepted Cathar teachings. One of his converts, a carpenter, reports that Giovanni taught him the Creed according to the usage of the Roman Church. Such claims to authority from a layman classed as illiterate may have lain behind challenges to his role by contemporary churchmen. They may also explain why the initial enquiry into his life and miracles in 1251 was renewed in 1253–4 with a further investigation of the same issues.

Perhaps these clerical anxieties account for the failure of the canonisation; Giovanni was beatified only in 1483. Unlike Malavalle, however, he had attracted numerous followers while alive, leading to the creation of a community, perhaps as early as 1217.[30] He never transferred from his cell, but as numbers grew, a house for the brothers was built a small distance away, with a church dedicated to the Virgin, for which they acquired the permission of the bishop of Cesena. The accounts of the witnesses suggest that there were also several cells close to his own for those more skilled in the difficult life of the hermit. This was a pattern of progress up the ladder of spiritual perfection also envisaged in the monasticism of Benedict, whose rule was intended for 'beginners' who might then move on to the struggles of the solitary life.

As the community expanded, the brothers sought approval for their form of life, and in 1225 adopted the rule of Augustine, in all probability as a result of restrictions imposed on new rules in the conciliar constitution *Ne nimia religionum diversitas* of 1215.[31] At first they wore the *habitus heremitarum,* a belt and habit of thin woollen cloth, a mark of humility. There were, however, tensions with the Franciscans. One witness in the 1250s claimed that the latter recruited some of Giovanni's brothers to their own rule. The larger order also objected to the similarity of their habits and in 1240, following an enquiry, Pope Gregory IX instructed the Bonites to take a black habit

---

[28] The change of the essence (*substantia*) of the bread and wine during the eucharistic rite into the body and blood of Christ, while the outward appearances remain unaffected.

[29] See P. Brown, 'The Rise and Function of the Holy Man in Late Antiquity', *Journal of Roman Studies* 61 (1971), pp. 80–101.

[30] Elm, 'Italienische Eremitengemeinschaften', p. 517.

[31] See above, p. 13.

with long sleeves and a very long belt, wear shoes and carry a stick, so that they must have appeared very similar to the Williamites, but certainly not like the Franciscans. When asking for alms they were to state explicitly to which order they belonged.[32] Such measures, formulated to avoid mistaken identities, also underline the special status in the Church already acquired by the Franciscans.

In the 1230s the Bonites had begun to expand rapidly across northern Italy, establishing houses mostly in or near cities. A decade later, Giovanni's followers were moving outside the hermitage, begging for food and attracting new followers, including clerics. Preaching (with episcopal permission) and pastoral care became increasingly important, a mark of the transition from an order of lay hermits to a clerical (and mendicant) engagement in the world.[33] By 1251 they had three provinces in north-east Italy and houses in cities including Treviso (1238), Verona (1240), Padua (1243), Vicenza (1244), Ferrara (1245) and Milan (1250).[34] They may already have reached Central Europe and Spain. From 1246 they enjoyed papal protection and the support of a cardinal protector, Guglielmo de' Fieschi, a nephew of Pope Innocent IV, whom they had approached in Lyons some time between 1244 and 1251.[35]

As the witnesses of 1251–4 make clear, Giovanni always remained a solitary recluse. He handed responsibility for the growing community to Matteo, one of his companions, some time before March 1238. After Giovanni's death, however, his followers rejected Matteo's authority. At a general chapter at Ferrara in 1249, conflict over the appointment of a successor and the nature of the relationship to the original community in Cesena split the order into opposing factions. Matteo resigned and Brother Ugo da Mantova was elected and confirmed by a papal legate. He was, however, faced by Brother Marco, elected in the same year as both prior and prior general by the members of Giovanni's own community at Budriolo and confirmed by the bishop of Cesena.

Marco's election, supported by the houses in Romagna, was probably intended to perpetuate the supremacy of Budriolo, but it was destined to fail. The choice of Ugo da Mantova had signalled a substantial change in the order, revealed in changes to the form of profession made by new brethren. The original vow had been made to the prior of Santa Maria of Cesena (Budriolo) according to the rule of St Augustine with the customs of Budriolo. This was now replaced by profession to the prior general according to the rule

---

[32] *Dudum apparuit*, 24 March 1240 (van Luijk, *Bullarium*, 22; Auvray 5122).

[33] *Vota devotorum*, 26 September 1246 (van Luijk, *Bullarium* 57; Berger 2103).

[34] F. A. dal Pino, 'Formazione degli eremiti di sant'Agostino e loro insediamenti nella terraferma veneta e a Venezia', in *Gli Agostiniani a Venezia e la chiesa di Sto Stefano* (Venice, 1997), pp. 27–85.

[35] *Religiosam vitam eligentibus* 26 April 1246 (van Luijk, *Bullarium* 56); *Admonet nos*, 14 April 1253 (van Luijk, *Bullarium* 102).

combined with the constitutions of the order.[36] The name of the order no longer referred to a motherhouse, but simply to friars of the order of hermits (*fratres ordinis heremitarum*), underlining its corporate constitution. Perhaps, as Elm suggests, this was because Budriolo maintained a more conservative structure, based on traditional eremitical lines, in isolated cells surrounded by a wall to keep out strangers. It is conceivable that the newer foundations drove a desire for mendicancy and pastoral care that characterised the last years of the Bonite order.[37] The division may even have been apparent as early as 1240, when a letter from Gregory IX refers to two separate elements, or at least two different ways of behaving in the order, distinguishing between those wearing a belt and carrying a stick (the traditional hermits) and those who had abandoned the stick and went about begging alms (embryonic mendicants).[38] The two sides were only reunited in 1252 when both Marco and Ugo were forced to resign. At a general chapter in Bologna, Brother Lanfranco da Settala of Milan, prior in Bologna and a companion (*socius*) of Ugo da Mantua, was elected in their place and confirmed by the cardinal protector, Guglielmo de' Fieschi.[39] By this date, as Cristina Andenna has recently pointed out, the Bonites formed a central nucleus together with the hermits of Tuscany, a precursor to the union of 1256.[40]

The Brettini

The first half of the thirteenth century also saw the emergence of a fourth group of hermits about seventy kilometres from Budriolo, near the small town of Brettino in the diocese of Fano (Pesaro), from which they acquired the name Brettini. Originally probably mostly laymen, these too were dedicated to an ascetic life of prayer, poverty and abstinence. In 1226 Honorius III granted papal protection to the prior, brothers and church of San Biagio and by 1228 they already had other houses subject to them.[41] A request for approval of their way of life was once again met with the requirement that they adopt a pre-existing rule, resolved by adoption of the rule of Augustine in 1228.[42] From a papal letter of 1235, *Que omnium conditoris*, confirming their *statutum* or institutes, it is clear that the Brettini hermits were following an austere form of traditional eremitical asceticism. The first text to give an extended account of the nature of their observance and spirituality, the

[36] *Admonet nos*, 14 April 1253 (van Luijk, *Bullarium*, 102; Berger 6493; Empoli 176–81).
[37] Elm, 'Italienische Eremitengemeinschaften', pp. 523–4.
[38] *Dudum apparuit*, 24 March 1240 (van Luijk, *Bullarium* 22; Auvray 5122; dated 1236 in Empoli 126–7).
[39] *Admonet nos cura*, 14 April 1253 as above n. 36.
[40] Andenna, '*Non est haec vita apostolica*', p. 604.
[41] *Sacrosancta romana ecclesia*, 26 November 1226 (Pressutti 6067; Potthast 7616).
[42] *Cum olim sicut*, 8 December 1228 (van Luijk, *Bullarium* 15; Empoli 123).

statutum emphasises fasting.[43] As well as Wednesdays, Fridays and the traditional periods of fasting in the Church, they were expected to fast from the feast of the Exaltation of the Cross (14 September) to Easter, except on Sundays or after blood-letting. Their diet on other days was to be eggs and cheese (not meat), eaten in a common refectory. Poverty was emphasised, both individual and communal: they were to be satisfied with a rough, belted habit of humble cloth and have no more than four tunics, one cloak and two scapulars. Like the Bonites, their original grey habit was similar to that of the Franciscans, again leading to controversy, a problem which still rankled for the Franciscan chronicler Salimbene de Adam decades later.[44]

The community was allowed to have no property outside the hermitage with its gardens and woods, so that revenues from rents, the usual means for supporting monastic communities at this date, were not possible. Although this was not the absolute destitution sought by Francis of Assisi, restrictions on property forced them to beg for some of their food, not unlike the early practice of the Franciscans themselves. In 1248 in *Circa opera pietatis*, the pope requested that bishops and other prelates allow them to beg because, 'dedicated to the service of God, they have no [other] means of sustenance'.[45] By the mid-1240s there were approximately ten houses, mostly in the March of Ancona, united by a general chapter and an elected prior general. A decade later there were probably two provinces – Ancona and Fermo, both on the east coast of Italy – and perhaps thirty houses. In 1243 the priests of the order had acquired the right to hear confessions and to preach, reflecting a commitment to the apostolate when they went out in search of alms.[46] They were also permitted to bury the faithful in their churches, another pointer to involvement in the care of souls, probably encouraged by the increasing clericalisation of the order. Foundations in cities such as Orvieto, Rimini and Terni accompanied these changes. A mark of their success is the incorporation in 1253 of the Benedictine monastery of Santa Maria Maddalena di Valle di Pietra in the diocese of Bologna which, after long negotiations, joined the order as a more austere observance.[47]

Montefavale

The last group named by Alexander IV in 1256 was the hermitage of Montefavale (Pesaro). Its origins are now the most obscure. The community was

---

[43] *Que omnium conditoris*, 13 March 1235 (van Luijk, *Bullarium* 19; Empoli 123–5) confirmed by Innocent IV, 17 September 1250 (van Luijk, *Bullarium* 79; Empoli 174; Berger 4831). See also Elm, 'Italienische Eremitengemeinschaften', p. 499.

[44] Salimbene de Adam, *Chronica/Cronica*, ed. G. Scalia, 2 vols, Corpus Christianorum. Continuatio mediaevalis, CXXV–CXXVa (Turnhout, 1998–9), I, p. 386.

[45] *Circa opera pietatis*, 4 July 1248 (van Luijk, *Bullarium* 69; Empoli 171–2).

[46] *Vota devotorum*, 24 September 1243 (van Luijk, *Bullarium* 27; Berger 128).

[47] *Oblata nobis ex*, 2 December 1253 (van Luijk, *Bullarium* 108; Berger 7097).

dedicated to St Benedict and may originally have used the Benedictine rule, but in 1225 acquired papal protection and permission to follow the rule of San Guglielmo.[48] Later connections to the recently centralised order of Williamites are not, however, clear, As we have seen, there were divisions amongst the latter by mid-century and it may be that Montefavale had broken away from Malavalle. In 1254 a general chapter, acting on papal directions, removed Giovanni, the Williamite prior general, for incompetence (*insufficientia*) and replaced him with a Brother Guberto, confirmed in office by the bishop of Forlì.[49] As Elm ingeniously proposes, it is possible that Montefavale had been an alternative centre for the Williamite order during this crisis, but this remains no more than conjecture.[50] The records of the union of 1256, which list Malavalle and Montefavale separately, make it clear that the latter was still independent of the Williamites. The Franciscan chronicler Salimbene de Adam later makes the same distinction, though this may of course merely reflect knowledge of the papal text.[51]

Magna unio: the Great Union of 1256

Like the Humiliati, Carmelites and several other orders both old and new, these distinct orders of hermits were administratively re-organised in the mid-thirteenth century. In this case, however, papal intervention amounted to the creation of a new entity. In 1255 Alexander issued a number of letters concerning the reform of hermits in French, German and English provinces.[52] In Italy he went a step further, charging his nephew Riccardo Annibaldi with the negotiations necessary to unite the various groups of hermits into one order. Whereas in 1244 the union of Tuscan Hermits had brought together autonomous, small and diverse houses, this time the union concerned well-established orders following a variety of approved rules. Once again each house was required by the pope to send two delegates to a meeting arranged by Annibaldi, held as before in Santa Maria del Popolo in Rome, which had been in the hands of the Tuscan Hermits since *c.* 1250, when the Franciscans moved to the church of Santa Maria in Capitolio. The original papal mandate was addressed only to the Tuscan and Williamite priors; the actual meeting, however, also included the Bonites, Brettini and Montefavale hermits.[53] The

---

[48] *Solet annuere sedes,* 9 May 1225 (Pressutti 5468). See also *Devotionis augmentum,* 27 August 1251 (Berger 5468), addressed to the prior general of the hermitage of San Benedetto di Montefavale, which identified the house as belonging to the *ordo sancti Guglielmi* and authorised the lay brothers of Montefavale to shave their beards like the clerics.

[49] *Dilecti filii fratres,* 18 August 1254 (Berger 7964).

[50] Elm, 'Italienische Eremitengemeinschaften', pp. 533–4.

[51] Salimbene de Adam, *Chronica/Cronica,* I, p. 386.

[52] *Quia salutem,* 5 July 1255 (van Luijk, *Bullarium* 133; F. Roth, *The English Austin Friars,* 2 vols (New York, vol. I 1966, vol. II 1961), II, p. 15).

[53] *Cum quedam salubria,* 15 July 1255 (van Luijk, *Bullarium* 142).

result was the unification of perhaps 180 communities, with over 2000 members, into an order to be known as the *fratres eremitarum sancti Augustini*, a title modelled on that used for the hermits of Tuscany since 1244.

This *Magna unio*, or Great Union, was approved by Alexander in *Licet ecclesie catholice* of April 1256.[54] The opening of the bull (the *arenga*) explains the purpose of the union from the papal point of view, using arguments reminiscent of those deployed by the chancery of Innocent III when faced with the Humiliati and other religious communities at the beginning of the thirteenth century: unity would make them stronger, while uniformity (in particular of name and habit) would avoid confusion in the Church.[55] This was more than convenient rhetoric. The range of habits the different groups had adopted meant they were unlikely to be easily distinguishable. Although not explicitly mentioned in the text, the Curia may have been particularly concerned about confusion between these groups and the Franciscans, already a cause of disquiet to the Bonites and Brettini. A newly delineated and easily recognised structure and habit also served to underline the difference between orthodox and heretic.

The new order of hermit friars adopted the constitutions and habit of the Tuscan Hermits, leading the Augustinian historian Balbino Rano to argue that the Great Union was not the creation of a new order but the unification of smaller ones to the Tuscan order founded in 1244.[56] This idea parallels that adopted by fourteenth-century Austin Friars themselves, who went on to develop a much longer pedigree for their order, tracing it back to Augustine.[57] Rano's argument draws attention to important continuities, but most modern historians now agree that while 1256 marked the culmination of a gradual process of aggregation, it was also the beginning of something new. In April 1256 Alexander gave the order exemption from tithes on their possessions and confirmed that privileges issued to the pre-existing communities should apply to all the houses of the new order.[58] He dispensed them from previous forms of profession and authorised them to reduce the number of houses in each town to one, disposing of any others. If nothing else, the order was now on a different scale from any of its precursors, and 1256 was to be celebrated as an important anniversary for many centuries.

Long-standing anxieties about diversity and the concomitant risks of confusion may have led Alexander IV and Cardinal Annibaldi to try to unite all hermits into one order modelled on the Franciscans and Dominicans. If so, they were unsuccessful. Not even all those who had attended the chapter

---

[54] 9 April 1256 (Alonso I, 1; van Luijk, *Bullarium* 163; Empoli 18–20).

[55] See Andrews, *The Early Humiliati*, p. 71.

[56] B. Rano, 'Agostiniani', *DIP* I, cols 278–381, 278.

[57] See below, pp. 158–62.

[58] *Ut eo fortius*, 9 April 1256 (Alonso I, 4; Empoli 21, dated 13 April); *Oblata nobis*, 20 April, 1257 (Alonso I, 27; Empoli 25–6).

in Santa Maria del Popolo were satisfied. The Benedictine Williamites were unhappy at the loss of their autonomy and the adoption of the rule of Augustine. As Andenna has shown, a later letter identifies the new observance as unacceptable because less austere than their own and blames the transition on human weakness.[59] As early as August 1256 the Williamites successfully petitioned to be allowed to remain independent. In 1261, after persistent disputes, a continuation of the earlier divisions in the order, Urban IV confirmed their independent status, observing the rule of Benedict with their own institutes.[60] A final settlement in 1266 (*Ea que iudicio*) returned to the Williamites all houses outside Germany and Hungary and three in Germany. Williamite friars who thereby found themselves in a house of Augustinians and might want to transfer had a month to decide.[61]

The hermits of Montefavale also left the union, choosing instead to move to the Cistercians, whom they had already petitioned to join in 1255. An enquiry was commissioned by the Cistercian general chapter at the request of the abbey of Santa Maria di Castagnola near Jesi, with which Montefavale was then incorporated. It may not be a coincidence that other orders whose form of life might have made them eligible for inclusion – the Servites (Servants of Mary), the Camaldolese and the Carmelites – also sought renewed papal approval at this point. Confirmation would make clear their exemption from any union.[62]

Despite such evident reluctance, Annibaldi and the pope remained keen to draw other groups into the union and enjoyed some success. In July 1256, Nicola, prior of the *domus sancti Augustini* in Milan and prior provincial of the Catholic Poor (*pauperes catholici*) in Lombardy, accepted membership of the order on behalf of the houses in his province. These Catholic poor had a more troubled past than the other religious adhering to the union, having originated from a group led by Durand de Huesca, a former disciple of Valdès of Lyons (†c. 1206) who had been condemned as a heretic. A merchant, Valdès had adopted a life of preaching and penance after hearing the story of St Alexius, a model for the emerging ideal of the *vita apostolica* as a life of poverty and preaching. Alexius had given up his wealth to adopt a life of penance, living as a beggar in his own home. He was unrecognised by his parents, who for seventeen years allowed him to live under the stairs, praying and teaching until his death. Valdès too gave up his property and began a life of poverty and evangelism, soon gathering followers calling themselves 'Poor of Spirit' as a mark of their humility, but widely identified as the 'Poor

[59] Andenna, '*Non est haec vita apostolica*', p. 607.
[60] *Licet olim pro unione*, 5 November 1261 (Alonso I, 73).
[61] *Ea que iudicio*, 30 August 1266 (Alonso I, 113). On the course and resolution of the dispute see K. Elm, 'Die Bulle "Ea quae iudicio" Clemens' IV. 30.VIII.1266', *Augustiniana* 14 (1964), pp. 500–22; 15 (1965), pp. 54–67, 493–520 and 16 (1966), pp. 95–145.
[62] Dal Pino, *I frati Servi*, I, pp. 656, 867.

of Lyons' or Waldensians (from Waldo, the latinised form of Valdès). As laymen they lacked authorisation to preach, and clerical opposition led to their condemnation as heretics alongside the Humiliati and others by Pope Lucius III in 1184 in the decree *Ad abolendam*.[63] Some of those who were condemned formed groups which remained outside the Roman Church and adopted increasingly distinct doctrinal views over the course of the late Middle Ages.[64] During a debate at Pamiers in 1207, however, Bishop Diego of Osma and his prior, Dominic of Calaruega, future founder of the Dominican order, convinced Durand to return to the Catholic mainstream. A group led by him were reconciled at the end of the following year, adopting the title Catholic Poor. Innocent III approved a *propositum*, a simple form of life committing them to poverty, prayer and mutual exhortation. Clerical brothers learned in doctrine were to debate against 'the errors of all sects' (heretics and in particular Cathars). They were to have *schola* or places for study and meetings where preaching might take place with the permission of the local bishop. Durand himself was a distinguished theologian and in the 1220s wrote a treatise, the *Liber contra Manicheos*, condemning Cathar teaching.

Alongside the literate and clerical central group, the Catholic Poor quickly attracted lay followers, who were not authorised to preach or wear the tonsure, but were to lead lives of simplicity and charity and work with their hands (like the lay Humiliati and other penitent groups). Perhaps inevitably the order faced episcopal opposition – some bishops were suspicious of these former heretics and their associates. They nonetheless established numerous houses in Catalonia, Provence, Languedoc and northern Italy. After 1237 they even adopted the rule of Augustine, so participation in the union need not have represented a traumatic change. The decision to renounce their previous ties was not, however, uncontested. Ten other named individuals had consented to the original agreement, but some of Prior Nicola's brethren, in Milan at least, refused to adapt to the new form of life and reasserted their autonomy. They were brought back into the order of hermit friars only in November 1272, when Odo Visconti, archbishop of Milan, instructed that their house at Sant'Agostino must revert to the Augustinian friary of San Marco.[65]

The reasons for the resistance of the Catholic Poor to the union are now hard to ascertain, but the reluctance of the Williamites and Hermits of Montefavale to join the new order may have been driven by the fact that *Licet*

---

[63] See Andrews, *The Early Humiliati*, pp. 39–40.
[64] See G. Audisio, *Les 'Vaudois': naissance, vie et mort d'une dissidence xiie–xvie siècle* (Turin, 1989), in English as *The Waldensian Dissent. Persecution and Survival, c. 1170 – c. 1570*, trans. C. Davison (Cambridge, 1999). See also E. Cameron, *Waldenses. Rejections of Holy Church in Medieval Europe* (Oxford, 2000).
[65] F. Roth, 'Cardinal Richard Annibaldi (Continuation)', *Augustiniana* 2 (1952), pp. 246–7. See also Elm, 'Die Bulle', p. 505.

ecclesie marked a step away from an eremitic identity, transition from the *vita contemplativa* of retreat, prayer and penance to the *vita activa* of preaching and teaching. As we have seen, preaching and begging played a part in the lives of some of the earlier communities, but these elements now became central: the Augustinian Friars would be defined by their pastoral, mendicant role. The closest model was now the apostolic ideal of the Dominican and Franciscan Friars, no longer the hermits of the desert. The Augustinian theologian and chronicler Jordan of Quedlinburg (†1370 or 1380) acknowledged this shift a century later in his *Liber vitasfratrum* (*c.* 1357).[66] No doubt benefiting from hindsight, he explained the motives of the Curia in 1256 in precisely these pastoral terms, while at the same time invoking the tradition that the preaching activities of the order had begun with Augustine:

> So that the friars of this holy religion united and gathered together in the Church of God like the Friars Preacher and Friars Minor could produce fruit just as they had once done before their dispersal, in the time of the blessed Augustine in Africa, that is [by] preaching to the people and hearing confessions ... Pope Alexander IV ordered them to move into cities, and have convents there, so as to bring forth fruit in the people of God, teaching, preaching, giving examples of holy life and deeds and hearing confessions.[67]

Jordan also, however, gives an idea of the tensions this transition caused:

> At which, some of them became difficult, preferring to serve God as they were accustomed to in solitude in the hermitage rather than live among seculars, exposing themselves to the danger of infection in the world.[68]

Jordan suggests that Alexander therefore determined that the order should keep its hermitages, so that those who wished might still live as solitaries. There is no trace of such a general disposition in the extant papal correspondence, but the order did keep many of its remote houses. Some of the men who joined the order after 1256 also renewed the hermit tradition while alternating it with the pastoral life of the mendicants. Agostino Novello (†1309), a former lawyer in the service of King Manfred, made his profession in Sicily after escaping from the Battle of Benevento (1266), but was attracted to Tuscany by accounts of the hermitages in the woods around Siena. At the end of his life, having spent years as a legislator dealing with the business of the order and as a papal penitentiary, he resigned after just two years as prior general in order to spend his last years in prayer at San Leonardo al Lago.

---

[66] Also known as Jordan of Saxony; not to be confused with the thirteenth-century Dominican of the same name.

[67] Jordani de Saxonia (Quedlinburg), *Liber vitasfratrum*, ed. R. Arbesmann and W. Hümpfner (New York, 1943), book 1, chapter 16, pp. 57–58. These are my translations, but the *Liber vitasfratrum* is also available in English as *The Life of the Brethren*, by Jordan of Saxony, trans. G. Deighan, ed. J. Rotelle (Villanova, Pa, 1993).

[68] Ibid.

Apart from preaching and pastoral care, the most characteristic feature of the early mendicants was their attitude to poverty. Whereas the traditional monastic ideal centred on individual poverty but communal property, Francis of Assisi had tried (with limited success) to establish absolute, collective poverty, leaving his followers dependent on their own labour and on begging, without any thought for the morrow (hence the name mendicants).[69] In April 1256 the pope pointed to a desire in the Augustinian order for the spontaneous collective poverty typical of the early Franciscans, but this was not interpreted as applying to all houses. In *Iis que* of 1257, Alexander authorised those who wished to have property to maintain it or to acquire more as needed, 'for the sustenance of the body and ... so that [the friars] need not run around hectic like Martha' (the biblical model of distracted industry, compared to the contemplative Mary). At the same time, those who preferred might choose greater poverty.[70] It was a compromise that probably did not satisfy those seeking a more mendicant identity, based on the idea of absolute personal and corporate penury. A drive for greater austerity in all probability lay behind a constitution reminiscent of Brettini practice issued in 1290, requiring that all lands outside the immediate enclosure of a priory should be sold. This was justified on the conventional grounds that it was necessary to be free of the preoccupations of this world in order to serve God more effectively. The friars were to live by begging. In practice, however, such restrictions were never fully enforced.

Over the course of the late thirteenth century the Augustinian Hermits accumulated the necessary papal privileges to support their new role. They were also protected from unwarranted competition: in 1259 Alexander IV warned the Dominicans and Franciscans not to admit members of the order without the authorisation of Augustinian superiors and vice versa.[71] In 1260 they were sufficiently established to participate alongside the Franciscans and Dominicans in the annual procession of the Roman clergy to St Peter's on the feast of St Mark.[72] Popes Urban IV (1261–4) and Clement IV (1264–8) further buttressed their institutional security. In 1262, they were again authorised to hear the confessions of the faithful and in the following year to preach – in both cases with the licence of diocesan authorities.[73] In 1265 the order was exempted from paying the usual tax (the canonical portion) on anniversary legacies for the building, furnishing and lighting of their churches.[74]

---

[69] See M. Lambert, *Franciscan Poverty. The Doctrine of Absolute Poverty of Christ and the Apostles in the Franciscan Order, 1210–1323* (London, 1961, reissued 1998).

[70] 13 June 1257 (Alonso I, 33; Bourel 1967).

[71] *Quanto preclara ordinis*, 11 June 1259 (Alonso I, 54; Empoli 29–30, 33; Potthast 17597).

[72] *Iurgia litium quibus*, 20 April 1260; *Vota devotorum*, 31 January 1263 (Alonso I, 61, 96).

[73] *Vobis ad hoc*, 26 May 1262 (Alonso I, 85).

[74] *Deuotionis augmentum*, 22 June 1265 (Alonso I, 104; Empoli 61; Potthast 19223).

The first prior general, Lanfranco da Settala, who had been the head of the reunited Bonites since 1252, had been given wide powers to impose uniformity of observance on the brothers.[75] In 1262 Urban IV again dispensed them from any observances required by professions made preceding the Great Union.[76] In spite of this, conformity was not easy to achieve. By this date some houses had acquired long standing urban ties and perhaps involvement in pastoral care. For individuals who had chosen the withdrawn life of the hermit, however, the transformation from eremitical and rural roots to an order centred on cities and towns cannot have been easy. The strains are neatly illustrated by continuing problems with the habit, also a marker of the complexities of carving out a space unique to the new order.

The precursors to the Great Union had adopted a variety of habits, and some had, as we have seen, faced pressure to change to a form and colour that could not be confused with the dress of the Franciscans. The typical Austin Friars' habit was already taking shape in 1253 when Riccardo Annibaldi approved black habits, a black leather belt and a straight stick for the Tuscan Hermits. Novices too were to adopt a black habit down to the ankles over a tunic, with a scapular, belt and stick.[77] *Conversi* (lay brethren) were to have black tunics, scapular and hood, again with a hermit stick. In 1255 the scapulars of all but *conversi* were to be white.[78] In *Licet Ecclesie* of 1256 the obligation to carry the hermit stick disappeared and all outerwear was to be black.[79] In *Litteras nostras* issued in October of that year the exclusive use of black was again emphasised.[80] From this date the formal habit of the order was to be black, with a belt covering a white tunic. According to later regulations (1290), the belt must be at least one-and-a-half fingers wide. In the heat of summer the prior might allow them to take off the outer habit, leaving just the white tunic. Even with the black habit, the white tunic could sometimes be seen at the hood and hem, a detail caught in images of Augustine as a friar painted two centuries later by Benozzo Gozzoli in the church of Sant'Agostino in San Gimignano, Tuscany (see jacket). Presumably in the 1250s some friars continued to wear white as well as black on the outer layer, since in October 1259 Alexander IV ordered the Augustinians to remove the 'habit of the friars preacher', who wore black and white, or anything similar.[81]

---

75 *Apostolice sedis provisio*, 9 April 1256 (Alonso I, 2; Empoli 20; Potthast 16335).

76 *Desideriis vestris* 9 December 1261 (Alonso I, 75; Empoli 370–1). C. Anenna, '... ut non sit confusio indiscreta ... La dispensa dalla professione di una regola: una eccezione o lo strumento per creare un nuovo ordine?', in *Viridarium Augustinianum. Studi storici in onore di Cosimo Damiano Fonseca*, ed. P. Piatti and R. Tortorelli (forthcoming 2006), follows B. Rano in dating the bull to 1262.

77 *Pia desideria deuotorum*, 22 July 1253 (van Luijk, *Bullarium* 105; Empoli 15–16 and Potthast 15942, both dated 1255; Berger 6834, dated 1 July 1253).

78 *Pia desideria deuotorum*, 22 July 1255 (van Luijk, *Bullarium* 148; Berger 6834, dated 1 July 1253).

79 9 April 1256 (Alonso I, 1; van Luijk, *Bullarium* 163; Empoli 18–20; Potthast 16334).

80 15 October 1256 (Alonso I, 17; Empoli 21–2; Potthast 16538).

81 *Meminimus nos per*, 15 October 1259 (Alonso I, 58; Potthast 17680).

Dress long remained a contentious issue. Thirty years later the provincial chapter of the Roman province deemed it necessary to stipulate that no brother was to wear a cord like the Franciscans or a cloth or silk belt.

Crisis: 1274 and beyond

Like the other mendicant orders, the Austin Friars faced criticism from the secular clergy in a controversy that was to continue for decades. Already before the Great Union there had been attacks on the pastoral mission of the mendicants largely because of the threat they posed to the role and revenues of the secular clergy. In the early 1250s this had exploded into a bitter struggle between the mendicant and secular masters at the University of Paris. In 1256 the most articulate of the seculars, William of Saint-Amour, published a treatise, *Concerning the Perils of the Last Days*, attacking the doctrine and practice of mendicancy and arguing that the secular clergy alone might take on the pastoral care of others.[82] No one, not even the pope, could change the traditional hierarchy, which excluded monks (and therefore also friars) from the apostolic succession.[83] These, he argued, had never had the right to the priesthood or to ministry. The friars were guilty of hypocrisy, false brothers who persuaded the faithful to hate their own priests (*proprius sacerdos*) to whom, since the decree *Omnis utriusque sexus* of 1215, all faithful were supposed to confess at least once a year. In Paris, William summarised his arguments in sermons also criticising King Louis IX, whose sympathy for the friars was well known and who frequently adopted their humble dress. This inevitably lost Saint-Amour the support of the Crown, and his treatise was condemned in the autumn of 1256, six months after the Great Union. The dispute was, however, far from resolved and the new order was soon drawn in. It could hardly be avoided. Like the other mendicants, their preaching in territory subject to a parish and the burial of the faithful jeopardised both the livelihood of the secular clergy and those holding parishes in advowson and disrupted the usual patterns of authority under the bishop.

In 1272 Pope Gregory X (1271–6) announced a new council of the Church which, amongst other issues, was to consider the standing of the religious orders. In the following year he requested reports on their condition; those which survive were not entirely favourable.[84] When the council finally met, at Lyons in the early summer of 1274, the very existence of the Austin Friars, as of the Carmelites, was brought into question. Invoking *Ne nimia*

---

[82] See M.-M. Dufeil, *Guillaume de Saint-Amour et la polémique universitaire parisienne 1250–1259* (Paris, 1972).

[83] In Latin the friars (i.e. mendicants) were always called *fratres* (brothers), not *monachi* (monks). The title *dominus* (lord, a polite form of address) was also used for monks (later reduced to 'dom') but not for friars. This distinction is reflected in modern English usage.

[84] See above, pp. 18–19.

religionum diversitas of 1215, the gathered bishops and prelates directed that orders established after that date were to be discontinued. The Franciscans and Dominicans were able to prove their 'evident utility' to the Church. The Augustinians, like the Carmelites, were not, or not yet, though one unofficial version of events at the council did include them among the orders to be preserved.[85] They must have claimed that they had been approved before 1215, but were allowed to continue only on a provisional basis until further judgement could be made. In the end just two smaller mendicant orders that had formerly acquired papal approbation were definitively suppressed, the Sack Friars and the Pied Friars, though others were certainly endangered.[86] The existing members of these revoked orders were destined to die out slowly: they might remain where they were, but might not recruit or take on new houses. Individual brethren could move to other communities and whole convents might also transfer, with permission. Neither ruling applied to the Austin Friars, but as recent arrivals, they must have felt vulnerable. According to Salimbene, Gregory X wished to suppress the hermit friars, but Riccardo Annibaldi persuaded him not to act at once and the pope then died before further action could be taken.[87] Salimbene was often happy to undermine other mendicants, and Francis Roth has shown that Annibaldi was in fact unable to attend the council.[88] But the cardinal's role was probably an important factor in the survival of the Augustinians in the months after Lyons. An extant letter shows that he was held in esteem by the pope and Andenna has recently drawn attention to a further aspect which may have encouraged the pope to relent. Both Gregory X and his predecessor Clement IV shared Annibaldi's pro-Germanic policy. The large number of Augustinian houses in German lands by this date and the support they enjoyed from both prelates and cities may have been a factor in the decision not to axe the order straight away.[89]

Papal records imply that the business of the friars continued as usual in spite of the decree. In March 1275 Gregory wrote to Annibaldi charging him with the confirmation of their new prior general, Francesco da Reggio (a former Bonite), to replace Clemente da Osimo, who had resigned in 1274.[90] However, it is telling that no new houses were founded in either England or Spain for over a decade. The impact of the uncertainty on the Augustinians is also evident in a letter of January 1275 sent to secular and ecclesiastical authorities by the archbishop of Salzburg. The letter reports that the friars

---

[85] See Roberg, *Das zweite Konzil von Lyon*, pp. 334–8.

[86] See below, pp. 208–9.

[87] Salimbene de Adam, *Chronica/Cronica*, I, p. 387.

[88] F. Roth, 'Cardinal Richard Annibaldi (Continuation)', *Augustiniana* 3 (1953), p. 30.

[89] C. Andenna, '*De introitu fratrum ad civitates*: una fondazione dell'*ordo fratrum eremitarum* a Regensburg', in *Studia monastica. Beiträge zum klösterlichen Leben im Mittelalter* (Münster, 2004), pp. 125–50, 137. See also Andenna, '*Non est haec vita apostolica*', p. 618.

[90] *Ex parte dilectorum*, 25 March 1275 (Alonso I, 129).

were being criticised and were losing customary assistance and benefits because it was the common opinion that the order had been suppressed. The archbishop therefore reminded his readers that the pope had only reserved judgement and they should continue to support the friars as before.[91] What effect the letter had on the friars in the region is unrecorded.

Gregory X's immediate successors took little direct interest in the Augustinian Hermits, but by the 1280s the friars were again enjoying the support of the popes in both general and specific terms. This may have been because in 1284 Clemente da Osimo was re-elected prior general. He was both an active legislator on behalf of the order and seems to have impetrated numerous letters at the Curia. In May 1286, Honorius IV (1285–7) allowed the friars to celebrate the feast of Augustine even during interdicts.[92] In the same year he renewed instructions to the bishop of Siena to protect the order in Tuscany and confirmed their ownership of a disputed site in Paris.[93] Honorius also used them for papal business, a sign perhaps of their newly acknowledged 'utility' in the Church. In December 1286, he instructed the Augustinian prior in Rieti, north of Rome, together with the superiors of the Dominicans and Franciscans, to investigate a purchase of land by a former bishop of Rieti.[94] Three months later he entrusted the Roman parish church of San Trifone to the prior of Santa Maria del Popolo, broadening the engagement of the order with the city.[95]

Under Nicholas IV (1288–92), the first Franciscan pope, papal interest continued in a similar vein. Annibaldi, who had been made cardinal protector in 1257, had died in 1276 and had not immediately been replaced.[96] In June 1288, perhaps prompted by Clemente da Osimo, Nicholas once again gave the friars an essential voice in the Curia by appointing Bernard de Languissel, cardinal bishop of Porto (†1291).[97] In 1289 the pope also gave an indulgence to all the friars' churches for the feasts of the Assumption, St Augustine and their own titular saints, following this with a number of indulgences for individual churches over subsequent years.[98] In January 1290 he asked the prior general and twenty 'mature and discrete' friars to preach the crusade

---

[91] *Salzburger Urkundenbuch*, ed. W. Hauthaler and F. Martin, 4 vols (Salzburg, 1898–1933), IV, pp. 85–6.

[92] *Pro reverentia beati*, 23 May 1286 (Alonso I, 140; Empoli 160–1; Prou 538).

[93] *Sub religionis habitu*, 13 June 1286 (Alonso I, 141); *Petitio vestra nobis*, 15 November 1286 (Alonso I, 142; Prou 688; Empoli 156–9).

[94] *Lecta coram nobis*, 9 December 1286 (Alonso I, 146; Prou 697).

[95] *Meritis vestre religionis*, 20 February 1287 (Alonso I, 147; Prou 962; Empoli 161–2).

[96] His authority was explicitly modelled on that of the Franciscan and Dominican general superiors; see *Inter alias solicitudines*, 29 March 1257 (Alonso I, 26; Empoli 23–4; Potthast 16806).

[97] *Immensi molem oneris*, 30 June 1288 (Alonso I, 148; Langlois 170).

[98] *Licet is*, 6 February 1289 (Alonso I, 151, Empoli 259–60; Langlois 481; Potthast 22873). See also Alonso I, 153–4, 164–5, 167–9, 172–3, 175–6 and, for comparable treatment of the Carmelites, above, p. 33n.

and eighteen months later requested thirty more.[99] He sent similar requests to the Dominicans and Franciscans, an indication of the Augustinians' now proven standing as preachers.

Nicholas IV was generous to the Austin Friars, but it was Boniface VIII (1294–1303) who was to provide the security they needed. As Benedetto Caetani, cardinal priest of San Martino ai Monti, he had known senior members of the order well. According to the Augustinian chronicler and theologian, Heinrich of Friemar (†1340), Clemente da Osimo had been Caetani's confessor and the cardinal had visited Clemente's body in Orvieto after his death, when the fame of his miracles was beginning to be known. Giles of Rome, the first Paris master of the order, was also a close associate of Caetani, whose election as pope in December 1294 probably explains his own election as archbishop of Bourges a few months later.[100] Already in February 1295 the order received the by now customary mendicant privilege precluding construction of churches or monasteries within 140 *canne* (rods) of their houses.[101] Most important of all, in May 1298 Boniface gave them papal confirmation, revising the Lyons decree in *Tenorem cuiusdam constitutionis* to allow both Augustinians and Carmelites to continue secure in their status as approved orders (*in solido statu*).[102] This may have been a reward for the support the Augustinians were providing during the pope's disputes with Philip IV over control of the French Church.[103] It was followed in 1299 by confirmation of their exemption from episcopal jurisdiction, under immediate obedience to the pope.[104] By the turn of the century the order was thus securely established within the Church, and in 1303 Boniface confirmed their participation in the same privileges concerning preaching, confession and the burial of the faithful as both Franciscan and Dominican friars.[105]

Rule and institutes

The rule observed by the Augustinian Hermit Friars was widely adopted by both male and female religious in the thirteenth century. This was in part due to the authority of its author, but also in part because of its flexibility. Unlike the rule of Benedict with its systematic and all-embracing framework, the text of Augustine's rule is a collection of exhortations or precepts, until recently

[99] *Necessitates miserabilis terre*, 5 January 1290 (Alonso I, 159; Langlois 2267; Empoli 260–2; Potthast 23152); *Terre sancte miserabilem*, 1 August 1291 (Alonso I, 171; Langlois 6805; Potthast 23762).
[100] See below, p. 149.
[101] *Ad consequendam gloriam*, 19 February 1295 (Alonso I, 181; Empoli 48–9; Digard 10; Potthast 24028).
[102] 5 May 1298 (Alonso I, 205; Empoli 46–7; *BC* I, 74; Potthast 24675).
[103] See below, p. 148–9.
[104] *Sacer ordo vester*, 21 January 1299 (Alonso I, 206; Empoli 44–5; Digard 2852; Potthast 24767).
[105] *Inter sollicitudines nostras*, 16 January 1303 (Alonso I, 236; Empoli 50–2, dated 1302; Digard 4983; Potthast 25210).

wrongly believed to have originated as a letter for nuns.[106] From its opening words it focuses simply on the need to share life in the monastery and 'to have one heart and one soul seeking God'. Its essence is the idea that the common life, based on shared property and common prayer, will promote fraternity and love, allowing religious of different abilities and economic backgrounds to live together in a spiritual community. To achieve this the text outlines the essential elements of the monastic life: fasting and abstinence, humble clothing, chastity, obedience and discipline, as well as the need to avoid jealousy and to forgive each other. There are almost no details on how to organise this community. What this meant in practice was that new or newly modified 'institutes' (or constitutions) necessarily accompanied the rule, allowing any group of aspiring religious the space to devise their own observance. Following the prohibition on new rules issued in 1215, Augustine's text therefore came into its own, providing a way to maintain the spiritual ideals of the *vita apostolica* aspired to by numerous new groups of religious men and women. This had been recognised by Dominic of Calaruega, who adopted the rule of Augustine and a modified version of the institutes or constitutions of Prémontré for his Order of Preachers. The same flexibility (and the model of the Dominicans) may explain why Augustine's rule had been accepted by many of the early hermits before 1256, and by those same men on creation of the order of Augustinian Hermit Friars.

The lack of detail in the rule was supplemented in two ways. As an official commentary the friars adopted the *Expositio in Regulam* erroneously attributed to Hugh of St Victor. The text stands as a gloss to the rule, explaining, for example, that common property means not calling anything your own (my tunic), but referring to everything as *ours* (our tunics). The accent of the *Expositio* is on the importance of fraternity, uniformity of life in the community and interiority – emphases already found in Augustine's own writings. Surprisingly few of the extant texts of this *Expositio* belonged to the friars,[107] though general chapters frequently insisted on its use. Nor are there many extant copies of the second body of auxiliary texts, the constitutions or institutes, which contain the mechanics of daily observance and determined the friars' interpretation of their rule.[108]

Statutes produced by the Brettini had received papal confirmation already

---

[106] For the textual tradition, discussion of its Augustinian authorship and original male audience, see G. Lawless, *Augustine of Hippo and his Monastic Rule* (Oxford, 1987) who summarises and develops the fundamental work on the manuscripts of L. Verheijen, in particular, *La Règle de saint Augustin, i, Tradition manuscrite; ii, Recherches historiques* (Paris, 1967).

[107] R. Goy, *Die Ueberlieferung der Werke Hugos von St Viktor. Ein Beitrag zur Kommunikationsgeschichte des Mittelalters*, Monographien zur Geschichte des Mittelalters 14 (Stuttgart, 1976). The most convenient version of the text is in *Patrologia Latina*, comp. J. P. Migne, 221 vols (Paris 1844–65), CLXXVI, cols 881–924, also available on line in the *Patrologia Latina* database.

[108] On the interface between rule and constitutions, see in particular Andenna, '*Non est haec vita apostolica*', pp. 585–92.

in 1235 and in 1244 the newly united Tuscan Hermits began drawing up constitutions with the assistance of Riccardo Annibaldi and the Cistercian abbots of Falleri Nova and Fossanova. These were finally confirmed by papal letter in February 1254 and, according to Jordan of Quedlinburg, were the basis for the constitutions of the order after 1256.[109] From the late 1270s, no doubt prompted by the crisis of the Council of Lyons, the friars set about producing new constitutions designed to promote uniform observance. The records of general chapters refer to various new regulations or *definitiones*, the first of which to survive date to the early 1280s. Thereafter Clemente da Osimo, perhaps assisted by Agostino Novello, drew up a definitive set of constitutions which were ultimately ratified and approved with minor modifications at a general chapter held in Regensburg in 1290.[110] As with other orders established in the later Middle Ages, earlier monastic institutions provided models for those of the Augustinians. There are parallels with the Cistercians, whose administrative structures, based around chapter meetings and visitation, provided the starting point for most orders after 1215. The text also owes much to Dominican practice, available in the revised Dominican constitutions drawn up by Ramon de Peñafort *c.* 1240. Thus the treatment of novices parallels that of the Order of Preachers, but the Augustinians also introduced elements not present in Peñafort's text, such as a complete account of the mechanisms for study in the order. These 'Regensburg Constitutions' were to remain the core legislative text for the Augustinians until the Reformation.

The Regensburg chapter instructed all priors to keep a copy of the new constitutions and make sure they were observed. Two years later Giles of Rome, newly elected prior general, again emphasised the importance of having a copy of the constitutions in every house. They were to be read out in chapter and in the refectory so that no failings could be excused on the basis of ignorance. Provincial priors were charged with visiting every house and energetically correcting any faults. Nonetheless in 1308 the general chapter meeting in Genoa registered concern that the diversity of rules and constitutions meant that neither ordinary friars nor their superiors knew which regulations they should observe. The chapter therefore instructed all priors to obtain for their convent a copy of the constitutions in a single volume, a copy of the rule of Augustine with the *Expositio* and the liturgical *Ordinarium* ('Ceremonial') which had also been drawn up by Clemente da Osimo.[111] Four years later observance of the Regensburg Constitutions was again stressed, this time with the requirement that earlier versions be

---

[109] *Cum a nobis*, 15 February 1254 (van Luijk, *Bullarium* III; Berger 371; Potthast 15236). See also Alexander IV's reissuing of *Cum a nobis* (Empoli 12–13).

[110] *Las primitivas constituciones de los Agustinos (Ratisbonenses del año 1290)*, ed. I. Arámburu Cendoya (Valladolid, 1966).

[111] On this see more below, p. 125.

annulled, but the problem of conformity was a persistent one. By their very nature constitutions were flexible: each general chapter issued new written instructions or *definitiones* which, if approved by successive chapters, were then added to the official text. Confusion was perhaps inevitable in such circumstances and later modifications to the standard copy were eventually undertaken. A first attempt at revision made in 1318 by the prior general Alessandro di Sant'Elpidio (1312–26) became known as the *Tolleramus*, from the opening word, but did not last long. In 1326 the general chapter again ordered that reliable brothers (*boni fratres*) be deputed to look at both new and old constitutions and establish a common text so that there would be no variations in observance in the order. Finally, the prior general Thomas de Strasbourg (1345–57) produced *Additiones*, approved in 1348, which replaced the *Tolleramus*, summarising intervening *definitiones*.[112] These were inserted as appendices to each chapter of the Regensburg text and like it, remained in force until 1551. Problems of distribution nonetheless remained: when the prior general Gregorio da Rimini visited the province of Naples in 1357–8, he found that some houses still had no copy of the constitutions.

Authority

The Augustinians, like the Carmelites, had no motherhouse. This meant that there was no prototype for the houses of the order and no fixed administrative centre. The central mechanism of government was the general chapter, which played a key role in the life of the order. Attended by provincial priors, two friars elected by provincial chapters and, from 1308, all masters of theology, its purpose was to regulate the business of the order and to issue *definitiones*. It might also act as a final place of appeal. Meetings were originally planned on a yearly basis, but as early as 1281 when the friars convened in Padua, it was determined that they should take place only every three years, a pragmatic decision which remained in force until 1430, when a general chapter at Montpellier decided on a four-year cycle. The Regensburg chapter of 1290 was the first to be held outside Italy and for eighty years from 1324 general chapters alternated between Italy and the other provinces. Thereafter most were again held in Italy, and from 1470, indeed, in Rome.

According to the Regensburg Constitutions, each general chapter opened with a sermon from the prior general or someone delegated by him, and notice of friars who had died since the last meeting. Within the general chapter diffinitors were chosen, who, together with the prior general, decided on petitions and questions of discipline. The prior general, who was elected by the general chapter, was required to hand back his seal to the diffinitors and

[112] Thomas was one of only two non-Italian generals during the Middle Ages. The other was Gui de Toulouse, elected 1371.

subject himself to assessment. In theory he might be absolved from office; in practice, of the first fourteen, eight died in office, two resigned, and two were promoted to the episcopate; none was rejected.[113] The diffinitors also had the authority to change the body of the constitutions or make new ones, though changes required approval by two successive chapters. The gathering closed with prayers and special masses for the pope, other prelates, kings, princes and benefactors both living and dead. The prior general or a diffinitor would then announce when and where the next chapter was to be celebrated and, after further prayers and the blessing of the friars, they would all return home, presumably carrying with them copies of the new *definitiones*, as well as news of the wider order.

Continuity between chapters was provided by the prior general, in office for three or four years at a time, with the possibility of renewal at successive meetings. The position was at first subject to papal confirmation, but from 1308 this was limited to a simple requirement that the new general present himself to the pope within a year of election (even this obligation was to be removed in 1475 by Sixtus IV). Should a general die in office, the superior of the province in which the next chapter was to be held acted as vicar. These men were not infrequently later elected as generals themselves. Each prior general kept a record of his activities comparable to an episcopal register. These are now important sources for the history of the order, but the first to survive is that of Gregorio da Rimini (†1358), prior general in the last year of his life. Only at the end of the fifteenth century did the general chapter introduce a *Liber ordinis* comparable to that used by the Carmelites, to be drawn up by the prior general with a catalogue of all the houses, provinces and observant congregations; none survive. The general was assisted by *socii* and by a proctor general who resided at the papal Curia to deal with the business of the order. To cover their expenses and other costs incurred at the Curia, each province was required to pay substantial taxes every year. The recurring expenditure necessary for general chapter meetings was such, however, that other resources were constantly needed: in 1289 Nicholas IV offered an indulgence of a year and forty days to those supporting the friars during a general chapter and attending their sermons.[114] Essential assistance came in the form of financial resources. In 1318, for instance, the Malatesta family paid for the general chapter in Rimini, while in 1335 Pope Benedict XII (1334–42) allowed the general proctor 50 gold florins towards the cost of a general chapter to be held in Grasse (Provence). Sometimes these payments were even retrospective: at Siena in 1339 the city gave the friars 100 *lire* in part payment of debts incurred on hosting the general chapter in the previous year.

---

[113] D. Gutiérrez, *The Augustinians in the Middle Ages 1256–1356* (Villanova, Pa, 1984), p. 61.
[114] *Pium est et*, 6 February 1289 (Alonso I, 150; Langlois 480).

The structure of the provinces mirrored that of the order as a whole. They were led by provincials, responsible for holding chapters attended by all priors, each accompanied by a friar elected by the brothers of the house and also attended by masters and lectors in theology. Like the general chapters, these meetings started on an annual basis but in some provinces were gradually reduced to every two or three years, a reality acknowledged by the popes in the 1430s and 1450s when the reduction was authorised for larger provinces because of the great distances between houses. Provincial chapters too might be costly: in 1298 Edward I gave the English friars £10 for their chapter in London and in 1319 Edward II gave the same amount towards the expenses of a provincial chapter held in Tickhill. Similar donations were frequently made by other royals in the following centuries.

At the bottom of the hierarchy, the fundamental unit of the order was the convent or priory, though this had relatively little autonomy. Each originally elected its own prior on a yearly basis, but from the late thirteenth century three names were proposed to the provincial chapter, which made the final choice. Later still, priors provincial chose the superiors of each convent. Decisions concerning debts or large payments could not be made without the authority of the majority or 'wiser' part of the community, usually through the chapter. Otherwise, the priors were responsible for everything that happened in the house: the economic management of its affairs, the spiritual and temporal needs of the friars. When the prior was absent a sub-prior elected by his brothers would conduct the normal business. If, however, the prior were to be absent for a longer period, or to attend a provincial chapter, a vicar would be elected to take his place. Priors presided at chapter meetings in their house, which were attended by both lay and clerical friars, though the former could not be chosen as priors or attend the provincial chapter as delegates. Nor might lay brothers supervise elections, since they were not expected to be able to read and, so it was claimed, might therefore be deceived.

This articulated network, held together by chapter meetings at each level, was very similar to and largely modelled on that of other orders. It worked in so far as it allowed rapid expansion and yet maintained a clear structure of authority for decision-making. It was also intended to support uniformity of observance across vast areas. Aready in the 1250s this had proved difficult. As the order expanded, it became ever harder to achieve.

CHAPTER TWO

In the World

A geographical sketch

By the late 1250s there were four main provinces in the order: France, Germany, Spain and Italy, but the last of these was probably already subdivided. The home of the order always remained central and northern Italy, where the number of houses far outnumbered those established elsewhere. Its relative importance is clearly underlined by a list of provinces from the end of the century, ten of which were in the peninsula: Ancona, Fermo, Lombardy, Naples, Pisa, Romagna, Rome, Siena, Spoleto and Treviso. Those outside covered France, Germany, Hungary, Provence, Spain and England.[1] Rapid expansion continued in the 1300s, so that by 1329 there were twenty-four provinces: southern Italy was divided into Naples, Apulia and Sicily, Germany had been separated into Bavaria-Bohemia (including Austria and further east), Cologne (including the Netherlands), Rhineland-Swabia (including the German-speaking Swiss cantons and Alsace) and Saxony-Thuringia (including north Germany). New provinces were created in Toulouse and Narbonne, whilst in the eastern Mediterranean a province of the Holy Land – Cyprus had houses in Crete, Corfu, Cyprus and Rhodes. In Spain, which encompassed Portugal, separate provinces were established in Aragon and Catalonia. Only one, Fermo, seems to have disappeared. By the mid-fourteenth century there were perhaps six thousand friars, of whom seventy-five per cent were clerics.[2] Although any figure is simply an educated guess, there were clearly far fewer Augustinians than either Franciscans or Dominicans.

Apart from the development of distinct observant congregations, the arrangement of provinces remained unchanged until the late fifteenth century, when further subdivisions produced the provinces of Abruzzo, Sardinia and Portugal. The last of these was to found a house as far away as La Laguna in the Canary Islands (1505).[3] By this date the 'Bavarian' province also had

[1] The precise number and identity of provinces at this date is still subject to discussion. The general chapter meeting in 1295 in Siena agreed to pay Giacomo da Viterbo one florin per province and then allocated him seventeen, *AA*, 2 (1907–8), pp. 371–2, leading the editor to argue for seventeen provinces, a number also adopted by Gutiérrez, *The Augustinians*, p. 44; Rano, 'Agostiniani', col. 323, proposes sixteen, as given here, but the two authors divide the territories differently.

[2] Gutiérrez, *The Augustinians*, pp. 47, 62.

[3] In the early sixteenth century there were various short-lived reorganisations of the provincial

houses in Poland and present-day Belarus. At its pre-Tridentine peak the houses of the order thus stretched from the Atlantic to the Aegean and north to the Baltic. The friars did not, however, expand into Scandinavia.

While the numerical importance of Italy is clear, the details of the early spread of the order here remain hazy. Recent accounts of the convents in the Marche provide radically conflicting information: van Luijk lists twenty-six houses before the union, Cicconi gives thirty-nine.[4] In part this is a factor of the difficulty in distinguishing Augustinian houses subject to the official supervision of the order from those defined simply by their observance of the rule. Either figure for the Marche would, however, confirm the early pre-eminence of the region in the history of the Augustinian Hermits. The picture suggested by lists drawn up by van Luijk in the 1970s is thus liable to revision, but nonetheless illustrates some general trends which are likely to be more or less accurate.[5] As we have seen, central, north and north-east Italy were of key importance before 1256 and expansion there continued to be significant in the second half of the century, so that by 1300 there were between 160 and 180 houses. This phenomenal growth was certainly assisted by Cardinal Riccardo Annibaldi. In 1258 he gave the friars the former Benedictine monastery of San Bartolomeo di Sestinga in the Maremma, and later requested that the local bishop give them the church of San Niccolò in Spoleto (1265). He also established a house on his own land at Molaria some time before 1274, when a general chapter was held there.[6] In the fourteenth century the level of expansion remained very high, with over sixty new houses in the region before 1400, but growth now also took off in the south, where there were fifty convents in the province of Naples alone by the Council of Trent.

Houses in Italy benefited from the proximity of the papacy, which provided privileges of protection and numerous indulgences to encourage lay support for their churches. Already in February 1257 for example, Santo Spirito in Florence received an indulgence for the feasts of the Holy Spirit and St Matthew. City patronage could also be particularly significant. In Siena, the church of Sant'Agostino, founded in 1259, was supported by donations in kind from the commune over the following century. Like the Carmelites and the other religious houses and hospitals in the city at this date, they received annual gifts of mortar or bricks (fifty thousand in 1262). At first these were

structure. See B. Estrada Robles, *Los Agustinos ermitaños en España hasta el siglo xix* (Madrid, 1988), pp. 33–5.

[4] The lower figure comes from B. van Luijk, 'Diffusione degli Agostiniani in Italia', *DIP* I, cols 327–40, who also lists just six houses for the period 1256–1300, and thirty-one for the remainder of the Middle Ages, while R. Cicconi, 'Gli insediamenti agostiniani nelle Marche e le relazioni del 1650', in *Arte e spiritualità nell'ordine agostiniano e il convento San Nicola a Tolentino* (Tolentino, 1992), pp. 139–46, gives much higher figures early on: thirty-nine houses before 1256, seventeen 1256–1300 and twenty-five for the fourteenth and fifteenth centuries.

[5] Van Luijk, 'Diffusione degli Agostiniani in Italia', cols 327–40.

[6] Roth, 'Cardinal Richard Annibaldi' (Continuation), *Augustiniana* 3 (1953), p. 25.

for the church, but later payments were for other parts of the monastic complex, reflecting the increasing size of the community.

In England the early history of the order is not easy to pin down. A cluster of fragmentary references suggests the friars may have arrived around the middle of the century. In 1249 King Henry III extended his protection to some 'brothers of the order of hermits of St Augustine' (*fratres heremitarum ordinis sancti Augustini*), which at this date probably meant the hermits of Tuscany. The Franciscan Thomas of Eccleston, writing *c.* 1258, records that the Franciscan provincial in England recommended the Austin Friars (*fratres de ordine sancti Augustini*) to his brethren at a general chapter held in Stamford some time in the 1240s or early 1250s. Again, according to the St Albans chronicler Matthew Paris (†1259), these years saw a flourishing of mendicant orders, including the *fratres de ordine sancti Augustini*. In 1254 the king granted land outside Shrewsbury to some *fratres de Coulon* who may have been attached to the order. In the following year, he allowed a hermit named Silvester *ordinis sancti Augustini* to have a (short-lived) hermitage in Sittingbourne, Kent. Whilst this sequence of references may suggest an influx of some size or stature, it is now impossible to be more precise. The origins or affiliations of these early communities remain undocumented. It is again likely that the influence of Riccardo Annibaldi was important, but in at least one case there may have been an invitation, which is probably how many of these early communities began.[7] A group of friars from France came to a site on the banks of the River Stour at Clare in Suffolk probably at the request of Richard, earl of Hertford and Gloucester, whose widow, Matilda, was later an important patron of the house, though the original land was given by a former steward of the honour of Clare. This was almost certainly the first house of the new province, or at least it became so by tradition, being so identified by the prior general in 1472. John Capgrave (1393–1464) an Augustinian chronicler from Lynn, dated it to 1248, but it can now be documented only from 1262 when Henry III ordered his bailiffs to arrest men who had abandoned the house. Despite this inauspicious beginning, Clare was to enjoy powerful connections. In 1296 King Edward I gave 29 shillings to provide for the friars during his own visit to the house and in 1307 his daughter Joan of Acre elected burial there in the chapel of St Vincent which she had founded. The heart and bones of Lionel of Clarence, third son of Edward III, who had died in Milan in 1368 were also interred at Clare, leaving the remainder of his body near the tomb of Augustine in Pavia.

These early English *loca*[8] were rural, as befitted the eremitical origins of the order, but the 1250s also saw the arrival of the friars in Leicester (1254?),

---

7 *The Cartulary of the Augustinian Friars of Clare*, ed. C. Harper-Bill (Woodbridge, 1991), pp. 2–3.

8 *Locus, loca*, literally meaning 'place(s)', is a term frequently used in contemporary sources to indicate a first religious colony before it had acquired the settled structures of a monastery or friary and was sometimes still used even once a convent was established.

Ludlow (1254), London (before 1256) and Huntingdon (1258). In 1266/7 the English prior provincial purchased land on the River Cherwell at Oxford and in 1268 Henry III gave them land for the construction of a chapel in the parish of Holy Cross, followed in 1270 by a gift of oaks for building. The Oxford friary was adopted for use by the theology faculty of the university, which remained there until the fifteenth century, and also became the first of the two *studia generalia* of the order in England, followed by Cambridge before 1289. By the end of the century there were at least twenty houses in England, mostly in the north and east.[9] By this date, the so-called English province, like others, was further divided into 'limits' (*limes*) for ease of administration: Cambridge, Oxford, Lincoln, York and Ireland. The structure highlights the general failure of the friars to spread to the south and west of England.

In the first half of the fourteenth new houses were founded at Boston (1317), Bristol (1313), Canterbury (1318), Droitwich (1331), Northampton (1323), Stafford (1344) and Stamford (1342). As before, the order enjoyed generous royal support. In the 1330s, Edward III, citing the 'special affection' in which he held the friars, granted them various plots of land in Cambridge. Similar grants were made in Oxford. Other planned settlements were, however, not so fortunate, particularly in the west. In 1331 the citizens of Dartmouth invited the friars to their town, but the opposition of the Premonstratensians at Torre Abbey led to a long appeal to Rome. Torre successfully argued that by papal privilege no new churches or oratories could be built in territory held in advowson by the abbey. Despite the secret consecration of their chapel, the friars were forced to leave in 1347. In the following year the bishop of Exeter, John Grandisson (1327–69), gave his permission for a friary in the town of Barnstaple (Devon) on land given by Sir John Audley, but only if the order kept no other house in his diocese. This time attempts to build a friary encountered the hostility of local Cluniac monks, who refused to make an agreement over revenues, again citing the privilege restricting new churches. No friary was built. An attempt to start a house at Sherborne in 1342–3 met a similar fate.

The limited number of papal letters addressed to the English Augustinians underlines the relative importance of royal support to the success or failure of these communities. The English friars automatically enjoyed any papal privileges issued to the order as a whole, but unlike Italy, particular provisions were rare. In 1261 the English houses were specifically authorised to have bells. Nearly half a century later they were named in a generic instruction

---

[9]   Besides those already mentioned there were houses at Berwick (1260), Grimsby (1293), Lincoln (1270), Little Yarmouth (i.e. Gorleston c. 1267), Lynn (1295), Newcastle on Tyne (c. 1290), Norwich (1289), Orford (1299), Penrith (1291), Tickhill (1256/68), Warrington (by 1272) and York (1272). The remaining houses are both traditionally assigned early dates but can only be documented from the early fourteenth century: Woodhouse (near Cleobury Mortimer, Shropshire) and Winchester. See Roth, *The English Austin Friars*, I, pp. 240–368.

to the prior general allowing him to accept *loca* in various kingdoms (1309) and a series of mandates from John XXII to the bishops of all the provinces in which the order then resided (1317) requesting their protection for the friars. But after 1261 the next extant papal letter addressed directly to the English prior provincial and friars dates to 1320. Moreover, it is simply the response to a royal petition requesting that the friars be permitted to accept the *locus* of Boston in Lincolnshire. By contrast, in that same period there are innumerable records of concessions of land, grants of protection and pittances made by the Crown. Nothing could make clearer the importance to the order of good relations with the royal court.

The later fourteenth century witnessed a further alternation of successful and unsuccessful English foundations. Those which survived were Atherstone in Warwickshire, a small house founded in 1374 on land given by Ralph, Lord Basset of Drayton; Newport (1377) on land donated by the earl of Stafford, Rye (1364) and Thetford (*c.* 1387–9), founded after a donation from John of Gaunt. All may have been in fulfilment of a papal licence issued by Urban V in 1364 authorising four new foundations in England.[10] The failed initiatives included Barnard Castle, where the earl of Warwick gave land for a friary in 1381 and the friars obtained the authorisation of the archbishop of York, but no house seems to have been founded. There were similar attempts at Coventry (1363) and Tawstoke (1385), but there is no evidence that the friars acted upon the initial donations.

Some of these difficulties may be attributed to the increasing isolation of the friars in England. The Hundred Years' War (1339–1453) made the English Crown suspicious of foreign mendicants. Already in 1333, after the taking of Berwick, all Scottish friars were expelled from the Augustinian house there and replaced with English men; a similar expulsion took place in August 1347 in Calais.[11] In 1351 the king further supported the Calais friars, granting them land next to a house of beguines in the town and two years later gave them financial assistance, but nothing further came of the new house.[12] It also became difficult for foreign friars to study at Oxford or Cambridge and the province did not provide senior figures for the order. It may be no coincidence that there were no new houses of Austins in England in the fifteenth century.

In the 1280s the Augustinians had spread from England to Ireland, settling at Dublin with royal assistance. This was followed in 1290 at Dungarvan in

---

[10] *Hiis que animarum*, 28 April 1364 (Alonso II, 23).

[11] Edward III also required that the Berwick Franciscans be dispersed to English houses, 'so that with a change of residence may come a change of spirit'. See W. M. Mackenzie, 'A Prelude to the War of Independence', *Scottish Historical Review* 27 (1948), pp. 105–13, 113.

[12] J. Röhrkasten, 'Local Ties and International Connections of the London Mendicants', in *Mendicants, Military Orders and Regionalism in Medieval Europe*, ed. J. Sarnowsky (Aldershot, 1999), pp. 145–84, 177n.

the diocese of Lismore and *c.* 1295 at Drogheda, County Louth, but it was in the fourteenth century that the Augustinians really took off in Ireland. There were ten new foundations, prompting the creation of a separate vicariate, and a further seven in the 1400s, a stark contrast with England, with whom the Irish vicariate was to have strained relations throughout the late Middle Ages. Apart from Newport, right on the border, no Augustinian friaries were ever founded in Wales and only three in Scotland, all in the 1500s: Linlithgow (1503), Manuel (1506) and Haddington (1511).

Unlike the British Isles, a substantial German province already existed at the time of the Great Union in 1256. The Tuscan Hermits and Bonites had established a number of houses north of the Alps which, together with the Williamite houses in German and Hungarian lands which chose to remain in the mendicant order after 1266, left a sizeable and widespread community. The Williamite houses included those named in the papal letter *Ea que iudicio*: Tübingen, Seemannshausen, Mindelheim and Schönthal in Bavaria, Lippene in Brandenburg, Marienpforte near Kreuznach, Weißenborn west of Erfurt, Oberried in the Black Forest and houses in or near Stockau (Johannistal) and Ostrov (Insula Sancte Marie in the diocese of Prague) in what is now the Czech Republic, as well as others unspecified.[13] There were also houses at Völkermarkt in Carinthia (Austria), Stettin (which later moved to Gartz on the Oder) and Holte near Osnabrück. Other early houses included Marienthal in the diocese of Münster (founded before June 1256) and a number of friaries in the Netherlands (then part of the German province): Leuven (1236), Mechelen (1242), Bruges (1250) and Maastricht (1254), followed by Enghien (1254–6). In what is now modern Switzerland the friars had a house at Freiburg in the diocese of Lausanne some time before 1255.

In the decades after the union, important new foundations, driven by the first provincial prior Guido de Stagia and his successors, were mainly but not exclusively to the west: Mainz (1260), Würzburg (1263), Worms (1264), Cologne (1264), Speyer (*c.* 1265) and Nürnberg (by 1265), followed by Erfurt (*c.* 1266), which, despite early disputes with the citizens, was to become an important *studium* for the order. Cardinal Annibaldi was again on occasion directly or indirectly involved. In July 1267 in Regensburg, where the friars had already been active for some time, the prior provincial Engelpert is described as acting on behalf of Annibaldi in accepting from the city (*universitas civitatis*) the donation of a chapel and cloister in the suburbs near the Jewish synagogue.[14]

Later decades saw the multiplication of houses all across the German provinces, with particular new growth to the north and east: the Cologne house founded the cloister of Lippstadt in 1280 with the help of Friedrich

[13] *Ea que iudicio*, 30 August 1266 (Alonso I, 113). See also Andenna, 'Non est haec vita apostolica', p. 607n.

[14] Andenna, '*De introitu fratrum*', pp. 137–43, A. Kunzelmann, *Geschichte der deutschen Augustiner-Eremiten*. Cassiciacum 26, 7 vols (Würzburg 1969–76), I, p. 133.

von Hörde, a Cologne *ministeriale* (a member of the lower nobility). By the end of that decade the Augustinians in Westphalia had moved into Osnabrück (from Holte) and to Herford, perhaps again a daughter-house of one of the Rhineland friaries.[15] In the Netherlands new houses were founded in Ypres (1265), Dordrecht south-east of Rotterdam (*c.* 1293) and Ghent in Flanders (1295), which was to become the most important of the houses in the region.

In Prague, King Wenceslaus II founded a friary in 1285 to complete a vow made by his father Ottokar II before he died in battle in 1278. He also gave the order a further house at Taus (1288) on the western edge of Bohemia, to which German friars came, probably from Regensburg or Schönthal. To the south, new friaries were founded, amongst others, in Constance (1268), Zurich (1270), Bern (1287) and Munich (1294), which was to become a key house in the later history of the order. By contrast, a house in the small town of Vevey, founded 1293/1301, disappeared by 1312. Another of the new convents, Falkenstein in Lower Austria, founded *c.* 1267, fell victim to the wars between Ottakar of Bohemia and the Habsburgs, but houses in Vienna (by 1266) and its vicinity, Marchegg (by 1278) and Baden (1285), were more fortunate. Vienna in particular was another of the major centres in the late-medieval order.

By the end of the thirteenth century then, through a combination of strong episcopal support, regular papal indulgences and energetic activity by the friars, there were some eighty male houses in the German provinces of the order.[16] This expansion continued throughout the fourteenth century, a golden age for the friars in the region. New houses were founded in all of the German provinces, but most spectacular growth was seen in the east. In Hungary, where the friars had some six houses by 1300, the number had more than tripled a hundred years later to twenty, centred on Esztergom, where a *studium generale* was founded after 1338. In mid-century the order settled in Kraków in Little Poland (1342) with the support of Kasimir the Great (1333–70), who had encountered the order in Prague and may also have founded a house at Wieluń. In the fifteenth century, in spite of the trauma of the Hussite wars which led to the destruction of numerous friaries, including Prague in 1420 (where the friars were able to return only in 1490), the order continued to expand and by the end of the 1400s had reached as far as Lithuania and present-day Belarus.

In the area of modern France early expansion was in the south; perhaps the oldest houses were Grasse, Arles and Marseilles, all of which may have preceded the Great Union, though the earliest documented house is Narbonne (1256). In the north, the first and only friary for some time was Paris (1259) where Louis IX, as reported by Joinville his biographer, bought the

[15] K. Elm, *Mittelalterliches Ordensleben in Westfalen und am Niederrhein* (Paderborn, 1989), p. 130.

[16] F. Rennhofer, *Die Augustiner-Eremiten in Wien. Ein Beitrag zur Kulturgeschichte Wiens* (Würzburg, 1956), p. 39.

friars a grange and had a church built for them outside the Montmartre gate, at Chardonnet.[17] In the east the order expanded from Germany to Strasbourg (1265), a daughter house of Speyer, Metz (1267) and Mulhouse (1268), which in turn founded Basel in 1276.[18]

Although there were only ten houses in the French province by 1275, seven of which were in the south, a further fifty-nine foundations were made by 1350, more than any other order in this period. In some areas this dynamism continued in the second half of the fourteenth century, as in Brittany, where three priories were founded in the space of twenty years. There were fewer new houses in the 1400s, but by the Council of Trent there were some 102 friaries in the area of modern France, closely comparable to the ninety-nine of the Carmelites in the same region.

In the province of Spain the first houses followed the Christianisation of lands taken in the *Reconquista*.[19] The earliest was in Játiva, one of the administrative centres of the kingdom of Valencia, founded in 1244 by the Bonites after Jaime I took the city from the Muslims, but already in the late thirteenth century the house had passed to the Dominicans. Other early houses included Cordoba in Andalusia, established at some point after Fernando III took the city in 1236 and Salamanca (in León), both of which probably predate the Great Union of 1256, as perhaps did the hermitage of S. Ginés de Cartagena (Murcia), but the surviving documentation for these early houses is very sketchy. There may also have been early houses in Portugal.[20] References immediately following the union include to the Balearic island of Formentera (documented by a gift from Jaime I in 1257) and in Toledo, where in 1260 Alfonso X of Castile, his wife Violante and their sons gave the hermits at Cartagena a house and church outside the city dedicated to Santo Stefano, which had belonged to a community of nuns. The donation came with clear conditions attached which demonstrate both the importance of royal patronage in stimulating the expansion of the order and the rewards royal patrons might expect to attain. Alfonso ordered that the house was to have twelve religious and be established within a year. No property could be alienated and the king maintained the rights of patronage for himself and his successors. There were to be daily masses for Alfonso and his predecessors; the friars were to celebrate the feast of St Clement (to whom the nuns had been dedicated), the birth of the founder and the anniversary of the death of his father in all convents of the order in his lordship. Similar aspirations lay behind most

[17] Jean de Joinville, 'The Life of Saint Louis', chapter 18, most easily available in Joinville and Villehardouin, *Chronicles of the Crusades*, p. 344.

[18] R. W. Emery, *The Friars in Medieval France. A Catalogue of French Mendicant Convents, 1200–1550* (New York and London, 1962), pp. 9–10.

[19] See the general account in Estrada Robles, *Los Agustinos ermitaños en España*.

[20] See L. Alvarez Gutierrez, *El movimento 'observante' agustiniano en España y su culminación en tiempo de los reyes católicos* (Rome, 1978), p. 8.

such foundations, if not always on this scale. By the end of the thirteenth century there were seven other houses in the Crown of Aragon, many of which enjoyed royal support: Aguas Vivas (by 1267), Alcira (1270), Zaragoza on the Ebro river (1286), Burgos (*c.* 1287), Valencia, Alcoy (1290) and Castellon de la Plana (1298).[21] There may also have been two late-thirteenth-century foundations in Andalusia: Badajoz and Seville, but neither can be securely dated before the early 1300s. The distances between them were so great that in the mid-fourteenth century, Gregorio da Rimini authorised the creation of vicariates in each region (*in singulis nationibus*) in the peninsula. In the late fourteenth century there was a further increase which, as before, depended on the involvement of lay and ecclesiastical patrons. In Salamanca in 1377 for example, Bishop Alonso Barrasa (1375–82) and the cathedral chapter gave the friars the church of San Pedro. The record of the donation makes specific mention of the importance of study in preparation for preaching. By 1422 it was recognised as a university. In Torroella de Montgrí (Catalonia), a new house was founded in June 1396 on land given by the city. By this date it was usual for the prior general to licence new settlements and in this case Bartolomeo da Venezia designated a friar Ramon Duran as first prior. The same process repeated itself again and again. In the early fifteenth century a house was founded in Valladolid in property given to the priors of Toledo and Dueñas by the constable Ruy López Dávalos and his second wife, Elvira de Guevara, who came to be considered the founder of the house. The friary was to be one of the first to join the Spanish observant movement.

In the urban landscape

As the account of the expansion of the order above makes clear, the transition from a predominantly rural to a largely urban order took place gradually over the course of the late thirteenth century. It was achieved by a variety of mechanisms. In some cases hermit groups simply moved into centres of population. Thus the small hermitage of San Pietro di Camerata south of Siena developed increasing ties with the neighbouring small town (*castrum*) of Monticiano and in 1288/9 the hermits moved into Monticiano itself, building a church and convent near the gate. Their new church, dedicated to St Augustine, soon became the preferred place of burial for the local population and a regular recipient of legacies. Such moves frequently meant houses at or near the gates of cities or in the suburbs, where land was still available. In Shrewsbury, the friars settled outside the gates, as they did at Lincoln, where the friary was founded in the suburb of Newport, north west of the cathedral. At Bristol, Simon of Montagu gave the order a plot inside the Temple Gate

---

[21] Burgos may be an early house, refounded with the support of Blanca, daughter of the king of Portugal and neice of King Sancho. See Alvarez Gutierrez, *El movimento "observante" agustiniano en España*, p. 13.

where their church was consecrated just seven years later, on 7 July 1320. At the other end of Europe, in Torroella de Montgrí the friars were given land at the extreme south of the town, near the River Ter. By settling on the edge, they were able to have more space but they also participated in the occupation and bonification of land surrounding settlements: this is most spectacularly evident in Venice, where in 1232 the hermits took a site surrounded by marshes which both they and the city wished to see drained.[22]

Location on the expanding fringes of cities placed the friars close both to their expected lay audience and to potential almsgivers; many houses always remained on the periphery, sometimes literally. In the small town of Cremieu near Lyons, the friary, founded in 1317 for ten religious, was built into the medieval town walls. Its stone chapel formed part of the defensive network and remains one of the most substantial buildings in the urban fabric. In some cases, however, growing wealth and lay assistance allowed the friars to transfer to better sites. In Mechelen, the original house was inconveniently placed behind a beguinage outside the city, but already in 1252 the friars were able to move to a more appropriate site on the so-called Nieuwland. In Toledo (Castile), because of the dampness of their original location at Santo Stefano outside the city, in 1311 the chancellor of Castile, with the permission of the archbishop of Toledo and of the pope, gave the friars the old palace of the kings inside Toledo itself. Similarly, in Vienna, where the Augustinians arrived before 1266, the first house was outside the Werder gate. From 1299, after the subdivision of the German province, the first prior of the new province of Bavaria-Bohemia chose to reside there. In 1306 it was named a *studium generale*. Twenty-one years later the friars moved into the city. Duke Friedrich der Schöne (1314–30) gave them land next to his Hofburg palace. It was the site of five houses and a bathhouse, where he had originally planned a Cistercian monastery. The friary became one of the most important religious communities in the city and the order. The prior generals and theologians Thomas de Strasbourg (†1357) and his successor Gregorio da Rimini (†1358) both died and were buried there.

At Winchester in the south of England, by contrast, an attempt to move failed. The friary was on the main road outside Southgate, but in the 1340s the friars obtained a parcel of land in the city, arguing that their original location was low-lying and dangerous. After the Black Death they acquired a further series of adjoining plots, tore down the original buildings and enclosed the site with a wall. This deprived the citizens of revenue in rents and the ensuing dispute was taken to the royal court, where the friars lost. They stayed at Southgate and the inventory taken at the Dissolution suggests the house remained impoverished.

[22] See A. Rigon, 'Ordini Mendicanti e politica territoriali urbana dei comuni nell'Italia centro-settentrionale', in *Gli ordini mendicanti in Val d'Elsa, Convegno di Studio* (Castelfiorentino, 1999), pp. 215–31, 220.

As well as the attitude of local clergy and laity, accidents, wars and other disasters also of course affected the fortunes of the friars. In Rye in 1364 an initial house was established on the cliffs with the support of the bailiff, William Taillour. After just thirteen years, French raiders burnt down both the town and the friary. This disaster turned to the friars' advantage two years later when they received a new site within Rye itself, near a ditch where new town walls were to be built and to which they were to allow access. Similarly, in Newport, a house founded in 1377 was rebuilt after its destruction during the revolt of Owain Glyndŵr in 1402.

As at Dartmouth, the arrival of the latest order of mendicants in the restricted urban context often exacerbated competition with pre-existing religious entities: parishes and cathedral clergy as well as the other regular orders. In 1261 the provost and chapter of St Martin at Ypres, who were later to oppose the Carmelites, obtained an injunction against the friar hermits who had begun to build a church within the parish boundaries of St Jacques. They were not to settle in either parish unless with special papal mandate. In Lincoln a dispute was pre-empted when the prior made agreement with the local parish of St John in 1273 not to accept gifts that would reduce its income. In Cambridge in 1290, the newly arrived friars agreed to pay 4 shillings a year to the rector of the parish of St Edward and undertook not to admit parishioners to the sacraments in their church. In 1294, by agreement with the abbot of Hirsau, the friars were able to settle in Weil der Stadt (Rhineland-Swabia) on land inside the walls belonging to the abbey. In the following summer, the mayor and gathered citizenry accepted them into the town with the agreement of the local parish. Conflict was avoided, but the friars lost freedom of action.

At Canterbury, where the Austins originally settled with archiepiscopal permission in 1318, a later move led to dispute. In 1324 the friars had taken over a messuage (house with land) in the parish of St George. A yearly sum was owed on this land to the priory of Christchurch, which vigorously opposed the transfer. The friars nonetheless opened their oratory to the public, thereby challenging both the parish and archiepiscopal authority. An enquiry led to a compromise which allowed them to stay put, on the understanding that they would pay St George's 9 shillings a year and 20 pence in rent to the monks of Christchurch. Over the following decades they acquired several new plots of land and unlike their brothers at Winchester were able to build a large friary, even enclosing two lanes which had, so they claimed, fallen into disuse. By contrast, in February 1283–4, when the friars at Tickhill planned to enclose a plot of land licence was not granted, though later attempts to expand were approved.[23]

To some extent relations with other regular religious were regulated by

[23] *VCH York*, ed. W. Page, III (London, 1913), pp. 280–1.

papal edict, but this did not always provide the easy solution to disputes that popes and Curia intended. In Treviso, a case studied by Daniela Rando, the Bonites had originally settled on the margins of the urban district, building a church dedicated to Santa Margherita. In 1265 they obtained a better site, at a bridgehead in Borgo San Paolo, and began building a new house. To this the city's Dominicans objected on the grounds of their privilege limiting new houses to more than 300 rods or *canne* from their own convent of San Niccolò. The bishop, a Franciscan, was inclined to accept the Dominicans' case, but the Augustinians objected that he had arbitrarily defined the length of a rod at twelve feet and had also allowed the Friars Preacher to make the measurement on their own terms. Since Treviso was a small town this would in effect mean that they could hardly have a house there at all. Pope Clement IV had already established the length of a rod at eight palms and a sample was now sent from Rome under papal seal. Remeasurement showed that the new church of Santa Margherita was more than three hundred *canne* from San Niccolò. The Austin Friars were not, however, yet free to build. A further dispute arose with the neighbouring nunnery of San Paolo, which had recently adopted the rule of Augustine but objected to the arrival of the friars next door on the basis of a hastily obtained episcopal privilege restricting building in their vicinity. This time the friars agreed to sell part of their land to the nuns, build their church on a newly acquired plot at a distance from the nunnery and enclose the remainder with hedges or walls. The bishop finally laid the first stone of their new church in November 1268.[24] Such problems were not easy to resolve. In 1296 the Franciscans complained to the pope that friars of various orders in the province of Tuscany had been building too close to their own churches, and in December Boniface VIII instructed the bishop of Arezzo to ensure that any offending buildings be pulled down. Two years later similar instructions were sent to the bishop of Siena on behalf of the Dominicans in the province of Rome.[25] It is not clear whether any friaries were in fact removed.

Once established, the Austin Friars, like their predecessors, were not necessarily easy neighbours. In Barcelona, friar Bonanat Zaguals founded a house in 1309 north of the city in the parish of S. Maria del Mar. Five years later the prior reached the usual agreement with the parish concerning the proportion of income from burials and other oblations to be shared with the parish rector. In 1315, Ponç de Gualba, bishop of Barcelona (1303–34), instructed his clergy to welcome the friars to their churches and to allow them to preach and hear confessions there like the Dominicans and Franciscans. However, at some point soon thereafter the prior incurred excommunication for failing

[24] D. Rando, 'Eremitani e città. L'esempio di Treviso', in *Religione e politica nella Marca. Studi su Treviso e il suo territorio nei secoli xi–xv* (Verona, 1996), pp. 199–235, 200–203.
[25] *Sua nobis dilecti*, 19 December 1296 (Digard 1488; Potthast 24443) and 24 April 1298 (Alonso I, 204; Digard 2535; Potthast 24665).

to pay the monies due to the parish. He was absolved only in 1318 when he paid up. Why he had failed to pay is not clear, but the friars were not deterred. In 1330 a petition to the king, Alfonso III of Catalonia, stated that their house was too small and that a neighbouring orchard into which they might expand was being sold at a price they could not afford. The king instructed his bailiff (*batlle*) to ensure a just price was applied. Whether he did so is undocumented. Two years later the friars complained about the smell from two butchers adjoining their church and the king instructed that the latter be moved to a more appropriate site. In the summer of the following year the friars complained that the noise made by a blacksmith planning to move in next to the church would disrupt their services. Again the king intervened. In June 1349 the first stone of their church was finally laid but work progressed very slowly. For some unknown reason relations with the secular clergy once more deteriorated and in November 1355 the bishop, Michael de Riçoma (1346–61), issued a ban on the preaching of the Augustinians in his diocese. In the absence of the prior, his vicar, Guillermo Pasqualis, refused to accept the letter, allowing it to drop to the floor when the messenger of the bishop tried to deliver it to him. Nothing further is known of the dispute but it cannot have helped the building works. Presumably relations had improved by 1365 when the new bishop issued an indulgence for those who made donations towards the building.[26]

As at Barcelona, the Augustinians were not always on the receiving end. In the 1280s in San Gimignano (Tuscany), they persuaded the commune to allow them to close off a road between their house and garden and to appoint arbiters to agree a price with the owners of further land and gardens, which they wished to purchase at a price the sellers did not accept. As we have seen, in the following decade the order received the privilege prohibiting construction of new religious houses within 140 rods of their own churches.[27] Even before the final confirmation of the order in 1298 they, like the other major religious and monastic orders, profited from the requirement that the houses of those discontinued in 1274 should be reserved for pious uses. In Esslingen am Neckar (province of Rhineland-Swabia) they may have taken over a site from the Sack Friars as early as 1282; in 1290 the house of the Sack Friars in Acre, where only three brothers remained, was assigned to the Augustinians by the patriarch of Jerusalem on the instruction of the pope.[28] The fall of the city in the following year put paid to any transfer, but the process continued elsewhere. In the French province numerous friaries acquired property from

[26]   J. Mutgé Vives, 'El convento de Agustinos de Barcelona en el siglo xiv, Noticias históricas y documentos', in *Conventos Agustinos: Madrid, 20–24 de octubre de 1997: Actas del 10 Congreso Internacional de Historia de la Orden de San Agustín*, ed. R. Lazcano, 2 vols (Rome, 1998), I, pp. 497–528.

[27]   See above, p. 93.

[28]   *Ad fratres eremitarum*, 10 October 1290 (Alonso I, 163; Empoli, 262–3; Potthast 23429); see R. W. Emery, 'The Friars of the Sack', *Speculum* 18 (1943), pp. 323–34, 328, and below, p. 215.

the Sack Friars, including Chalons-sur-Marne (1292), Paris (1293) and later Angers (1307), Rouen (1309), Verdun (1316) and Reims (1320).[29] In 1317 the king petitioned the pope to allow the Augustinians to take over the houses of the order of the Sack in the dioceses of Reims, Orléans and Tours. By that date the duke of Brittany had handed a Sack house on his own land at Lamballe to the Augustinians.[30] A similar pattern, on a smaller scale, is identifiable in England. In the 1290s the friary at Leicester probably acquired a former Sack house as part of its holdings. In 1318 in Canterbury the friars briefly occupied a site that had belonged to the order of the Sack until 1314. In Stamford in 1342, following a petition to the pope by Edward III, the Augustinians acquired a site abandoned by the Sack near St Peter's gate in the western suburbs.

Buildings

Many of the early hermitages were very simple constructions: small oratories or their ruins are all that survive at numerous sites dotted across central Italy. At Santa Maria di Rupecava on Monte Pisano, the church, now abandoned, is just 6.2m by 9.5m. At San Leonardo al Lago west of Siena a first small oratory was built on the site of an early-medieval cave chapel. Trace of the cave was, however, lost when a larger church and enclosure replaced the original hermitage, turning it into a fairly substantial complex, with a cloister already documented at the end of the twelfth century.[31] After 1256, the size of buildings expanded in proportion to the growth of the order. The fundamental model was that of the other mendicant friars and the same functionality which drove their buildings: within the church, a rood screen (*tramezzo, pontile*) enclosing the choir for the community and the high altar; a proliferation of chapels for the private masses of priests in the community and increasingly for confraternities and lay patrons; large spaces to house the laity attending sermons and where possible, open squares in front of the façade for the same reason, often with a raised wooden platform as a pulpit, later sometimes replaced in stone. The absence of a mother church, however, meant that there was no template for churches and cloisters in the order, no great exemplar like Cîteaux or San Francesco in Assisi. New friaries were frequently established in buildings that had previously belonged to a different order or served a different function. At Warrington, for example, the friars may have taken over an earlier hospital. Like those of the other mendicants, then, the churches and convents built by the Austin Friars were heterogeneous: some were great hall churches dominating their surroundings, others

---

[29] On Paris, see below, pp. 141 and 219–20.
[30] H. Martin, *Les Ordres mendiants en Bretagne (vers 1230 – vers 1530)* (Paris, 1975), p. 34. See also below, pp. 212–21, on the fate of Sack houses in general.
[31] G. T. Radan, 'Archeological Excavations at San Leonardo al Lago and Sta Lucia di Rosia', *AA* 60 (1997), pp. 149–72. M Pellegrini, 'La cattedra e il deserto', p. 34n.

were small and unimposing: the difference was likely to be dictated by space and resources (and especially patronage). In 1281 the general chapter determined that if a large church or house was to be founded, then the decision must be made with the advice of experts with the appropriate technical skills. Indeed the friars frequently came to be considered specialists in building matters: in Florence Augustinians were called on as experts together with Dominicans and Franciscans to advise on the building of the new cathedral in 1357. There is, however, no normative evidence for the great concern about the finer points of their buildings shown in different ways by the Cistercians, Dominicans or Franciscans. When new buildings were undertaken, local architectural styles most often dictated the details. Thus at Padua, the Eremitani church was built by one of the friars (Giovanni degli Eremitani), an architect and engineer who also worked on other projects in the city in the early fourteenth century, including the Palazzo della Ragione. The resulting church is a typically Lombard structure, built in brick with a wooden ship's keel roof and four apsidal chapels flanking a large choir.

In Italy and France a substantial number of great hall churches built for the Austin Friars are still standing. But in innumerable cases, both here and elsewhere, the architecture and layout of early Augustinian conventual buildings is not easy to discern from present structures. Like so many medieval edifices, rebuilding and redesigning in later centuries has obscured the original construction. In Spain, the golden age of the order in the sixteenth century led to the rebuilding of numerous medieval foundations and later the Wars of Independence saw the closure and reuse of convents: Torroella de Montgrí was one of many used as a barracks by French soldiers. In England, the vast majority of conventual buildings were pulled down, pillaged for building materials or otherwise rendered unrecognisable after the Dissolution. At Stafford, twenty loads of stone from the demolished church were sold in 1542 to the church of Bradley west of the city, whilst in Cambridge in 1545, slate from the Austin friary was used for the new steeple at Great St Mary's. Even the early building history of a key friary such as Oxford can only be reconstructed by guesswork: we can assume a first house and chapel were completed by 1288 because the provincial chapter was held there.[32]

This dearth of information makes a report on excavations at the priory site at Leicester in the 1970s a precious rarity. When the buildings were pulled down in the early modern period, the area of the church was covered with a garden. Evidence from this relatively undisturbed site allows us to reconstruct the form and evolution of a typical small friary.

The traditional date for the foundation of Leicester is 1254, in which case it predates the Great Union, though no written records survive until the beginning of the following century. It was certainly not a particularly wealthy or

---

[32] Roth, *The English Austin Friars*, I, p. 321.

large house: there were perhaps twenty friars in 1300 and the same number in 1329.[33] At the dissolution in 1538 its property was valued at just £1 2s a year. The house stood on the River Soar outside the west gate of the city, a low-lying area liable to flooding. The original building was probably a timber structure, which may have provided temporary accommodation while work progressed on the stone church, which was in use by 1306. The friars accumulated land gradually: in the 1290s they may have acquired a house originally held by the Sack Friars and in the early fourteenth century the earl of Lancaster gave them three messuages adjoining their own, creating a site something under four acres in size. In the same period a new phase of buildings was begun and earlier timber and stone structures were pulled down to provide space for a traditional, enclosed cloister. The size of the foundations and the nature of masonry finds indicate that this was a substantial sandstone building with upper floors. The excavations also suggest that the cloister alley was narrow (*c.* 2.5m), while the size of the cloister may have been about 19.25m x 17m, comparable to the 18.5m x 18.5m cloister of Austin Friars in London. This was not, however, deemed sufficient. The Constitutions of Regensburg insist on the need for two cloisters so that different tasks could be kept apart and in the mid-fourteenth century work began on a second 'little' cloister beyond a culverted ditch. This was to provide workshops and other ancillary build-ings and should probably be seen as the continuation of the earlier building works. In mid-century construction was abandoned, probably because of a decline in numbers after the plague. Rubbish piled up on the site. Then at the end of the century building resumed, with the partial construction of a west range. The community seems to have been flourishing in the second half of the century: a *studium particulare* is documented and the original cloister acquired an inlaid tile floor, decorated with the arms of England and of several local families, including the earls of Lancaster. Imposing walls were built to enclose the complex. There was a separate building for the prior of the community and the varying standard of other accommodation across the friary is reflected in higher quality tiles and pottery finds to the south, nearer the church. In the fifteenth century the second cloister was finally completed with an impressive south range. Although the friars continued to receive generous bequests from the citizens of Leicester, and housed a guild of 'Our Lady beyond the Water' (1522), by the early sixteenth century there was already some reduction in use of the buildings. The community was pre-sumably dwindling and by the Dissolution only four friars remained.

Adaptation to the nature of the site at Leicester and to evolving economic circumstances, with intermittent building works throughout its two centu-ries of existence, is characteristic of the Austin Friars, as of the other orders

---

[33] *The Austin Friars, Leicester*, ed. J. E. Mellor and T. Pearce, CBA Research Report 35 (London, 1981), p. 1.

discussed in this book. Building often post-dated the foundation by some years. Thus in Brittany at Carhaix, founded *c.* 1355, building started only in 1372; at Vitré, founded 1363, building started only in 1376. At Lannion, founded 1373, the dormitory was under construction in 1400 when a legacy of wheat was given 'to help make the building of their dorter' (*pour ayder a faire ledifice de leur dortouer*).[34] The first construction was usually the choir, as at Seville, where the double structure, with the high altar above and a crypt below was begun in 1314 under the patronage of the Arias Yáñez de Carranza family. Thirty years later the counts of Arcos took over the *iuspatronatus* (patronage) and burial rights and the crypt became the family burial vault. The refectory, a gothic structure with fine ribbed vaults was added in 1362–6, but the church, with five lateral chapels, was completed only in the late fifteenth century.

Once started, maintenance, extension and embellishment of buildings were constant concerns and not just to the friars living in a house. A provincial chapter in Rome in 1290 decreed a payment of 50 gold florins to the priory in Orte north of the city, because its poor state was alleged to be causing embarrassment: Curial prelates and great barons passed through there on their way to Rome. The house also received annual payments from the commune for the cost of repairs and 'ornament'. By 1335, building was presumably more or less complete, since a local man whose son may have been in the house chose the church for his own burial. In 1363 a testamentary bequest of 30 *solidi* was again made 'for necessary repairs'.

Leicester and Orte are representative of small Augustinian churches. In more important centres, with more powerful patrons, much larger buildings were conceived, though once again building might take a very long time. In Vienna the Bavarian architect Dietrich Ladtner von Pirn was employed from 1330 to build a very tall three-aisled *Hallenkirche* typical of high-gothic architecture with ribbed vaults and shafts. A long choir with polygonal apse was still in construction in 1399 but the main church was completed sixty years earlier and consecrated to Augustine in 1349. Next to it stood the chapel of St George (constructed 1337–41), which served as the chapter hall of the Augustinians but had originally doubled as a meeting place for a short-lived knightly order founded by Duke Otto der Fröhlich (1330–9). To the east stood the conventual buildings, with a cloister completed in 1341 to which were attached chapels dedicated to St Leonard (1368) and St Sigismund (1386). The east wing of the cloister housed the refectory with dormitory above.

In Barcelona the friars' church, pulled down in 1718, was a vast single nave with buttresses on the model of the neighbouring gothic church of Pino. From the mid-fourteenth century it acquired several square lateral chapels:

---

[34] Martin, *Les Ordres mendiants en Bretagne*, p. 37.

Corpus domini (1352), St Raphael (by 1362), Our Lady of Grace (1367), St Martin (1387) and St Julian (1397). The presbytery and high altar were built by 1367 and consecrated thirty years later. The last bay of the nave was, however, only completed in 1517. One of the most popular chapels was that of Nuestra Señora de la Piedad (Our Lady of Mercy), originally built in the cloister in 1399, but at the end of the fifteenth century a canon of Barcelona was still exhorting the faithful to make contributions for its decoration.

In London the friars were building and expanding throughout the fourteenth century. In 1321 they were accused of raising walls without any right in the parishes of Allhallows on the Wall and St Peter's, Broad Street. In 1334 they obtained ground to extend their buildings and in 1345 Reginald de Cobham granted them three further messuages. Other tenements were obtained from the priory of St Mary without Bishopgate. In 1349 they made an arrangement with the rector of St Peter's, Broad Street, over tithes and oblations, which probably indicates recent acquisitions in the parish. The church was rebuilt in 1354 with the aid of Humphrey de Bohun, earl of Hereford and Essex, an heir of their founder of the same name, and in 1361 he left 300 marks for masses. Three years earlier, in August 1358, Gregorio da Rimini had written to the prior, John of Arderne, concerning a planned infirmary, reminding him to take the advice of master builders and not to allow the healthy to stay in the infirmary once built. The friary's tall and slender steeple required repairs after a storm in 1362. The final church was vast: at the end of the nineteenth century an architect observing excavations noted that the nave was about 27m wide and 47m long, so that with the choir the whole building may have been some 90m in length. The original building had nine large windows on each side, but a fire in 1503 led to substantial changes. After the Dissolution, the friary and cloister were torn down, leaving only the church, which survived until it was bombed in the 1940s.

At Clare in Suffolk the building must have been habitable and with a chapel by 1265 when the first English provincial chapter was held there, attended by at least eight priors and their companions (*socii*). Donations towards the costs of building were encouraged by a series of episcopal indulgences issued at intervals between 1279 and 1324 and the church was finally consecrated in August 1338. In spite of its primacy in the province, and use for the burial of members of the royal family, the building was much smaller than London – about 50m long, with a chancel of six bays. There was no south aisle but in the north, a chapel probably consecrated to the Annunciation was established and furnished in 1361. A new bell-tower was also built *c.* 1363. In the same decade the roof was leaded and the chapterhouse and other conventual buildings seem to have been in use, though they were only dedicated in 1381, when a new cemetery was also consecrated. As at Leicester, the presence of noble patrons was reflected in the decoration of the buildings: the windows of the church and cloister showed the descent of the lords of Clare from Earl

Richard and the arms of other benefactors. Similar decoration was installed at Norwich in 1419 where the east window of the chancel included 107 coats of arms, whilst at Gorleston (Little Yarmouth) the church had armorial tiles comparable to those used at Leicester.

In Florence the surviving records again allow us a sense of the continuous process of expansion and rebuilding that went on in mendicant churches throughout the late Middle Ages. In this case wealth and civic pride produced a very substantial building. The hermits had first settled on a site a mile outside the city, but in 1250 acquired a plot in the thinly populated Oltrarno, the area on the left bank of the river enclosed by walls only in the late twelfth century. The location was favoured by the building of a bridge across the Arno, the ponte Santa Trinità, in 1252. The first church and convent, begun in the same year, was already in use by 1265. Known as Santo Spirito, it was originally dedicated to Mary, All Saints and the Holy Spirit, changing by the end of the century to Mary, the Holy Spirit and Matthew, this last probably a reference to an earlier suburban church.[35] The church itself was already paved by 1279 but communal funding can be documented from 1292 to 1301, so building must have been ongoing. Indeed, in the summer of 1301 houses were purchased in order to make space for squares in front of the façades of both Santo Spirito and the Dominican church in Florence, Santa Maria Novella. By 1317 Santo Spirito had seven altars and the number of family chapels included in the fabric continued to grow throughout the fourteenth century. By mid-century there was also a very substantial conventual complex, including a large cloister and a refectory with a Crucifixion and Last Supper painted by Andrea Orcagna and his workshop in the 1360s.

After the Florentine victory over the Milanese in 1397 on the feast of Augustine (28 August), the *signoria* decided to rebuild the church to honour the saint, placing it under the patronage of the city. Despite this decision, nothing much happened until 1443–4, when rebuilding began on a grand Renaissance design by Filippo Brunelleschi, with thirty-eight niche chapels along the walls of the nave and transepts and a cupola over the crossing. The architect even hoped to re-orientate the church and open a square connecting the façade with the Arno (matching the much smaller Humiliati church of Ognissanti on the other side of the river) but this ambitious scheme was never undertaken. Work progressed slowly until a fire in the original building in March 1471, which prompted greater speed. Some standing walls were re-used, but the redesign was so substantial that it is no longer possible even to be certain about the position of the original church. The result is an imposing temple reflecting the glory and wealth of the Renaissance city as much as the order of friars.

---

[35] See F. Quinterio, 'Il complesso di Santo Spirito dal primo insediamento agostiniano al progetto del Brunelleschi', in *La chiesa e il convento di Santo Spirito a Firenze*, ed. C. Acidini Luchinat (Florence, 1996), pp. 33–47.

Churches built by the friars were frequently designed as great open halls suitable for preaching, but these were soon filled with liturgical furnishings, stained glass, votive panels, great altarpieces and monumental fresco cycles. As at Santo Spirito, they also included the many tombs and separate chapels of lay patrons and confraternities. The impression on entering must frequently have been of a cluttered and brightly coloured hall. The convent spaces were also increasingly complex; at Freiburg in 1447 the friary seems to have had a clock tower, paid for in part by the local community: as so often, the church was the principal building in the district.[36]

Along with the fixed furnishings, the liturgy also required innumerable smaller and valuable items, usually stored in the sacristy, which was therefore often a particularly substantial and secure construction. Conveniently for historians, in 1345 the general chapter of the order required that all houses keep inventories of their property, including both moveable and immoveable goods, an obligation inserted in the *Additiones* by Thomas de Strasbourg. A typical example of a surviving list of liturgical items comes from Gubbio (Umbria) which already in 1341 included nine chalices, gilded and silver crosses (one with a piece of the True Cross), silver and bronze thuribles and navicellas, three wooden crosses for funerals, fifteen sets of paramenta, many of silk, seven pluvials, six silk chasubles and numerous others for ordinary days, stoles, shirts, cingula, cushions, innumerable pallia, cloths and towels, a chest with reliquaries and a set of tools for making the host. Some of the items in this and later inventories for Gubbio are identified as gifts from friars or laymen (including a pluvial which had been a layman's cloak), or as belonging to earlier members of the community. In 1341 the house also had twenty-one books for celebrating the Office including antiphoners – one in five volumes – lectionaries, psalters, missals, gospels, a chained breviary, the Office of the dead and ordinaries, six other manuals for the Office and four booklets for use in processions.

Gubbio was by no means unusual, but was fortunate when compared to the equipment listed for Stafford, drawn up by Richard Ingworth, bishop of Dover, to whom the friars surrendered the house at the Dissolution in August 1538. Ingworth's inventory of the property stated that 'the Austin Friars . . . is a poor house, with small implements, no jewels but one little chalice, no lead in the house, in rents by year 51s. 8 d.'. The church ornaments were sparse and well worn: four sets of vestments, old or stained altar-cloths, 'one plain cross of copper with a little image of Christ, silver upon it . . . one little wooden cross plated over very thin with silver', a chalice weighing thirteen ounces (which he took), a pair of organs, a Mass book which was sold for 1 shilling at the subsequent sale in September and some 'old books in the choir' which fetched 6 pence. The tower had one large bell valued at £8 and one small

[36] B. Stüdeli, *Minoritenniederlassungen und mittelalterliche Stadt* (Werl, 1969), p. 120 and n. 274.

one worth 8 shillings. There was very basic furniture, crockery and pots in the hall, brewhouse and kitchen. The total receipt from the sale was £32 6s 8d.[37] The contrast between the grandeur of the churches at Vienna, London and Florence and the smaller structures in Clare, Leicester or Stafford again underlines the importance of patronage and location in determining the size and ambition of ecclesiastical buildings and their communities.

[37] *VCH Stafford*, ed. R. B. Pugh, III (London, 1970), p. 274.

CHAPTER THREE

The Community within the Walls

Size

The first hermitages of the orders preceding the union of 1256 generally housed small numbers: in the Sienese countryside they seem never to have exceeded ten men, mostly recruited locally. The move into an urban context certainly involved expansion in numbers but records are frustratingly incomplete. One of the best indications of size is provided by contracts or other agreements listing the friars present, but these often name only representatives acting on behalf of a larger community. Calculating the size of that larger number is a hazardous business. Francis Roth and Keith Egan used royal pittances to estimate the size of English houses in the thirteenth century, giving results which varied from about sixty-four in London in October 1289 to four or six at Berwick in December 1299, but the London figure fluctuates between perhaps forty in the early 1280s to sixty again in 1324.[1] Although most recruits to houses without a *studium* were local, the itinerant life of the friar meant that numbers could and did vary substantially. Later foundations frequently depended on an apostolic minimum of twelve, as prescribed in papal privileges and carried out in practice at Weil der Stadt (1294), Stafford (1343), Carhaix in Brittany (1355) or Atherstone (1374), amongst others. But this rule did not always apply and once established, some houses inevitably shrank, while others grew exponentially.

The move into the cities necessarily changed the contours of the order. Hermitages and the life of the recluse remained important: occasional urban houses even had a hermit living within the precinct, as at Droitwich in 1388, where the earl of Warwick paid for a cell for a recluse next to the choir and retained the right to choose who should occupy it.[2] Urban communities involved in pastoral care came to predominate, however, in part because they attracted larger numbers of friars and more substantial donations. Thus the Siena commune gave alms to each of the Augustinian houses in their territory, but the sums reflect the increasing significance of the urban church. Whereas Montespecchio and the other rural hermitages in the district received 10 *lire*

---

[1] Roth, *The English Austin Friars*, I, pp. 32 and 463–72, including data supplied by Egan.
[2] The anchorite was to pray for the earl and his family. See *VCH Worcester*, ed. J. W. Willis-Bund and William Page, II (London, 1902), pp. 173–4.

each year, from 1274 the priory of Sant'Agostino in Siena received 40 and later 100 *lire* a year, on a par with the Franciscans and Dominicans. In the mid-fourteenth century, a record of a communal salt donation to the religious in the city and district makes the same point. The urban Augustinians, like the Franciscans and Dominicans, received a quantity based on sixty mouths. This was probably a negotiated figure but nonetheless an indicator of a large friary in each case. By contrast, the nine Augustinian communities named in the *contado* of Siena were each alloted a donation for six mouths, except the hermitage at Santa Lucia in Valle Rosia which received eight and Lecceto which received ten.[3]

Convents housing *studia* like that in Siena were likely to be more sub-stantial communities but also to oscillate considerably as students came and went. Even rural houses were affected by these fluctuations as students were assigned to them during the breaks in their studies. Comparative numbers for Oxford and Cambridge in the fourteenth century show that Oxford had approximately fifty students in both 1305 and 1377, while Cambridge had thirty-six in 1297, but this had doubled to seventy in 1326.[4] The Austin communities in both cities were roughly equivalent in size to the Carmelite houses and rather smaller than those of the Dominicans and Franciscans, probably a fair reflection of their status as the 'third' order of mendicants.

The life of a friar

Entry and the renunciation of property

In keeping with the practice of all regular orders by this date, some individu-als were automatically excluded, at least in theory: those who were married, in debt or slaves, because not free to make the decision on their own authority. Nor was anyone under the age of fourteen to be accepted (reduced to eleven in 1348) whilst those with hidden infirmities were debarred on the grounds that they would be unable to bear the strain (*pondus religionis*). From the very beginning the early constitutions emphasise the importance of learning and it is clear that what the order sought was men who could already read or sing competently or at least showed aptitude.

If deemed qualified, a petitioner would be brought to the conventual chapter where, following the instructions of the Regensburg Constitutions, the prior was to explain the difficulties likely to be encountered, enumerating the loss of personal autonomy, the poor quality of the food, the rough cloth-ing, the nocturnal vigils, the daily labours, the exhausting fasts, the humilia-tion of poverty, the embarrassment of begging, the torments of the flesh, the

---

[3]   M. Ascheri, 'Le "bocche" di conventi e ospedali di Siena e del suo stato nel 1360', *Bullettino senese di storia patria* 92 (1985), pp. 323–33.

[4]   See table above, p. 37–8.

tedium of the cloister and so on. If he was not put off by the austerity on offer, the petitioner was to have his hair cut and to put on the habit, which differed from that of the professed brethren only in that it was not yet blessed. He would then be taken to prostrate himself before the high altar and receive the kiss of peace from each member of the community.

Any assets a novice had were to be used to buy books (if he was to be a cleric and likely to study), bedding and clothing as needed. Habits could be substantial items: in 1280 and again in 1281 the commune of San Gimignano gave the Austin Friars in the city 25 *lire* for tunics and other clothing;[5] in 1312 the general chapter legislated that no one was to wear a black hood or cloak worth more than 5 gold florins. Clothing was also expected to last: the general chapter frequently ordered that the habits of deceased friars should be passed to poor novices by the prior. Once the essential purchases had been made, a note of all other property was drawn up so that it could be restored should the novice leave.

Noviciate and profession

All novices lived under the authority of a master and, if the convent had space, apart from the professed brethren. During a probationary year the novice master, who was to be of proven virtue and learning, was to read the rule and constitutions with the novices and teach them how to maintain the observance. They learned the customs and gestures of the order and chant, while from the beginning the constitutions also instructed novices to read the Scriptures avidly and devoutly. At the end of the probationary period, the novice was brought to the chapter and asked whether he wished to leave and go his own way or offer himself to God and the order. If he chose to stay, the first thing to happen would be the blessing of his hood either in the chapter or during Mass. Profession was made wearing the newly blessed hood and kneeling at the feet of the prior. Taking the rule of Augustine the novice would hand this to the prior and make his profession to God, Mary and the prior of the house as representative of the prior general of the order. The new friar promised obedience, to live without property and to remain celibate, essentially the monastic vows of poverty, chastity and obedience. Unlike other orders, the promise was made to live according to the rule, with no mention of constitutions. Nor of course, was there any promise of *stabilitas*, the monastic commitment to stay in one place, since this could not apply to the itinerant life of the friar. The prior received his new brother with the kiss of peace. From 1368 the profession was then publicly recorded in the *Liber professionum* of the house.

On professing, any friar, lay or clerical was expected to give up all

---

[5]   Florence, Archivio di Stato, Comune di San Gimignano 143, fol. 60v, and 146, fol. 38r.

possessions irrevocably, but it is clear that this did not always happen: in 1290 the general chapter ordained that houses, fields, vineyards, olive groves or farm animals belonging to any individual were to be sold and the money used to buy books or other goods needed by that friar or the community. Anyone failing to respect this regulation was to lose the property, which was to be sold and the proceeds used for the *studium* in Paris. Nonetheless friars frequently continued to retain and administer family land: Redon cites the case of Giovanni Fedini who joined the house at Monticiano near Siena in 1312 and was followed by his brother Benedetto five years later. Benedetto was to become prior of Monticiano, but he and his brother continued to oversee family property, paying a dowry for their sister Manta and exchanging property with other brothers who had stayed outside the cloister.[6]

The emphasis on poverty and the common life gradually faded over the course of the fourteenth century. Most professed brothers were expected to sleep in a shared dormitory, but increasingly in cells which were not closed or had transparent doors so that what was going on inside could be observed, while the individual could have the quiet necessary for study, day or night. Constitutions allowed pillows, a straw mattress, a cloak and a rush mat. No linen was allowed, nor any cloth other than wool. Coloured or special materials were forbidden as unsuited and embarrassing to those professing poverty, but an inventory from 1374 lists eleven cells at Gubbio, furnished with a variety of straw mattresses, coloured pillows, striped blankets and walnut chests.

Special dispensations allowed the elderly, sick and weak, but also the order's theologians, to sleep on feathers and use linen. By the time of the *Additiones* of 1348, masters of theology were assigned separate cells. Priors too lived in separate accommodation: in 1358 Gregorio da Rimini confirmed the right of the London prior, John of Arderne, to keep a chamber given to him by the convent and previously authorised by Thomas de Strasbourg. Similar instances are legion. In 1371 a newly appointed lector in the house at Gubbio was assigned a special cell next to the dormitory to be his for life. In 1439 a friar in the same house was able to leave property exclusively to a nephew who was a novice.

The community that the new friar joined was constructed around a clear hierarchy. At the head was the prior, but there might be numerous other office-holders. As well as the sub-prior, cantor and master of novices there was also a proctor responsible for the property belonging to the convent and to individual friars if allowed to them for books or other necessities. A sacristan was responsible for looking after everything in the church, the oblations of the faithful and striking the hours. Both proctor and sacristan were to keep a register. Other offices included a porter, almoner, infirmarer, hospitaller and supervisor of building works. Smaller communities did not have

---

[6] Redon, 'L'eremo, la città e la foresta', p. 31.

all these positions, but the hierarchy of the community based on seniority and learning would be clear to any new member.

In theory, once professed, the friar belonged to the order first, his blood family a remote second. Spiritual ties to the family were not, however, ignored: each friary commemorated the parents of friars, other relatives and benefactors every year. Moreover, in 1319 the provincial chapter of France held in Paris stipulated that friars might only have their priors' permission to stay away from their convent at night for two reasons: if either a great person or a close relative were seriously ill or on point of death. Similarly, the provincial chapter of Rome in 1321 allowed friars to visit relatives in monasteries, if accompanied by a companion provided by their prior, though by the following year all visits to monasteries required the written permission of the provincial.

For clerical brethren, the first years in the order would be spent on study. Even those who were not destined for scholarship spent at least a year studying grammar and three on logic and basic philosophy. Those qualified would then progress to the study of theology in one of the *studia generalia*. This was usually funded by the priory or province, which sent the money to the *studium* at the beginning of each academic year. However, some students remained longer, paid for by parents or benefactors, whilst others were there *de gratia*, sent by the prior general. Study was so important to the tasks of the friars that a prior was allowed to oblige all his friars to attend lessons in theology unless otherwise occupied. The constitutions of 1290, however, banned those over thirty-five from going to Paris to study unless particularly brilliant or intending to prepare for the *magisterium*.

In 1287 the general chapter ruled that no friar was to be promoted to the priesthood under the age of twenty-four (this was reduced to eighteen in 1507). For the first year of his priesthood he was not to hear confessions, but thereafter, the life of the average friar would involve close concern with pastoral matters in the community around the friary: saying masses, preaching, hearing confessions and administering the sacraments. He might also be involved with confraternities, or in supervising charitable organisations such as hospitals, as at Santa Maria della Scala in Siena, where the Austin Friars provided pastoral care for the patients, as portrayed by Domenico di Bartolo in 1441, in a fresco of a busy ward scene showing an Augustinian friar listening to the confession of a bed-ridden patient, which must have been a regular event.

The rhythm of life

Surviving normative texts allow us to reconstruct the routine of activities in a typical, if imaginary, friary. Ordinary days began with matins, to which the community was called by the ringing of a bell or other signal. As it sounded the friars got up, went to the church or oratory, sprinkled themselves with holy water, genuflected before the high altar and took their place in order. As the ringing ceased, they began the Office.

Following in the footsteps of both the Franciscans and the Tuscan Hermits (1244), the Austin Friars used the rite of the Roman Curia: *secundum modum Romane curie* (1290), which meant the rite of the papal chapel. The brevity that made this practical for the busy life of the Curia also recommended it to the life of itinerant friars. How this was observed in the order can be seen in the work of Clemente da Osimo, prior general 1272–4 and 1284–91, who produced instructions (*ordinationes*) and an *Ordinarium* ('Ceremonial') with directions and notation for the liturgy, presumably based on material already in use in the order. From the 1290s the general chapter reminded the friars that all singing was to accord with Clemente's text. His *Ordinarium* was to remain the liturgical norm for the order until reforms introduced by Girolamo Seripando in the mid-sixteenth century.

Augustine's rule refers to singing the Office and in 1290 the Roman province decided that the prior of any convent with a friar who knew how to sing the chant was to arrange for him to teach the others. By 1308 this had evolved into a requirement that each house was to have a choir. Seven years later each province was instructed to have two song schools (*studia in cantu*), to which friars with the appropriate talent were to be sent. By the mid-fourteenth century, if not earlier, all the hours were sung.

In 1295 the chapter had adopted an *Ystoria in cantu* about St Paul, the first hermit, by a friar Pietro Romano, to be distributed throughout the order. Numerous metrical poems were also produced for the feasts of the saints in the order and sung to traditional melodies. By the late fifteenth century, friar Johannes von Dorsten (†1481) reports that on a feast day in Erfurt lay members of a community might even intersperse the usual Office with devout songs in the vernacular, such as *Crist ist erstanden* ('Christ is risen') at Easter.[7] Organs were used to accompany the liturgy, and in 1387 Bartolomeo da Venezia authorised a friar Philip of Brünn to construct and repair organs in the houses of the order as needed, including at the shrine of San Nicolò in Tolentino. There were also friars who wrote about music, including the humanist Aurelio Brandolini of Florence (*c.* 1440–97), author of a treatise *De laudibus musice*. But the order did not produce original composers before the sixteenth century. Perhaps this was because Clemente had provided notation in his *Ordinarium,* including for the order's own Marian vigil, *Benedicta tu.* The lack of composers presumably signals conformity in music at least.

.

---

[7]   A. Zumkeller, 'Augustiner-Eremiten', in *Die Musik in Geschichte und Gegenwart: allgemeine Enzyklopedie der Musik* (Kassel 1994–), I, cols 1033–9.

After matins the friars proceeded to chapter, bowing to the cross on entering the chapter hall and again taking their assigned places. The lector announced the saints and any feast for the next day from the Calendar or Martyrology. Prayers and readings for the day and the commemoration of deceased brethren, servants, relatives and benefactors of the order followed. On Fridays, any alms received during the week would be announced and the souls of the donors, living or dead, recommended to the prayers of the community. The second part of the chapter was concerned with discipline: the lector would read from the constitutions and if necessary the prior might then expound them. On Mondays and Fridays, all friars were required in turn to confess any faults of which they were aware and to accuse each other (the chapter of faults, a tradition of humility in monastic communities). Visiting friars and *conversi* were to do the same. This might be followed by a sermon. In houses with a *studium* the prior could dispense friars who were studying from attending the chapter during the winter except on the days when faults were to be heard. All friars were nonetheless required to confess privately at least once a week and to take communion on fifteen feasts in the year (increased to seventeen in 1348).

Everyone was expected to attend Mass, unless sick or by special permission. Friars who were priests were also expected to say masses for both the living and the dead of the community. Lay brothers attended the hours of the clerical brethren, substituting the Office with set numbers of standard prayers (such as the *Pater noster, Ave Maria, Gloria Patri* and *Deus in adiutorium meum intende* (Psalm 69 [70]). The Constitutions of Regensburg forbade lay brethren from reading unless they could read the Psalter well, which had to be a skill already acquired before entry because any friar teaching them to read would be punished with a diet of bread and water for three days. No lay brother, however well he could read, was to have the tonsure. For the others, the tonsure was to be shaved every fifteen days from Easter to the feast of St Michael (29 September) and then eight times before the following Easter. All the brethren were also to be bloodlet four times a year: after Christmas, at Easter, around the feast of John the Baptist (24 June) and in September, after which there was to be no fasting for three days.

The community was called to the refectory by a bell or cymbal and having first washed and then gathered in the cloister, they entered together. No one was to eat until the readings had started. The nature and quantity of food was carefully regulated. In times of fasting there was one meal a day. From Easter to All Saints and from Christmas to the Sunday of Quinquagesima the friars were authorised to season their food with fat or oil, except on days of solemn fast, Fridays, Saturdays and certain vigils. The rest of the time they could eat eggs, cheese, butter and milk. From Easter to All Saints they were not required to fast except on those same days. On Good Friday, they were to have just bread and water on a bare board, with no dispensations allowed.

At table, silence was to be observed except by the most senior person present, though priors general and provincial might dispense with silence as needed.

From lunch until nones the friars in the house either slept, read, prayed or did something useful in their cells, as long as it did not disturb others. The day ended with collations (a drink) and compline, after which they recited the vigil of the Blessed Virgin. In the late fifteenth century evening prayers were added, which invoked the members and benefactors of the order, both living and dead. The friars then went to their dormitory cells where they could either pray, read or sleep.

Everyone was expected to observe silence at certain times and places: throughout the enclosure from the second sign for compline in the evening until after prime on the next day in spring and summer (from Easter to All Saints), or until after Mass on the following day during the rest of the year. To maintain the peace gestures were used or, when directing the Office in the choir, the cantor was encouraged to whisper in his brothers' ears. Within the community, tasks were divided by location: in the dormitory they were allowed to read and pray and do other work. Houses with *studia* usually had separate spaces for teaching and study. In the cloister, manual work and singing were permitted, as long as the rules of silence were not broken. If there was a second cloister, friars might be allowed to go there to talk, but an indication of the incidence of incomplete buildings is the provision that where the cloister was unfinished, the prior should decide where talking was permitted. Any second cloister or garden was not normally to be accessible to secular clergy or lay visitors and the door of the main cloister was to be kept fastened so that entry could be restricted. Churches were to be closed when the community was in the refectory or asleep, but guests, especially other religious, were to be welcomed by the porter. Convents usually had a room near the entrance for receiving lay visitors, who might also be admitted to the chapter house, but not to the other spaces of the enclosure.

Liturgy and saints

Like the Carmelites, the Dominicans, the Sack Friars and for that matter the Cistercians, the Austin Friars were particularly attached to the Virgin Mary, as is evident from the profession of new friars (to God and Mary), and her presence alongside Augustine on their seals and above all in the *Ordinarium*. As we have seen, at the end of each day they participated in the vigil of the Blessed Virgin Mary, a combination of prayers and short readings attributed to Augustine and documented as an established custom already in 1284. Particular devotion is also evident in their feasts: the Annunciation (25 March) was already mentioned in the constitutions of 1290, and by the mid-sixteenth century, the order was celebrating the whole series of major Marian feasts, including the Visitation (2 July), Assumption (15 August),

Nativity (8 September), Presentation at the Temple (21 November), Conception (15 December) and Purification (2 February).[8]

Mary was also honoured with a number of titles, reflecting her various qualities and her intercessory role: Our lady of Grace was particularly venerated in Spain, Portugal and Sicily (Messina), while a holy image of Our Lady of Perpetual Aid (*de succursu*) in Palermo was already venerated by 1306. From the late fifteenth century, the cult of Our Lady of Good Counsel was linked to an image in Genazzano (Italy), said to have been carried by angels from Scutari in Albania and soon a major Marian sanctuary. Similar devotion developed around Our Lady of Consolation, portrayed from the fifteenth century with the leather belt of the Augustinians and the focus for a confraternity. Thomas de Strasbourg (†1357) was one of those who undertook the defence of the doctrine of the Immaculate Conception and a century later in Paris there was a confraternity of the Immaculate Conception (from 1440), which received indulgences from Eugenius IV and his successors. Others followed.

Mary was a universal saint. Other feasts were more specific to the order, giving a better sense of its particular spirituality and the rhythm of the friars' liturgical year. By the mid-fourteenth century the order was celebrating both the tradition of the translation of Augustine's body from Hippo to Sardinia (11 October) and his further translation from Sardinia to Pavia in the eighth century on the last day of February (first mentioned 1343). These were in addition to the principal feast of the saint (28 August), his conversion (5 May) and the founding of a friary at Pavia next to his tomb (5 June), though this last was suppressed in 1343. Other important feasts in the order were those of saints associated with Augustine: his mother Monica, whose feast on 4 May is first documented in 1365 (and whose remains were rediscovered at Ostia in 1430 and brought to Rome),[9] St Ambrose, who baptised Augustine (7 December) and San Simpliciano, Ambrose's successor as bishop in Milan (13 August).

Most specific of all were saints and blessed (*beati*) either related to the heremitical tradition, such as Anthony (17 January), or members of the order itself. The first of these to be canonised was Nicolò da Tolentino (†1305) in 1446, when the feast of his canonisation was established on 5 June and the major feast on 10 September, but his cult was active long before this: a process of enquiry had been undertaken as early as 1325. There was also an ever-increasing number of Augustinian holy men and women venerated as *beati* with more geographically limited cults. While none were formally acknowledged until the modern period, a survey of the better-known figures illustrates the variety of approaches to spirituality in the order. Guglielmo

8   'De Caeremoniali ordinis eremitarum sancti Augustini', *AA* 15 (1933–6), pp. 181–227, 192–9.

9   See I. Holgate, 'The Cult of St Monica in Quattrocento Italy: Her Place in Augustinian Iconography, Devotion and Legend', *Papers of the British School at Rome* 71 (2003), pp. 187–212.

da Malavalle's cult flourished in the area of his hermitage near Castiglione and, despite the secession of the Williamites and their separate existence after 1266, the Augustinians considered him a member of their order and celebrated his feast on 10 February. The feast of Giovanni Bono, hermit founder of the Bonites (beatified by Sixtus IV) whose tomb was in Budriolo, was observed on October 23. Two early priors general, Clemente da Osimo (†1291) and Agostino Novello (†1309) were formally beatified respectively in 1761 and 1759, but were also venerated very quickly after their deaths. Novello himself was the subject of a remarkable panel by Simone Martini representing the friar as a saint surrounded by scenes of his miracles, which was probably placed over his tomb in Siena in 1328. He was to become one of the most popular figures in the city's pantheon of holy men.

There was no shortage of candidates for sanctity in the order, both men and women. The Florentine Simone Fidati da Cascia (†1348) was a charismatic preacher who founded a nunnery and a house of penance for women.[10] He was also the author of a work of spirituality, *De gestis domini salvatoris*, emphasising the imitation of Christ and praising the *vita eremitica*, which was to be enormously influential in Germany, but once again, he was beatified only in 1833. The observant friar Juan de Sahagún, who joined the order relatively late in life, was a tireless preacher and peacemaker (†1479) and was venerated in Spain soon after his death, but canonised only in 1690. There were also numerous holy women honoured by the order. Chiara di Montefalco (†1308) was not juridically a member of the order but followed the rule and after her death her community was incorporated into that of the friars, while perhaps the most famous Augustinian female saint in the modern Catholic Church is Rita da Cascia (†1456), a widow who became an Augustinian nun, canonised in 1900. It is probably not a coincidence that most of the holy men and women of the order were Italian. Before the sixteenth century Italy dominated the spiritual life of the order. Although Heinrich of Friemar mentions a John of England as one of the illustrious holy men of the order, this may simply have been the early prior provincial of that name. There is no other evidence for this or any other English cult before John Stone, an Augustinian from Canterbury executed in 1539 for refusing to accept King Henry VIII as head of the Church. He was beatified only in 1886 and canonised in 1970.

The lack of papally sanctioned saints from the order during the late Middle Ages was not for want of trying. In 1329, according to one version of the *acta*, the general chapter instructed that all miracles performed by any of the brethren were to be recorded in legal form and collected in each province, to be sent to the general for presentation at a future chapter. Provincial priors were also encouraged to ask for information about the deeds of Giles of

---

[10] See below, p. 136.

Rome, presumably out of a similar desire to promote his cause as a holy man. The case of Nicolò da Tolentino, however, had been the first to be formally adopted and provides a well-documented example of how such cults related to the order. Nicolò seems to have joined as a boy, studied in the provincial *studium* of the March of Ancona for ten years (1259–69), was a priest by 1270, but never rose to high office. He spent the rest of his life in a typical career of preaching and hearing confessions in the area of Tolentino. Already in life, however, Nicolò was referred to as a saint, and on his death pilgrims in search of miraculous cures began coming to his tomb. The general chapter at Montpellier in 1324 authorised the imposition of a tax on each province to promote the cause. In the summer of the following year a commission of enquiry into his sanctity deliberated at his former convent in Tolentino. Numerous witnesses attested to miracles: a mother whose small son's teeth, broken in a fall, were preventing him from eating, reported that he had been healed by the saint, as did the mother of a boy suffering from falling sickness who was healed once she offered his weight in grain to the shrine. As part of the same promotion of his *fama* as a holy man, a substantial fresco cycle was painted in the 1320s in the Great Chapel (Cappellone) at Tolentino, in which his tomb stood and which may also have been a chapter hall. Here, beneath images of the Evangelists, fathers of the Church and episodes from the life of Christ and the Virgin Mary, a Riminese workshop produced a cycle of the life and miracles of the as yet uncanonised Nicolò. The narrative begins with the elderly parents of Nicolò on pilgrimage in Bari, where an angel informs them that they will have a child. It follows his childhood and conversion, death and the ascent of his soul to heaven in Christ's arms. There is also a series of portrayals of the saint as miracle worker: healing a blind woman, freeing a man captured by bandits, saving a ship from a storm. The cycle was directed at the friars meeting in the Cappellone, but also of course at the laity coming to the tomb. It undoubtedly helped the spread of the cult, which was soon acknowledged across Italy: in 1371 a boy who suffered from epilepsy had a vision in which Nicolò told him that if he joined the order he would be freed from his illness. His parents therefore brought him and placed him on the altar of the local house at Gubbio.

The unruly and apostates

The concern with details of the routine evident in the constitutions described above was designed to inculcate uniformity. Observance of these rules, as in all religious orders, was shored up by the requirement that individuals suffer penalties for failure. Some of these were very simple, from standing waiting before the high altar for the prior's permission to take a seat if late for the Office, to sitting on the floor in the refectory during meals. For more serious crimes, the penalties were removal from office, or loss of the right to speak in chapter. Those guilty of the 'unspeakable' crime of sodomy[11] were to be imprisoned for ten months of fasting and then expelled. From 1327 prior provincials were required to keep a record of any crimes they had not been able to punish, citing the witnesses, reason for the delay and other information, so that when found the delinquent could be disciplined.

Some chose to escape. Already before the union hermits were subject to excommunication and imprisonment if they left without permission and in the spring of 1262 Urban IV again authorised general and provincial priors to excommunicate or arrest apostates.[12] In that year in England Henry III ordered the arrest of vagabond friars who had abandoned the house at Clare. By 1281 apostates returning to the order, if they had adopted secular clothes without causing a scandal, might be accepted without imprisonment and absolved from excommunication, but must return to their own province. An apostate who had been absent for a year was never to be elected as provincial. Three years later the penalty for apostates shows that study in Paris was both a privilege and a risk: an absentee was not to be allowed to go to Paris for at least five years after his return. If he had run away more than once or had been imprisoned, he was never to go. The first extant register of a prior general, that of Gregorio da Rimini (1357–8) includes numerous disciplinary measures concerning brothers accused or guilty of sexual misconduct, violence and fighting, gambling, theft, or leaving the order without permission.[13] He dealt with the case of Friar Gualtero of Spoleto, who had left the order, lived with an unnamed woman and had children, but now wanted to return. Gregorio instructed the prior provincial to imprison him until further notice. The numbers involved, however, seem to have been small. Donald Logan's study of runaway religious in England lists only twenty-three Austin Friars between 1301 and 1515, two of whom appear to have been Wyclifite sympathisers.[14]

Death

For those who stayed, the community could supply support and protection to the end. If a friar or novice became gravely ill, his brothers were instructed to take particular care of him, providing comfort and prayers. He was not to be left alone and at his death, the whole community was to come together

---

[11] Whether this was limited to the physical act or understood to include modern concepts of homosociability/sexuality is not clear, nor would the legislators wish to make it so.

[12] *Provisionis nostre*, 17 April 1262 (Alonso I, 80). For earlier bulls, see, for example, *Provisionis vestre cupimus*, 27 April 1254 (van Luijk, *Bullarium*, 114; see also ibid., 123; Empoli, *Bullarium* 2, 7, 14, 366; Berger 7469–71).

[13] On Gregorio and his register see now E. Saak, *High Way to Heaven. The Augustinian Platform between Reform and Reformation 1292–1524* (Leiden, 2002), pp. 315–44. The register itself is *Gregorii de Arimino OSA, Registrum Generalatus 1357–1358*, ed. A. Meijer (Rome, 1976).

[14] Logan, *Runaway Religious in Medieval England*, pp. 248–50.

and say the Office over him. The brothers were to wash the corpse and then dress it in the habit and belt of the order before burial. Priests in the province were to say three masses for his soul, clerics a Psalter, and lay brethren fifty *Pater nosters* and the *Requiem eternam*. The same commemoration of all the dead of the order was repeated three times each year. Burial was within the enclosure and, as in life, placement depended on status: senior members of the community would be buried closer to the high altar or in the chapter hall, particularly favoured for the eminent. Cloisters were also preferred places of burial.

Nuns

The discussion so far has focused on the male order, but all over Europe in the thirteenth century there were also houses of women religious following the rule of Augustine, members in the generic sense of the *ordo sancti Augustini*. They all depended on the services of male priests to provide the sacraments and often also employed men to act on their behalf in business affairs. This need not mean association with or incorporation into the order of hermit friars: numerous communities of women following the Augustinian rule or wearing a black-belted habit turned to the regular canons or the Dominicans, while themselves belonging in administrative terms to no specific order. Other women did, however, become associated with the Augustinian mendicant order. It is often now difficult to ascertain the precise status of many of their houses. Balbino Rano has proposed that if a house followed the rule of Augustine according to the institutes of the Augustinian Friars modified to suit women, wore the black habit with a belt, was visited and supervised by Augustinian friars and acknowledged their membership of the order, then they can be counted as members of the order.[15] In many cases, however, these strict criteria cannot be established and in the thirteenth century, as later, the status of many houses was disputed.

Women's houses were taken into the order already in the first decade after the union: in May 1264, for example, at the German provincial chapter in Seemanshausen the provincial, Guido de Stagia (later prior general 1265–70) accepted a nunnery in Oberndorf. The prioress and her sisters had requested incorporation and Guido offered them the assistance and protection of the order. Two years later Cardinal Annibaldi instructed the new prior general and German prior provincial to provide for the religious women in German lands who had been incorporated into the order. His letter uses the plural so, as Rano argues, presumably there were already other nunneries in the province in addition to Oberndorf.[16] The letter also conveniently outlines

[15] Rano, 'Agostiniani', cols 164–8.
[16] Ibid., col. 158.

the responsibilities of the friars: on one hand the regular duties of the Office and administering the sacraments, including confession and preaching, and on the other visitation, correction and reform. They might enter the monastery itself for the consecration of novices or for funerals, but never alone. Otherwise they were to go to the open grill or the parlour (*parlatorium*).

Other women's houses were incorporated to the order during the following decades but the phenomenon seems to have been limited to Germany and Italy. The general chapter of 1295 confirmed the acceptance of the nunnery of Santa Maria Maddalena in Orvieto by the former prior general Clemente da Osimo, who had entrusted it to the supervision of a specific friar named Agostino Seneca. In jurisdictional terms the community was now instead to be administered by the prior of Orvieto whose authority was required for the election of the prioress. The nuns also enjoyed all the privileges and immunities of the male order. In some cases this privileged status led to difficulties with the secular church, just as it did for the male houses. At Oberndorf, Guido da Staggia had explicitly mentioned the need to protect the rights of the parish, but the nuns' church, dedicated to the Virgin Mary, was already a concern to the parish clergy in 1278. In that year an agreement was drawn up awarding the parish a share in donations from the city and outlining the responsibilities of the two sides.

Just as the status of many houses is unclear to modern historians, so it was sometimes disputed by contemporaries. In 1318 eight women were received by the subprior of the Augustinians in Gubbio, marking the beginning of a new monastery of recluses dedicated to Santa Cecilia outside Porta Sant'Agostino. In 1327 the bishop authorised their oratory and claimed the right to visit (oversee) the community. This was, however, disputed by the friars, who claimed that as they had been ministering to the women the house was exempt from episcopal intervention. The decision of the ensuing enquiry does not survive, but twenty years later the friars were still to be found providing pastoral care for the nuns.

In the fourteenth century nuns frequently adopted the liturgy and constitutions of the friars and the male order seems to have been happy to accept membership in the order of women who, like the men, identified Augustine as their founder. The number of houses that can be identified as belonging to the order thus greatly increased and came to include new areas, including Spain and Bohemia. Some of these were foundations sponsored by lay patrons, as at Prague, where in 1354 Charles of Bohemia gave land for the foundation of a nunnery dedicated to St Catherine which was to be immediately subject to the provincial and general priors. In the same decade, a house of women dedicated to Santa María de Gracia was founded outside the walls of Madrigal de las Altas Torres, north of Avila in Castile. It was to enjoy particularly close ties with the royal family: various members of the household joined the monastery and in September 1424 the infanta Catalina, daughter of King Juan II, was buried there. Women were also important founders of communities: in the fifteenth century, Maddalena Albrici (†1465, beatified 1907), from Brunate above Como in northern Italy, founded the monastery of Sant'Andrea, which was soon followed by nine other monasteries in the region. Rano, however, estimates the number of nunneries belonging to the order as most likely never more than two hundred and probably less.[17] Nor do they seem to have included houses in England, though there are certainly references to English Augustinian sisters, who may of course have been canonesses.[18]

Often precarious, foundations for women (as for men) depended on a network of different individuals for survival. The case of Santa Monaca in Florence, founded in the 1440s, provides a detailed account of how a nunnery might take shape and the role of the women themselves in creating a community.[19] The origins of the house lay with a group of Augustinian women living in a monastery at Castiglione near San Miniato, under the authority of the friars of the province of Pisa. The passage of troops in the area in 1441 made them aware of how vulnerable they were to attack and, with the support of noble relatives from the city, they moved to a site near the church of the friars in Florence. The original abbess disappeared not long after arriving in the city, leaving just four nuns, soon reduced to three. Francesco Mellini, a friar of Santo Spirito, took an active interest in the community, bringing in a new abbess from Pistoia, together with two nuns, to whom he gave the habit of the order. Mellini wrote a chronicle recording his activities and the history of the first twenty years of the convent, including an account book. The original community settled in two adjacent houses with a courtyard, given to them in 1442, in which at first they had a small oratory. An initial legacy of 500 florins allowed them to begin work on a new complex with domestic buildings and a refectory in which, in 1445/6, Bicci di Lorenzo painted a crucifix, now lost. The Bardi family were the principal funders of the project. In 1447 the neighbouring Carmelite friars at Santa Maria del Carmine objected to the new monastery and tried to block its construction, appealing to the archbishop and citing the restriction on constructions within 140 rods of their own convent. The friars did not stick to legal means. On the night of 3 August 1447 a group pulled down and removed the doorjambs of the new church. Nonetheless, in 1449, with the support of one of the Bardi family, the community obtained papal permission to complete work on their church, which already served thirty nuns.

---

[17] Ibid., col. 184.

[18] For example, *Calendar of Patent Rolls, Henry III 1266–1272*, p. 536: 17 May 1271: Henry III grants protection to a group of women described as 'sisters of the order of St Augustine'.

[19] See the excellent study by M. M. Simari, 'Profilo storico-architettonico di un monastero fiorentino del quattrocento: Santa Monaca', *Rivista d'arte* 39 (1987), pp. 147–214. See also A. Thomas, *Art and Piety in the Female Religious Communities of Renaissance Italy* (Cambridge, 2003).

The archbishop confirmed their right to build, but with strict limitations: they were not to extend their monastery beyond the block where it currently stood; there was to be no bell-tower and the bell used was to remain small; there was to be no more than one Mass celebrated in the church each day; the laity were to be admitted only on the feast of St Monica and for the vestition of novices; no lay man or woman was to make confession or be buried in the church. The activities and influence of the Carmelite friars in the district, and also of their community of nuns, established at much the same time, were thereby protected. By the late 1450s the church was completed and in the 1460s the Santa Monaca nuns acquired permission to expand their site despite the earlier restrictions, in part because of the support of a secretary to Pope Pius II, whose sister became a nun there. Over the course of the next century it was to become one of the main female religious communities in Florence, with 112 nuns in 1562. They enjoyed close relations with the Austin Friars, having a chapel in Santo Spirito dedicated to Monica, and benefiting from the support of some of the friars' patrons, including the Capponi family, whose arms are still visible on the façade of the nuns' church.

As was typical for female communities, the church of Santa Monaca in Florence was much smaller than that of the neighbouring friaries at Santo Spirito or Santa Maria del Carmine. After it was suppressed in 1808 the art works were dispersed and the building continually subdivided. Simari has shown, however, that it was originally a simple hall nave with wooden beamed roof, plain façade with oculus and single central grey-stone (*pietra serena*) doorway surmounted with a lunette. Details of the building such as doorways and plastered walls imitated those of other buildings in the city at this date.[20] The sisters also commissioned Neri di Bicci to paint another Crucifixion, presumably for their high altar, in which he included St Monica and St Augustine and, as Anabel Thomas has shown, otherwise tailored the iconography to suit a community of enclosed nuns. In the 1480s, they may also have commissioned a panel now in Santo Spirito showing St Monica as the founder of the female branch of the Augustinian order.[21] By this date all houses of the order were required to have a painted image of Monica, as ordained at the general chapter in Montpellier in 1430.

Santa Monaca was not the only female Augustinian house in Florence: just outside the walls stood the monastery of Santa Caterina or San Gaggio, founded in an abandoned hermitage in 1339 by friar Simone Fidati da Cascia with the support of numerous wealthy citizens. The founding abbess was Mona Nera, widow of Lapo Manieri who had already spent several years as a holy recluse in her mother's home before Simone persuaded her to found a monastery. It too was under the spiritual guidance of the friars of Santo

[20] Simari, 'Profilo storico-architettonico', pp. 177–90.
[21] Thomas, *Art and Piety*, pp. 68–70.

Spirito. Fidati was also involved in the foundation of a house for former prostitutes (often referred to as *convertite*), a project put into practice by the *laudese* (praise) company of Santo Spirito. By 1333 it already housed more than fifty women.[22]

Women's houses were often small and not particularly wealthy. There are therefore relatively few surviving records, and convents were more inclined to disappear or reappear in a new form. At Oberndorf, the dukes of Teck and local citizens were generous donors to the house throughout the late Middle Ages. By 1352 it had fourteen sisters, all from the region, including both lesser nobility, women from the citizenry and local farming families. The prioress was usually from the nobility. In the fifteenth century, however, the house suffered economic difficulties and in the mid-1500s, when there was only one sister remaining, it was transformed into a male friary. By contrast, the monastery of St Catherine in Prague, which was undermined by Hussite forces in 1420 so that falling stones killed twenty-seven nuns, was immediately re-established and under the leadership of their prioress continued to observe a life of strict observance.

In general late-medieval churchmen increasingly insisted on the enclosure of women religious. This followed the lead of Boniface VIII's constitution *Periculoso* (1298), which severely restricted the movement of nuns outside the convent and led to initiatives against beguines. Thus it was in keeping with the mood of the times when in 1329 the general chapter at Paris instructed that all nuns of the order were to be kept in strict enclosure. Friars were not to enter their monasteries unless to hear confessions, in cases of illness or to carry out visitation. They must not eat or drink with the nuns. The same regulation was to make its way into Thomas de Strasbourg's *Additiones*.

These restrictions were aimed at regulating relations between nuns and friars. For the women themselves, many of whom were not expected to know Latin, various versions of modified constitutions were prepared in the vernacular. One of the most complete to survive was prepared in Spanish, probably in the early fifteenth century. Although produced for one house, its provisions are likely to be representative and confirm that the nuns lived according to a version of the male constitutions tailored to their needs. Like the friaries, their communities were divided into fully professed nuns dedicated to the Office and lay nuns or *converse* who undertook the necessary manual work. The structures of life in the community were comparable to those of the male houses. Profession could be made from the age of twelve. Only after three years could a nun participate in elections and speak at chapter. The superior was elected for three years. The formal habit was black with a belt, over a white tunic, with a black and white veil. Like the men, however, when in the

---

[22] See A. Benvenuti Papi, 'Devozioni private e guida di coscienze femminili nella Firenze del due-trecento', *Ricerche storiche* 16 (1986), pp. 565–601, 581.

house the sisters often wore just the white tunic. The rhythm of the day was structured around the canonical hours, starting with matins and closing with the vigil of the Virgin and compline. The main divergence from the life of the men was the lack of *studia* or the floating communities that went with them. Although fully professed nuns could and did study or copy books, and might be admired as exemplars of the Christian life, they could rarely participate in the intellectual or pastoral life of the Church.

Variations from these norms are not difficult to find. Some communities were strictly enclosed, others allowed the nuns to go out to confess or as necessary for the community. Some enclosed nunneries obtained permission for visits from relatives: in 1424, the prior general Agostino Favaroni (1419–31) allowed four nuns in Toledo who were also blood relatives to invite their female family members to the cloister, eat with them and accommodate them for the night if they could find nowhere else. He also authorised the nuns to maintain their own personal property and pass it to a relative should she join the order. There were also communities of tertiaries, often known as *mantellate, clamidate* or sometimes as oblates, who followed a more open regime so as to be able to support themselves: for many women enclosure was simply not practicable.[23] In 1399 Boniface IX confirmed their juridical status, allowing them the right to wear the habit and enjoy the privileges of the Augustinian order, but they remained independent and were not subject to the prior general.

Relations between the male and female members of the order were not always easy. In 1357, for example, Innocent VI reaffirmed the enclosed status of a nunnery in Valencia (Catalonia). Following unspecified scandals twenty-five years earlier, the friars who had provided pastoral guidance for the community since its beginnings had wanted to impose claustration on the nuns to prevent further difficulties. The prioress had agreed but some of the nuns had objected. The community had therefore placed itself under the supervision of the local bishop. According to a letter issued by the pope, the nuns found this unhelpful because the secular clergy were unfamiliar with the institutes and rule of the order. Innocent therefore confirmed their return to the jurisdiction of the friars and the requirement of enclosure, entrusting the bishop with the task of enclosing the nuns. The monastery was to be subject to the prior provincial of Aragon.

In Valencia the friars seem to have wanted to win the argument, but there was always some tension about the supervision of women's houses and the men often sought to avoid responsibility for women. The general chapter held in Naples in 1300 ruled that because of the risk of scandal, no brother

---

[23] The terminology is often confusing: *mantellata*, literally meaning cloaked, might also be used for 'second-order' enclosed nuns. See K. Gill, 'Open Monasteries for Women in Late Medieval and Early Modern Italy: Two Roman Examples', in *The Crannied Wall. Religion and the Arts in Early Modern Europe*, ed. C. A. Monson (Ann Arbor, 1992), pp. 15–47, with bibliography.

was to accept into the order or into the order's care *bizocche* (beguines), nunneries or any religious women without the permission of the prior provincial. By the fifteenth century there is increasing evidence of reluctance to supervise women, and in the mid-sixteenth century the prior general Girolamo Seripando was delighted when Cosimo de' Medici petitioned the pope, requesting that the friars in Medici lands be relieved of the supervision of nuns. Augustinian women increasingly came under the jurisdiction of bishops.

In spite of the reluctance of many friars, in the fifteenth century Holland and France certainly had houses of nuns belonging to the order and by the following century they had reached Portugal and probably Poland. Nuns living according to the rule of Augustine continued to be a disparate group: some were reformed to strict observance, others were provided with pastoral services by a local male community but remained independent, and as before such provision was not necessarily made by the Austin Friars. Moreover, still at this date houses that used Austin Friars for these services need not observe the rule of Augustine: the Benedictine nuns of San Lorenzo in Como and of Santa Giustina in Lucca were both entrusted to the supervision of Augustinian friars of the observant congregation of Lombardy and remained so, despite the latters' unwillingness.

Lay brethren

From the earliest days, Augustinian houses, both male and female, also included *converse, conversi* and oblates, lay women and men whose status is not always immediately clear.[24] In essence they offered themselves and their property in service to the friars and nuns, but did not acquire clerical status. After a probationary year, according to the 1290 constitutions, *conversi* in the male order were required to make simple promises of obedience, chastity and poverty to the prior of the house and to the rule. There was, however, in practice no standard formula and the terminology used was often vague.

The status of a *conversa* may have been particularly attractive to women, who were excluded from many confraternities, such as those for flagellants which involved some nakedness in public, but it was also attractive to men, as powerfully evoked in surviving records from the thirteenth century. In 1267 Alberto, a Sienese man, joined the friary there, 'wishing to abandon the world and worldly things with their noise and greed and to serve God'. In 1293, Druda Iacobi, the widow of Mantie Fortis, gave herself and her property to the Augustinians in Gubbio 'wishing to adhere to the contemplative life' (*volens adherere vite contemplative*). She became a *conversa* and *familia* (servant), acting for the redemption of her own soul and those of her husband,

---

[24] On the terminology see D. Osheim, 'Conversion, *Conversi* and the Christian life', *Speculum* 58 (1983), pp. 368–90.

children and parents. The use of the term *familia* seems to define Druda as working for the community, but also underlines the holy humility of her new state. She presumably did indeed undertake some form of contemplative life since in 1336 she is referred to with another sister as a *recarcerata*, a term often used for anchoresses. Numerous other women followed in her footsteps as oblates or *converse* sharing in the community and prayers of the friars.

The category of *conversi* overlaps with what historians now refer to as oblates, though the terminology of the time is often less clear. They need not take vows, nor did they participate in conventual chapter meetings, but males often acted on behalf of both friars and nuns in the acquisition of land or in other administrative and legal business. This could be extremely useful but was not always straightforward. Secular governments often saw unprofessed lay brethren of the Augustinians (as of other orders) as tax-evaders, falsely profiting from the tax-immune status of religious houses. They therefore attempted to restrict the definition only to those living in a religious community, wearing the tonsure and having given up all personal property, but these distinctions did not match those of the orders themselves, which limited the tonsure or veil to clerical brothers and fully professed nuns. Some members of the order were equally concerned about lay members. In 1290 the general chapter ruled that, as there was perplexity about the status of *conversi*, they should only be received in future with the special licence of the prior general. As we might expect, extant notarial records confirm that such rulings were frequently ignored. The number of *conversi* does, however, seem to subside as the fourteenth century progressed and confraternities increasingly replaced them, in Italy at least.

CHAPTER FOUR

Beyond the Cloister

The communities described above had land and property in varying amounts, intended to support the friars or nuns, but they also always depended on gathering direct donations. Described as a limit, limitation or *terminus*, each priory had a territory within which limitors (*questors*) of the house were authorised to preach and beg for alms. This sometimes led to dispute, as between Clare and Orford in 1373 or between Clare and London ten years later. New foundations thus necessitated that borders be established between houses of the same order. In 1388, the provincial chapter held at Newcastle instructed the prior provincial to determine the limitations of Clare and of a new priory to be established at Thetford. Clare gave up forty-seven villages to the new house. Controversies over limitations or *termini* nonetheless continued in England and elsewhere: in the 1360s Cologne disputed rights in the city of Dortmund with its former daughter-house in Lippstadt. A century later, a conflict between the limitors of the friaries at Enghien (province of Cologne) and Tournai (province of France) was initially resolved by appeal to the prior general, Guglielmo Becchi, who entrusted the case to two masters, Bernardo di Volterra and Andrea di Alessandria. These two divided the disputed area between the houses, but the argument continued. In the same decade controversy erupted between Trier and Thionville (then in the French province) over the right to beg in Luxemburg. Once again the general entrusted resolution of the case to one of the masters of the order.

Begging was not an attractive activity. In some cases convents with *studia* were able to call upon friars from another house to act as limitors on their behalf in order to leave their own friars free to study, as at Oxford in 1391. By the mid-fifteenth century in the province of Cologne, there is evidence that *questors* were allowed to keep the income collected, passing only a percentage to their house and living more or less free of the community. This practice seems to have been unknown amongst friars in England, though Chaucer's famous satire on the limited repertoire and grasping behaviour of 'hooly freres', including the Austins, suggests they were not perceived as immune.[1]

Already by the late thirteenth century the friars were much in demand

---

[1] See, for example, the general prologue of the *Canterbury Tales* and the opening lines of the *Wife of Bath's Tale*, in *The Riverside Chaucer*, pp. 26–7, lines 208–69, pp. 116–17, lines 865–81.

as preachers and confessors and their activities were increasingly regulated: by the 1290s only those who had the appropriate reputation and were sufficiently learned (*sufficientis litterature*) were to be permitted to preach and to hear confessions from the age of thirty (reduced to twenty-five in 1357). In the same decade Giacomo da Viterbo wrote a *Summa* on sin which was the first Augustinian contribution to the vast pastoral literature of the late Middle Ages.

Friars of all orders were also involved in the public life of the church in their localities, organising and encouraging processions and other festivities. In 1338 in Gubbio for example, the friars persuaded the city to institute the feast of St Catherine of Alexandria to protect them, marking it with a torchlit procession to their church of Sant'Agostino on her feast day. Friars of all orders were also regularly called upon to meet the requirements of royal patrons: Austins, like other friars, frequently preached in the royal court in England.[2] In 1309, they participated as chaplains and confessors in the Almería campaign of King Jaime II of Aragon.[3] Powerful individuals also often requested the personal services of a friar, taking them away from the order for long periods: Friar Thomas Edwardstone of Clare, for example, went to Italy in 1368 as confessor to Lionel of Clarence. More generally, royal patrons expected support. In 1346 Edward III issued a mandate addressed to the prior of the Austin Friars in London requiring the friars to explain the English royal claims to the French Crown in their sermons. A similar mandate was sent to the prior provincial of the Dominicans. In some circumstances such political expectations rendered life difficult for the friars, as at Paris at the end of the thirteenth century. By this date the Paris house had become a major intellectual powerhouse in the order and the wider Church and was recognised as such by the French king, Philip IV. Because of pressure of numbers and for the sake of convenience, the community of Les Grands Augustins moved in 1295 into buildings vacated by the Sack Friars at the western edge of the Latin Quarter.[4] They obtained this site through the Crown and also received gifts of income from the king and his queen, a marker of their goodwill towards Giles of Rome. Thus, when Philip sought assistance for his confrontation with Pope Boniface VIII in 1303 there was a tradition of support from – and for – the Crown. There was also, however, a strong tradition of papal support in the order.[5] Giles of Rome both had close personal ties with the pope, and had written pro-papal treatises, including *De ecclesiastica potestate* in 1302, which articulated the hierocratic principle of papal power, diverging notably

---

[2] Roth, *The English Austin Friars*, I, p. 202.
[3] J. Webster, *Els Menorets. The Franciscans in the Realms of Aragon from St Francis to the Black Death* (Toronto, 1993), p. 190.
[4] See below, p. 219–20.
[5] Saak, *High Way to Heaven*, makes this the centre point to his discussion of the Augustinians' relations with the papacy.

from his earlier *De regimine principum* dedicated to the king as a young man. His treatise was to influence Boniface's great statement of papal supremacy, the bull *Unam sanctam*, issued in November of that year.

This identification with the pope went deeper than Giles: Giacomo da Viterbo, the second master in the order, also wrote a treatise supporting the primacy of the papacy. In December 1297 Boniface had identified the Austin Friars in central Italy, together with the Franciscans and Dominicans, as suitable to preach a crusade against the Colonna family, his enemies in Rome.[6] He presumably knew he could rely on their support. It is thus unsurprising that in response to a demand for aid from the French Crown in 1303, only twenty-seven members of the Paris house initially declared their adherence to the royal *appellatio*. A day later, when it became clear that non-adherence would mean exile, a further eleven names were added to the list of adherents. The total number signed up was thirty-eight, but the community probably had some sixty brothers, so over twenty chose to leave.[7]

By this date the friars were providing an essential supplement to the pastoral care of the secular clergy. In some cases they also provided an international element that could not be supplied by the local church. As Jens Röhrkasten has shown, the London community included friars from overseas who might serve as spiritual advisors for foreign merchants and artisans otherwise excluded from the parochial system.[8] The Austins were uniquely well placed to do so since their church stood in an area surrounded by overseas merchants. Dutch, German and Italian friars all played this role in the fifteenth century. A Friar Georgius acted as confessor to the Dutch goldsmith Gisbert van Dist in 1431 and to the German merchant Arnold Soderman in 1441. In similar vein, in 1402 an English friar, Richard Clay, long resident in Prussia and Livonia, acquired papal permission to say Mass for English merchants and their families in the region.[9] Like other friars, the Augustinians also acted as executors for individuals and in some cases received personal bequests. In London in 1391 for instance, a Friar Andrea de Alice received a legacy from an Italian merchant.

The Italian who made a bequest to Friar Andrea was one of thousands all over Latin Christendom who left legacies to the friars and their churches, witnesses to the enthusiasm engendered by the order. The reputation of the Augustinians for preaching and teaching made them one of most popular targets for lay generosity after the Franciscans and Dominicans, though the final choice was probably frequently determined by proximity to the home of the donor. Innumerable men and women left property to Augustinian

---

6   *Olim Iacobum de Columpna*, 30 December 1297 (Alonso I, 198–9; Digard 2383; Potthast 24611).
7   W. J. Courtenay, 'Between Pope and King: The Parisian Letters of Adhesion of 1303', *Speculum* 71 (1996), pp. 577–605.
8   Röhrkasten, 'Local Ties', pp. 180–2.
9   Roth, *The English Austin Friars*, I, p. 204.

houses hoping to benefit their own and their relatives' spiritual fortunes. In 1290, Bartholomew of Acre, a merchant and citizen of Norwich, gave a messuage to the Austins of that city 'for the good of his soul and those of his forebears'. Fifty years later (1341) in Gubbio, Massacio Hostii left houses and land for the building of a chapel in the church of Sant'Agostino to the honour of the saints Augustine, John and the as yet uncanonised Nicolò da Tolentino. Similar examples could be cited for almost any mendicant church by this date. In many cases, through donations and purchases, the friars became major property-holders, their archives full of leases and records of rent payments, sales and acquisitions.

The greatest spiritual assistance obtained by benefactors was, as with other orders of this period, burial in one of their churches. This would attract the prayers of the friars but also of pilgrims brought to a church by episcopal and other indulgences. In Siena in 1331 the commune disbursed 713 *lire* for the funeral of Pietro de la Branca di Gubbio, their *podestà*, who had died in office, and for his burial in the convent of the Austin Friars in the city.[10] Most lay patrons were buried in the nave or, if they could afford it, in their own chapels. Thus as we have seen, Joan of Acre was buried in her own chapel in Clare. Further north, Robert de Wodehouse, archdeacon of Richmond, who had sponsored the foundation of the priory in Stamford in 1342, was buried in the choir of the church, probably in 1344–5.

Connections with the laity might also take more formal shape during life, including what historians usually refer to as letters of confraternity, similar to those issued by traditional monastic communities, hospitals or other ecclesiastical institutions, though this term is rarely found in the texts themselves.[11] In 1265 an early donor to the friars at Clare, Roger de Scaccario, was admitted to the confraternity of the order and recognised as patron and advocate. The document recording it was a cyrograph in two halves, one for the friars with Roger's seal, the other for Roger with the seal of the provincial chapter (the first reference to this body).[12] In 1279 Brian of Brampton and his wife Emma received an analogous letter of confraternity from the English provincial chapter in return for their support of the Austins in Ludlow. The letter accorded them and their antecedents and descendants participation in the spiritual good works of the order as accorded to their own brethren, including vigils and fasts, and the assurance of a priest to say masses at the altar of the Virgin in their church in Ludlow.

The terminology of fraternity used shows that these patrons were part of the community in a broad sense, as was a widow, Margaret Delowe (†1457),

---

[10] Siena, Archivio di Stato, Consiglio generale 110, fols 108v–109v.
[11] See R. N. Swanson, 'Mendicants and Confraternity in Late Medieval England', in *The Religious Orders in Pre-Reformation England*, ed. J. G. Clark (Woodbridge, 2002), pp. 121–41.
[12] *The Cartulary of the Augustinian Friars of Clare*, p. 35.

who described herself as a *suster* of the Augustinians in London.[13] Despite their fragile nature, Roth found nineteen such letters extant from the English Austins, a mark of their popularity in England.[14] Similar agreements were made elsewhere: in 1289, a wealthy donor to the friars in Vienna was included in the necrology of the house and her name was thereafter to be read out every year on the anniversary of the foundation. As Robert Swanson has noted, such promises of posthumous commemoration were particularly important given the emphasis on purgatory in late-medieval spirituality.[15]

Although obviously popular, confraternity letters were both targeted by critics such as Wyclif and lampooned as the sale of spiritual benefits in satires such as *Piers the Plowman's Crede*, who has an Austin friar say to Piers:

> Helpe us herteliche therwith; and here I undertake
> Thou schalt ben brother of our hous, and a boke habben,
> At the next chaptire, clereliche enselaed;
> And thanne oure Provinciall hath power to assoilen
> Alle sustren and bretheren that beth of our order.
> And though thou conne nought thi Crede, knele downe
> here.
> My soule I sette for thyn to asoile the clene,
> In covenaunt that thou come againe and katell us bringe.[16]

Concern that such confraternity should be a special privilege to be granted rarely is implied in instructions like those to William Wells, the English prior provincial in 1438, allowing him to grant just ten letters of affiliation. Twenty-six years later, however, another new provincial, John Halam, was authorised to grant fifty.

Closely linked to the activities of limitors and the issuing of confraternity letters was the promotion of indulgences to assist building and other projects in the Church. In the thirteenth century these usually amounted to time-specific indulgences for those attending a church on a feast day and making donations to the order. Already before the Great Union, the Brettini acquired from Innocent IV an indulgence of forty days to anyone making gifts to their new church at Gubbio. In the summer of the following year a man named Iacomellus gave them a house, vineyard, woods and various

---

[13] Röhrkasten, 'Local Ties', p. 175.

[14] Roth, *The English Austin Friars*, I, pp. 213–14.

[15] Swanson, 'Mendicants and Confraternity in Late Medieval England', p. 124.

[16] *Piers the Plowman's Crede*, ed. James Dean, originally published in *Six Ecclesiastical Satires* (Kalamazoo, Michigan: Medieval Institute Publications, 1991), online at http://www.lib.rochester.edu/ camelot/TEAMS/credefrm.htm, lines 325–33: 'Help us heartily therewith [making donations] and here I undertake/ you shall be a brother of our house and have a book/ (at the next [provincial] chapter), sealed by a cleric/ and then our provincial [prior] has power to absolve/ all sisters and brothers of our order/ And though you do not know your Creed (kneel down here)/ I set my soul for yours, to absolve you clean/ with the agreement that you will come again and bring us cattle.'

lands.[17] Other donations soon followed. Building began in 1251 and the church, outside the Porta Romana, was completed by 1294. The indulgence surely helped. The friars in Bologna also acquired an indulgence from Alexander IV in June 1259, awarded to those who assisted in building their new church. A similar privilege was issued for Paris in June of the following year.

By the end of the fifteenth century, in keeping with practices throughout the Church, the friars were obtaining indulgences on a new scale. In Cambridge they acquired a plenary indulgence for combined donations to St Peter's, Rome, and the houses of the Austins in England. A donor would receive the same participation in spiritual benefits and post-mortem commemoration associated with confraternity letters. A similar indulgence was purchased for Oxford, with collecting boxes to be placed in all Austin churches. In 1515 the prior general Giles of Viterbo obtained a plenary indulgence for the general chapter in Rimini. These were potentially fruitful sources of income for the order, but in northern Europe the practice was increasingly criticised, in part a response to the attacks of Martin Luther, himself originally an Augustinian friar. It is telling that by the 1520s in England, the sums collected for the Oxford indulgence dropped dramatically, from £494 in 1517 to £129 in 1521.[18]

Confraternities

Surrounding almost all Augustinian churches, like those of the other mendicants, were groups of laywomen and men organised into confraternal and guild associations. In England these seem never to have been very large or to have involved either flagellants or *laudesi* (praise) companies. By the fifteenth century, however, even a remote house such as Tickhill, in a small town in a secluded South Yorkshire valley, though still referred to as a hermitage, had three guilds linked with it: the Assumption (documented from 1395), Holy Cross (from 1405) and St Christopher (from 1429). By the same period the church of the Austins in York had altars for the Guild of Corpus Christi and for a confraternity attached to the altar of St Catherine of Alexandria, whilst in 1487 the friars agreed to perform two trentals (30) of masses each year for the deceased members of the Union of Carpenters. In 1488 a guild of St Augustine is documented at Clare, and in Canterbury in the early sixteenth century the shoemakers, curriers and cobblers' Guild of the Assumption of Our Lady attended Masses for the souls of their deceased members in the Austin Friars' church on the feasts of the Assumption, St Cyprian and St Crispin.

Many of these confraternities were tied to cults which were taking shape

---

[17] See P. S. Lopez, 'Documenta Eugubina', *AA* 16 (1937), pp. 41–58, 42–5, 132–46.

[18] Roth, *The English Austin Friars*, I, pp. 433–4.

in the late Middle Ages, such as that of Corpus Christi, and were linked with processions. According to a later tradition, in mid-fourteenth-century Ghent, a confraternity of the Holy Blood was founded after the report of a miracle. Thieves who had stolen a container holding the Host from the Augustinian church had buried it, but one of the criminals later returned and found the buried Hosts full of blood. The Augustinians took them in procession back to their church and from then on held an annual procession, displaying the relic on the Sunday or octave of the Holy Sacrament. Whether or not this was really a fourteenth-century episode, miracles were associated with the site and a chapel was built over it, first documented in 1444. By this date there were also other brotherhoods of the Holy Blood associated with Augustinian houses in the region, including Maastricht (1428).[19] Other confraternities were very specific to the order: according to a story the origins of which are obscure, Mary consoled Monica on the death of her husband and over the errors of her son Augustine before his conversion, encouraging her to dress in black and wear a black leather belt. Inspired by this tradition (which competed with others associated with Augustine on the origins of the belt), a Confraternity of the Belt and Habit of St Monica was founded in Bologna in 1439, transformed in 1495 into the Confraternity of Our Lady of Consolation. Similar confraternities were founded in Treviso and Venice.

Whilst in continental Europe confraternities might be very large indeed, the numbers involved in English guilds such as that of St Augustine at Clare are much more difficult to establish and were probably smaller. The responsibilities they entailed for the friars, however, are likely to have been very similar on both sides of the Channel and can be illustrated from the records of a confraternity of flagellants which met in the crypt of Sant'Agostino in Orte, north of Rome. The friars in this case seem to have been reluctant hosts: in 1362 the provincial prior, Bonifacio da Castello, instructed the prior not to obstruct the meetings of the confraternity or to impede their celebrations of the Office in his church. He was also to allow them to bury members in their chapel, reserved to them alone. This exclusive right was confirmed thirteen years later (1375), when the prior also promised the confraternity that he would ensure that a friar was nominated to celebrate their daily Mass, hear their confessions and act as their spiritual guide. They in turn were not to obstruct his ministry.[20]

In the much bigger community of Santo Spirito in Florence, the confraternity of Santa Maria delle Laude, dedicated to the Virgin and her praise and founded before 1322, was responsible for an annual Pentecost play celebrating the descent of the Holy Spirit to the Apostles. Like the Ascension play performed at the neighbouring church of Santa Maria del Carmine,

---

[19] See P. Trio, *De Gentse broederschappen (1182–1580)*, Verhandelingen maatschappij voor geschiednis en oudheidkunde te Gent XVI (Ghent, 1990), p. 37.

[20] *Le pergamene medievali di Orte (secoli x–xv)* (Orte, 1984), pp. 54–5, 89–90.

it enjoyed communal subsidies and was a substantial spectacle requiring months of preparation, complicated equipment and even fireworks. It was after a performance of the play in 1471 that the church caught fire, destroying books, paintings and other furnishings. Understandably, the play was never performed there again.

CHAPTER FIVE

Learning

Unlike the Carmelites, the superiors of the Augustinians understood the importance of study from the very beginning. Whereas the hermits had focused on contemplation and withdrawal with limited engagement in pastoral care, the new order would need learned brothers to act as preachers and teachers. In 1259 the prior general, Lanfranco da Settala, purchased a house in Paris for students and by 1260 it was already functioning. There also seems to have been a *studium* in Bologna by 1264. Within twenty-five years the Paris house was so successful that it was too small to accommodate all those attending and, although a larger house was acquired in Chardonnet, numbers had to be restricted on a temporary basis to one per province. In May 1287 the general chapter therefore ruled that there were to be at least four *studia generalia* in Italy: in the Roman Curia, Bologna, Padua and Naples (the last three all university towns). As David Gutiérrez has argued, these had probably all already been established as schools before 1287, since in June of that year the Roman province designated a student for the last three and for Florence, indicating that this last too was now established as a *studium generale*.[1]

A key figure in the early development of study in the order was Giles of Rome. He had been one of the first to live in the Paris house and from 1269 to 1272 attended the classes of the Dominicans led by Thomas Aquinas. He belonged to the first generation of scholars faced with the main corpus of Aristotle's works and in particular his moral philosophy. His *De erroribus philosophorum* (*c.* 1270) played a fundamental role in the acceptance of the doctrine of 'philosophers' in Christian learning. Some of his ideas were, however, condemned after the prohibition on Aristotelian propositions by Bishop Tempier in 1277. The impact of this set-back on his career or the fortunes of the Austin Friars in Paris is not clear, but cannot have been long-lasting. Presumably he withdrew to Italy, where he reappeared at the general chapter in 1281. This may be when he first introduced the practice of debating theological and philosophical issues (*quaestiones*) at the general chapter. In 1285 the condemned propositions were re-examined and he was permitted to

---

[1]   D. Gutiérrez, 'Los estudios en la orden agustiniana desde la edad media hasta la Contemporánea', *AA* 33 (1970), pp. 75–149, 86.

return to Paris, where he was the first member of the order appointed Regent master in Theology. From now on, the hermit friars in Paris could study in their own *studium generale* and at the same time acquire university qualifications and the licence to teach (*licentia docendi*).

As the most experienced in university matters Giles drove the organisation of study in the order. He saw learning as the means to success: in a letter written to the provincial priors in the year he was elected prior general he emphasised the importance of the study of theology, which, he argued, together with regular observance, would lead to the growth and prestige of the Austin Friars. He also explicitly linked both these to obtaining the much-desired confirmation (*firmum statum*) of the order in the Church. Thus in 1295, after his designation as archbishop of Bourges, Giles attended the general chapter in Siena and held a disputation *de quolibet*, the standard form of learned debate in the universities. His belief in the power of learning went beyond the scope of the order. He placed the same emphasis in his *De regimine principum*, a mirror of princes for the future king, Philip IV, written in the years after the condemnation of his propositions in Paris. It was quickly translated into numerous vernaculars, widely read and imitated down to the beginning of the sixteenth century. Giles exhorted rulers to increase the number of schools and surround themselves with men of learning. Indeed he went so far as to argue that a ruler who did not promote study and did not wish his subjects to be knowledgeable was no king but a tyrant. By the time of his death his writings encompassed some sixty-five philosophical, theological and other works on a variety of subjects: he was undoubtedly the most prolific and original of the Augustinian Hermit Friars and his careful scholarship earned him the epithet *doctor fundatissimus*. Such was his fame that already at the general chapter in Florence in 1287 his writings and interpretations, present and future (*opiniones, positiones et sententias scriptas et scribendas*), were instituted as the standard for all students in the order, to be studied and diligently defended. Giles was the only master in the order at that date, so this may have been an attempt to ensure conformity across the different *studia*. Nonetheless, his writings were still invoked as the guide for study in the order in reform statutes introduced in 1539. Later scholars in the order took liberties with his work, but this early insistence on his authority encouraged the creation of a fairly coherent school of theology centred on profound knowledge of his works. Since this was in turn heavily indebted to Aquinas, this gave the Dominican's work great influence. It does not, however, seem to have led to the creation of a distinct 'Augustinian' school in the order, as has in the past been argued.[2]

Giles's prestige as a master undoubtedly assisted the Augustinians to

---

[2] M. W. F. Stone, 'Augustine and Medieval Philosophy', in *The Cambridge Companion to Augustine*, ed. E. Stump and N. Kretzmann (Cambridge, 2001), pp. 253–66, 259.

expand into the world of the universities, but alongside the *studia generalia* the order also developed a series of schools of more limited scope. These usually aimed at teaching the skills of logic, philosophy and basic theology and are often referred to as *studia particularia* but, when theology was taught, also (confusingly) sometimes as *studia generalia* for the relevant province. In some cases the two types of *studia* overlapped: Bologna was both a *studium generale* at the superior, international level and a *studium* for the province of Romagna. Thus in Bologna there were both students training for the lectorate and others taking the more basic course to prepare them for preaching and pastoral care. At Paris too, as well as students from further afield the community accommodated men for whom it was their home convent and men from the province of France undertaking primary studies in logic and natural philosophy.

After about three years in a provincial *studium* (later reduced to one or two) the promising friar chosen to go to Paris or to one of the other *studia generalia* was to spend up to five years studying theology. His day would start with the *lectiones ordinarie* of the master expounding the Old or New Testament with the aid of glosses and the works of the Church fathers. This was followed by reading of the *Sentences* of Peter Lombard and then of the Bible guided by *baccalarii*. There might also be supplementary courses in philosophy and the students were expected to attend disputations and listen to sermons. At the end of five years they would be examined at either the general or provincial chapter. If successful they could then be appointed as lectors and assigned to teach in one of the houses of their province. Later they might be chosen to undertake a further programme of study at a *studium generale*, leading to the university degrees and, eventually, to the position of master.

Involvement in *studia* changed the order fast. The earliest legislation extant (1281) insisted that only those who could read the Breviary and Missal well (*distincte*) might be elected as priors 'since ignorance is the mother and mistress of error'. In 1287 the general chapter presided over by Clemente da Osimo still found it necessary to specify that even the priors of houses with *studia* must know Latin well, an indication that this was not necessarily the case. There were still so few university-trained friars that newly qualified lectors were appointed to teach in the *studia generalia*. But by the 1290s, at least three years' experience was required before qualifying for such posts. The Constitutions of Regensburg named the promotion of study as the foundation of the order (*fundamentum ordinis*), identifying it as one of the primary activities of the prior general.

By the end of the century study in the order was genuinely international, as demonstrated by the list of friars provided when Philip IV demanded written support from the house in Paris in 1303. These included fifteen men from France (including Brabant and the south), eleven from Italy, two from England, one who was perhaps German, one from the Low Countries, as well as the new and former regent masters (from Hungary and Provence).[3] Twenty years later study in the order was sufficiently international to require examiners to be competent in different languages for those promoted to the lectorate: those named were allocated to the German provinces, to the Occitan *studia*, to Italy and to Paris. By this date Oxford and Cambridge were almost as important as Paris and in 1318 they were allowed the same rights, reflecting their genuinely international status. Over the course of the late Middle Ages other *studia generalia* were to be found at Bruges, Cologne, Lyons, Mainz, Metz, Milan, Montpellier, Siena, Toulouse and Vienna. Another series of *studia generalia* were mainly serving the students in their own provinces: Aix, Bordeaux, Cahors, Esztergom, Lleida, Lisbon, Toledo and Valencia. In Italy, a whole series of *studia generalia* were established in the first half of the fourteenth century, but none in practice operated as such: Arezzo, Ascoli Piceno, Asti, Barletta, Genoa, L'Aquila, Lucca, Pavia, Rieti, Rimini, Treviso, Venice and Viterbo. In spite of this proliferation, Paris remained the model for all other *studia* and that most aspired to by the friars. In 1321, to avoid dispute, the general chapter ruled that there must be an alternation between those north and south of the Alps going to Paris to read the *Sentences* or the Bible.

The pattern of studies laid out here is based on normative sources, but the experience of individual friars suggests that it is not far from the reality. Friar Vittorio di Camerino, one of the witnesses in the canonisation process for Nicolò da Tolentino (1325), describes his own scholastic career in the late thirteenth century in recognisable terms: as a novice he was sent to Tolentino for a total of three years, where he studied grammar and then logic and theology. He then went to a *studium generale* for an unspecified period before being appointed lector. On the other hand, a few decades later the career of Friar Johannes Klenkok, studied by Ocker, shows just how itinerant a learned friar's career could be. Klenkok was born in Lower Saxony *c.* 1310, the son of a knight. He became a subdeacon in the secular Church and joined the order relatively late, probably in Osnabrück in the 1340s. He began a career as a student, which may have taken him to Strasbourg and Bologna, and certainly included a *studium generale* somewhere in the German provinces, followed by Paris and then Oxford, where he was regent master 1359–61. He returned to his home province as lector (probably at Erfurt) and as provincial prior from 1363 to *c.* 1370. Here he began a campaign against various elements of the Saxon law, the *Sachsenspiegel*, which contradicted his view of papal authority, provoking an outcry. The next step took him to Moravia as an inquisitor, resident at the richly endowed new friary at Brno. He seems also to have enjoyed access to the imperial chancellery, but did not stay long. By the early summer of 1372 he was at the Curia in Avignon, a minor penitentiary specialising in hearing the confessions of those whose sins were reserved

---

[3] Courtenay, 'Between Pope and King', p. 602.

to the papal see. Once there he persuaded Pope Gregory XI to set up a commission to investigate the *Sachsenspiegel*, which resulted in the condemnation of fourteen articles in 1374. Just a few months after this victory, Klenkok succumbed to the plague.[4]

In the mid-fourteenth century, the prior general Thomas de Strasbourg (1345–57), who was himself a master of theology (like most of the generals after Giles of Rome), revised the regulations for study in the order. He paid particular attention to Paris, giving it a whole series of norms in 1353. He clarified the curriculum for lectors and the exams they were to take and raised the qualifications expected so that those sent there must now have some experience of teaching. No province, except France, was to send more than two students at a time to Paris and they were not to remain for longer than three years at the expense of their province and not more than five even at their own or a benefactor's expense. He also established precise sanctions against lectors who failed to 'read' at least four times a week. Thomas was himself the author of a commentary on the *Sentences* which was to remain the most complete and appreciated course in theology in the order until the eighteenth century.

By the mid-fourteenth century the Augustinians were playing a prominent role in the universities. In Italy, the first master of theology in the university of Florence was an Augustinian friar. The chronicler Matteo Villani describes the resulting celebrations:

> On 9 December 1359 in the church of Santa Reparata, publicly and solemnly, Friar Francesco di Biancozzo de' Nerli of the order of hermit friars (*romitani*) became a master in divinity and took the symbols of a master in theology; and the commune, showing its gratitude for the privilege of being allowed to do this [by the pope], had its bells pealed for a long time. . . . all the officials of the commune and a great number of citizens were present . . . which was a notable and beautiful thing.[5]

Five years later friar Ugolino da Orvieto was entrusted with drawing up the statutes for the new faculty of theology in the University of Bologna. He was assisted in the task by another Augustinian, Friar Bonaventura da Padova, who in 1378 – by this date a cardinal – was chosen together with a Franciscan and a Dominican to update the statutes of the other Italian universities, completed in 1380. In the same decade, another Augustinian friar, Leonhard of Carinthia (†1402), together with a Cistercian, a Carmelite and a Dominican, contributed to the foundation of the theology faculty of the University of Vienna (1389).

At first, friars who had already studied medicine or surgery before entering the order were allowed to continue practising, with the licence of the provincial prior. As for other friars there was, however, increasing concern

---

[4]   C. Ocker, *Johannes Klenkok: A Friar's Life c. 1310–1374* (Philadelphia, 1993).

[5]   *Matteo Villani Cronica, con la continuazione di Filippo Villani*, ed. G. Porta, 2 vols (Parma, 1995), II, p. 370 (book 9, chapter 58).

about the potential for conflict with their duties as professed religious. From 1281 they were not allowed to practise outside the cloister and in 1290 they were explicitly forbidden to undertake any sort of operation. A Friar Arnold is recorded as physician to the king of Hungary in Gregorio da Rimini's register of 1357–8, but thirty years later (1388) the general chapter banned medicine altogether. One or two continued thereafter: Roth notes the case of Friar Robert Waldeby, who became archbishop of York (†1397). His epitaph in Westminster Abbey calls him a skilled physician (*ingenuus medicus*) and he was reputed to have been physician to Richard II.[6] But Waldeby had also studied law in Toulouse and was an active bishop, first in Dublin, then in Chichester, before moving to York. There can have been little time for medicine. In 1443 at the request of the prior general and diffinitors, Pope Eugenius IV authorised a Friar Paolo da Viterbo to practise among the religious and poor alone, as long as he made no profit or other reward. This was, however, exceptional.

A few brothers seem to have been unhappy about the emphasis on learning. William Flete († *c.* 1383), an English friar, wrote three letters to the members of the English province questioning the purpose of study in the order. He may have come to Italy to attend a general chapter, but chose to stay, withdrawing to Lecceto. He was soon known for his austere asceticism and holy life: according to a contemporary account he spent each day out in the woods, taking his books with him and returning to the hermitage at night. He warned against the dangers of excessive emphasis on learning, distancing the friars from the holy simplicity (*sancta stultitia*) of the fishermen whom Christ had chosen as his disciples and apostles. It was an appeal rooted in the original idea of solitary contemplation of the hermits who had been united to produce the mendicant order of friars in 1256.[7] He was also a friend and spiritual advisor to Catherine of Siena (†1380).

Despite such pessimists, theologians in the order participated in the major learned debates of the time. They remained prominent papal supporters, as evinced in the disputes of the 1320s, when Friar Agostino da Ancona produced a *Summa de potestate ecclesiastica* (1326). Guglielmo da Cremona, the prior general and Friar Hermann von Schildesche, amongst others, also provided Pope John XXII with responses to the critiques of Marsilius of Padua and William of Ockham.[8] A decade later, Friar Geoffrey *de Anglia* was one of sixteen theologians summoned to discuss the doctrine of the Beatific Vision by the pope (1335). Members of the order also became deeply

---

6   Roth, *The English Austin Friars*, I, p. 89. See also A. Montford, *Health, Sickness, Medicine and the Friars in the Thirteenth and Fourteenth Centuries* (Aldershot, 2004), p. 125.

7   On Flete and the observants, see below, pp. 164–71.

8   See M. J. Wilks, *The Problem of Sovereignty in the Later Middle Ages. The Papal Monarchy with Augustinus Triumphus and the Publicists* (Cambridge, 1963), and Saak, *High Way to Heaven*, pp. 40–138.

involved in the on-going controversy about the mendicant ideal and skilful defenders of their interpretation of the apostolic life. Little interest seems to have been shown in Italy, but in the German provinces and the British Isles the issues were hotly debated. An emblematic case is provided by the activities of Richard FitzRalph, a theologian and originally a mendicant sympathiser who turned against them, perhaps because of his experiences as archbishop of Armagh (1347–60).[9] In a sermon before the pope in Avignon in 1350 FitzRalph preached against the role of the mendicants who engaged in pastoral concerns exempt from the jurisdiction of bishops. He may have been prompted by an appeal from the friars requesting a reconsideration of *Super cathedram*, issued by Boniface VIII in 1300. The original bull had been intended to resolve the conflict with the secular clergy by imposing restrictions on the activities of the mendicant orders.[10] FitzRalph may also have been responding to a request from the pope that he and two other theologians investigate the thorny issues disputed amongst the friars: property, and the implications of the evangelical poverty adopted by the Franciscans. In his Avignon sermon and in a later dialogue on the poverty of Christ (*De pauperie salvatoris*, 1356), FitzRalph picked up on the by now century-old arguments about the pastoral role of the mendicants and the scriptural basis for their poverty. In an investigation of the whole theory of lordship, possession, property and use, he introduced the question of lordship founded on grace. FitzRalph himself was careful to avoid the suggestion that a state of sin and consequent loss of dominion might have an effect on the valid exercise of priestly powers, but these implications were to be adopted by Wyclif in the 1370s. Paradoxically, many of FitzRalph's ideas can be traced back to Augustinian friars, and especially to Giles of Rome's *De ecclesiastica potestate*.

In London in the winters of 1356 and 1357 FitzRalph preached a series of sermons summarising and clarifying the arguments contained in his dialogue. According to his own later account he did so initially by invitation and in response to an existing dispute in the city between mendicant theologians and secular clergy over the poverty of Christ. Whether this theoretical issue was hotly debated or not, there had certainly been recent attacks on the role of the mendicants, summed up in a complaint to a provincial council held in London in May 1356. The clergy of the province of Canterbury renewed old accusations that the friars abused their privileges, failed to observe poverty, rode fine horses, lived in grand houses, slandered the clergy and flattered the nobility, meddling in their affairs in order to boost their own wealth. Such criticisms were also familiar in contemporary satire. Whether or not his audience in London was familiar with the intricacies of the debate, it is likely that FitzRalph's criticisms would have found an echo.

[9] See the excellent account by K. Walsh, *A Fourteenth-Century Scholar and Primate. Richard FitzRalph in Oxford, Avignon and Armagh* (Oxford, 1981), pp. 349–451, on which this summary is based.
[10] See above, p. 49.

Geoffrey Hardeby, the Augustinian regent master in Oxford, took up the challenge of answering FitzRalph's attack. In his *De vita evangelica* he responded to FitzRalph's theory of dominion as applied to the poverty of the mendicants and defended the pastoral role of the friars. Still more importantly, in London, the four principal mendicant orders acted in unison against the archbishop. Following a meeting of their representatives in the Franciscan house in March 1357, John of Arderne, London prior of the Austin Friars, acting as proctor for all four orders, had the resulting list of twenty-one alleged errors in FitzRalph's sermons copied out and presented to him. Two days later, in a powerful sermon, FitzRalph responded to each of their criticisms. He drew attention to the wealth of mendicant churches and, enumerating it clause by clause, reminded his audience of the rule of St Francis with its emphasis on poverty – though he did not draw attention to the fact that this rule did not apply to three of the four orders criticised. He also repeated an earlier attack on confession to friars, arguing that even if a parish priest's education were defective, he at least would know the penitent, whilst as an outsider a friar would not.

The friars now appealed for royal support. Mandates were issued forbidding FitzRalph and other religious and Austin Friars in particular to leave the country, so as to prevent them taking the case to the Curia. FitzRalph and John of Arderne were both, however, in Avignon by the following autumn. Each side petitioned the pope. FitzRalph was allowed to respond to the friars' criticisms in person before the cardinals' tribunal, repeating and clarifying his views on Christ's poverty, on the illegitimacy of voluntary mendicancy and on the need for confession in a parish church. He also picked up on another current criticism of the friars, accusing them of unprincipled admission of young boys into the mendicant houses in Oxford. The general proctors and advocates of the friars responded in kind, with detailed criticism of Fitzralph's account of mendicant poverty, accusing him of doctrinal errors and culminating in an accusation of heresy. They attacked him as a scandalmonger, even as the Antichrist, or the devil incarnate. As Walsh argues, they also, with 'an ironic twist ... turned FitzRalph's own doctrine, that those who committed grave sin (i.e. by slandering the friars), were deprived of their ecclesiastical and temporal dominion' against the archbishop himself.[11] The friars had enormous resources at their disposal. In November 1358 the prior general raised a tax of 10 florins on each province for the expenses of the case. He even allowed money to be diverted from the fund for the canonisation of Nicolò da Tolentino. FitzRalph had no such resources. Although there were certainly secular clergy who shared Fitzralph's views of the friars, few contemporary churchmen would have accepted the full implications of FitzRalph's critique, which amounted to a demand for an end to the mendicant

---

[11] Walsh, *A Fourteenth-Century Scholar and Primate*, p. 433.

privilege of confession and outright condemnation of the mendicant orders. In practice diocesan bishops often relied on the services of the friars and FitzRalph's views were dangerously close to those of the heretical spiritual Franciscans, while also implicitly challenging the power of the pope to issue such privileges. In October 1358, while acknowledging that the case was still pending, the pope issued *Gravem dilectorum*, recognising the friars' value in the pastoral field and condemning all interference and disruption by the secular clergy. It was an interim solution, but in practice it amounted to defeat for FitzRalph. The polemic dragged on – with FitzRalph increasingly isolated – until his death at the Curia in November 1360. The case thus inevitably came to an end, but the dispute did not end there: manuscripts of FitzRalph's anti-mendicant case were widely circulated and he came to be regarded as the 'father of Wyclifism'.

Books

The intellectual and political energy of the Austin Friars is evident in their conduct of the FitzRalph controversy or later in the debates over Wyclifism. It was also manifest in disputes with the Dominicans and Franciscans over poverty, but surviving evidence about their books provides a more measured indicator of their intellectual interests. The earliest extant constitutions already refer to sharing of books for students and the general chapter frequently took direct interest in the provision of books for individual friars. The constitutions of 1290 ordained that new lectors should receive 40 *livres tournois* from their provinces to buy the books necessary to teaching before leaving Paris. At death these reverted to their province. There was also provision for a library, or at least a book cupboard (*armaria*), in each *studium generale* and a copyist to transcribe works for the collection. Later constitutions detail extensive provisions for the *studia generalia*, student friars and their needs. These were sometimes *ad personam*: in 1295 the second master to qualify in the order, Giacomo da Viterbo, who had succeeded Giles of Rome in Paris in 1293, was required to write some sort of biblical commentary (*Opera in sacra pagina*) for which the general chapter allocated a florin a year from each province, to cover the cost of scribes and vellum and other expenses involved. Scholars might build up substantial libraries: Giles of Rome left a large collection of philosophical, theological, legal and other texts to the Paris convent at his death.

Ordinary houses also acquired libraries of liturgical and theological works. Many of these were purchased by the brethren themselves: in 1283 two brothers of the house in Gubbio were allowed to use an inheritance from their family to buy books necessary 'to the gaining of wisdom'.[12] The

---

[12]   S. López, 'Documenta Eugubina', *AA* 16 (1937), pp. 41–58, 132–46, 134.

inherent value of books was such that in 1324 the general chapter deemed it necessary to instruct priors not to alienate or pawn books on pain of excommunication. By 1368 the house in Gubbio had fifty books in the sacristy in a single chest. As we might expect, the list includes various Bibles (including one with illuminations), the *Sentences* with *Commentaries*, books of saints, homilies on the Gospels, various sermon collections (including Jacopo da Voragine), theological *Quaestiones*, Boethius on the Trinity, glossed books of the Gospels, Giles of Rome on the Body of Christ, Augustine's *Confessions*, Innocent III's *De contemptu mundi*, and various *Summae*.

A much more substantial library is recorded at York. This included some 647 books of which a single friar, John Erghome, master of the *studium* there, donated 306. Most codices contained several different works, leading to a total of around 2188. An extant inventory, drawn up in 1372, is organised by subject matter, beginning with Bibles. There were numerous copies of the works of Augustine, the writings of prominent members of the order, the rule and constitutions and a vast number of treatises on preaching, sermon collections, theological and philosophical *summae*, music, logic and geometry. There were also the works of classical historians such as Caesar's *Gallic Wars* and more recent chroniclers such as Ranulf Higden. Perhaps more surprisingly, there was only one copy of pseudo-Hugh of St Victor's *Expositio* on the rule, but there was a copy of an unspecified work by William of Saint-Amour, which was almost certainly his attack on the practice of mendicancy. Remarkably few of these works can be identified in extant manuscripts.

The library at York was unusually rich and complex, but there were also good libraries in the houses in Paris, Avignon, Bordeaux, Toulouse, Erfurt, Magdeburg, Munich, Vienna and Prague, to name only those outside Italy. By the late fourteenth century most friaries seem to have had separate collections of books for the choir and of library books for borrowing by the friars and students. Some also had chained reference collections, or occasional chained volumes. Surviving fifteenth-century books from the Augustinian Hermit Friars at Mülln, now in Salzburg University Library, include several which originally had chains.

Scriptoria were present in numerous key houses of the order: producing and illuminating both liturgical and secular books is one area where both male and female members of the order were very active.[13] In 1389 Friar Pietro, working in the important scriptorium in Pavia, produced an illuminated copy of Pliny's *Natural History* for a lay patron, Pasquino Capelli, and signed it, adding a self-portrait in the Augustinian habit.[14] In 1453 a Sister Maria

[13] For the role of religious women from several different orders in book production and consumption in the fourteenth to sixteenth centuries, see K. Gill, 'Women and the Production of Religious Literature in the Vernacular 1300–1500', in *Creative Women in Medieval and Early Modern Italy: A Religious and Artistic Renaissance*, ed. E. A. Matter (Philadelphia, 1994), pp. 64–85.

[14] 'Frater Petrus de Papie me fecit'. Now Milan, Biblioteca Ambrosiana MS E. 24, inf.

Ormani wrote and illuminated a Breviary now in Vienna. She too signed her work and included a self-portrait in a lower margin adorned with a banner with the phrase 'The serving-maid of Jesus Christ, Maria, daughter of Ormani, wrote [this] in 1453' (*Ancilla Iesu Christi Maria Ormani filia scripsit MCCCCLIII*).[15] Some produced very high-class objects: in 1478 Friar Alessandro di Antonio Simone, *baccalarius*, produced a prayer book for Lorenzo Strozzi with miniatures in the style of Mantegna, now in the Fitzwilliam Museum in Cambridge.[16] Others were very prolific. In the second half of the fifteenth century, Friar Apollonio da Calvisano (Brescia) illuminated large numbers of works for the monasteries of the city and for Santa Maria del Popolo in Rome.[17] Six Antiphoners produced for the cathedral in Cremona are the work of Friar Apollonio. In 1503 in the *explicit* (closing sentence and signature) of a Gradual for feast days now in the cathedral in Ventimiglia (Liguria), an observant friar, Damiano da Genova, recorded that he had illuminated fifty-two volumes.

Augustine and the friars

The Augustinian Friars, like the nuns, were part of the order of St Augustine in the broad sense, as were the long-established regular canons who also observed the rule. The immediate founder of the male order, however, was the papacy and more particularly Cardinal Riccardo Annibaldi. This allowed Jordan of Quedlinburg to argue that the Austin Friars were superior to others because (re)united not by a single man but by the Church, and therefore essentially by the Holy Spirit acting through the Church.[18] Nonetheless, like the Carmelites and also like the Humiliati, the friars soon felt the lack of a founding figure: a charismatic body around which to centre their ideals and aspirations. Whereas the Carmelites focused on Elijah, the Augustinian Hermit Friars increasingly and perhaps inevitably linked themselves to the figure of Augustine. Their churches were very often dedicated to the saint and by 1272 the prior general Clemente da Osimo referred to him as 'our holy father'. In 1286 Honorius IV allowed them to celebrate the feast *solemniter* even during interdicts.[19] Seals of the order almost always included a figure of Augustine, often with kneeling friars on either side, as in the case of the seal used in Florence in 1287 which showed Augustine dressed as a bishop, or the seal of the theologian Hermann von Schildesche (†1357), which included both a crucified Christ at the top, Augustine with the Virgin and child in

---

[15] These works are briefly described in G. Sabazio, *Gli artisti agostiniani* (Genoa, 1938), now also available on-line at http://web.tiscali.it/ghirardacci/sabazio/sabazio.htm
[16] Cambridge, Fitwilliam Museum, MS 153. M. R. James, *A Descriptive Catalogue of the Manuscripts in the Fitzwilliam Museum* (Cambridge, 1895), pp. 346–8.
[17] Now in the general archive of the Augustinian order in Rome.
[18] Jordani de Saxonia (Quedlinburg), *Liber vitasfratrum*, book 1 chapter 19.
[19] *Pro reverentia beati*, 23 May 1286 (Potthast 22452).

two niches in the middle and Hermann himself kneeling beneath them.[20] In Fabriano, one of the earliest surviving frescoes from an Augustinian church (late thirteenth century) shows Augustine dressed as a bishop giving the rule to a group of black-habited friars. In 1306 the general chapter ordained that all the brethren should fast on the vigil of his feast, so that he would intercede on their behalf.

This wholesale adoption of St Augustine was not uncontroversial, for a range of perhaps predictable reasons. Augustine was a father of the Church, author of a rule observed by several orders. Moreover, whereas the Carmelites' claim to Elijah involved no surviving body or relics, the body of Augustine was in San Pietro in Ciel d'Oro Pavia, a long-established house of Augustinian regular canons. The canons were justifiably reluctant to allow any other claims to their saint. In 1326 the friars, led by their prior general, Guglielmo da Cremona, nonetheless requested permission to establish a house near the tomb. In 1327 they were successful: John XXII issued *Veneranda sanctorum patrum*, acknowledging that they should be permitted to 'sing with greater joy and intimacy' at the place where they believed the relics of their 'teacher, father, general and head, Augustine, were buried' and so to share the custody of the body of Augustine.[21] John set out the terms by which the two orders were to carve up rights and responsibilities in the basilica concerning the Office, burials, confession and oblations. He also asserted the prior right of the superior of the canons to preside on feast days such as Christmas, Easter or the feasts of Augustine. Notwithstanding these precautions, conflict broke out between the friars and canons almost immediately and, despite a legal settlement in 1331, rumbled on for centuries.[22]

Veneranda sanctorum patrum also had a powerful but certainly unforeseen impact on the historians of the order and their opponents. John XXII was simply evoking the same sort of Augustinian paternity ascribed to all those who observed the Augustinian rule. Within the order of friars, however, this coincided with the growth in the early fourteenth century of a tradition claiming Augustine as both patron and founder of the order. The Carmelites had been inspired to define and record the origins and history of their order by the challenge to their existence at the Second Council of Lyons (1274). The Austin Friars faced similar questions over their legitimacy, but the dates of extant written claims suggest that they were prompted to write only by the struggle to obtain custody of Augustine's relics in Pavia half a century later.

[20] Illustrated in A. Zumkeller, *Hermann von Schildesche O.E.S.A.* (Würzburg, 1957), after p. 92.
[21] Alonso I, 397–8; Empoli, 195–202; *Bullarium Lateranense* (Rome, 1727), 94–99, 95.
[22] K. Walsh, 'Wie ein Bettelorden zu (s)einem Gründer kam. Fingierte Traditionen um die Entstehung der Augustiner-Eremiten', in *Fälschungen im Mittelalter* 5 (Hannover, 1988), pp. 585–610, and K. Elm, 'Augustinus canonicus – Augustinus eremita. A quattrocento cause célèbre', in *Christianity and the Renaissance. Image and Religious Imagination in the Quattrocento*, ed. T. Verdon and J. Henderson (Syracuse, 1990), pp. 83–107. Saak, *High Way to Heaven*, pp. 166–74, now gives the fullest account of the early stages of the dispute.

Legends and earlier texts about Augustine, such as Possidius's short *Vita* or Jacopo da Voragine's *Legenda aurea*, as well as the saint's own *Confessions*, were reworked both to assert and to shape the self-perception of the Augustinian Hermits. The earliest accounts are a *Vita* of Augustine written by an otherwise unidentified prior of Santo Spirito in Florence (by 1331) and an anonymous *Initium sive processus ordinis Heremitarum sancti Augustini* (*c.* 1330) which may also have been written in Florence. A third text, which survives in the same manuscript as the first two, was produced in Paris in 1332, by Friar Nicola di Alessandria, a master of theology who may have intended it as a sermon for the friars in the *studium*. Nicola divides his work into two parts, first praising Augustine and then giving an account of the origins of his order, which picks up on and sometimes embellishes the accounts of the two earlier texts.[23] His version of their history begins with the originators of monasticism, Paul the Hermit and Anthony, some of whose followers allegedly came to Italy and established hermitages in Tuscany. There they eventually received their rule from Augustine at the hermitage of Centumcelle. After a short description of Augustine's career in Africa, Nicola then turns to the history of the hermits in Italy, the translation of the body of Augustine to Pavia, the eventual union of the various groups scattered across central Italy (triggered by a vision of Augustine seen by Pope Alexander IV) and the beginnings of the move into the cities. He takes the story down to the moment when the order acquired custody of Augustine's body and ends with a list of proofs that the saint was a hermit and not (by implication) a regular canon. This account sustained his assertion that unlike the canons regular or the Dominicans, who had simply constructed new orders using Augustine's rule, the hermit friars were the saint's direct progeny, created by him (*sumus filii immediate ab eo geniti*). They also pre-dated the canons regular. He repeated and embellished two claims made in the *Initium* which further promoted the special status of the order. Thus he asserted that Francis of Assisi had originally lived with an Augustinian community near Pisa, perhaps even as one of them, before obtaining permission to leave for a stricter observance. He also identified the hermit friars with the prophecies of Joachim of Fiore on the rise of an order of black-belted religious who seem new but are not, who preach the faith and strive to imitate the life of the angels, burning with zeal for God.[24] Neither claim would endear his mendicant contemporaries to the order of hermit friars.

Nicola's text is brief and may not have circulated widely, but it seems to have been known to Heinrich of Friemar, who produced his *De origine et progressu ordinis fratrum eremitarum S. Augustini* in Erfurt in 1334. Heinrich

---

[23] B. Rano, 'Las dos primeras obras conocidas sobre el origen de la orden agustiniana', *AA* 45 (1982), pp. 329–76.

[24] Ibid. See also M. Reeves, 'Joachimist Expectations in the Order of Augustinian Hermits', *Recherches de théologie ancienne et médiévale* 25 (1958), pp. 111–41.

again integrated the recent history of the order into a longer perspective in which Augustine was identified as the founder and father of the friars. He also worked on some of Nicola's formulations, such as the papal vision of Augustine, which in Heinrich's account inspired Alexander both to unite the hermits and to direct them towards preaching and pastoral care. As already asserted in the version of Nicola, Augustine appeared to Alexander with almost no body so that, Heinrich explained, the body was to be filled out by the members of the order, literally the limbs of his body. As Eric Saak has argued, for Heinrich, the Augustinian Hermits became 'the embodiment of Augustine'.[25] This was also potentially a forceful response to the claims of the Canons Regular in Pavia. It is conceivably significant in this context that Heinrich's text was the basis for a fresco cycle of the life of Augustine dressed as a hermit painted in the Eremitani church in Padua by Guariento d'Arpo some time between 1334 and 1368.[26]

Perhaps the best known of the early histories was Jordan of Quedlinburg's *Liber vitasfratrum* (completed by 1357). A lector and successful preacher who had worked in Erfurt with Heinrich and later became provincial prior of Saxony-Thuringia, Jordan's early work included a *Vita* of Augustine (before 1343). This developed the ideas present in Friemar and introduced a further pseudo-Augustinian text, the *Sermons to Brothers in Hermitages* (*Sermones ad fratres in eremo*).[27] The alleged words of Augustine himself could now be brought to bear on the hermits' case. In his *Liber vitasfratrum*, which made extensive use of the earlier *Vita*, Jordan's main purpose was, as his title suggests, to explain and describe the life of the friars. In particular, as he told his dedicatee, Johannes Hiltalingen of Basel (then a lector at Avignon) he intended to explain how to be a true son of Augustine through perfect observance of his rule. Like Nicola and Friemar, he was keen to strengthen the friars' claim to Augustine and introduced the story of a vision seen by Guglielmo da Cremona which reflects awareness of the dispute in Pavia. According to Jordan, after the prior general had petitioned for custody of the body, Augustine appeared to Guglielmo and a group of friars in the form of a raised episcopal tomb figure in a church covered in dust, a sign that it was not being properly cared for by another (unspecified) order. The target would have been lost on few of his readers. The figure of the bishop woke up and spoke to Guglielmo and other brethren who were with him, revealing his identity as Augustine. Less than two months later the papal letter (*Veneranda sanctorum patrum*) entrusting the hermits with shared custody of the body reached the order.[28]

---

[25] Saak, *High Way to Heaven*, p. 218.

[26] L. Bourdua, 'De origine et progressu ordinis fratrum heremitarum: Guariento and the Eremitani in Padua', *Papers of the British School at Rome* 66 (1998), pp. 177–92.

[27] Saak, *High Way to Heaven*, appendix D provides a description and transcription of the *Vita*.

[28] See most recently *Hermits and History. Art and the Augustinian Order in Early Renaissance Italy*, ed. L. Bourdua and A. Dunlop (forthcoming, Aldershot, 2006).

Such legitimatory claims were also furthered in the iconography of the order, which became increasingly distinctive. As well as the cycle in Padua showing Augustine as a friar, in mid-century the friary in Pavia itself commissioned a new tomb for the saint, which highlights his roles as both bishop-saint and founding father of the order.[29] A century later, Benozzo Gozzoli completed a cycle of seventeen scenes from the life of Augustine for the church of the friars in San Gimignano (Tuscany) where, once again, the saint is depicted as a hermit friar.[30] Augustine was also sometimes portrayed giving the rule to both friars and nuns, as in a Missal now in Toulouse produced in 1362 which shows him giving the text to both men and women, all in black habits. Later in the fourteenth century the 'friar' Augustine was also portrayed in images which paralleled those of the 'Triumph' of the Dominican St Thomas Aquinas: allegorising the victory and inspiration of learning.[31]

Such claims to a special relationship could not be left unchallenged by other followers of the rule of Augustine. In 1354 a canon regular, Durand of Aln, wrote a refutation of the hermits' claims, aiming to prove that Augustine 'is not the father of the Hermits alone, nor is he their patron alone . . . furthermore the blessed Augustine never wore the habit of these brother hermits . . .'. Instead, the canons claimed that Augustine had given his rule to them, thereby creating the order of canons, whereas the hermits had been founded only by Guglielmo da Malavalle. The controversy haunted the two orders over the next two centuries, ramifying into disputes over how to portray the saint. In 1474, a plan to erect a statue of Augustine on the roof of Milan Cathedral initially foundered on the question of how he should be dressed: in the tunic of the canons or the scapular and belt of the hermit friars? A veritable pamphlet war ensued, profiting from the arrival of printing and involving members of both orders as far afield as England and Germany. The canons regular argued for Augustine as the 'form and norm of canonical life'. As Elm has argued, the dispute in practice went much deeper than the habit or tunic of Augustine. It was about 'how to live the "perfect" Christian life', each side claiming that their own spirituality was superior, the truly apostolic life (*vita vere apostolica*).[32] In spite of numerous appeals to the Curia, the dispute was not to be settled before the Council of Trent and indeed took on still broader dimensions thereafter.

[29] L. Bourdua, 'Entombing the Founder. St Augustine of Hippo' (forthcoming, in *Hermits and History*).

[30] D. Cole Ahl, 'Benozzo Gozzoli's Frescoes of the Life of Saint Augustine in San Gimignano: Their Meaning in Context', *Artibus et historiae* 13 (1986), pp. 35–53.

[31] D. Hansen, *Das Bild des Ordenslehrers und die Allegorie des Wissens. Ein gemaltes Programm der Augustiner* (Berlin, 1995).

[32] Elm, 'Augustinus canonicus – Augustinus eremita', pp. 86–8.

CHAPTER SIX

Reform and the Observance

Throughout the history of the order some of the friars were concerned to encourage a purer observance of the rule and the ideals of poverty; in the fourteenth century some even supported the extreme position of the Franciscan Spirituals. The first extant register of a prior general, that of Gregorio da Rimini (1357–8), is less radical but opens with *Ordinationes* addressed to the provincial priors in which he exhorted them to reform the observance in their areas, insisting for example on the importance of attending the Office, eating together in the refectory, supervising young friars, and attending sermons preached in the community. It was to be followed by numerous letters to individuals and provincials directing them to reform particular abuses.

There were certainly serious difficulties in the order by this date. A general decline in the number of students was in large part due to the Black Death. The plague of 1348 left numerous communities decimated: in the province of Saxony-Thuringia alone, the prior provincial Jordan of Quedlinburg reported 244 deaths. Such losses may have encouraged inappropriate recruitment. In 1351 the general chapter relaxed the usual qualification requirements in an attempt to make up the numbers. Seven years later, nonetheless, in response to a request from the provincial prior of Spain, the prior general Gregorio da Rimini was still able to send him only one non-Spanish lector, Francesco di Amelia, protesting that he could not even fill all the vacant positions in Italy. Numerous *studia* remained without sufficient teachers and examinations were now in the hands of local regent masters rather than the general chapter. It is probably for related reasons that in 1357 the general chapter approved a regulation allowing those who could not speak Latin, but were otherwise qualified, to be ordained as priests. The privileged position of masters within the order meant that some aspired to the position without the appropriate years of study: in the mid-fourteenth century seculars complained about 'wax masters', men who had obtained their status by papal dispensation (a problem not limited to the Augustinians). In 1400 the general chapter excommunicated those who had procured the *magisterium* through a papal dispensation, but the practice continued.

A further difficulty was caused by divisions in the Church. In 1379 schism was introduced into the order when the Avignonese Pope Clement VII appointed as prior general the theologian Johannes Hiltalingen of Basel

(†1392) (earlier the dedicatee of Jordan of Quedlinburg's *Vitasfratrum*), in opposition to Bonaventura da Padova who supported the Roman obedience and Urban VI.[1] Remarkably, Johannes had begun as a supporter of Urban VI but had swapped sides. For the next four decades the order, like all those with international networks, was split along the lines of the two papal obediences. The registers of the 'Avignonese' priors general have disappeared, so a great deal of information about France or Spain in these years is now lost, but Hiltalingen was a powerful advocate of the Avignonese cause and a keen reformer, promoting the foundation of new houses in France and acting against *fratres bullati*, friars who had become papal chaplains and therefore released from the discipline of the order. The next 'Roman' general, Bartolomeo da Venezia (1385–1400), condemned Hiltalingen (who became bishop of Lombez in 1389) and in 1391 even forbade his own friars to attend the university of Paris, thereby rewarding the Spanish and French with easier promotion to the *magisterium*. Bartolomeo also placed houses in Aquitaine under an English friar, Robert Waldeby, removing them from the province of Toulouse. Conflict continued under Bartolomeo and Hiltalingen's successors. For three years after the failure of the Council of Pisa to elect a single pope (1409), there were even three priors general, two in the obedience of Alexander V and one under Benedict XIII. The chaos was only finally resolved in 1419, two years after the papal schism had been settled with the election of Pope Martin V (1417–31), when the general chapter meeting at Asti (northern Italy) accepted the resignation of both priors general. The meeting was presided over by Johannes Zachariä, provincial of Saxony-Thuringia. A key figure in the condemnation of Jan Hus, Zachariä used his casting vote to effect the election of Agostino Favaroni (1419–31), formerly a master of theology in Florence. Favaroni immediately appointed one of his predecessors, Thomas Fabri, as his *socius* and later his vicar in Aragon and Castile, while the other, Jerome Paul, was given complete control over his own mother friary in Pistoia.

The observance

While the late fourteenth century witnessed crises in recruitment and the emergence of various distortions of the original mendicant model, probably encouraged by the lack of consolidated authority in the order, the spiritual life of religious orders was animated by a wave of reform which resulted in new 'observant' congregations over much of Europe. In the most famous case, the Franciscan observants were eventually entirely separate from their 'conventual' brothers. By contrast, in the order of Austin Friars, the new 'observants' remained subject to the prior general. If the majority of friars

---

[1] See F. Roth, 'The Great Schism and the Augustinian Order', *Augustiniana* 8 (1958), pp. 281–98.

in a community wished to adopt a reformed observance they could request permission to become autonomous from the province in which they resided and subject only to the prior general and a vicar appointed by him. Although they were increasingly independent, the continued connection gave the reformers direct influence on the order as a whole and they were in most cases favoured by the order's leaders.

Apart from a self-evident and generic emphasis on reform based on observance of the rule without dispensations, it is not easy to trace the early motives of the early Augustinian observants since, as Walsh has noted, the first documents usually concern the introduction of the observance and its approval by the priors general, not the reasons for these decisions. Moreover, in the case of the Austin Friars a return to origins might well be interpreted either as a return to the withdrawal of the hermit life or to the life of study, preaching and pastoral care of the mendicants. A Milanese friar-humanist Andrea Biglia (†1435) provides the most eloquent early explanation of the observance in the order. Between 1429 and 1435, during a period of retreat at Lecceto while teaching at Siena, Biglia wrote the first treatise on its character for a former student. In his emphasis on the need for a return to a more faithful observance, he underlined the particular dangers of *studia* such as Siena and Paris where standards of observance were inevitably affected by the demands of university life. Hermitages were the most promising ground for reform, since they allowed a combination of devotion with study of the wisdom of antiquity.[2] Ascetical monasticism was to be combined with learning, a factor that, as Elm has argued, helps to explain why the Augustinians produced so many friar-humanists.[3] Biglia himself was an active member of humanist circles, having taught at Santo Spirito in Florence where he had encountered men such as Leonardo Bruni and the Camaldolese Ambrogio Traversari and later in Bologna, where he enjoyed associations with Leon Battista Alberti, Filelfo and others. His was an intellectual approach to pastoral care, which led to conflict with the popular observant Franciscan preacher Bernardino of Siena over expressions of charismatic piety. Whereas the Franciscan observants emphasised poverty above all, the Augustinians focused on an inner existence of prayer and meditation, following the common life. This was to be achieved by an insistence on attending the refectory and canonical hours together and the removal of all special provisions, dispensations or the *peculium* (personal property).

---

[2] See R. Arbesmann, 'Andrea Biglia. Augustinian Friar and Humanist (†1435)', *AA* 28 (1965), pp. 154–218, who includes an edition of the text. See also K. Walsh, 'The Augustinian Observance in Siena in the Age of Sta Caterina and San Bernardino', in *Atti del simposio internazionale caterinianobernardiniano*, ed. D. Maffei and P. Nardi (Siena, 1982), pp. 939–50, 945–6.

[3] K. Elm, 'Mendikanten und Humanisten im Florenz des Tre- und Quattrocento. Zum Problem der Legitimierung humanistischer Studien in den Bettelorden', in *Die Humanisten in ihrer politischen und sozialen Umwelt*, ed. O. Herding and R. Stupperich (Boppard, 1976), pp. 51–85, 58.

The first of the Augustinian observant congregations was formed from Lecceto in 1385–7, supervised closely by the 'Roman' prior general Bartolomeo da Venezia, who appointed two friars to oversee the reform. It had acquired a reputation for holiness in part due to the association of the Tuscan hermitages with Augustine, which had, as we have seen, attracted figures such as Catherine of Siena and the English friar William Flete. By the end of the century Santa Maria del Popolo in Rome had joined Lecceto and though it was never a large congregation, other key houses followed, creating their own constitutions, distinct from those of the order as a whole.

As in the thirteenth century, so in the fifteenth, Italy dominated the order and the observant movement. Several congregations owed their beginning to the inspiration of an individual, charismatic preacher. In Liguria, the congregation (1471–3) came to be known as Battistini after their founder and first vicar Giovanni Battista Poggi (†1497). His insistence on poverty was much closer to that of the Franciscans than other Augustinian observants, but after his death the prior general insisted that they conform to the Augustinian norm. At the other end of Italy, the congregation of Calabria (1509), inspired by Francesco da Zumpano, began with just five houses: Aprigliano, Soverato, Nocera, Francavilla and Bombile, but, in spite of problems of discipline, had grown to fifteen by 1539. Other Italian congregations were formed in Naples (1421), Perugia (1422), Santa Maria di Monte Ortone near Padua (1433–6), Lombardy (1439) and Deliceto in Puglia (1487). Of these Lombardy was the most extensive with nearly eighty houses by 1539, including nunneries closely affiliated to it and sharing all papal privileges, such as Santa Monica in Crema. The vicar general of the congregation served as *ex officio* visitator and superior for the women.

Although only three of the congregations were established outside the peninsula, the Italian example and the activities of the priors general were major impetuses for the spread of the observance elsewhere. The first Irish observant house was founded at Banada, county Sligo (1423) with the licence of the prior general Agostino Favaroni. Twenty-two years later the pope gave the community an indulgence for the feast of Corpus Christi. By the sixteenth century eight of the communities in Ireland were observant. They were perhaps encouraged by the opportunity observantism presented to express Gaelic revivalism and escape the hegemony of Anglo-Irish superiors,[4] but they never formed a separate congregation. The congregation in Saxony (1419), to which Martin Luther later belonged, was again strongly supported by Favaroni, who authorised the first observants to receive friars from other houses. Two leading figures, Heinrich Zolter (vicar 1432–58) and Andreas Proles (vicar 1461–7 and 1473–1503), had studied in

---

[4]   B. Bradshaw, *The Dissolution of the Religious Orders in Ireland under Henry VIII* (Cambridge, 1974), pp. 9–10.

Italy and brought ideas back north of the Alps with them. Italy may also have inspired Juan de Alarcón (†1451), who had been a lector in Florence in 1420 before introducing a stricter observance in Castile in 1431 (though houses are already documented from 1412).[5] Like most of the congregations, this Spanish observance began very small, with just two houses, at Villanubla de los Santos (Palencia) and Santa María del Pilar (Avila), soon followed by Dueñas (Palencia), Valladolid and the nunnery of Santa María de Gracia in Madrigal de las Altas Torres.[6] Alarcón travelled to Rome to obtain the approval of the prior general Gerardo da Rimini and Pope Eugenius IV (1438) for a separate congregation under a vicar general and was himself appointed to this position for life. Salamanca joined the congregation in 1454 and was quickly its most important house. Thereafter growth came to a standstill until the end of the century when, encouraged by the support of the Catholic kings Ferdinand and Isabella, the observance extended across much of their kingdom, led by friar Giovanni Battista who had been sent by the prior general from the Carbonara congregation of Naples.[7] Although Giovanni Battista was deprived of office in 1505, in 1511 an agreement originally prepared in Toledo in 1504 was confirmed, briefly uniting all the houses in Spain, both observant and conventual, thereby removing the autonomy of the vicar. It was an arrangement which was to last until 1527, when the houses were again divided into two provinces, Castile and Andalusia. By this date there were also observant congregations in Dalmatia (1511) and Sardinia (1512), which included houses in Mallorca, Menorca and four in Spain, but no observant movement ever took root in England.

The success of the observance certainly stemmed from spontaneous initiatives, driven by members of the order themselves, but also benefited from the support of popes, councils and kings, pious individuals such as Catherine of Siena and learned humanists intent on reform. Not all observants were, however, engaged in intellectual pursuits. Gutiérrez notes that in 1439 the Spanish congregation denied the claim of their conventual brethren (*fratres claustrales*) that they were simple untaught idiots, but in the process they rejected higher learning:

> because by God's grace nearly all our priests know how to read and sing and understand what they read, and there are many among us who are lettered and good preachers, although they take no interest in academic qualifications.[8]

5   See L. Alvarez Gutiérrez, *El movimento 'observante' agustiniano en España y su culminación en tiempo de los Reyes Católicos* (Rome, 1978).

6   T. Vinas Roman, 'El convento agustiniano extramuros de Madrigal de las Altas Torres', *Ciudad de Dios* 214 (2001), pp. 705–32.

7   See L. Alvarez, 'Fusión de la provincia de Castile o de España con la congregación homónima, culminación de la Reforma "Observante"', *Revista agustiniana* 12 (1971), pp. 371–405.

8   Gutiérrez, 'Los estudios', p. 101.

Scepticism about learning amongst Spanish observants was obviously still evident in the early 1450s when some friars of the house in Salamanca were reluctant to join the observance because of the threat to the continuation of studies. The ensuing divisions in the community were only resolved when the prior general intervened in 1453, insisting on the importance of both.

In December 1445, Eugenius IV and the cardinal protector had instructed the vicars and rectors of the various Italian observant congregations then existing to hold a chapter in Santa Maria del Popolo, Rome, and choose one vicar to unite them. In practice, under his successor Nicholas V (1447–55), the Italian congregations met at Montespecchio and decided to keep their separate vicars, and to hold their own chapters annually or every other year. Decisions of these chapters were subject to the approval of the prior general, but in some areas priors provincial were opposed to the observants, who became exempt from their authority. The hostility of the German provincials contributed to the limited early growth of the Saxon congregation to just five houses by 1458. In 1460 the provincial of Saxony-Thuringia briefly succeeded in having the congregation placed under his authority, but it was a dead letter. There were also frequent controversies between the vicars of the various congregations and the priors general of the order keen to maintain their authority over the increasingly autonomous observant congregations. In the Saxon congregation, the vicar, Andreas Proles came into conflict with the priors general over issues such as the removal of houses into the observance and refusal to allow friars to leave.

Already in the 1430s tensions between conventuals and observants had led to insistence by the general chapter that all *observantinos* (probably, as Alvarez notes, a disrespectful term) were to pay the usual annual taxes (*collecta*) to provincial priors. These instructions were renewed in 1465 and again later in the century, when, in Spain for example, there was an attempt to prevent the takeover of conventual houses by the *observantinos*. The general chapter in Siena in 1486 also tried to reimpose the authority of the provinces over observant houses, but later generals continued their support for the observants: Giacomo di Aquila (1470–6) renewed privileges issued by Gerardo da Rimini (1436) and although controversy continued, particularly over jurisdiction and fiscal matters, his successors increasingly backed the spread of the observance.

In spite of a feeling of superiority among the reformers, there was also a problem with standards in some houses of the observance itself in the later fifteenth century: as well as the reforming activities of Giovanni Battista in Spain, renewed reform measures were imposed at Lecceto in 1473 and in the congregation of S. Giovanni a Carbonara in Naples in 1485, amongst others. In 1499 the will of the Dominican bishop of Palencia, Alonso de Burgos, referred to the recent reform of the Augustinian observants in Valladolid and assigned them a legacy to help them maintain the observance.

The observant movement was to produce numerous prominent and learned figures in the order. Indeed from the mid-fifteenth century it was common for the prior general to be elected from one of the observant congregations. Before his election as prior general in 1497, Mariano da Genazzano had been vicar general of the congregation of Lecceto and then of the Lombard congregation as prior of Santa Maria del Popolo in Rome, which had been transferred to the Lombards by Sixtus IV in 1472, prompting a major rebuilding of the church.[9] Mariano was keen to prevent further divisions, and at the general chapter which elected him he introduced measures to re-establish uniform practices across the order. He was, however, opposed by the superiors of the Lombard congregation, who obtained reconfirmation of their autonomy from Pope Alexander VI and his premature death halted any further action. Mariano's successor, Graziano Ventura da Foligno (vicar 1499–1501, general 1501–4), likewise planned to re-establish the regular life throughout the order, but with little effect.

The year 1506 saw the election of the humanist scholar Giles of Viterbo (†1532), a leading preacher and reformer.[10] A friend of humanists such as Pontano, Ficino, Bembo and Manuzio, he combined the skills of a scholar with those of a diplomat and orator, the humanism of the Renaissance with the zeal of the reformer. Already before his election Giles had worked successfully for the spread of the observance and in 1503 identified himself as a member of Lecceto. He also laboured to persuade the priory in Viterbo to join the Lecceto congregation (1505). In the same years he wrote *De Ilicetana familia*, addressed to the community at Lecceto, which evokes the spiritual heights of the rural eremitic life.[11] Like his predecessors, as prior general 1506–17, he set out to abolish abuses and re-establish uniform observance. He was close to Pope Julius II, and gave the opening oration for that pope's Fifth Lateran Council in 1512, constructed around the programmatic idea that 'men should be changed by religion, not religion by men'. After the pope's death, however, the seculars renewed their attack on mendicant privileges in a furious controversy over their property and exemption from episcopal jurisdiction. Giles's desperate defence of the order undoubtedly drove his desire for renewal: in letters to the friars he warned that unless they undertook true reform, they would lose their exempt status.

Giles was a keen promoter of the ideals represented at Lecceto and his registers as general are littered with references to *reformatio* (reform) and the *vita communis* (common life).[12] He was even prepared to bring in the secular

---

[9]   D. Gutiérrez, 'Testi e note su Mariano da Genazzano (†1498)', *AA* 32 (1969), pp. 117–204.

[10] J. W. O'Malley, *Giles of Viterbo on Church and Reform. A Study in Renaissance Thought* (Leiden, 1968).

[11] See F. X. Martin, 'Giles of Viterbo and the Monastery of Lecceto: The Making of a Reformer', *AA* 25 (1962), pp. 225–53.

[12] O'Malley, *Giles of Viterbo*, p. 150.

arm if needed to punish delinquent friars. Like all reformers in the order, he was determined to restore the common life according to the early traditions, down to relatively minute details. His letters refer to the need to avoid using linen instead of wool for habits, the importance of silence, and of eating in common, or always having a friar companion and behaving appropriately when outside the enclosure. He was also concerned about financial affairs, illicit alienation of Church property and, of course, inappropriate contact with nuns.

Like Mariano, Giles was keen to re-establish the central power of the general over the order and in particular over those of the observant congregations which had become virtually independent. He was equally determined to maintain the order's privileges and made careful use of visitators as outsiders to reform lax houses. Under his leadership there were also the beginnings of serious reorganisation of study in the order. His immediate successor as prior general, Gabriele della Volta (1518–37), described his proposal as impossible, but Egidio's plans formed the basis for the reforms of Girolamo Seripando (†1563), prior general 1539–51. New statutes were issued for study and in 1539–42 Seripando himself ensured that these and his own reform measures were applied during visitations of the provinces of Italy, France, Portugal and Spain. He was later the principal Augustinian theologian at the third session of the Council of Trent, 1562–3.[13]

In spite of the efforts of reformers such as Giles of Viterbo and Seripando, the sixteenth century witnessed divisions in the order which were to resonate for centuries. Indeed, it was from within the Augustinian observant movement that one of the most powerful voices of the Protestant Reformation was to come: Friar Martin Luther, originally a master of theology in the Saxon congregation. Luther presented his theses against indulgences to the pope in 1519 while still a friar, left the order in 1525 and married Katherina von Bora, a former nun. His writings against the satanic papacy were a complete reversal of the Augustinian position of the late Middle Ages. Many of his former brethren preached and taught against him. Others sympathised: the vicar-general of the Saxon congregation, Wenzel Link (†1547), resigned from the order in 1523, married and became a Lutheran preacher at Altenberg. Two friars, Hendrik Vos and Johann van den Esschen from the observant house in Antwerp, became the first martyrs of the Reformation period, burnt as heretics in Brussels after refusing to recant their Lutheran views. An account of their execution was printed in sixteen editions in seven different German towns in the same year.[14] Luther himself praised them in a hymn.

In the year of Luther's death, 1546, the Council of Trent was in session and

---

[13] H. Jedin, *Girolamo Seripando. Sein Leben und Denken im Geisteskampf des 16. Jahrhunderts*, 2 vols (Würzburg, reprinted 1984).

[14] B. S. Gregory, *Salvation at Stake. Christian Martyrdom in Early Modern Europe* (Cambridge, Mass., 1999), p. 143.

the Roman Church was beginning the task of forming a new 'post-Tridentine' identity. Unlike many other regulars, the Augustinian Hermit Friars and nuns survived this transition, driven by new leaders and both old and new concerns. The legacy of the medieval friars was to remain a powerful presence in the life of the modern order.

PART THREE

The Orders Discontinued after Lyons, 1274

Unlike the other friars discussed in this book, the Friars of the Penitence of Jesus Christ and the friars of the Blessed Mary, popularly known as the Sack Friars and the Pied Friars, did not survive long. Whereas the Carmelites and the Augustinians were able to resist the force of sanction at the Second Council of Lyons in 1274, these orders succumbed. Their historiography failed to attract much attention from early modern antiquarians and has been largely ignored by the confessionally driven works on orders still existing in the contemporary world. Since neither substantial archives nor texts survive, only a very piece-meal account of their histories can now be attempted. Each reference is a valuable, but sometimes problematic, piece in a puzzle that cannot be complete, though new sources for individual houses will undoubtedly come to light. Even so, their histories powerfully demonstrate both the wide diffusion of the ideals of mendicancy initiated with the Franciscans and Dominicans, and the newly acquired force of centralism in the Church, focused on the pope, whose constitutions, approved in a general council, put an end to successful and popular institutions. They also provide an uncommon angle on the life of the thirteenth-century Church in Latin Europe: what it meant to fail.

CHAPTER ONE

The Friars of the Penitence of Jesus Christ, or Sack Friars

The Friars of the Penitence of Jesus Christ first appeared in Provence at some time in the 1240s.[1] The year 1248 is often given as a precise foundation date, on the grounds that the fullest narrative, provided by the Franciscan Salimbene of Parma, is in a section of his chronicle describing that year.[2] The phrasing, however, only specifies that in that year Salimbene himself was in Hyères visiting Hugh of Digne, a fellow Franciscan, and does not specify that the order was initiated at that point. Another Franciscan, Thomas of Eccleston (*c.* 1258), reports instead that the order was founded at the time of the (First) Council of Lyons, held in 1245.[3]

Salimbene records that two laymen were so impressed by the preaching of Hugh of Digne that they tried to enter his order. Although Hugh's high standing meant that, according to Salimbene, he had the authority to admit brothers, he instead told them to 'go into the woods and learn to eat roots, for tribulations are at hand'.[4] The two men therefore went and had multi-coloured cloaks made (which Salimbene compared to those originally worn by the early servants of the order of St Clare), began begging for bread like the other mendicants and

---

[1]   The official title of the order in papal bulls is 'Ordo/fratres de penitentia Iesu Christi', but other contemporary sources identified them by a range of names, including 'fratres saccati/sacciti/saccorum/de sacchis'. For a fuller list of the Latin variants see R. W. Emery, 'The Friars of the Sack' (as above, p. 111 n. 28), p. 324n. In Marseilles and Avignon they were called 'fratres Fenoilletis/Fenolhetis', the result of an early association with Mont-Fenouillet near Hyères. The name was later used for the quarter where they settled in Marseilles. See P.-A. Amargier, 'Les Frères de la Pénitence de Jésus Christ ou du Sac', *Provence historique* 15 (1965), pp. 158–67, 163n, 165. Other vernacular names include 'frères sachets/des Sacs, Zackbroeders, broeders van den zacke, frati saccati, Sackbrüder'.

[2]   Salimbene de Adam, *Chronica/Cronica*, I, pp. 385–8; G. M. Giacomozzi, *L'ordine della penitenza di Gesù Cristo, contributo alla storia della spiritualità del secolo XIII: excerpta ex dissertatione ad lauream in facultate historiae ecclesiasticae Pontificiae Universitatis Gregorianae* (Vicenza, 1962), p. 11n., argues that this marks the origins of the order.

[3]   In a marginal note to Thomas de Eccleston, 'De adventu minorum' (as above, p. 24 n.3), p. 72, also ed. F. Liebermann, *MGH SS XXVIII* (Hannover, 1888), p. 569: 'fratres de Penitentia Iesu Christi . . . . qui in Provincia, tempore concilii Lugdunensis ortum habuerunt, per quemdam novicium qui expulsus erat'.

[4]   In official Franciscan sources authority to admit new brethren was strictly limited. See, for example, Gregory IX, *Quo elongati*, 1230, now most conveniently in *Francis of Assisi. Early Documents*, ed. R. J. Armstrong *et al.*, 3 vols (St Bonaventure, NY, 1999), I, pp. 570–5.

copying his own order: 'for we and the Friars Preacher taught all men how to beg'. Their numbers immediately expanded and the Friars Minor in Provence ironically and inaccurately called them *Boscarioli* (men of the woods).

Salimbene, who was himself from northern Italy, reports that the Sack Friars 'poured into the cities of Italy and took places in which to live, copying every practice of the Friars Minor and Preacher in preaching, hearing confession and begging'. This, he suggests, put no little burden on seculars, leading a laywoman from Modena, Iulitta de Adelhardis, who was devoted to the Friars Minor, to joke when she saw these new friars, that the city already had 'so many sacks (*sacculos*) for emptying granaries that they hardly needed the Order of the Sack (*saccatorum*)'. Such ridicule, underlined by wordplay, is latent throughout Salimbene's brief account. He was very ready to criticise those who copied the Franciscans and Dominicans, and the Sack Friars were a sitting target, since he was writing after the Council of Lyons, which had effectively disbanded the order, although large numbers of friars were still around. In his account of the council itself he makes it clear that he shared the view that the proliferation of mendicant orders should be halted so as to 'avoid overburdening the Christian people'. He can hardly be considered a neutral source for the order's character or spirituality. Nor is his information all necessarily reliable: he suggests for example that a member of the order was later archbishop of Arles, though this does not appear to fit the biography of any of the known prelates.[5] Nonetheless Salimbene identifies some of the salient features of the new order and seems to have found them impressive. Their life was indeed based on explicit imitation of the Friars Minor and Friars Preacher. All medieval religious orders adopted some elements of previous forms of regular life and were increasingly encouraged to do so in this period by papal legislation; it is clear that the Franciscans and above all the Dominicans had become the primary model. Like them, the new order quickly moved into the towns, engaged in pastoral care and relied on begging to support themselves. At first, however, if Salimbene is to be believed, they chose to withdraw from the world (caricatured as 'going into the woods'). The location of at least one of their early communities, on the island of Porquerolles off Toulon, and the name attributed to them in Marseilles and Avignon – *Fenolhet/Fenouilhet*, derived from Mont-Fenouillet near Hyères[6] – may indeed mean that there was an eremitical element in

---

[5]   C. Eubel, *Hierarchia Catholica medii aevii*, I (Münster, 1898), p. 104, lists no individual with such links. Salimbene's phrasing links this man to Athenulf: *Chronica*, ed. Scalia, pp. 387–8, lines 25–30, 'Primus ordinis saccatorum dictus est Raimundus Attanulfi . . . et fuit miles in seculo et fuit in ordine fratrum Minorum, sed in novitiatu fuit licentiatus et emissus de Ordine quia infirmus erat. Filium habuit in ordine saccatorum, qui postea fuit Arelatensis archiepiscopus.' This is presumably also the source for Robert Burns's statement that Athenulf was 'married and had at least one child' (Burns, 'The Friars of the Sack in Barcelona', *Anuario de estudios medievales* 28 (1998), pp. 419–35, 421), but the use of *filium* (son) need not imply either prior marriage or a blood relative.

[6]   See above, n. 1.

the early movement. Like several contemporary groups they began by doing penance in poverty and solitude, but later adopted the life of mendicants engaged in pastoral care. A parallel transition can be traced in the life of the early Servites, a lay fraternity of seven men who withdrew to Monte Senario, north-east of Florence, to pursue a life of penitential solitude and contemplation, probably in the early 1240s, but acquired approval as a quasi-mendicant order.[7] The hermits preceding the creation of the Austin Friars, in their distinct groups, experienced a similar transition from 'desert' solitude to urban mission.[8] Hugh of Digne's warning 'for tribulations are at hand', is typical of his Joachite eschatology, and it is not unlikely that a desire to prepare for the Last Judgement through penance and withdrawal drove the early friars.[9] Salimbene was a keen Joachite himself in his early career, but it is also possible that he put the lapidary phrase 'tribulations are at hand' into the mouth of Hugh as a means to further ridicule a competing order: the tribulations were to come, but in the form of the Council of Lyons.[10]

Salimbene also draws our attention to the importance of dress as an identifier. His suggestion that the Friars of the Sack wore multi-coloured or perhaps even chequered cloaks, as implied by the reference to the early habit of the followers of Clare of Assisi, may of course be satirical.[11] A multi-coloured habit would have required expensive dyed cloth. On the other hand, the Carmelites at this date still wore striped habits, and it may indeed be that the Sack Friars too had a parti-coloured habit. It is less likely that they wore expensive tunics under their sack cloaks as Salimbene also claimed. Such accusations of false humility were a convenient way of undermining a religious opponent or competitor. It is more probable, as the English chronicler Matthew Paris observed, that the Friars of the Sack were so named because of the humble sack-like cloth which they wore.[12] It was a standard form of penitential dress and one on which the Dominican Humbert de Romans wrote a model sermon. Like Salimbene he made play on the word sack, but also pointed to the dangers of false humility, perhaps with members of the order in mind:

> for sometimes what is in the sack is different from what is expected: it must be carefully established whether the religious man [wearing] the sack has in him what the sack implies, for in the past men wore the sack for three reasons: to preach penance more effectively . . . for more efficient prayer . . . and to do great penance.[13]

[7] See F. dal Pino, 'Servi di Maria', *DIP* VIII (Rome, 1973), cols 1398–1405, with extensive bibliography.

[8] See above, pp. 71–93.

[9] On Hugh, see T. de Morembert, 'Hugues de Digne', *Dictionnaire de biographie française*, XVII (Paris, 1989), pp. 1494–5, with bibliography.

[10] For Salimbene's career see R. Manselli, 'Adam, Ognibene (Salimbene) de', *Dizionario biografico degli italiani*, I (Rome, 1960), pp. 228–31.

[11] For the potential difficulties of a variegated habit, see above, p. 21.

[12] Matthew Paris, *Chronica Majora*, ed. H. R. Luard, Rerum Britannicarum medii aevi scriptores, V, 57 (London, 1880), p. 621.

[13] Humbert de Romans, 'De eruditione praedicatorum', in *Maxima bibliotheca veterum patrum* XXV

The idea that the friars adopted this particularly humble form of dress is also substantiated by the view of Rutebeuf, a contemporary poet, who commented on their attempts to imitate Christ's 'habit'.[14] The friars may also have gone barefoot, as asserted by a contemporary Austrian poet.[15]

Salimbene tells us that the Franciscans criticised Hugh of Digne for indirectly founding the order of the Sack rather than admitting the laymen who approached him when he might have, a clear indication of the larger order's anxiety about rivals. Hugh died in 1255 and there is no other suggestion of a link with the Sack Friars. Nor is there any evidence that he shared Salimbene's view of them. Rather, the remaining details provided by Salimbene concern Raymond Athenulf, a man he had known and whom he identifies as the first member of the new order. If Hugh was in any way involved it was as a source of inspiration, not leadership.[16] According to the chronicle, Athenulf was a former knight from Hyères in Provence whose first companion was a Friar Bertrand de Manara, a neighbouring settlement.[17] Athenulf had been a Franciscan novice but had not been allowed to profess as a friar because of illness. The same information is confirmed in a blunt reference from Thomas of Eccleston to the foundation of the order of the Sack by a former novice, 'who had been expelled'.[18] Little is currently known about Athenulf, beyond the bare outlines of his career. In 1251, when the rule of Augustine was given to the order, he was listed as sub-prior (*tenentis locum*) of their house in the university town of Montpellier. Later he was prior provincial of Provence, and in 1258 during a general chapter was elected to succeed as rector general of the order.[19] In 1261 he was negotiating the status of his friars in Palma de Mallorca. By 1264, however, he had been replaced as rector by a Friar Juvenis, documented 1264–7.[20] Athenulf had presumably either retired or died.

The lay identity of Athenulf and Bertrand has led historians to link their spirituality with lay penitential movements such as the beguines and Beghards, and in particular with the ideals of the community of women established by Douceline (†1274), Hugh of Digne's sister.[21] At the root of such ideas was an emphasis on poverty and penance, often without a secure

---

(Lyons, 1677), p. 461.

[14] See below, p. 200.

[15] Anonymous, 'Chronicon rhythmicum Austriacum', ed. W. Wattenbach, *MGH SS* XXV (Hannover, 1880), p. 358.

[16] T. de Morembert, 'Hugues de Digne', p. 1495, describes him as the founder of the friars.

[17] Amargier, 'Les Frères de la Pénitence de Jésus Christ ou du Sac', p. 159n., suggests that the section on Athenulf and Bertrand, which is in a larger script, is a later insertion. The modern editor of the chronicle, however, identifies it as Salimbene's hand (*Chronica*, ed. Scalia, I, p. 387n). Amargier also suggests that there is a mistake in the transmission of the name of Bertrand de Manara which should read Guillaume de Manara, the name of the rector general elected in 1256.

[18] See above, n. 3.

[19] *Sua nobis dilecti*, 11 December 1258 (Bourel 2731).

[20] K. Elm 'Ausbreitung' (as above, p. 20 n. 41), pp. 288–9.

[21] For example, ibid., p. 295.

means of support. It was an extreme rejection of the comforts of daily life, justified as a return to the ideals of the Desert Fathers, the primitive Church and imitation of Christ. Such values were rooted in the long history of Latin monasticism but had acquired new force amongst the laity in the twelfth and thirteenth centuries. There were certainly close parallels and associations between such groups and the Sack Friars. As we shall see, however, the pattern the order took as it developed suggests that the immediate model was, as Salimbene claimed, the mendicant friars themselves, rather than lay communities inspired by them.

A bald outline of the stages in the emergence of this new urban-oriented institution can be sketched from the few surviving papal letters concerning the Sack Friars issued before 1274. By the early 1250s they had already achieved sufficient size and stability to seek papal approval. In *Debet ex nostri* of 31 March 1251, Pope Innocent IV, responding to a petition from the 'rector and brothers of the penitence of Jesus Christ', instructed bishops Benoît d'Alignan of Marseilles and Rostan of Toulon to provide them with advice and assistance and assign them the rule of Augustine, as chosen by the order, which already had some thirteen houses.[22] No *propositum*, or proposed form of life from the friars survives and they simply assumed an established rule. The papal bull refers to their rejection of the honours of the world and riches, preferring to follow the fathers of the Church in the 'truth of the spirit and habit of poverty', a formula typical of the spiritual language of the period. They chose penance as a means to spiritual benefit (*facere penitentie dignos fructus*), rejecting the vanity and pomp of the world.[23] The name adopted, Friars of the Penitence of Jesus Christ, underlines the same approach to spiritual perfection and a link with Jesus also to be found in their constitutions, where the friars were encouraged to imitate 'our poor Lord Jesus Christ' (*pauper dominus noster Jhesus Christus*).[24] The language of the bull, insisting on the need to live by a rule and *ordo*, was in line with those sent to the various groups of Augustinian hermits five years later: the petition of the Friars of the Sack chimed conveniently with a growing Curial desire to regularise the life of professed religious.[25] In May the bishops duly attended the general chapter of the order assembled in the refectory of their convent in Marseilles. They approved and confirmed the decision of the chapter to adopt the rule of

---

[22] *Debet ex nostri* was inserted in *Ut que fiunt* of Alexander IV and is therefore to be found in Bourel 659. Giacomozzi, *L'ordine della penitenza di Gesù Cristo*, p. 114. See also P.-A. Amargier, 'Benoît d'Alignan, évêque de Marseille 1229–1268. Le contexte et l'esprit d'une théologie', *Le Moyen Âge* 72 (1966), pp. 443–62. According to Salimbene, he was a Benedictine who became a Franciscan for the last ten years of his life. Salimbene de Adam, *Chronica/Cronica*, II, p. 833. Bishop Rostan is not listed in Eubel, *Hierarchia Catholica*, but is so named in the text of the letter (Bourel 659). On the rule of Augustine, see above, pp. 93–4.

[23] Giacomozzi, *L'ordine della penitenza di Gesù Cristo*, p. 114.

[24] Ibid., p. 104.

[25] On the various bulls sent to the Augustinian hermits see above, pp. 83–4.

Augustine. Their letter *Noverint universi*, reporting events, records that the friars celebrated by exultant singing of the *Te Deum*.[26] Among the witnesses was Gaufridus, provost of the see of Marseilles, who was later to negotiate an agreement with the friars concerning their activities in the city.

Once the rule had been confirmed by the bishops, the new order was all set to acquire the papal privileges necessary to the life of mendicants, but nothing seems to have happened immediately. The reasons for the delay are not clear. Perhaps, as Franco dal Pino has proposed, Innocent IV was in no mood to support new orders of mendicants once the dispute between the secular masters and the friars in Paris was under way: in November 1254 indeed he issued *Etsi animarum*, severely restricting the activities of all the friars.[27] The new pope, Alexander IV, elected in the winter of 1254, quickly overturned Innocent's anti-mendicant measures and in July 1255 authorised members of the order of the Sack who had the appropriate theological training to preach, as long as they had the licence of the diocesan bishop.[28] His letter opens with an allusion to the importance of the link between the way of life of a preacher and the results of preaching, implying that both a reputation for holiness and the potential of the friars as professional preachers were accepted. A few days later Alexander finally confirmed the approval of the rule by the bishops of Marseilles and Toulon.[29] Then in August the friars received the usual broad-ranging privilege, *Religiosam vitam eligentibus*, according them papal protection and specifying further details of their life.[30] They were to observe the 'canonical *ordo . . .* according to God and the rule of St Augustine' (*ordo canonicus. . . secundum Deum et beati Augustini regulam*). Their property was to be inviolate and they were authorised to accept both laymen and clerics into their community. Those who made profession were not to leave unless for a stricter observance. During interdicts (unless themselves the cause), the friars were authorised to celebrate the daily Office as long as they excluded anyone subject to the ban, kept doors closed, rang no bells and spoke quietly. For holy oil, consecration of altars and ordination of clergy they were to turn to the diocesan bishop. Archbishops and other prelates were not to burden them with undue taxes. Their superior, the rector general, was to be elected

---

[26] Bourel 659. Also in Giacomozzi, *L'ordine della penitenza di Gesù Cristo*, pp. 114–15.

[27] See most recently F. A. dal Pino, 'Papato e ordini mendicanti-apostolici "minori" nel duecento', in *Il papato duecentesco e gli ordini mendicanti*, Atti del xxv convegno internazionale. Assisi 1998 (Spoleto, 1998), pp. 107–59, 132–3, 136.

[28] *Cum in ore*, 22 July 1255 (Bourel 667) and Giacomozzi, *L'ordine della penitenza di Gesù Cristo*, p. 115.

[29] *Ut que fiunt*, 31 July 1255 (Bourel 659), Giacomozzi, *L'ordine della penitenza di Gesù Cristo*, pp. 114–16.

[30] 20 August 1255 (Bourel 714); Giacomozzi, *L'ordine della penitenza di Gesù Cristo*, pp. 116–17. The same bull was presented to Bishop Arnau of Barcelona by the friars when they arrived there *c.* 1260 and was reissued by the bishop: see L. Feliu, 'El monestir de Frares de Penitència de Jesucrist de Barcelona (1260–1293)', *Analecta sacra Tarraconensia* 10 (1934), pp. 45–59, appendix 1. One of the signatories of the original bull was Cardinal Annibaldi, on whose comparable activities reorganising the regular life of hermits as mendicants see above, pp. 83–5.

by common consent or the majority and wiser part and indeed in February of the following year Alexander asked the bishop of Marseilles to approve the election of Friar Guillaume as the rector general of the order, his predecessor having resigned.[31] In the same month he prohibited others from copying their habit and in July 1257 renewed the protection of the papal see.[32] Like other new groups, there seems to have been anxiety about their distinct identity: in 1260, the pope repeated his instruction that other religious must not use the habit of the order or collect alms in their name.[33] None of this cluster of provisions was novel or unusual: they simply enabled the development of a new, autonomous body within the Church and the creation of structures of authority comparable to those in contemporary orders. Extant constitutions mention a proctor general resident in the Curia to deal with the business of the order and it is very likely that he impetrated these letters.

Geographical spread[34]

The origins of the order lay in Provence, where early expansion was extraordinarily rapid and, like that of the other orders of friars discussed here, far outstretched early development in the rest of modern France. Already in 1251 thirteen houses are named, of which ten are easily placed: Marseilles and Toulon on the coast, the island of Porquerolles off Toulon, Aix, Barjols, Le Luc, Draguignan and Cuers inland, Tarascon further north, and the university city of Montpellier to the west. Two locations have not so far been identified and of those given, the friary at Cuers together with another at Belmont (or Beaumont) are known only from the documentation of 1251.[35]

[31] *Pro parte dilecti*, 18 February 1256 (Bourel 1169), and Giacomozzi, *L'ordine della penitenza di Gesù Cristo*, pp. 117–18. The precise sequence of early rectors of the order may never be clarified, but Amargier, 'Les Frères de la Pénitence de Jésus Christ ou du Sac', p. 164n., notes that in September 1254 a Friar Guillaume 'de Almanarra' was identified as rector general of the order and was witnessing a contract stipulated by Bishop Benoit d'Alignan. He proposes that this was the same Guillaume approved as rector general by Alexander IV in 1256. See also above, n. 17.

[32] *Quia ex habitus*, 18 February 1256, and *Religiosam vitam eligentibus*, 31 July 1257 (Bourel 1170 and 2119); Giacomozzi, *L'ordine della penitenza di Gesù Cristo*, p. 118.

[33] *Exhibita nobis vestra*, 13 April 1260 (Bourel 3100). For parallels with treatment of the other friars, see above, pp. 21, 79–80, 82.

[34] A map of the houses in the order, as known in 1970, is given in Elm, 'Ausbreitung', following p. 272.

[35] The houses are identified by their priors and sub-priors in the text of the letter *Cum autem nos* issued by the bishops of Toulon and Aix in May 1251 and confirmed by Alexander IV in *Ut que fiunt*, 31 July 1255 (Bourel 659 and ed. Giacomozzi, *L'ordine della penitenza di Gesù Cristo*, pp. 114–16). The two houses which have not so far been identified are 'Tenoleum' and 'Roenum'. Micheline de Fontette plausibly proposes Rians (Var) for Roenum though there is no other evidence for a house there or this name, 'Les Mendiants supprimés au 2ᵉ concile de Lyon 1274: Frères Sachets et Frères Piés', in *Les Mendiants en Pays d'Oc au 13e siècle*, Cahiers de Fanjeaux 8 (1973), pp. 193–216, p. 212. A house at Fréjus is the product of confusion by Giacomozzi and does not seem to have existed; see de Fontette, 'Les Mendiants supprimés', p. 211. There may also have been a hermitage on Mont Fenouillet. See above, n. 1 and p. 176.

These may have been temporary settlements, or hermitages, rather than long-standing friaries.

The extant constitutions acknowledge the status of Provence, naming it the 'mother and beginning' (*mater et principium*) of the other provinces. The register of Archbishop Eudes Rigaud in Rouen even refers to the friars as 'of the *Provence* order of Jesus Christ (*de ordine provincie Ihesu Christi*), underlining its Provençal roots.[36] But by the 1270s the order had also spread across much of western Europe. Like all international orders at this date, they were divided on geo-political grounds into provinces, identified in the consitutions as Provence, France, Spain and England. There was also a province of Germany at the latest by 1264[37] and two were created in Italy, identifiable in 1269 as Bologna and *Lombardia*. A single friary was also established at Acre in the Holy Land, some time before 1274. The order never reached eastern or northern Europe, but by the time of the Council of Lyons there were at least 122 friaries, probably more than either the Carmelites or Augustinians then had and the product of phenomenal growth in under thirty years.[38]

The substantial difficulties involved in identifying short-lived houses which turned to other uses in the decades after 1274 and the fragmentary nature of the sources render any detailed account of the spread of these communities provisional, subject to further research which will undoubtedly nuance what follows.[39] By the time of the adoption of the rule in the early 1250s, Provence was newly attached to the French Crown through Louis IX's younger brother, Charles of Anjou, but the expansion of the order ignored political boundaries, extending rapidly into Catalan lands and the Crown of Aragon on both sides of the Pyrenees. In the Iberian peninsula the friars had settled in Barcelona by 1261 and in the same year reached Palma de Mallorca and Valencia where, as Burns notes, they long preceded the arrival of the Augustinian and Carmelite friars on this Reconquista frontier.[40] Burns also lists houses in Zaragoza (1263), Játiva in the south of the dependent kingdom of Valencia (by 1269), the new Pyrenean town of Puigcerdà (1270), the episcopal city of Tarragona on the coast, and a series of smaller centres such as Calatayud, Girona, Lleida, Peralada north of Barcelona, Teruel and Tudela. Several of these remain undated or can only be documented after 1274 but

---

[36] See below, p. 193.

[37] Elm, 'Ausbreitung', p. 285.

[38] For the most recent totals see L. J. Simon, 'The Friars of the Sack and the Kingdom of Majorca', *Journal of Medieval History* 18 (1992), pp. 279–96, 285.

[39] The dates supplied here are the first, sometimes indeed the only, reference for a house, not necessarily a date of foundation.

[40] R. I. Burns, 'Friars of the Sack in Valencia', *Speculum* 36 (1961), pp. 435–8, 438; he dates the Barcelona house 1252–7 (Burns, 'The Friars of the Sack in Barcelona', p. 421), although his first document is 1261. Feliu, 'El monestir de frares de Penitència de Jesucrist de Barcelona', p. 45, dated the house to 1260. R. W. Emery, 'A Note on the Friars of the Sack', *Speculum* 35 (1960), pp. 591–5, 592, seems not to have known Feliu's work and therefore dated the house only pre-1274.

must have been established earlier. The furthest south the order ever reached was Seville in Castile.[41]

North of the Pyrenees the friars again targeted urban centres, including Narbonne (1256), Villefranche, Perpignan, Toulouse (1264), Figeac (1268), Avignon (1270) and Cahors (1273). Louis IX supported foundations further north, in Paris (1258), Caen (1268) and Rouen (1269) and also in the diocese of Carcassonne at Montréal (1264).[42] Other friaries to the north included Orléans (1265), Sens (1266), Limoges (1269), Poitiers, Rouen (1270), and La Rochelle on the Atlantic coast, where the friars received gifts from Alphonse of Poitiers.[43] Before 1272 there was also a house in Bordeaux, presumably linked to the English province.

In Italy, just as Salimbene reported, the order settled quickly in the cities of the north, though only seven friaries can currently be dated before 1274. As early as 1254 they were in Venice,[44] followed by Bologna (1256), Ferrara (1264), Parma (1264), Todi (1269), Modena (1272) and Asti (1273).[45] Other houses can only be identified after the Council of Lyons but must have existed earlier; all were in sizeable urban centres.[46] The Sack Friars never extended south of Rome, a pattern which parallels the slow progress of the other mendicant orders in the south of the peninsula.[47]

In England the Franciscan Thomas of Eccleston records that, like the Augustinian Hermits, the Friars of the Sack were welcomed by his provincial minister, Peter of Tewkesbury, who 'received ... [and] recommended' them at a chapter meeting of his order in London.[48] Royal support was also significant. In August 1256 Henry III granted them protection and agreed

---

[41]   See Burns, 'Friars of the Sack in Valencia', pp. 435–6, 438, and Simon, 'The Friars of the Sack and the Kingdom of Majorca', p. 286 for more on the location of these houses.

[42]   Emery, 'The Friars of the Sack', p. 326n. Amargier, 'Les Frères de la Pénitence de Jésus Christ ou du Sac', p. 161.

[43]   For the French houses see Emery, *The Friars in Medieval France* (as above, p. 106 n. 18), but also the corrections in de Fontette, 'Les Mendiants supprimés', pp. 198–213. Lists of Alphonse's alms in 1264 include 60 *solidi* each for Paris 'per fratrem Stephanum procuratorem' and Orléans 'per magistrum Stephanum'; in 1266–7 these gifts were halved, as they were for other religious houses, E. Berger, *Layettes du tresor des chartes*, IV, Archives nationales. Inventaires et documents (Paris, 1902), pp. 119–23, 210–15.

[44]   Rigon, 'Ordini Mendicanti e politica territoriale', p. 220, provides an earlier date than previously known for this house.

[45]   On Parma, see *Statuta communis Parmae digesta anno mcclv, Monumenta historica ad provincias Parmensem et Placentinam pertinentia*, I, ed A. Ronchini (Parma, 1855), p. 435, with an addition to the statute, dated 1264, referring to 'fratres de sacchis' as recipients of communal alms. This corrects Emery, 'A Note on the Friars of the Sack', p. 593, who found only much later evidence for the order in the city.

[46]   Alessandria, Florence, Lucca, Milan, Pavia, Perugia, Pisa, Reggio, Rome, Siena, Spoleto and Viterbo. See Emery, 'A Note on the Friars of the Sack', pp. 591–5.

[47]   See, for example, the case of the Augustinians, above, p. 100.

[48]   Thomas de Eccleston, 'De adventu minorum', ed. Brewer, p. 72: 'Frater Petrus recepit primo fratres de Poenitentia Jesu Christi et recommendavit in capitulo Londonensi, qui in provincia...'

to ratify all gifts they received.[49] Eighteen houses can now be identified, the first of which was London itself (1257). Matthew Paris commented on the unknown and unexpected nature of the friars there (*fratribus ignotis et non previsis*), incidentally confirming that this was the earliest English foundation.[50] London was followed by Norwich (1258), Cambridge (1258), Oxford (1262), Rye (1263), Lincoln (1266), Bristol (1266), Newcastle on Tyne (1266), Northampton (1271), Lynn and Worcester (1272).[51] The remainder, as elsewhere, can only be dated in or after 1274: Canterbury, Chester, Leicester, Stamford and York.[52] The only Scottish house stood in the border town of Berwick (1267), while in 1268 two friars going to Ireland on the business of their order were granted royal protection for three years: presumably they founded the Dublin house which is otherwise only documented in 1282.[53]

Compared to the Augustinian Hermit Friars, who inherited a large number of Williamite houses north of the Alps, there were relatively few houses of the order of the Sack in the vast lands of the German Empire. Once again the evidence is fragmentary and subject to revision, but Kaspar Elm provides a valuable outline.[54] The friars first reached the Rhine at Cologne some time before March 1260 when they received a legacy of 3 marks; four years later they were to be found at Worms. On the upper Rhine they arrived more or less simultaneously at Strasbourg (1267) and Basel (1268). At Freiburg im Breisgau an indulgence from the bishop, Hartmann of Augsburg (1250–86), issued in 1277, refers to the building of their church in the suburbs at Neuburg, which must have started before 1274.[55] The furthest east they reached was Erfurt in Thuringia, where once again they must have settled before 1274, but can only now be documented from 1282. To the south the friars arrived in Esslingen in 1268, and the last German house known to Elm was in the Altstadt in Augsburg, dated to 1275, when it was already empty. Hans-Joachim Schmidt has suggested that a further community at Trier, identified as *fratres sacciti* already in 1242, may also have belonged to the order.[56] It

49 *Calendar of Patent Rolls Henry III 1247–58* (London, 1908), p. 493. See also H. F. Chettle, 'The Friars of the Sack in England', *Downside Review* 63 (1945), pp. 239–57, 245.

50 Matthew Paris, *Chronica Majora*, p. 621.

51 The house in Rye was apparently one of the only buildings left standing when the town was destroyed by the French five days after Richard II came to the throne in 1377. The house in Leicester is first documented in 1283, when the prior Richard was involved in a dispute over a messuage in Bruntingsthorp. See W. Dugdale, *Monasticon Anglicanum. A History of the Abbies and Other Monasteries Hospitals Frieries and Cathedral and Collegiate Churches in England and Wales*, VI, part 3 (London, 1846), p. 1607; in 1295 at least part of its property transferred to the Austin Friars; see above, p. 114.

52 A. G. Little suggests that the York house was founded *c.* 1260 but the first record is the ordination of two friars as priests in 1274 – see below, p. 212.

53 *Calendar of Patent Rolls Henry III 1266–72* (London, 1913), p. 256.

54 Elm, 'Ausbreitung', pp. 262–76.

55 F. Hefele, *Freiburger Urkundenbuch*, 2 vols (Freiburg im Breisgau, 1940), I, no. 303. Elm, 'Ausbreitung', p. 267.

56 H.-J. Schmidt, *Bettelorden in Trier. Wirksamkeit und Umfeld im hohen und späten Mittelalter* (Trier, 1986), pp. 33–5 and map, p. 44.

is possible, as Schmidt suggests, that this was a community established on similar lines to the Provençal houses but without formal connections to the later order – wearing sack cloth as a means of expressing humility and penance was after all a long-standing tradition in the medieval Church. Whereas the Marseilles founders were laymen, it is clear that the Trier community already included clerics in 1242, since they undertook duties of pastoral care. An agreement concerning the treatment of the excommunicate associated them with the other mendicants then resident in the city, the Dominicans and Franciscans.[57] It may be that the house later joined the order: records from 1271 and 1284 continue to use the name, which by that date was strongly associated with the *ordo fratrum poenitentie.*

Unlike the heartland of the Empire, in the much smaller, but highly urbanised area of the Low Countries, the Sack Friars were very numerous: perhaps a third of the known settlements of all orders of mendicants belonged to them. The earliest recorded is Utrecht, where the bishop, Heinrich of Vianden (1250–67), supported them with a legacy in May 1267. A will of 1271 also mentions friars at Middelburg on the island of Walcheren, though it is not clear whether this, or a friary at Biervliet at the mouth of the Scheldt, whose prior is documented in the same year, were long-term settlements.[58] As Walter Simons suggests, it may be that Biervliet was founded in expectation of the development of the harbour town, which never reached its potential.[59] On the other hand Elm proposes that references to Middelburg and Biervliet were in practice records of friars linked to the new foundations of Bruges (documented in a will of the same year) and Ghent (1269). It is equally possible that they were simply hermitages associated to one or other of the urban friaries. The house at Bruges belonged to the province of France, as did Tournai, documented in 1264. Liège was founded by August of the following year and Brussels by December 1270. A single document also refers to a house at Douai in 1272.[60] Simons has tentatively proposed that in Flanders in particular, the unusually high number of houses may be explained by early ties with the Spirituals (presumably through Hugh of Digne), which attracted the 'urban proletariat', textile workers near whose homes the friars tended to settle.[61] There is, however, too little evidence either for substantial links with Digne or for the social status of individual friars to make this more than conjecture.

---

[57] Ibid., pp. 167, 297.
[58] Elm, 'Ausbreitung', pp. 271–2. W. Simons, *Bedelordekloosters in het graafschap Vlaanderen* (Bruges, 1987), p. 93.
[59] W. Simons, *Stad en apostolaat: de vestiging van de bedelorden in het graafschap Vlaanderen (ca. 1225 – ca. 1350)* (Brussels, 1987), pp. 97, 238.
[60] Simons, *Bedelordekloosters*, p. 94.
[61] Ibid., p. 245.

The life of the friars

No copy of the rule of Augustine known to have belonged to the order has yet been identified and no liturgical text or formula for the profession of new friars is now known. But their surviving constitutions fill some of the gaps. As a category, such texts are always prescriptive rather than descriptive, and in this case there are very few other sources by which to ascertain whether they were ever fully implemented; nonetheless they give us a sense of the shape early members of the order intended the life of the community to take. The extant manuscript was written in a late-thirteenth-century English hand.[62] It is very small, on re-used parchment, and is both incomplete and full of mistakes, the sign of a poor copyist.[63] It is now impossible to say which friary it may first have belonged to, but presumably the codex passed to the community which replaced the friars in one of the English houses. In the comparable case of Bologna, a copy of the Sack constitutions no longer survives, but in the late Middle Ages was to be found in the library of the prior of San Frediano, Lucca which had acquired the Bologna house.[64]

The text of the constitutions or *Liber constitutionum* is a modified version of the primitive constitutions of the early Dominicans, composed in the 1220s and early 1230s before the revisions of Ramon de Peñafort *c.* 1240, but with additions made by capitular authority down to *c.* 1252. It is not clear why the order used this outdated text. The modern editor, Gabriele Giacomozzi, speculates that they were given a codex which was no longer needed by the Dominicans. It may equally be that the friars explicitly chose the version closer to St Dominic and the early ideal of the mendicant life centred on study and preaching epitomised by him.[65] Their use confirms the status of the Dominicans as authorities on the administrative structures of the religious life in the mid-thirteenth century, comparable to the position of the Cistercians a few decades earlier.[66] It also made sense for a group that, like the Dominicans, had adopted the rule of Augustine. Precisely when the Sack version of the text was produced is not clear: there is no mention of constitutions in the papal bulls of either 1251 or 1256, but the evidence for chapter meetings and the election of a general superior makes it likely that

---

[62] London, British Library, MS Cotton Nero A XII, fols 155r–174v. G. M. Giacomozzi, 'Le "Constitutiones fratrum de poenitentia Jhesu Christi"', *Studi storici dell'ordine dei Servi di Maria* 10 (1960), pp. 42–99, also in Giacomozzi, *L'ordine della penitenza di Gesù Cristo*, pp. 63–113.

[63] G. G. Meersseman, review of Giacomozzi, *L'ordine della penitenza di Gesù Cristo*, in *Revue d'histoire ecclésiastique* 58 (1963), pp. 610–12.

[64] Giacomozzi, *L'ordine della penitenza di Gesù Cristo*, p. 65n. The sale of the house for 300 *lire* is documented in two bulls of Honorius IV, *Dilectus filius magister*, 5 April 1285, and *Sane petitio vestra*, 8 April 1286 (Prou 9, 456).

[65] Giacomozzi, *L'ordine della penitenza di Gesù Cristo*, p. 67.

[66] See above, p. 75. The Dominicans were also an important model for the Humiliati at this date. See Andrews, *The Early Humiliati* (as above, p. 11 n. 9), pp. 207–8, 252.

it was drafted by the end of the 1250s at the latest.[67] As in the Dominican original, the text is divided into two parts or distinctions: in this case the first covered the life of the convent, the second provincial and general chapters, study and preaching. Much of the content is a straightforward account of how life should be carried on in the community, lifted from the Dominican text. This begins with the behaviour expected of the friars from the moment they awoke for matins, observance of the hours, meals and abstinence. Meat was excluded and fasting was observed for long periods, though it is a sign of planned expansion of the order that allowance was made should the friars find themselves in a place where practices about food were different (*aliter comeditur*).

Changes to the Dominican text first noted by A. G. Little in the 1890s give the most direct clues to the particular way of life of the order of the Sack.[68] The instructions concerning property and money are extensive, reflecting the concerns of the author(s) to maintain the original ideals of poverty. Indeed a whole chapter 'On poverty', although derivative of earlier texts, is not taken from the Dominican source. It opens with a reference to the blessed status of those imitating the poverty of Christ, and stipulates that, like the other mendicants, the order was not to have fields, vineyards or income from rents.[69] The only land or buildings permitted beyond the convent and church were gardens and workshops, a provision paralleling that of the Brettini hermits who joined the order of Austin Friars at just this juncture (1256).[70] Property left to the order was to be distributed to charitable causes as soon as possible and in the meanwhile was to be looked after by servants and friends, not by the friars themselves, an arrangement strongly reminiscent of the practices of the early Franciscans, and much stricter than that of the Dominicans. The friars were to live by begging and, like the other mendicant orders, each house had its own *terminus*, the area outside which the prior was not to send his brothers to beg. Every friary was to elect two friars responsible for receiving all alms and for recording both receipts and expenditure in a register. If any of the friars were nominated as the executor of a will, they were to be assigned a companion (*socius*) by the friary, with whom all decisions about distributing legacies were to be reached. Choices made by all these individuals were to be reported to the prior and more discreet friars. Finally, two other members of the house were responsible for goods held in the friary and acted as holders of the keys. The anxious detail of this chapter reflects the concern of the drafters to keep the temptations of money and property at bay and maintain the ideals of mendicancy and poverty. There is some evidence that

---

[67] Elm, 'Ausbreitung', pp. 292–4, argues for 1255/6. Simons, *Stad en apostolaat*, p. 23, suggests *c*. 1250.

[68] A. G. Little, 'The Friars of the Sack', *English Historical Review* 9 (1894), pp. 121–7.

[69] Giacomozzi, *L'ordine della penitenza di Gesù Cristo*, p. 104: 'Verum quia pauper dominus noster Jhesus Christus imitatores beatificat et exaltat, statuimus...'

[70] See above, p. 82.

this was successful, at least at the level of contemporary perceptions: from the account of Salimbene and in later papal correspondence it is clear that the order was identified as living in poverty: two bulls issued in November 1265 by Clement IV, for example, list the Sack Friars after the Dominicans and before the Carmelites amongst those orders, 'founded in poverty' (*in paupertate fundatis*).[71] The poet Rutebeuf also made play on the particular poverty of the Sack Friars, which suggests that they may have been yet more emphatic about the issue than the other mendicants.[72]

The constitutions also prohibited 'unnecessary painted images' (*inutiles ymagines picturarum*), a requirement similar to that of the Franciscans or Dominicans and, before them, the Cistercians.[73] Doubtless altarpieces and liturgical furnishings would not have been considered *inutiles*, but as we might expect, no paintings or sculpture produced for or by members of an order dedicated to poverty and soon disbanded appear to survive. On the other hand, each house did have its own seal, kept in a chest under lock and key. Some of these are now scattered in libraries and archives across Europe. The iconography varies considerably. That of the community of Bologna published by G. B. Grossi in the eighteenth century shows a grazing animal and a star.[74] The seal of the Norwich house portrays the martyrdom of St Edmund.[75] Of two seals from the Cambridge friary, one from *c.* 1262 shows the Cross, with saints Mary and John, below which is a kneeling figure in a niche. Another has the standing figure of Christ and a kneeling St Thomas with his hand outstretched; beneath is a friar in prayer.[76] This is not unlike a seal from Basel which shows the Virgin and Child with a praying friar below.[77] Artistic imagination and an interest in images are certainly evident

---

[71] *Ad consequendam gloriam*, 20 November 1265 (Jordan 172; Potthast 19455) and *Sane non sine*, 22 November 1265 (Jordan 1886; Potthast 19462). The other orders mentioned are the Augustinian Hermit Friars and the order of Clare. The bull concerned the restriction of buildings of these orders within 300 rods of a Franciscan house. The fossilisation of the language of papal letters is neatly illustrated by the re-issuing of *Ad consequendam gloriam* for the Augustinian friars by Boniface VIII in 1295 (Digard 10; Potthast 24028), in which the houses *in paupertate fundatis* not permitted to build near them still included the Friars of the Sack, though by this date they can no longer have been planning any new buildings.

[72] See below, p. 200.

[73] On Franciscan avoidance of *curiositas* see L. Bourdua, *The Franciscans and Art Patronage in Late Medieval Italy* (Cambridge, 2004), p. 25.

[74] Illustrated in R. I. Burns, 'Penitenza di Gesu Cristo, Frati della', *DIP* VI (Rome, 1980), cols 1398–1403, 1400. The inscription reads 's[igillum] fratru[m] penite<n>cie d bon[onie], which may of course link it to the friars of penance or tertiaries.

[75] Giacomozzi, *L'ordine della penitenza di Gesù Cristo*, p. 34.

[76] Cambridge, Peterhouse Deeds Collegium F 3 and Collegii Situs B 6.

[77] Elm, 'Ausbreitung', p. 291, n. 218, refers to this seal as Staatsarchiv Basel, Klosterarchiv St Clara Nr. 51 (9 January, 1273). In practice this is now Klosterarchiv Klingenthal no. 51 (1 January, 1273). Elm also lists a seal in the Gemeente Archief, Utrecht Regulierenklooster, no. 884 (14 July, 1289). The archive is now Het Utrechts Archief and the seal, described in *Oorkondenboek van het Sticht Utrecht tot 1301*, IV, ed. F. Ketner ('s-Gravenhage, 1954) 2390 as a (fragment of a) seal, is identified as belonging to the chapter of St. Mary in Utrecht, the 'author' of the charter, cf. *Corpus sigillorum Neerlandicorum*

in these pieces: other works of art produced in or for the order may yet be identified.

An indication of the gap between constitution and practice is also provided by evidence for the dedication of altars. According to the constitution, high altars were, where possible, to be dedicated to Jesus and his mother Mary, a reflection of the chosen title of the order. This requirement was respected (for example) at Cambridge, but in Strasbourg the high altar was consecrated to the Virgin alone, in Tournai to St Bartholomew and in Liège to Saint-Didier.[78] Although the sample is small, the variation suggests that like most churches, a determining factor was local devotion or pre-existing cults and indeed the case of Freiburg confirms this: their church was dedicated to the Virgin Mary, the Holy Trinity and 'other saints of the diocese of Constance'.[79] Surviving indulgences for this church reveal how devotion might be directed (and changed) in a particular community. In 1277 the first indulgence was offered for the day of dedication of the church and feasts of the saints listed above. In 1284 this had become a longer list: the day of dedication, the first Sunday of Advent, the fourth Sunday of Lent and the first Sunday after the feast of St John the Baptist. In 1288 the list was extended again: the four feasts of the Virgin Mary, All Saints, Holy Trinity, St Augustine, Saints Peter and Paul and 'all the other saints to whom the altars of their church are consecrated'. However, in 1289, an indulgence was offered to those attending and offering alms on the four feasts and octaves of the Virgin Mary and on the day of the dedication of the church alone.[80]

Devotion to Mary was fundamental, but as we should expect, the constitutions also reveal a shared emphasis on the cult of Augustine: as the author of their rule, he is identified as the 'father' of the order, a claim also made by the Augustinian Hermit Friars.[81] His day was to be celebrated as a major feast, as were the feasts of St Michael and of Mary Magdalene, a cult universally celebrated in the Church but particularly important in southern France, and above all Provence.[82]

As well as encouraging devotion to the Magdalene, the Provençal origins

---

('s-Gravenhage 1937–40), p. 188, but is no longer legible. Elm lists another seal in the Archive departmentale Strasbourg, G. Fasc. 4713 (18 January 1267) and one in Rijksarchief, Arnheim, Archief Bethelehem, 14 April 1292. The latter is now Gelders Archief Archive 0314 Klooster Bethlehem bij Doesberg, inv. No. 121bis. The pointed oval seal is now very fragmentary and may not have belonged to the friars.

[78] Elm, 'Ausbreitung', p. 274. On Cambridge, see below, p. 205

[79] Hefele, *Freiburger Urkundenbuch*, I, no. 303: 17 February 1277, 'in honore beate Marie virginis et sancte trinitatis ac aliorum sanctorum Constanciensis dyocesis consecratam'.

[80] Hefele, *Freiburger Urkundenbuch*, I, no. 303 (1277), II, no. 8 (13 March 1284); no. 59 (1288), no. 77 (1289). The dedication to All Saints survived the transfer of the property to the regular canons of Marbach. See below, p. 218.

[81] See above, p. 158.

[82] K. L. Jansen, *The Making of the Magdalen. Preaching and Popular Devotion in the Later Middle Ages* (Princeton, 2000), p. 3.

of the order may have inclined contemporaries to see the spirituality of the friars in Joachite terms, as one of the orders heralding a new age: the region was undoubtedly strongly associated with such ideas. Contemporaries such as Thomas of Eccleston, writing before the suppression of the 1270s, suggested that they fulfilled a prophecy of the Franciscan William of Nottingham, that 'Jesus would bring forth a new order to excite their own'.[83] The Dominican Robert d'Uzès (†1296) later wrote of a forthcoming revival through authorised bodies, while denouncing 'one contemporary, would-be agency', the 'sect commonly known as of the Sack' (*secta, que vulgo saccatorum dicitur*).[84] In the late fourteenth century Bartholomew of Pisa may also have had the Sack Friars in mind when he wrote in Joachite terms of an order dressed in sack-cloth (*ordo saccis vestitus*) and destined to a very short life, which would herald the coming of the Antichrist.[85] There is a slender possibility that the friars had indeed inherited such thinking from Hugh of Digne, who was certainly a Joachite and to whose eschatological ideas Salimbene alludes in his account of their foundation. But accusing a competing order of Joachism, by this date tinged with heresy, was a convenient strategy for Salimbene, as for later mendicant commentators. There is no evidence from within the order for such beliefs, though the lack of sources makes any analysis inconclusive.

Like numerous male orders, the friars rejected from the outset any responsibility for religious women, the *cura monialium*. Their constitutions specifically forbade them to look after congregations of nuns or to accept them as professed members of the order. In a chapter which is a combination of provisions instituted in other orders, but original as drafted here, the legislators also instructed that women were not to be admitted to the cloister, workshop or oratory of the friars except to attend the consecration of a church or on Good Friday. The friars were particularly warned to avoid beguines, 'suspect places' or unnecessary visits to women, which in any case were only permitted with the specific licence of a superior. Women were, however, authorised to follow processions and listen to the preaching of the friars – they could hardly have been prevented – and in practice, the status of religious women in relation to the order is not so straightforward. In spite of the restrictive measures of the constitutions, Giacomozzi suggested that a number of houses of women – in Strasbourg, Paris, Montepulciano and Viterbo (Proceno) – were incorporated in the order as convents of *Saccate*. Against this Kaspar Elm, putting together the work of several other historians, has argued that these women were penitents and beguines with no link to the order. Elm is probably right about these particular houses but, following work on

---

[83] Thomas de Eccleston, 'De adventu minorum', ed. Brewer, p. 71: 'quod suscitaret dulcis Jesus Ordinem novum ad excitationem nostram'. See also Elm, 'Ausbreitung', p. 322.

[84] Cited in M. Reeves, *The Influence of Prophecy* (London, 1969), p. 168.

[85] Ibid., pp. 181–2. The texts are also discussed in Elm, 'Ausbreitung', p. 322.

beguines and Beghards in the Low Countries, he also argued that names such as *Sachettes, saccite* and *de Sacho* were simply generic terms customarily applied to penitent women.[86] More recently, Mario Sensi, following the lead of Giovanna Casagrande and other historians of central Italy, has associated with the friars a second order of religious women in the region, known as *fratelle* or, less often, as *saccate/de sacchis*.[87] If we are to accept Elm's view that the epithet *de sacho* is insufficient to indicate a formal link for female houses, the same rule must also apply to many of the houses of men, documented by a single reference of the type *fratres de sacco*. In both male and female cases it may simply indicate an individual or group adopting a penitential life and wearing sackcloth as a form of humble clothing – like the numerous penitents referred to by contemporaries as 'minors' yet with no official connection to the order of Friars Minor.[88] Equally, it may disguise some more substantial link. The problem of identification may not be resolvable, but it is clear that well-documented male houses did have ties with religious women: in 1271 the prior of the friary in Cologne approved the acquisition of a house by two beguines.[89] In Valenciennes, according to Hélyot, the friars were known as *frères beguins* because they were responsible for beguine women in the town.[90] Both references imply an association with religious women beyond simple preaching. Like many other monastic communities, in at least one case a friary also took on an older woman as a corrodian: in Barcelona Joana Villela, a widow, was fed and supported by the friars. On her death a sum paid for her support by her sons, Bernat and Pere, remained to the house.[91] By contrast the only surviving pastoral text produced by a member of the order particularly criticises women, who are accused of trying to lead men astray.[92] Comparison with other orders is instructive. Numerous male communities initially rejected the *cura monialium* but in the end accepted responsibility for female houses. Others were not explicitly hostile, but were slow to absorb women. The Augustinian Hermit Friars seem to have been an entirely male order when formalised in 1256, but started to incorporate female houses in 1264. This was only eight years after final approval, but several decades after the creation of the various communities that made up the order. Even so, the

---

[86] See Elm, 'Ausbreitung', pp. 264–5, for Strasbourg and Elm, 'Penitenza di Gesu Cristo, Frati di', parte seconda: Il ramo femminile', *DIP* VI (Rome, 1980), pp. 1403–4, referring to Giacomozzi, *L'ordine della penitenza di Gesù Cristo*, pp. 46–9.

[87] M. Sensi, 'Monachesimo femminile nell'Italia centrale (sec. XV)', in *Il monachesimo femminile in Italia dall'alto medioevo al secolo XVII*, ed. G. Zarri (Verona, 1997), pp. 135–68, 141n., with substantial bibliography.

[88] Discussed in Andrews, *The Early Humiliati*, pp. 58–9, with bibliography.

[89] J. Asen, 'Die Begarden und die Sackbrüder in Köln', *Annalen des historischen Vereins für den Niederrhein* 115 (1929), pp. 167–79, 179.

[90] P. Helyot, *Histoire des ordres monastiques, religieux et militaires*, 6 vols (Paris, 1714–18), III, p. 176.

[91] Burns, 'The Friars of the Sack in Barcelona', p. 427.

[92] See below, p. 196–8.

status of many of these houses of women is now unclear.[93] By analogy, there may have been particular hostility to women amongst the Sack Friars, there may be a gap in the documentation, or there may simply not have been time or space to develop the sort of formal links established by other orders of friars with women's houses.

Authority

The first tier of authority in the order was the conventual prior, elected by his brethren, but subject to the confirmation of the rector and of the provincial prior. In each province the latter enjoyed powers comparable to those of the rector general in the order as a whole. The rector was elected at the general chapter but, like the early Augustinian Hermit Friars, the appointee was subject to papal approval.[94] The election was also to be explicitly endorsed by the provincial priors, who were to place their seals on the document of election sent to the Curia. In practice, Alexander IV's letter recording the choice of Raymund, notes that the friars had omitted to refer his election to the Curia. The pope accepted that this had come about through simplicity rather than design and reported that he had been told that Raymund's life and knowledge (*scientia*) were praiseworthy. Nonetheless, following normal procedures, he now required the bishop of Fréjus to establish whether he was suitable to be rector and if so to confirm the appointment.[95]

The constitutions anticipate that the general chapter or assembly would serve as a forum for discussion of the affairs of the order and, as was usual for monastic orders at this date, only through this chapter could the constitutions themselves be modified. The chapter also received petitions and letters from conventual chapters and heard reports on the study, preaching and needs of the friars from visitators appointed to inspect their activities. In theory they were to be held after Pentecost every third year, with provincial chapters in the intervening years which, like the Dominicans, were to elect diffinitors to send to the general chapters. Only two general chapter meetings are now known: 1251 and 1258, when Raymond Athenulf was elected as rector general. There must have been others: in 1270 Alphonse of Poitiers left 100 *sous* annually to the chapter general of the order.[96]

---

[93] See above, p. 132–8.

[94] The choice of the title 'rector' set the order apart from the other mendicants and contemporary orders: the Dominicans used 'master general' and were copied in this by the Humiliati. The Franciscan superior was known as 'minister general', while both the Augustinian and Carmelite friars favoured 'prior general'.

[95] *Sua nobis dilecti*, 11 December 1258 (Bourel 2731). Amargier, 'Les Frères de la Pénitence de Jésus Christ ou du Sac', p. 161n.

[96] Berger, *Layettes du tresor des chartes*, IV, p. 458.

The friars

Twelve, the apostolic number, may have been the number of friars expected in a new convent – there were twelve in Narbonne in 1266 and in Basel in 1274[97] – but several houses were much bigger than this: Zaragoza had twenty and Villefranche de Conflent thirty friars. In Barcelona, Robert Burns has traced only about ten friars at any one time, but he identified fifty-one names over two decades, just six repeated over several years, which suggests substantial turnover, as we should expect in a major centre in the province.[98] By contrast, in Puigcerdà in the Pyrenees, apart from the occasional visitor, extant names suggest that the friars were local men, recruited for the most part from the district, who stayed put.[99]

Alexander IV authorised the admission of both lay and clerical recruits. The ordination lists of Eudes Rigaud, archbishop of Rouen (1248–75), in the years between 1261 and 1267 include twenty-five ceremonies for members of the order: seven acolytes, twelve subdeacons, four deacons and two priests. Allowing for the likely repetition of some names, this accounts for perhaps fifteen individuals, at least seven of whom must have been laymen on entry, like the founders themselves.[100] The economic and social status of members of the order is less easy to determine: Athenulf was a former knight, and in Paris, according to an *exemplum*, the friars recruited the son of a noble.[101] However, for houses in the lands of the Empire, Elm concludes on the evidence of wills from relatives, and the kind of support they attracted, that the friars came from the urban laity, the sons of burghers.[102] In Barcelona the order attracted a Friar Berenguer d'Ape, who brought with him 7500 *solidi*, which may explain why this house appears particularly wealthy.[103] In 1264 King Jaime of Aragon acknowledged a loan of nearly 5000 *solidi* from the house, provided when he sent a noble, Garcia Ortiz, to Tunis, presumably on a diplomatic mission. Burns notes that the interest rate on such loans was high, so this was an attractive proposition for perhaps increasingly entrepreneurial friars.[104] Comparable examples are not, however, currently documented.

---

[97] 'Annales Basileenses', ed. P. Jaffe, *MGH SS* XVII (Hannover, 1861), cols 193–202, 196.

[98] Burns, 'The Friars of the Sack in Barcelona', p. 425.

[99] Burns, 'The Friars of the Sack in Puigcerdà. A Lost Chapter of 13th-Century Religious History', *Anuario de estudios medievales* 18 (1988), pp. 217–27, 220, 221.

[100] *Regestrum visitationum archiepiscopi Rothomagensi, Journal des visites pastorales d'Eude Rigaud*, ed. T. Bonnin (Rouen, 1852), pp. 678, 683, 685–7, 690–1, 695, 698, 700, 706, 709, 711, 716, 721, 724–5, 731.

[101] See below, p. 194.

[102] Elm, 'Ausbreitung', p. 280.

[103] Burns, 'The Friars of the Sack in Barcelona', p. 424. He brought 1500 Barcelona and 6000 Melgorian *solidi*.

[104] Burns, 'The Friars of the Sack in Barcelona', pp. 430–1.

Learning

Judging by the section of the constitutions on study, the Sack Friars were quick to recognise the need for involvement in the universities, a necessary preparation for any professional preacher. Provincial priors were authorised to take on brothers who could not sing or read competently, or were not yet eighteen, without dispensation from the rector, but the order's commitment to learning was already evident in Alexander IV's authorisation of preaching only by those trained in theology (*Cum in ore*, 22 July 1255). The constitutions refer to *studia generalia* in Montpellier, Paris, Oxford, Cologne and Bologna, to which each province might send two friars (four from Provence), though it is not clear whether all of these were ever formed. The house in Bologna was one of the most important in the order, becoming the centre of a province named for it before 1269, in which year a Friar Suillus is identified as provincial. The bishop, Giacomo Boncampi (1244–60), gave them accommodation near Porta San Mammolo and the house, linked to the *studium generale*, had fifteen religious at least. In 1270 Rolandino of Pavia, as representative of the friary, contracted a Master Lapo from Florence to live in the Bologna convent to teach logic and natural philosophy to the friars in return for his board and lodging and a salary of 30 *lire*.[105] There is also indirect evidence for the *studium* in Paris. A thirteenth-century collection of *exempla* written by an English mendicant, probably a Franciscan, refers to an anonymous Paris scholar, the son of a French noble, who entered the order of the Sack and remained there despite paternal fury: when his father arrived to take him away, the young man asked him,

> 'Father, if I returned to the world and lived well, could you give me heaven?' To which his father replied 'No'. 'And if I live badly, will you be able to save me from hell?', 'No', 'So I must rightly serve him who can offer me either'.[106]

A friar from Ghent is mentioned among the eight men left in Paris in 1293 when the house was finally closed, perhaps a sign of what was left of an international community of friars from other provinces brought to Paris to study and teach.[107] The evidence is, however, even sketchier for other *studia*: in Cologne, when the house transferred to new owners in 1298, it had a church, workshops and other unspecified buildings (*edificia alia*),[108] which may (or may not) have been teaching spaces; in Montpellier after the friars left, their house was used by monks coming to the university to study. However, in

---

[105] Giacomozzi, *L'ordine della penitenza di Gesù Cristo*, p. 43.

[106] J. T. Welter, *Le Speculum laicorum* (Paris, 1914), p. 12. See also Giacomozzi, *L'ordine della penitenza di Gesù Cristo*, p. 28.

[107] E. Ypma, 'L'Acquisition du couvent parisien des Sachets par les Augustins', *Augustiniana* 9 (1959), pp. 105–17, 108–10. On the transfer of the Paris house, see pp. 219–20.

[108] Elm, 'Ausbreitung', p. 270.

neither case is there evidence for the activities of the friars themselves.[109] On the other hand, the friars also had houses in other university towns, including Cambridge, Toulouse and Orléans, where members of the order may have studied.

Those who went to study were to be provided with at least three theological books by their province: the Bible, the *Sentences* of Peter Lombard and unspecified 'Histories' – almost certainly the *Historia scholastica* of Peter Comestor, abbreviated versions of the Biblical stories.[110] At death any books would revert to the friary. Like the Dominicans, from whom these regulations came, study was to be allowed to distort the usual routines of communal life: those advanced in study were assigned cells in which they could have a light at night to allow them to carry on working. Students and qualified preachers were not required to be present at conventual chapter meetings except on the fourth and sixth days of the week, unless expressly called to attend. They were also to be dispensed from office-holding should this get in the way of their studies.

In view of the attacks on the activities of the mendicants by men such as William of Saint-Amour in the years when these constitutions were being drafted,[111] it is no surprise that they refer explicitly to the need for care about relations with the secular clergy. Sack preachers were to remind their lay audiences to pay tithes and other dues to the Church and were also to request the permission of parish clergy before preaching in their territory. Were permission refused, they were not to preach, unless with special papal or episcopal licence. Like all regular religious the friars were instructed to extend warm hospitality, but members of the Franciscan and Dominican orders in particular were to be received and provided for 'with love and joy' (*caritative et hylariter*), as if they were Sack Friars, an acknowledgement of the kinship status of other mendicants which is paralleled in the regulations of other religious groups.[112] Finally, the friars were not to chase benefices or join the service of prelates or princes, unless with the licence of the rector or general chapter: presumably the Friar Bernard who was chaplain of the bishop of Marseilles in September 1254 had obtained such permission.[113]

The omissions in these constitutions are as interesting as the additions. The section of the Dominican text prohibiting involvement in secular affairs is not included, but the friars are warned not to act as judges, arbiters or advocates in the affairs of seculars. The only role they might adopt was as

[109] A survey of matriculation lists from thirteenth-century universities may yet provide further evidence.

[110] Giacomozzi, *L'ordine della penitenza di Gesù Cristo*, p. 107n.

[111] On this see above, pp. 18–19, 90.

[112] The issue of monastic and lay hospitality and its links to honorable behaviour is explored in new work by Julie Kerr, 'Monastic Hospitality: The Benedictines in England, *c.* 1075–1245', *Anglo-Norman Studies* 12 (2001), pp. 97–114; Kerr, 'The Open Door: Hospitality and Honour in Twelfth/Early-Thirteenth-Century England', *History* 87 (2002), pp. 322–35. A monograph study is forthcoming.

[113] Amargier, 'Les Frères de la Pénitence de Jésus Christ ou du Sac', p. 164n.

peacemakers, advising or supervising peace agreements between conflicting parties. As Burns has shown, the friars certainly undertook such tasks: in 1271, Friar Bertran de Auriach (Oriach), prior provincial of the Friars of Penitence in Spain, was chosen as arbiter in a debt dispute between laymen. When a first meeting in the house of the order in Puigcerdà failed because one of the men fled, Auriach was able to refer the case to the court of the prince, Jaume. The status of the friar as a prominent and trustworthy figure in the local community, if not the sort of peace-maker envisaged in the constitutions, can hardly be disputed. Catalan friars were also involved in resolving more overtly spiritual issues. Burns records the case of a young couple in May 1270 who wished to divorce on the grounds that the woman had slept with the brother of the groom before their marriage, which had never been consummated. Having failed to get the desired solution from the diocesan clergy, and 'seeking a better opinion', they turned to Friar Pere d'Albareda of the Friars of Penitence in Barcelona. He listened to them both in confession and then turned the case over to Ramon de Peñafort, the former Dominican master general who was then living in Barcelona, aged eighty-five. Ramon enjoyed authority as a papal judge and, having heard the case, allowed them to divorce. The witnesses were three friends of the couple and Pere d'Albareda.[114] What the diocesan clergy made of this is not recorded.

Bertran and Pere were clearly well integrated into public life. Very few writings of the friars survive, however, so the nature of the preaching and teaching undertaken by such men remains largely obscure. Just one text currently fills the void: in the third quarter of the thirteenth century an anonymous Provençal Sack Friar produced a short collection of *exempla*, persuasive moral stories for use in illustrating sermons. The material is not particularly original, often repeating anecdotes from a range of earlier sources, including the *Vitae patrum*, Gregory the Great's *Dialogues*, Caesarius of Heisterbach and, above all, two prolific producers of *exempla* in the thirteenth century, Jacques de Vitry, bishop of Acre (1216–27), and the Dominican Étienne de Bourbon (†1261), who was based at Lyons for most of his career.[115] Its Sack origins are not spelled out in the opening of the text, which may have assisted the collection's later survival, such that three copies were made in the 1300s.[116]

---

[114] Burns, 'The Friars of the Sack in Barcelona', pp. 427–9. The friars are identified only as 'de ordine fratrum Penitencie'.

[115] The text survives in a late-thirteenth-century manuscript in the Bibliothèque municipale in Arras. First discussed by J. T. Welter, 'Un receuil d'exempla du XIIIᵉ siècle', *Études franciscaines* 30 (1913), pp. 646–65, and 31 (1914), pp. 194–213, 312–20. See also Welter, *L'Exemplum dans la littérature religieuse et didactique du Moyen Âge* (Paris, 1927), pp. 254–7. On Étienne and on the preaching of the friars in general, see D. d'Avray, *The Preaching of the Friars. Sermons Diffused from Paris before 1300* (Oxford, 1985), p. 147.

[116] See I. Rava-Cordier, 'La Proximité comme élément de persuasion: les références géographiques, sociales et culturelles dans les *exempla* d'un Sachet provençal au XIIIᵉ siècle', in *La Prédication en Pays d'Oc (XIIe – début XVe siècle)*, Cahiers de Fanjeaux 32 (1997), pp. 225–48, 226, who reports that she is preparing a critical edition of the text, otherwise available in summary form in the work of

The topics are typical of the genre: the exaltation of Christ and the Virgin, the behaviour expected of good Christians, moralising against various categories of sin: avaricious or indiscrete clergy, ineffective monks, bad judges, usurers, deceitful women. There is little here to distinguish the preaching of the Sack Friars from that of the other mendicants. It is worth pausing to examine, however, both because of the rarity of texts produced by the Sack Friars and because in a few cases the author reveals something of the particular circumstances and claims to holiness of his order and a less prescriptive view of its relations with the secular and regular clergy. He also provides brief insight into the personal world of the thirteenth-century Church, reporting the stories circulating among the friars. Thus he used as an *exemplum* the case of Bertrand Agerat, a canon of Toulon who had, incidentally, been present with his bishop at the general chapter in Marseilles in 1251 which approved the adoption of the friars' rule. According to the anonymous friar, Bertrand was also prior of the church of Ollioules, north-west of Toulon, and one Sunday he set off for the village, leaving at dawn. On arrival, instead of saying matins, hearing Mass or listening to the sermon given in the village church, he played chess. Nor, so the story goes, did he say all the Hours as he should have done as a deacon. Instead, he went on playing chess until nones, after which he got up with a pain in the head and returned to Toulon. There, having gone mad, he suffered a serious illness and died after a few days.[117] The use of a man whose identity can still be traced now need not mean that Bertrand's fate is accurately reported, but the story was certainly intended to frighten the audience and encourage them to attend to their Christian duties. The reference to a local man gave the *exemplum* the power of gossip, encouraging agreement with the moral intended by the friar, whose principal audience was presumably the members of his own order, some of whom may well have remembered Bertrand.

The nature of the intended audience is also clear in an *exemplum* which exposes the inevitable difficulties of a community dedicated to endless repetition of the same prayers. An unnamed friar of the Sack reported that in a vision, an angel carried his spirit to a cathedral church, in which he saw clergy burying Christ, so that only his head and feet were visible. The angel revealed that this was because the clerics were singing the beginning and end of verses but were silent in the middle and thus they were 'burying Christ'.[118] The moral of course was that better and more attentive singing was needed, both by the clergy in the vision and by members of the order.

The *exempla* collection also provides a unique intimation of the development

---

Welter, 'Un recueil d'exempla du XIIIe siècle', and Welter, *L'Exemplum dans la littérature religieuse et didactique du Moyen Âge*, pp. 254–7.

[117] For the identification of Bertrand, see Rava-Cordier, 'La Proximité comme élément de persuasion', pp. 236–8.

[118] Welter, 'Un recueil d'exempla du XIIIe siècle', p. 660.

of a pious tradition within the order, reporting a miracle purported to have taken place in the house at Marseilles. One year, at the end of the sermon and solemn Mass on the feast of the Assumption (15 August), the friars found that that the *questors* (beggars) of the house had been unable to find any bread. The community therefore came together in praise of the Virgin, and immediately, abundant, beautiful loaves were to be had. Similar tales imitating Christ's miracle of the loaves and fishes were associated, amongst others, with Saints Dominic and Clare of Assisi, as portrayed on the tomb of Dominic in the 1260s and echoed in a panel in Assisi showing the life of Clare, painted in 1283.[119] They reinforced the message of the holiness of the friars' lives and justified their dependence on begging, an endlessly disputed issue.

The sources for these Provençal *exempla* give some sense of the kind of things members of the order were reading, and they are exactly what we should expect: pastoral works useful to a preacher: the Bible, saints' lives, miracle and sermon collections, occasional histories and one contemporary romance, the *Roman de Renard*.[120] A list of books belonging to the Barcelona friars in 1271 is very similar, but more theological and wide-ranging: in a single chest they kept some thirty-two volumes, starting with a large Bible and the standard works necessary for theological study and pastoral training, including Peter Lombard, Aquinas, various other commentaries, sentences and *Summae*, saints' lives, sermons and scholastic *quaestiones* by various masters of theology. They also had Augustine's *Confessions*, several canon-law texts (including the *Decretals* with apparatus), books on natural philosophy and other volumes in verse and prose.[121] It is not a substantial library, but bears comparison with those of analogous houses in the other orders of mendicants at this date.[122]

Beyond the cloister

All religious orders, of the Middle Ages and beyond, depend on lay support: the Sack Friars were no exception. In Worms, according to the *Chronicon Wormatiense*, the friars were totally unwanted by the citizens (*civibus totaliter irrequisitis*) and only admitted by the bishop, but this seems to be a unique

[119] On the tomb of Dominic see J. Cannon, 'Dominic *alter Christus*? Representations of the Founder in and after the *Arca di San Domenico*', in *Christ among the Medieval Dominicans. Representations of Christ in the Texts and Images of the Order of Preachers*, ed. K. Emery and J. Wawrykow, Notre Dame Conferences in Medieval Studies, VII (1998), pp. 26–48. On the Clare panel, see E. Lunghi, 'La decorazione pittorica della chiesa', in *La Basilica di S. Chiara in Assisi*, ed. M. Bigaroni, H.-R. Meier and E. Lunghi (Perugia, 1994), pp. 137–282, 164–88.

[120] Listed in Welter, 'Un recueil d'exempla du XIIIᵉ siècle', p. 650.

[121] Feliu, 'El monestir de frares de Penitència de Jesucrist de Barcelona', pp. 47–8 (also numbered as pp. 3–4), provided a partial transcript of the list, but was not able to decipher all the terms used. In 1998, Robert Burns ('The Friars of the Sack in Barcelona', p. 426) reported that the list is now 'displaced and perhaps lost'.

[122] See above, p. 60–2, 156–8.

bad-tempered example, if we discount the witty hostility of Iulitta de Adelhardis of Modena, cited by Salimbene.[123] Although Elm found only three donations to the order in Worms, two of which were from the clergy, in Basel and Strasbourg he identified numerous burghers as patrons of the houses of the order and a similar picture can be painted elsewhere. Throughout the Empire the friars were listed along with the other mendicant orders as recipients of largesse from urban donors, and also with beguines, Beghards, hospital brothers and hermits, a good indication of their relative position in popular understanding.[124] In general, the support of the laity was generous, if not as substantial as that available to the Franciscans and Dominicans. To the south in Mallorca, Larry Simon has found that testators usually left money to all the mendicant houses, both male and female and including the Sack Friars, again a convenient guide to their relative position in the esteem of lay believers. Thus in 1270 Pere Serra left 150 *solidi* to the Franciscans, twenty each to the Dominicans and Sack Friars, and ten each to the Clares and the nuns of Santa Margarida.[125]

Whereas Elm found relatively limited evidence for higher-status donors to the order in the Empire, elsewhere this was certainly not the case. The French royal family in the form of Louis IX and his younger brother Alphonse of Poitiers were generous to the order, as to all the mendicants. According to an undated manuscript now in Auxerre, when the friars first came to Paris they complained to Louis about the number of insults they were suffering, so that they wanted to leave. He allegedly replied: 'What were you looking for in this religion? If honour, then you were stupid, if dishonour then you have what you sought, so you should be happy.'[126] The tone of this exchange matches the wit of Louis conveyed in sources such as Joinville's biography of the king. He seems to have understood perfectly the ideal of poor humility professed by these friars, and took a close interest in them. As well as support for individual houses, in his will, drawn up in 1270, he left them 60 *livres*. This was substantially smaller than his legacies to the Friars Minor and Preacher (whose Paris houses each received 400 *livres*) but three times what he left to the Carmelites and four times his bequest to the Augustinian Hermits.[127] Such evidence seems to confirm the assessment of the poet Rutebeuf, whose account of the 'Orders of Paris' emphasised the Sack Friars' dependence on Louis:

---

[123] 'Chronicon Wormatiense', cited by Elm, 'Ausbreitung', p. 267. See also above, p. 176.

[124] Elm, 'Ausbreitung', p. 282.

[125] Simon, 'The Friars of the Sack and the Kingdom of Majorca', p. 288.

[126] Auxerre, Bibliothèque Municipale MS 35, fol. 232v (my English version is a paraphrase). It is cited in numerous previous accounts of the order, but never dated. See for example, Elm, 'Ausbreitung', pp. 287–8n.

[127] Berger, *Layettes du tresor des chartes*, IV, pp. 419–21, 420; Elm, 'Ausbreitung', p. 288. To the Dominicans and Franciscans, he left respectively 400 *livres* in Paris and a further 600 for the convents of the orders in his kingdom.

L'Ordre des Sas est povre et nue
Et si par est si tart venue
Qu'a paines seront soustenu.
Se Diex ot tel robe vestue
Comme il portent parmi la rue
Bien ont son abit retenu
De ce lor est bien avenu
Par un homme [Louis] sont maintenu
Tant comme il vivra, Diez aiüe!
Se mort le fet de vie nu,
Voisent la dont il sont venu
Si voist chascuns a la charrue![128]

Alphonse of Poitiers also left money to the Paris friars in his will, drawn up in 1270, and in the same year Hugh of Lusignan bequeathed them 100 *solidi*.[129] There is plenty of other evidence for high-status support for the Sack Friars. Jean, duke of Brittany, gave them a house on his land at Lamballe. In Angers, Godfroi de Chateaubriand gave the order a house and land for building in 1263 and the Benedictine nuns of the abbey of Ronceray, in whose fee the house stood, licensed the building of a church.[130] It is not clear how far building had got by the time of the Council of Lyons. In Utrecht in 1271 the house was supported by a legacy of £5 from Countess Aleidis, sister of William of Holland.[131] Likewise, in Ferrara (Italy) in 1264, the will of Mambilia Pelavicino, widow of Azzo VII d'Este, assigned the friars money for the works on their church and its decoration, though the sums involved were significantly smaller than those left to the Franciscans and the other mendicant orders.[132] In the Iberian peninsula, all but two houses lay within the lands of the Crown of Aragon, which was to prove generous to the friars. Burns has drawn particular attention to the various gifts of land and alms to the friars in the dependent kingdom of Valencia: in 1261 the Infante Pere (later Pere III), gave alms of 10 *solidi* to the friars of Valencia itself. In 1272 Jaime I left them 200 *morabatins* for their building works.[133] Three years earlier the

---

[128] 'The order of the Sack is poor and naked/ and has come so very late/ that they will hardly be supported./ If God had worn such dress as they wear in the street/ they have done well to keep his habit:/ from that it has turned out well for them;/ they are kept by one man [Louis]/ for as long as he will live, may God help him./ If death strips him of life,/ let them go there whence they came/ and let everyone go to the plough' (i.e. let them do an honest day's work, either as peasants or as proper monks). Rutebeuf, *Oeuvres complètes*, ed. E. Faral and J. Bastin, 2 vols (Paris, 1959), I, pp. 325–6. The identification with Louis IX is made by the editors, p. 326n. For other references to the Sack Friars, see ibid., pp. 332–3 and 367–8. Rutebeuf makes the same point about the late arrival of the friars in 'La Vie du monde', ibid., p. 406, and see below, p. 228.

[129] Berger, *Layettes du tresor des chartes* iv, pp. 413, 456.

[130] P. A. Feutry, 'Conventus Andegavensis OESA', *AA* 5 (1913), p. 130.

[131] Elm, 'Ausbreitung', p. 271.

[132] A. Samaritani, 'I frati Saccati a san Paolo di Ferrara (1260 *ca.* – 1295 *ca.*)', *Carmelus* 31 (1984), pp. 40–64, 50.

[133] *Thesaurus novus anecdotorum*, ed. E. Martene and U. Durand (Paris, 1717), I, col. 1144.

Játiva house had received from the Crown all the goods of a woman named
Bernarda deAlila, who may have been a relative of a Ramón de Alila who had
given them a plot of land. Bernarda had disinherited her son because he had
become a Muslim.[134] In lands heavily populated by Mudéjars, the order was
understandably and inevitably identified with the campaigning Catholicism
of the Reconquista. Nikolas Jaspert's study of legacies to the friary in Barcelona between 1257 and 1274 also confirms both the continuing support of
high-status individuals and the resulting wealth of the house.[135] In England,
similar evidence for the continuing enthusiasm of nobles and royals is not
hard to find – indeed royal grants are often almost the only evidence remaining for a friary. In February 1260 the friars in London were included in a long
list of recipients of alms issued by Henry III on his return from meeting Louis
IX in France.[136] Later that year, when his half-brother Aymer de Valence died,
the king asked all the friars in Oxford, where Aymer had been a student in
the 1240s, to say Masses for his soul and gave them money for food on the day
of liturgical commemoration.[137] Those benefiting included the Sack Friars.
Similar grants continued throughout Henry's reign and he also provided
building materials: in 1266 he gave six oaks from Selwood Forest to the friars
in Bristol and in Oxford in the following year. In Worcester in 1272 Henry
increased the land available to the friars, as also in Newcastle, where the grant
was requested by a Robert Bruce, probably the grandfather of the future king
of the Scots.[138] In London in the 1270s, Henry III responded to a complaint
from the friars about the wailing of the Jews and gave them the synagogue
(*scola*) next to their property, forcing the Jews to move further away.[139] The
building was to become the friars' chapel.[140] Edward I's queen, Eleanor of
Castile (†1290), also gave them buildings in the city and took them into her
protection.[141] English nobles were equally important patrons: the countess
of Warwick supported them in building their new house in Oxford with a

---

[134] Burns, 'Friars of the Sack in Valencia', p. 436. R. I. Burns, *Diplomatarium of the Crusader Kingdom of Valencia. The Registered Charters of Its Conqueror Jaume I, 1257–1276*, 3 vols (Princeton 1985–2001), III, nos 881, 972.

[135] Jaspert, *Stift und Stadt* (as above, p. 2 n. 2), p. 108n.

[136] *Close Rolls of the Reign of Henry III 1259–1261* (London, 1934), pp. 238–9, 12 February 1260. Other friars were also beneficiaries: the Dominicans, Franciscans and Carmelites, but not it seems the Austin Friars, who had arrived in the city some time before 1256.

[137] See S. Dixon-Smith, 'Feeding the Poor to Commemorate the Dead: The *Pro Anima* Almsgiving of Henry III of England, 1227–1271', Ph.D. thesis, University College London, 2003, p. 158.

[138] *Calendar of Patent Rolls, Henry III 1266–1272*, p. 633. He allowed the friars in Worcester to 'enclose a street called Dolday 120 feet long by 11 feet wide', granting it to them in frank almoin. See also Knowles and Hadcock, *Medieval Religious Houses* (as above, p. 38 n. 3), pp. 248–9.

[139] *Close Rolls of the Reign of Henry III 1268–1272* (London, 1938), p. 522: 'per strepitum judeorum confluentium ad scolam suam … et eciam per ipsorum judeorum continuum ululatum in eadem scola juxta ritum suum impediuntur …'; Chettle, 'The Friars of the Sack in England', p. 246.

[140] *Calendar of Patent Rolls Edward I 1301–1307* (London, 1898), p. 316; Chettle, 'The Friars of the Sack in England', p. 246.

[141] Dugdale, *Monasticon Anglicanum*, VI, part 3, p. 1607.

chapel near the church of St Budoc, acquired from the Crown in 1264–5.[142]

In just one documented case, that of Barcelona, while the friars were acquiring land and building their convent and church (including the purchase of a bell), they took on a lay proctor or syndic, Pere de Copons, to represent them. In 1264 they also appointed him manager (*iconomum*) of their property.[143] This seems to be close to the requirement of the constitutions that an outsider handle money and property on behalf of the friars. It was also a convenient financial arrangement. Pere later loaned them 3525 *solidi* and provided surety for other loans to be repaid from future legacies to the house. Similar syndics are not documented elsewhere, but the absence may well reflect the lack of sources.

One of the fullest accounts of the presence and activities of the friars is now to be found in a series of surviving agreements drawn up before they settled in a new parish or diocese. Many if not most of the towns in which they were located already had friaries of the other mendicant orders, an indication of their attraction as centres for preaching and begging. But the new arrivals put added pressure on the resources available and contributed to the tension between regular and secular clergy. The Provençal *exempla* collection discussed above reports an exchange between a friar of the Sack from Brignoles and a monk from the Benedictines at La Celle in which the problem is manifest. The monk reproached the friar for taking temporal goods which should have gone to the parish church.[144] The friar suggested to the monk that he should be grateful for the spiritual assistance provided by his order through its ministry and prayers, to which the monk retorted (in a wonderful mixture of vernacular and Latin): 'What the devil have we to do with the care of their souls, as long as we get the secular property'.[145] The anecdote personalises the strained relations between the mendicants and their regular neighbours. The author surely intended his audience to be shocked and to remember the avaricious monk, neatly contrasted to what his own brethren were offering. Agreements stipulated between friars and their secular and regular neighbours were an attempt to pre-empt such tensions; often they were an essential prerequisite for the formation of a new house. In Norwich in 1258, for example, the Sack Friars had to agree an annual payment to a local parish before acquiring property.[146] Again, in 1267, the friars in Strasbourg reached an accord with the dean and chapter of Jung-St Peter allowing them to build an oratory, the altar of which was consecrated in the following year

---

[142] *VCH Oxfordshire*, ed. W. Page, II (London, 1907), p. 150.

[143] Burns, 'The Friars of the Sack in Barcelona', p. 423n.

[144] Welter, 'Un recueil d'exempla du XIIIᵉ siècle' (1913), p. 646, and (1914), pp. 194, 312. See also Amargier, 'Les Frères de la Pénitence de Jésus Christ ou du Sac', p. 162.

[145] 'Che deablos aven nos afar de animabus ipsorum, dummodo possimus habere temporalia', quoted in Rava-Cordier, 'La Proximité comme élément de persuasion', p. 244.

[146] Jotischky, *Carmelites and Antiquity* (as above, p. 9 n. 2), p. 21n.

by the Dominican Albertus Magnus.[147] In the same way in Avignon in 1270, before starting building the friars agreed to pay a yearly sum to the rector of the parish of Saint-Symphorien in which their house was to stand.[148] In all these cases and again in Brussels, the friars gave up a substantial percentage of any future income to the local parish clergy.[149] In some cases, perhaps because the local friars encountered particular difficulties, senior members of the order were involved. In Liège in 1265, after a long wait, Friar Juvenis, the rector general, obtained permission from the provost, dean, archdeacon and chapter of the cathedral of St Lambert for his friars to celebrate the Office in the house they planned to establish in the town, but only on condition that they found no other houses in the diocese.[150] Three years later the German provincial prior reached agreement with the chapter of Speyer Cathedral which had held the rights over the parish of Esslingen since 1213. The contract granted the friars land in Esslingen on which to build a church and convent.

The purpose of such undertakings is particularly well-illustrated in the 'amicable convention' (*amicabilis compositio*) drawn up in the summer of 1260 in Marseilles between on the one hand Gaufridus Rostagnus (the provost of Marseilles who had witnessed the giving of the rule to the order nine years earlier), the precentor, *operarius* (master of the works), and four canons of the cathedral chapter and, on the other, Prior Gui de Soleriis, of the Friars of the Sack in Marseilles, together with three of his friars acting on behalf of the convent.[151] Each side declared that they were making the pact explicitly to 'avoid disputes and altercations which arise unexpectedly at the instigation of the devil'. The contract was stipulated in the canonry in the room of the provost and gave precise form to the obligations and opportunities of the friars. They could build a church or oratory and have as many altars in it as they chose. They might also allow anyone to attend the Office in their church and have a cemetery for the burial of their own brethren and any others who should choose to be buried there. They were permitted to accept oblations and legacies. In return, on Christmas Eve each year, they were to pay the provost of Marseilles 20 *solidi*, half of which was to go to the parish of St Cannat, whose current prior was a member of the chapter and also one of the four canons participating in the agreement. The provost himself was to collect the canonical portion, a quarter of all proceeds from legacies. Finally, the friars must attend any general processions called by the bishop, his deputy or the provost to mark occasions such as the advent of the pope, or

---

[147] Elm, 'Ausbreitung', p. 264. Albertus Magnus was a famous Dominican theologian, master in the Dominican *studium* in Cologne and briefly bishop of Regensburg (1260–2).

[148] De Fontette, 'Les Mendiants supprimés', p. 211.

[149] Elm, 'Ausbreitung', p. 281.

[150] Ibid., pp. 274, 278.

[151] Giacomozzi, *L'ordine della penitenza di Gesù Cristo*, pp. 118–20.

(more likely) cardinals, papal legates and other prelates. The whole text was predicated on the status of the Sack Friars as subject to the authority of the diocesan bishop, who duly gave his seal of approval on 1 August, by which date the friars had already received their first donation towards the costs of work on their church from the will of Leone, daughter of Surleon and widow of Pierre Bermond de Saint-Félix.[152]

The Marseilles settlement left the friars unusually free to preach and participate in the spiritual life of the laity. By comparison, in Palma de Mallorca in the following year, the arrival of the friars prompted a more restrictive settlement with the secular clergy, which unusually, makes no reference to sharing of revenue, perhaps because the seculars hoped to prevent accumulation of resources by the friars.[153] In August 1261 the bishop and chapter of Mallorca reached agreement with Raymund (Athenulf), rector of the order. Arnau, the provincial prior of Spain, Pere, the prior of the friary and the provincial priors of France and England, amongst others, all also gave their approval. Activities which might present competition for parish clergy were to be strictly controlled. The friars were to be obedient to the bishop and attend annual diocesan synods; they were not to have a cemetery except for their own brethren, parishioners were not to be admitted to their churches on Sundays or feast days (when they would be expected to attend either their parish church or the cathedral). Nor were the friars to preach or hear confessions without specific licence from the bishop. Appeal to the pope against these constraints was forbidden. As far as we can tell, the agreement was observed, or at the least none of the wills traced by Larry Simon refers to burial in the Sack Friars' house, though the popularity of the friars as beneficiaries in those same wills suggests that they nonetheless succeeded in building contacts with the laity.[154]

In other orders such agreements often fell by the wayside as the friars became entrenched in a diocese; in the case of the Sack Friars too little time passed for this to happen before 1274. But initial agreements were not always sufficient to prevent conflict: in Brussels in 1270 the Sack Friars, together with the Carmelites were involved in a dispute with the chapter of St Gudule.[155] The context in Brussels is now obscure, but in the same year in Toulouse the friars again found themselves at odds with the local chapter. They had initially settled outside the walls and paid an annual fixed sum and a quarter of all legacies to the chapter of Saint-Étienne. The site was, however, unsatisfactory and they sought to move to land given to them in the city. The chapter of Saint-Étienne objected. In 1270 the friars petitioned the *parlement*

[152] Amargier, 'Les Frères de la Pénitence de Jésus Christ ou du Sac', p. 162n.
[153] Simon, 'The Friars of the Sack and the Kingdom of Majorca', pp. 292–4.
[154] Ibid., pp. 288–91.
[155] *Chartes du chapitre de Sainte Gudule a Bruxelles 1047–1300*, ed. P. Lefèvre, P. Godding and F. Godding-Ganshof (Louvain, 1993), p. 148.

of Alphonse of Poitiers, requesting that he intervene on their behalf and authorise them to build. No action was taken and after 1274 it was in any case too late. Ironically, in 1290 the convent was itself sold to the chapter of Saint-Étienne, which took possession in 1295, though it later passed to the Dominicans.[156]

In some cities the friars did manage to settle in the centre straightaway, as for example in Augsburg, Utrecht, Brussels or Cologne. In other cases they had time to move to a better site before the crisis of 1274: in London, they started off outside Aldersgate but later moved to Coleman Street near Guildhall and also acquired properties in other areas of the city by bequest.[157] In Cambridge, where they arrived before 1258, they began in the parish of St Mary in the Market, but later moved to a large stone house given to them by John le Rus, held in fee of Barnwell Priory, which gave licence for the transfer in that year. Ten years later Henry III confirmed the grants of the le Rus family and those from various other donors. The friars replaced an original chapel dedicated to St Lucy with a church in honour of 'Jesus Christ and his Blessed Mother', but the le Rus family required that Lucy's feast day continue to be celebrated.

At times the friars succeeded in acquiring houses previously occupied by another order, as in Erfurt, where they took over the former Franciscan house outside the walls, or used for another purpose, as in Asti, where they occupied a former hospital near the church of San Marco.[158] In Viterbo they obtained the church of San Pietro del Castagno, which had belonged to the Cistercians.[159] In Ferrara the archbishop of Ravenna assigned the friars the parish church of San Paolo. But in most cases, where the position of the house can now be established, it generally reflects the late arrival of the order in the urban context: the restricted space within the walls was beyond their reach. In Venice, currently the earliest known house outside Provence, the friary was on land surrounded by marsh, like the early Augustinians and Carmelites in the city. In Valencia the friary stood next to a market-place outside the *Buatella* gate.[160] In Palma de Mallorca it lay within the third ring of medieval walls, near the Sitjar gate in the lower city. In Basel the house lay close to the city wall in newly formed 'Klein Basel' on the right bank of the Rhine.[161] In Aix-en-Provence the house again stood near the city walls, but must have been an unusually substantial and convenient property, since it was later identified as an excellent site (*locum valde bonum*) when passed to

---

[156] Dossat, 'Opposition des anciens ordres à l'installation des mendiants', p. 294. *Lecta coram nobis*, 7 October 1290 (Langlois 3508). See also below, p. 218.

[157] *VCH London*, ed. W. Page, I (London, 1909), p. 516.

[158] Giacomozzi, *L'ordine della penitenza di Gesù Cristo*, p. 39.

[159] Ibid., p. 45.

[160] Burns, 'The Friars of the Sack in Valencia', p. 436.

[161] P. Zimmer, 'Die Augustiner-Eremiten in der Schweiz', *Helvetia sacra*, IV, 6, ed. P. Braun (Basel, 2003), pp. 21–182, 28.

Dominican nuns, whose previous house was much farther out.[162] In Strasbourg, the house was in a suburb of the city, with a small oratory and convent in 'Steinstrasse'. In Oxford, the friars were in a thinly inhabited area where they gradually acquired a plot some 20.5 perches long.[163] In Lincoln, they had a substantial plot of land in suburban Thornbridgegate Street which included eight properties given to them by a series of lay donors and an area of the common pasture given to them by the town of Lincoln. In 1268 the king allowed them thirteen oaks for the construction of their church.[164]

The constitutions set down that the houses of the order should be small and humble but gives no further details. According to a later account the buildings of the friars in Norwich were a 'carefully planned and compact block'.[165] Presumably carefully planned buildings were being put up in many of the locations cited above. Later disputes over the rights to their houses, such as that at Paris, suggest that some had been or become desirable properties.[166] Jaspert notes that the house in Barcelona was so large that the community which took over had no need to add new buildings to the friary for nearly a century.[167] It is now, however, impossible to say much about the structure of their buildings anywhere. Elm argues that they were in no position to build solid churches and cloisters, or for that matter to acquire valuable liturgical equipment and celebrate with splendid liturgy.[168] As we have seen, they inherited some buildings, but many of their friaries must have been incomplete in 1274. Construction was certainly encouraged at Freiburg, with the support of episcopal indulgences, but in numerous other cases the decision to continue lay in the hands of their new owners.[169] All that seems to remain in England is one building of their convent at Rye, a rubble-walled construction, which was turned to secular use after the friars departed,[170] while the present simple structure on the site of their house at Brignoles in Provence later passed to the Templars (soon in their turn to be suppressed), and must largely date to the latters' tenancy and beyond.[171]

The evidence presented here is piece-meal, but it shows an order which, from simple beginnings in Provence, had expanded rapidly across Europe.

[162] Giacomozzi, *L'ordine della penitenza di Gesù Cristo*, p. 24n. See also de Fontette, 'Les Mendiants supprimés', p. 210.

[163] *VCH Oxfordshire*, II, p. 150.

[164] *VCH Lincoln*, II, ed. W. Page (London, 1906), p. 225.

[165] Chettle, 'The Friars of the Sack in England', p. 247.

[166] On Paris see below, p. 219–20.

[167] Jaspert, *Stift und Stadt*, pp. 108n., 359.

[168] Elm, 'Ausbreitung', p. 281.

[169] For the Freiburg indulgences, see above, p. 189.

[170] B. Harbottle, 'Excavations at the Carmelite Friary, Newcastle upon Tyne, 1965 and 1967', *Archaeologia Aeliana*, 4th series 46 (1968), pp. 163–223, 169. It was known in the twentieth century as 'Old Stone House' on Church Square. See *VCH Sussex*, ed. L. F. Salzman, IX (London, 1937), p. 43, which refers to a thirteenth-century moulded string-course, window arch and jambs.

[171] For Brignoles, see the photograph in de Fontette, 'Les Mendiants supprimés', following p. 216.

They received approval as a mendicant order before the Austin Friars, but like them risked the fate of late arrivals. As we have seen, Rutebeuf drew attention to the problem when he wrote of the difficulties of supporting them.[172] Poverty, nakedness and lateness on the scene combined to make them difficult to sustain. Yet it was their very poverty which inspired the assistance of lay patrons in innumerable cities and towns and earned them the acceptance, if not always the support, of both secular and regular clergy for their activities. Frequently the first reference to the arrival of the order is now a will, marking the interest of both lay and clerical donors and indicating that the friars had impressed with their holiness: giving to them was recognised as a way to improve the chances of the soul of the donor and his or her family.[173] In at least one case, that of Marseilles, a bishop who was later a Franciscan chose a member of the order as his chaplain, clear evidence of esteem.

The friars had also had a sequence of rectors general. Friars Guillaume (documented *c.* 1254–6) and Raymond (documented 1258–61) were followed by Juvenis (documented 1264–7), and Otto (documented *c.* 1274). Iuvenis had probably earlier been provincial prior in France (1261) and was active in Amiens, Liège and Barcelona in the 1260s.[174] All were presumably working to promote and secure the future of their order, as were the various provincial priors who can now be identified.[175] Yet in the last quarter of the thirteenth century this structure was to be pulled apart. It is a marker of the potential of papal and conciliar authority within the Church that there seems to have been very little challenge to the decision of 1274.

The Council of Lyons and its aftermath

In July 1274, the last session of the general council presided over by Pope Gregory X at Lyons decreed the end of orders founded since 1215.[176] Constitution 23 repeated and expanded on *Ne nimia religionum* of 1215, which had restricted new orders or the adoption of new habits. Two categories of order were now to be discontinued. All religious and mendicant orders established after the Lateran Council of 1215 which had not had papal approval were placed under perpetual ban. Regulars professed in orders which had obtained papal approval after the Lateran Council, but whose profession, rule or constitutions forbade them to have appropriate income or possessions, so that they lived by the uncertainty of begging (*incerta mendicitas*), might

---

[172] See above, p. 200.
[173] On this see J. Chiffoleau, *La Comptabilité de l'au-delà. Les hommes, la mort et la religion dans la région d'Avignon à la fin du Moyen Âge* (Rome, 1980).
[174] For a 'frater Iuuenis prior prouincialis Francie' see Simon, 'The Friars of the Sack and the Kingdom of Majorca', p. 293. Activities summarised in Elm, 'Ausbreitung', pp. 288–9.
[175] As well as those already named, a Friar Achardus is identified as the provincial of the brothers in the *regno francie* in 1271. Simons, *Bedelordekloosters*, p. 91.
[176] See also above, pp. 18–20, 90–1.

continue as they were, but only on the basis that they admit no one to their profession and acquire no new houses or *loca*. They were to die out slowly. Nor might they dispose of their property without special papal licence: it was to be reserved to the papal see and used for the Holy Land, the poor, or other pious purposes, as instructed by local bishops or others authorised by the Curia. Any who disobeyed were subject to excommunication. Those in orders affected by the constitution were particularly forbidden to preach, hear confessions or provide burial for outsiders. Individuals were authorised to transfer to other approved orders immediately, but specific papal permission would be required for the transfer of a whole order to another, or of a convent with its property to another convent.[177]

Senior prelates had recommended the dissolution of some of the 'multitude of mendicant orders' before the council and some regulars certainly expected their ideas to be implemented: in their provincial chapter in Toulouse, meeting four days *before* the decree of the general council, the Dominicans warned against admitting unsuitable friars from the disbanded orders who would burden them. Someone was obviously in the know. However, neither the council nor the pope produced a list specifying which orders were to be closed down, leaving plenty of room for uncertainty. The Dominicans and Franciscans were explicitly exempted in the decree itself and the Carmelites and Augustinians were allowed a stay of execution. Over the following decades, canon lawyers and chroniclers commented on the decision and its effect, variously identifying the orders concerned, but confusion reigned.[178] Some contemporaries clearly thought the decree was aimed mainly at the Sack Friars: the *Annals of Dunstable*, for example, reported that 'many orders were prohibited', but named only the Sack Friars.[179] Others thought the regulation covered the Augustinians too or the Williamites and Trinitarians, all of which in practice survived.[180] The most complete list is provided by the chronicle of St Catherine *de Monte* in Rouen, which catalogues a whole series of discontinued orders. It is not, however, always accurate. As well as the Sack and Pied Friars, it names the *Ordo martyrum* who were otherwise known as 'Friars of Penitence of the Martyrs'. These had spread from France, to Spain, Italy, Bohemia, Poland and England, where, according to Eccleston, they arrived during the priorate of Peter of Tewkesbury.[181] Their community in Rome was approved in April 1256 as an *ordo canonicus*, following the 'rule

---

[177] Constitution 23, 'Concilium Lugdunense II, 1274', *Conciliorum oecumenicorum decreta* (as above, p. 49 n. 2), pp. 326–7.

[178] Elm, 'Ausbreitung', pp. 258–9.

[179] 'Annals of Dunstable', ed. R. Pauli, *MGH SS* XXVII (Hannover, 1885), p. 512; Chettle, 'The Friars of the Sack in England', pp. 239 and 255.

[180] Elm, 'Ausbreitung', p. 259. On the Augustinians see above, p. 91–3.

[181] Thomas de Eccleston, 'De adventu minorum', ed. Brewer, p. 72 (from a marginal note): 'Tertio anno administrationis fratris Petri venerunt fratres de Ordine Marytrum in Angliam, quorum fundator erat quidam Martinus, qui fuerat Parisius, quasi fatuus nobilium Alemanniae.'

of Augustine and the institutes of the brothers of penitence of the order of martyrs'.[182] Four years later they had a house in Guildford and after 1274 became an order of regular canons, obtaining papal confirmation in 1295.[183] According to an anonymous Austrian poet, they wore a sign of the cross on their chests over a white habit.[184] On the other hand, another of the groups in the Rouen list, the *Ordo apostolorum* or Apostolic friars, described disparagingly by Salimbene, were followers of Gerardo Segarelli, who sought to reclaim the absolute barefoot poverty of Francis of Assisi in imitation of Christ and the Apostles. In 1269 the bishop of Parma recommended Gerardo's female followers to all believers, but they never acquired papal approval and refused to obey the decree of 1274. By 1285 they had spread beyond Italy and, influenced by Joachite ideas, had become strong critics of the clergy. Some of their members were eventually to be burned as heretics.[185]

Not all on the Rouen list can now be identified with any certainty: no group calling itself an *Ordo evangelistarum* or 'Order of evangelists', has so far been traced, while perhaps the most difficult to distinguish now are the *Ordo sanctae Crucis* and *Ordo crucifixorum*. There were several contemporary groups calling themselves by names associated with the cross or crucifix (the Friars of the Holy Cross, Crucifers, *Cruciferi*, *Croisiers* or Crutched Friars), but whether those referred to in the chronicle are those of Belgian or Italian origin or those who reached England is unclear: certainly none were suppressed and the English Crutched Friars were in any case not mendicants but canons regular.[186]

One thing is certain: of the orders discontinued as a result of the council, the Sack Friars were the largest and most established – numerically they were probably in third place among the mendicants, after the Franciscans and Dominicans.[187] But whereas the Carmelites and Augustinians were able to regain ground even during the council, the Sack Friars seem to have been caught unawares. The years leading up to 1274 had seen considerable growth: in April 1272 they may have acquired general protection from the English

---

[182] *Religiosam vitam eligentibus*, 9 April 1256 (Bourel 1310), addressed to 'priori ecclesie sancte Marie de Metri de Urbe'.

[183] Knowles and Hadcock, *Medieval Religious Houses*, p. 250; Elm, 'Ausbreitung', pp. 297, 316.

[184] Anonymous, 'Chronicon rhythmicum Austriacum', p. 358.

[185] See most recently G. G. Merlo, *Eretici ed eresie medievali* (Bologna, 1989), pp. 99–105 and dal Pino, 'Papato e ordini mendicanti-apostolici "minori" nel duecento', pp. 107–59.

[186] See J. M. Hayden, 'Religious Reform and Religious Orders in England, 1490–1540: The Case of the Crutched Friars', *The Catholic Historical Review* 86 (2000), pp. 420–38, 422–3. H. F. Chettle, 'The Friars of the Holy Cross in England', *History* 34 (1949), pp. 204–20; Elm, 'Ausbreitung', p. 316, and Emery, *The Friars in Medieval France*, who documents houses of Crutched friars in Buzançais (1419), Caen (1290), Carignan (1341), Chauny (1484), Lannoy (1474), Paris (1258), Saint-Georges in Ille-et-Villaine (1346), Saint-Ursin in Mayenne (1316), Salignac (1337), Toulouse (1256), Troyes (1343), Varennes (1391) and Le Verger in Maine-et-Loire (1490).

[187] As suggested by K. Elm, most recently in 'Sackbrüder', *Lexikon des Mittelalters* 7 (Munich, 1995), col. 1244.

Crown, authorising them to build further oratories and houses.[188] Numerous new friaries were founded or appear in the documentation for the first time in these years, and of the latter many may have been very recent. In February 1274, just a month before the opening of the Second Council of Lyons, the commune of Perugia in central Italy was discussing how to provide a place for the friars to settle and build a church.[189] Nothing ever came of it. Even the pope may not have expected such drastic change in the case of the Sack Friars. As late as March 1274, as the council opened, Gregory X seems to have criticised attacks on their convents in the kingdom of France and renewed papal protection.[190]

Juridically the decision was straightforward. In 1215 the Fourth Lateran Council had called a halt to the expansion of new *religiones* (rules), instructing those wishing to adopt the religious life to choose an existing text, lest diversity 'lead to serious confusion in the Church of God'.[191] The Lyons Council invoked this decree, and whereas the Carmelites and Augustinians had indeed had houses before this date, if not in the form later approved, the Sack Friars could not, or simply did not, claim any earlier history. They had, as we have seen, acquired papal approval, though this was soon forgotten. In a letter copied into a formulary produced for one of the offices of the papal chancery in the time of Boniface VIII (1294–1303), the original approved status of the order was cautiously reported only as an assertion, not as fact.[192] And in any case, constitution 23 explicitly disbanded even those who had been papally approved since 1215, if they lived by begging, which the Sack Friars certainly did.[193] In the immediate context of the council, the lack of a cardinal protector aware of what was going on and able to act on behalf of the order in the Curia must have been critical. The friars also lacked a powerful lay advocate on their side, such as Louis IX, who had died four years earlier. The criticisms of the new orders by, amongst others, Humbert de Romans, the former Dominican master general, do not appear to match what we know of the Sack Friars, but the preference of such men for fewer

---

[188] Chettle, 'The Friars of the Sack in England', p. 245, citing *Calendar of Patent Rolls Henry III 1266–72*, p. 645 (21 April 1272), which refers, however, to the friars of the 'order of St Mary and Jesus Christ' and may, as he suggests, refer to the Servites, or, perhaps more likely, to the Pied Friars.

[189] D. M. Montagnana, 'Una progettata fondazione a Perugia dei frati della penitenza di Gesù Cristo (1273–1274)', *Studi storici dell'ordine dei Servi di Maria* 24 (1974), pp. 272–3.

[190] The bull is cited by Giacomozzi, *L'ordine della penitenza di Gesù Cristo*, p. 19 and n.71, on the basis of F. J. Marquez, *Origine delli frati eremitani dell'ordine di sant'Agostino e la sua vera istituzione avanti al gran Concilio lateranense* (Tortona, 1620), pp. 246–7. As Giacomozzi notes, no record of the bull is to be found in *Les Registres de Grégoire X 1272–1276*, ed. J. Guiraud (Paris 1892–1906), or in Potthast.

[191] On this see above, pp. 13, 18, 90–1.

[192] P. Herde, *Audientia litterarum contradictarum*, Bibliothek des deutschen Historischen Instituts in Rom 31–32, 2 vols (Tübingen, 1970), II, pp. 380–2, K 227: 'qui ut asserit, extitit post generale concilium institutus per sedem apostolicam confirmatus fuisse dicatur...'

[193] The importance of this issue is underlined by the activities of the Servites, who employed canon lawyers to provide *consilia* defending their status and insisting that they were not begging. See above, p. 20.

orders was powerfully voiced.[194] By contrast it is not even clear whether Otto, the rector general of the Friars of the Sack, was present at the council, or whether, like the prior of the Servites, who were also threatened with suppression, he then went to the Curia to plead their case.

The emotional effect on the members of the order is laid bare in a letter written by Otto, at some point soon after the council.[195] He wrote to inform his friars of the disastrous outcome and enclosed a copy of the relevant constitution, to give them a better idea of what to do. He warned them not to despair, but his own opening address sets an anguished tone: 'To men whose order has been rejected, to all the desolate brothers of the Penitence of Jesus Christ, Brother Otto, greeting and a message of most bitter death, full of tears and grief.'[196] He made no reference to the legal argument for the suppression of the order, instead criticising those who may have objected to their increasing numbers, comparing them to the conspirators against the Jews in the Book of Esther and identifying himself with the wronged innocence of the Old Testament figures Job and Jeremiah. He acknowledged that they may have done some wrong, yet he also tried to console his friars, clearly hoping that the pope might yet change his mind. If they served God in simplicity and ignored others' derision, they might yet acquire an 'eternal name and receive the power to regenerate'. The letter reminds the friars that they can still go on celebrating the Office and begging for alms. At the same time it acknowledges the authority of the pope, whose sentence is to be 'feared and observed, not judged'. Otto warns them not to challenge the force of the prohibition and to be careful to avoid the criticisms and detractions of men or, above all, of the pope and other religious. He also repeats the provision in constitution 23 that they could now leave the order: those who wished to, should do 'whatever seemed good in their own eyes', a direct contradiction of the normal stipulation that regular religious must submit to the will of the superior without hesitation. It is symbolic here of the sudden change in the status of the order.

Otto's letter reveals a desperate man; whether or not he was capable of being an effective advocate for the order it is impossible to say. As Elm commented when writing about the friars in general before this text was known, he appears law-abiding, perhaps too much so. It may also be, as Elm suggests, that their origins in Provence, home to well-known heretical groups, made them vulnerable to the accusations of Joachite links which were exploited by other mendicants to suggest that heresy might arise among them.[197] A similar

---

[194] J. D. Mansi, *Sacrorum conciliorum nova et amplissima collectio*, 31 vols (Florence and Venice, 1759–98), XXIV, p. 130. See also Giacomozzi, *L'ordine della penitenza di Gesù Cristo*, p. 53.

[195] Oxford, Bodleian MS Digby 166, fols 48rb–48va. Brought to light by A. G. Rigg, 'The Lament of the Friars of the Sack', *Speculum* 55 (1980), pp. 84–90.

[196] Rigg, 'The Lament of the Friars of the Sack', p. 88.

[197] Elm, 'Ausbreitung', pp. 321–2.

case can be made for the closing down of the Pied Friars. In the end, however, it must simply have been the insurmountable absence of any history pre-dating 1215, combined with poverty and a lack of resources, perhaps also the humility inherent in the ideal of penance by which they lived, which prevented any campaign to restore the order.

Perhaps surprisingly, there is scant evidence for disruption or problems of discipline: in August 1278 Pope Nicholas III wrote to his legate in France, Simon de Brion, about a scandal involving a conspiracy against King Philip III and his queen, Marie of Brabant. At the end of the letter Nicholas instructed Simon to ensure that an unnamed friar of the Sack, guilty of blasphemy, should be imprisoned until he repented.[198] The nature of the blasphemy is not stated: it may be that the friar was raging against the treatment of his order, but it may equally be that he was involved in the conspiracy, or neither.

In some houses, life continued as before: in York, the register of Bishop Giffard (1266–79) lists two friars of the house, Thomas de Harepam and Hugh of Leicester, who were ordained as priests in September 1274.[199] In Barcelona in 1276 the friars themselves referred to a hoped-for reversal of the decree, whilst in Valencia in August 1278, a man named Ramon Armer gave up his goods to his sister Marie and brother-in-law Geraldo, declaring that he wished to enter the order of the Friars Penitent of Jesus Christ.[200] In Florence in 1286 the friars were to be found exchanging property, with papal permission.[201] Despite the ban, some friars continued their pastoral activities: in 1288 Cologne friars were present at the burial of men who had been killed in battle at Worringen,[202] while the continuing relevance of the Sack Friars to spiritual life in Ferrara is underlined by a city statute of 1287 which ordained that those returning monies acquired through usury should give them to either the Dominicans, the Franciscans, the Augustinian Hermit Friars or the Sack Friars.

There is also evidence for continuing generosity from churchmen. In Bordeaux in 1277 the Sack Friars received a remarkable gift from the local Dominicans, Franciscans and Carmelites: a silver chalice valued at 6 *livres tournois* for the celebration of Mass.[203] Were the friars particularly poor or

---

[198] R. Kay, 'Martin IV and the Fugitive Bishop of Bayeux', *Speculum* 40 (1965), pp. 460–83, 472, citing *Super amaritudine carissimi*, 23 August 1278 (Gay 297).

[199] *The Register of Archbishop Walter Giffard*, ed. W. Brown, Publications of the Surtees society 109 (Durham, 1904), p. 198. The ordination and examination also included a Carmelite from York, three Augustinians from Tickhill, five Dominicans (four from Derby), four Friars Minor from Beverley, monks from several of the Yorkshire Cistercian houses, three from St Mary's, York, two canons of St Oswald's and numerous other canons and regular religious.

[200] Jaspert, *Stift und Stadt*, p. 109 n. 37; Burns, *The Crusader Kingdom of Valencia, Reconstruction on a Thirteenth-Century Frontier* (Cambridge, Mass., 1967), p. 209.

[201] *Significavit nobis*, 23 May 1286 (Prou 521), grants permission for an exchange of land with Fulco Portenari, a Florentine citizen, who was building a hospital outside the city walls.

[202] Asen, 'Die Begarden und die Sackbrüder in Köln', p. 179.

[203] De Fontette, 'Les Mendiants supprimés', p. 205.

their neighbours simply generous in victory? In 1277 Bishop Hartmann of Augsburg gave the friars in Freiburg an indulgence for the building of their church and later Bishops Simon of Worms (1283–1291) and Johannes of Litthauen (*c.* 1273–*c.* 1285) provided similar support.[204] In 1284 the cantor of Trier Cathedral gave the Sack Friars in the town 20 *solidi*, the same as he gave the Williamites, Carmelites and two houses of Clares, though half the sum given to the Dominicans and Franciscans.[205] In 1285 the bishop of Toulouse made bequests to the Sack Friars in his will.[206]

A few houses were particularly long-lived: in England at least twelve lasted until the turn of the century and beyond, including York, London, Newcastle, Stamford, Lincoln and Norwich. Friaries in Mallorca, Brussels and Rouen were also all still occupied at the end of the century. The friars were no longer supposed to preach, hear confessions or bury outsiders, and thus were removed from the usual means by which to build relationships with the laity and acquire alms and oblations. Yet the evidence suggests that it was above all continuing lay support for the order across Europe which maintained these communities in the decades after 1274. In 1275 a Valencia notary, Pere Marqués, left the friars in the city 5 *solidi*.[207] In Siena in 1278 and 1279 they received money for clothing.[208] In Ferrara in 1275 a widow left the order more than either the Dominicans or Franciscans, though as Samaritani notes, the will avoids naming the friars, referring instead to their church of San Paolo, which was also a parish. Four years later, a Ferrara noble, Gerardino Contrari, left 20 *lire* to each of the mendicant orders in the town, but chose burial in the church of the Dominicans.[209] In April 1282, before departing for the Holy Land, William of Stafford left legacies to various churches in Dublin, including 2 shillings to the Brothers of the Sack.[210] In Palma de Mallorca, Larry Simon has traced continuing legacies throughout the late 1270s and 1280s and down to 1301. Although by the end of the century the size of bequests was shrinking and they were almost always smaller than those to other friars, the order of the Sack was clearly still popular.[211] Nikolas Jaspert has found similar evidence for Barcelona.[212] Again, in Marseilles, the support of the populace resulted in continued donations throughout the late thirteenth century: in 1286 Bertrand de Bellomonte left 20 *sous* for an anniversary Mass in their church and in 1293 Gullielma Thomasia, the widow of a sailor, left 20 *sous* to the prior, Pierre de Narbonne, to have himself some clothes made.

[204] Elm, 'Ausbreitung', p. 266.

[205] Schmidt, *Bettelorden in Trier*, p. 153. On the doubtful status of this house, see above, p. 184–5.

[206] De Fontette, 'Les Mendiants supprimés', p. 212.

[207] Simon, 'The Friars of the Sack and the Kingdom of Majorca', pp. 288–90.

[208] Giacomozzi, *L'ordine della penitenza di Gesù Cristo*, p. 45.

[209] Samaritani, 'I frati Saccati a san Paolo', p. 52.

[210] Roth, *The English Austin Friars* (as above, p. 83 n.52), II, p. 41 no. 73.

[211] Simon, 'The Friars of the Sack and the Kingdom of Majorca', p. 289.

[212] Jaspert, *Stift und Stadt*, p. 109n.

Royal alms to the order also continued, though no longer, it appears, for building works. In 1277 the Sack Friars in Norwich were still included together with Franciscans, Dominicans, Carmelites and Pied Friars as beneficiaries of royal alms.[213] Edward I gave the house in Canterbury alms for food in 1289 and again in 1297.[214] In 1289 he also gave alms to the friars on his lands in south-west France (Bordeaux) and further north in Poitiers, Tours, Paris and Amiens. The Sack Friars also benefited alongside the other orders of friars from a gift of money seized from the Jews of Guyenne who were expelled that year.[215] Eight years later he was similarly generous to the friars in Ghent during his military expedition to Flanders.[216] In 1300 he gave the house in Lincoln 2 shillings and 8 pence for two days' food – from which we may infer there were perhaps four friars each since the English Crown usually calculated the cost at four pennies per day – and in the same year gave pittances to a similar number of friars in Stamford, three in Newcastle and two in York.[217] In Paris in 1285 Philip III gave the Sack house the same in alms as he gave to the Carmelites and more than to the Augustinians.[218]

Some houses may have gathered the friars from several abandoned properties, as has been suggested for Cambridge, where there seem to have been only six friars in 1277, but twenty in 1289.[219] Most vigorous of all was Puigcerdà in the Pyrenees, where some two hundred wills from 1299 to 1328 document the continuity of a prosperous community. Like most religious houses, some of the donations came from members of the friars' families: in 1306, Ramona Galaub made a bequest to her two sons, Friar Simó and Friar Pere Galaub; but the majority were gifts from men and women asking for post mortem masses and prayers. In one case, Joan Pellisser, himself a priest, had a priest of the Friars of Penitence present at his deathbed.[220] Many of the legacies were personally directed to the prior, Mateu, whose great activity leads Burns to suggest that in this Pyrenean stronghold even in the early fourteenth century the friars and the lay community among whom they lived may still have been hoping for a reversal of the decree of 1274.[221]

Some friars obviously expected that the decree would be reversed and

[213] R. W. Emery in a review of the first edition of Knowles and Hadcock, *Medieval Religious Houses* in *Speculum* 29 (1954), pp. 290–2.

[214] *VCH Kent*, ed. W. Page, II (London, 1926), p. 205.

[215] A. G. Little, 'Aumônes faites par Édouard I aux frères mendiants en Guyenne et autres parties de la France en 1289', *Revue d'histoire franciscaine* 2 (1925), pp. 178–85. The sums were generally much smaller than those for the four main orders of friars.

[216] Simons, *Bedelordekloosters*, p. 152.

[217] Harbottle, 'Excavations at the Carmelite Friary, Newcastle upon Tyne', p. 167. See also *VCH Lincoln*, II, pp. 225, 230 and *VCH York*, III, p. 296. On the calculation of four pennies a day see Little, 'Aumônes', p. 180.

[218] Emery, 'The Friars of the Sack', p. 330n.

[219] Knowles and Hadcock, *Medieval Religious Houses*, p. 248.

[220] R. I. Burns, 'The Friars of the Sack in Puigcerdà', p. 225n.

[221] Ibid., p. 220.

numerous lay and clerical testators continued to support the friars who remained in houses of the order. Others were not so confident. There is plenty of evidence that transfers of property and friars were taking place according to the instructions of 1274: where there had been thirty religious at Villefranche de Conflent in 1266, by 1279 there were just three remaining and these now moved to the Franciscans.[222] Houses emptied fast: Augsburg was already sold to the Carmelites in August 1275,[223] Pisa and Basel were abandoned by 1279, Narbonne in 1280, Viterbo by 1283, Acre by 1285,[224] Metz in 1289. The Ferrara community seems to have dissolved by the early 1290s, to be replaced by the Carmelites in 1295,[225] and the Cologne house disappeared just a few years later. The friars frequently took the initiative themselves. In Montpellier in 1288 the remaining five friars chose to transfer to the Benedictine monastery of Saint-Pons-de-Thomières (Herault). They sold the convent to the Benedictines, who used it for monks sent to Montpellier to study.[226] In Cologne, Archbishop Wikbold (1297–1304) reported in 1298 that the material needs of the small number of friars remaining had led them to give him their property. He now granted the house to the Antonites, whom Elm identifies as an order which had settled in the early twelfth century at Rossdorf near Frankfurt.[227] In some cases transfers took place *en masse*, as envisaged by the council: in Metz the Cistercians of Clairvaux received the house and all the friars as a body in 1289. At La Rochelle in 1295, the friars successfully petitioned to be allowed to transfer to the Austin canons, taking with them the property of the friary, on the grounds that they were too elderly to continue begging. Again, in Strasbourg in 1297, the friars acquired papal and episcopal authorisation to join the Premonstratensians, taking with them both their house and chapel, which now became a priory of the new order.[228] Some individual friars also took matters into their own hands, just as Otto, the rector general in 1274, had authorised them to do. An extant form letter for the *Audientia litterarum contradictarum* of the papal chancery (a body designed to resolve disputes arising from conflicting papal letters) recommends a priest of the order to the abbot and monks of an unspecified monastery to which he wished to transfer, asking them to accept him out of reverence for the papal

---

[222] *Nuper exponentibus vobis*, 27 June 1279 (Gay 511; Potthast 21618).

[223] Elm, 'Ausbreitung', pp. 300 and 310n.

[224] *Exhibita nobis dilectorum*, 30 November 1285 (Prou 255), records the sale to the Knights Templar of Jerusalem, the proceeds to go to the aid of the Holy Land, but in 1290 Nicholas IV authorised sale to the Augustinian Hermit Friars, *Ad fratres heremitarum*, 10 October 1290 (Langlois 3379). See Emery, 'The Friars of the Sack', p. 328.

[225] See Samaritani, 'I frati Saccati a san Paolo', pp. 52–4.

[226] *Lecta coram nobis*, 27 June 1288 (Langlois 278). Cited by Giacomozzi, *L'ordine della penitenza di Gesù Cristo*, p. 24 and note.

[227] Elm, 'Ausbreitung', p. 305; A. Mischlewski, 'Antoniusorden, Antoniter', *Lexikon des Mittelalters*, I (Munich, 1977), cols 734–5, however, places the origins of the Antonites in La-Motte-aux-Bois/ Montmajour, and identifies them as originally a fraternity caring for pilgrims.

[228] Elm, 'Ausbreitung', p. 301.

see. The friar, identified only as B., must have impetrated the letter himself and also explained the circumstances, citing constitution 23 both for the reasons for the discontinuation of the order and for Gregory X's licence to the friars to either stay or transfer to another approved order. The pope invited the abbot and his community to accept Friar B. as a monk and brother, but did not (perhaps could not) command them.

We do not know where the anonymous Friar B. ended up, but in 1277 Friar Berenguer d'Ape who had brought a substantial sum with him when he joined the Friars of the Sack in Barcelona (since expended on the convent's buildings and bell), chose to transfer to the military order of the Knights of St James of Santiago. Despite the vow of poverty taken on joining the friars, he now wanted to take his inheritance with him, and his brethren agreed to an arrangement whereby the two orders would hold the house jointly until the last friar of the Sack had died.[229] In the end, however, in the 1290s the remaining friars agreed to unite with the neighbouring house of regular canons of the Holy Sepulchre, though this union seems to have taken effect only in the early fourteenth century, when the canons were still debating the price to be paid with the bishop of Barcelona, finally settled at 10,000 *solidi*.[230]

As these cases demonstrate, bishops were frequently involved in the transfer both of property and of the friars themselves, and in many cases were key players in assisting the friars. In 1280 before giving the Basel house to the Clares, the bishop transferred five friars to the Franciscans and installed Heinrich of Weissenburg, the order's provincial prior in Germany, as provost of the newly reformed regular canons of St Leonard, where he was to prove a very active leader of the new community.[231] In Tournai, Strasbourg and Brussels it was again the bishop who made the final decision about the fate of the house.[232] In Narbonne the friary was sold by the bishop in 1280 for 300 *livres tournois*.[233]

In some cases the popes intervened directly to protect the friars. In 1286 Honorius IV ordered the Franciscan Guardian and the Dominican prior in Barjols to enquire into the activities of Gaufridus, provost of Barjols, who was reported to have mistreated the Sack Friars and handled their property as his own. Presumably the pope was concerned about the fate of the property, the profits from which were to go to the Holy Land, but the letter also shows concern for the Sack Friars themselves.[234] Similarly, in September 1291,

---

[229] Feliu, 'El monestir de Frares de Penitència de Jesucrist de Barcelona', appendix 4; Burns, 'The Friars of the Sack in Barcelona', pp. 432–3.

[230] Jaspert, *Stift und Stadt*, p. 328.

[231] 'Annales Colmarienses maiores', ed. P. Jaffé, *MGH SS* XVII (Hannover, 1861), pp. 202–32, 203; Emery, 'The Friars of the Sack', p. 330; Elm, 'Ausbreitung', pp. 300 and 313n.

[232] Elm, 'Ausbreitung', p. 308.

[233] De Fontette, 'Les Mendiants supprimés', p. 203.

[234] *Venerabilis frater noster*, 31 May 1286 (Prou 532; Potthast 22473). Cited in de Fontette, 'Les Mendiants supprimés', p. 208.

Nicholas IV, then in Orvieto, wrote to the bishop of Florence telling him to stop troubling the friars.[235] Many papal letters refer to the needs of the Holy Land: between 1285 and 1291 in Játiva, the Dominicans purchased the house with the permission of Honorius IV and the proceeds were destined for the Holy Land.[236] In June 1285 the bishop of St Andrews in Scotland was instructed to see to the sale of the friary in Berwick to the Dominicans and use the proceeds for the benefit of the Holy Land (though four years later the sale had not yet been finalised).[237] The same conditions applied to the disposal of the house in Montpellier and to numerous other sales.[238] But the pope and Roman church were also often direct beneficiaries of the sales of friaries, at least in the first instance. The destination of proceeds to pious purposes often came to mean money going to the Curia. In December 1289 Nicholas IV authorised the friars of Perpignan to sell land in order to pay off loans acquired before 1274. He entrusted the task to the bishop of Elne and any money left over was to be held on behalf of the pope and the Roman Church.[239] In June 1291 the Benedictines at St Michael de Cuxa successfully petitioned to be allowed to buy the house itself because they needed somewhere to stay when they went to Perpignan to do business, so as not to have to stay in public hospices and other 'inappropriate places'. The sale was to go ahead once the friars had left or died and the money was again to be held by the bishop of Elne, on behalf of the pope and the Roman Church.[240] In 1300 Boniface VIII wrote to the bishop arranging for the 15,000 *solidi* acquired from the sale to be sent to the Curia.[241] Similarly in January 1290 Nicholas IV had instructed the bishop of Maguelonne to deposit 630 *livres* acquired from the sale of the Montpellier house with Pucio Raynerii, a banker from Pistoia then living in Nîmes, to be held in account for the Roman Church.[242]

The papal registers are full of correspondence concerning the transfer of Sack houses. Micheline de Fontette, writing about southern France, has argued that this was perhaps because the bishops were insufficiently active.[243] Yet as we have seen, in practice bishops frequently were involved. Moreover, as Richard Emery noted, the initiative in numerous cases came from the prospective purchasers, neither pope nor bishops.[244] Neighbours with an eye to the property kept a close watch on the declining numbers of friars. In June

---

[235] *Ad audientiam nostram*, 20 September 1291 (Langlois 6114).

[236] *In ordine fratrum*, 7 June 1285 (Prou 83).

[237] *Ex parte dilectorum*, 17 Jun 1285 (Prou 77); *Sua nobis dilecti*, 7 February 1289 (Langlois 461).

[238] Similar authorisations for the sale of houses are to be found for Guingamp, diocese of Tréguier, 7 June 1285 (Prou 81), Venice, 8 June 1288 (Langlois 551), Poitiers, 1 and 17 June 1289 (Langlois 899, 965), Bayeux, 20 December 1289 (Langlois 1791) and Le Puy, 12 July 1290 (Langlois 2912).

[239] *Exhibita nobis dilectorum*, 10 December 1289 (Langlois 1819).

[240] *Dilecti filii abbas*, 9 June 1291 (Langlois 5529).

[241] *Cum, sicut ex*, 29 January 1300 (Digard 3472).

[242] *Transmisse nobis tue*, 13 January 1290 (Langlois 7241).

[243] De Fontette, 'Les Mendiants supprimés', p. 202.

[244] Emery, 'The Friars of the Sack', p. 328.

1289 King Charles of Sicily obtained permission to acquire and build a chapel on the *locus* of the friars in Brignoles, 'which would soon be deserted'.[245] In the same year the Lyons convent was described as belonging to the apostolic see when Nicholas IV ordered the church of Lyons to sell, but five days later he instructed that the proceeds pass to the Franciscans, presumably after a petition from the latter.[246] Again in that year, the Templars noted that the house in Verdun would soon be empty and secured papal authorisation to purchase, though twelve years later it was derelict and, after its sale to the bishop, passed in 1316 to the Augustinians.[247] In 1290 the English Gilbertines successfully petitioned to be allowed to purchase the Cambridge friary which, so they reported, was soon to be abandoned. Not unlike the monks of Cuxa, they justified the purchase on the grounds that they otherwise had to stay with seculars when they were studying, and stated that they planned to have a house in the town. The pope gave leave for the remaining friars to join the Gilbertines if they so wished and directed that the proceeds from the sale be kept in a safe place, to be used for the Holy Land or other purposes, as he would provide.[248] In practice, nothing seems to have happened and the Sack friary continued for some years yet.

Although the council had claimed exclusive papal and episcopal control over the fate of the friars and their houses, lay authorities inevitably became involved. Occasionally the two sides worked together. In 1300 Count Egino of Freiburg approved the foundation of a convent of Augustinian regular canons in the former Sack house by a knight, Johannes Amman of Waldkirch, using religious from Marbach. On the same day, Konrad, provost of the church of Constance and rector of the parish church in Freiburg, agreed to the foundation and a short time later, the bishop, Heinrich of Constance, also gave his assent.[249] In 1304 Charles of Sicily was authorised to transfer the now empty house of the Sack Friars in Toulouse to the order of Preachers.[250] In 1307, when Edward I assigned the Sack house in Newcastle to the Carmelites and the friary in Norwich to the Dominicans, he instructed them to support for life the last remaining Sack Friar in each; Walter of Carleton, the last prior of Newcastle, had been living alone in the house for seven years, but now received papal licence to enter the Carmelite order.[251] In other cases,

---

[245] *Significavit nobis carissimus*, 28 June 1289 (Langlois 1059).

[246] *Cum sicut accepimus*, 8 June 1289; *Ex parte dilectorum* 13 June 1289 (Langlois 925, 946).

[247] *Significarunt nobis dilecti*, 10 December 1289 (Langlois 1901); Emery, *The Friars in Medieval France*, p. 93.

[248] *Ex parte dilectorum*, 9 June 1290 (Langlois 2731).

[249] Hefele, *Freiburger Urkundenbuch*, II, nos 286–7 (23 March 1300), 291 (24 April 1300).

[250] *Affluentis devotionis*, 17 February 1304, *Le Registre de Benoît XI*, ed. C. Grandjean (Paris, 1905), no. 731.

[251] Emery, 'The Friars of the Sack', p. 330; Chettle, 'The Friars of the Sack in England', p. 248. In 1286 Honorius IV had instructed the archbishop of York and the bishop of Durham to sell the house in Newcastle to John de Veti, who planned to build a monastery of Clares there. *Dilectus filius nobilis*, 30 October 1286 (Prou 679).

secular interest in the land and houses of the order was sometimes manifest before it was clear whether the decree would take full effect. In Valencia in July 1275, King Jaime granted that 'should the house of the order of penitence of Jesus Christ . . . be changed, or should the friars abandon it in accordance with the papal ordinance', then Artal Esquerre, a member of the royal household, might have the open space 'which lies in front of the residence of the Dominicans'.[252]

Jaime and Artal were prepared to wait, but as time passed, lay authorities, often in any case the original donors or patrons of a house, simply took matters into their own hands or made sure that papal choices matched their own. Lay intervention was sometimes decisive: in 1317 the French king successfully petitioned the pope to allow the Augustinians to take over the houses of the order of the Sack in the dioceses of Reims, Orléans and Tours. In England, the Crown eventually took over five houses, including Lincoln and Cambridge, which was given to Peterhouse College *c.* 1307–9. Oxford passed to the Franciscans in 1309. Inevitably, the lines between the jurisdictions of secular and ecclesiastical authorities were not necessarily interpreted in the same way by all concerned. An emblematic case, studied by E. Ypma, is that of Paris, where in April 1293 Philip IV promised the convent to Giles of Rome, the prior general of the Augustinians, once the last Sack Friars had departed or died.[253] The king did so subject to papal or other competent authorisation. Only eight elderly friars remained and in September 1293 they chose to hand the keys of the house to the Crown for re-allocation to another pious use, as they believed they were required to do by the terms of the original donation from Louis IX. The representatives of Philip at the ceremony included Giles of Rome, to whom the convent was then immediately given. Although Giles explicitly accepted possession of only temporal (not spiritual) goods and acknowledged that the donation was made pending the right of superior authority to intervene, a group of clergy led by an official of the bishop of Paris turned up to demand that the friars leave the house. When they refused, the bishop's men tried to get them out by force. Giles immediately wrote a petition to the Holy See (then vacant), but the bishop's official refused to read it, excommunicated him, suspended the friars and placed the house under interdict, on the grounds that the Augustinians had infringed the instructions of the Council of Lyons by accepting a house from a layman. The Augustinians did not, however, admit this line of argument and made renewed representations to the bishop's official. On re-consideration the latter accepted the friars' version of events and in November the excommunication was lifted. The bishop then confirmed the royal donation in December, but not until September 1296 was the dispute finally resolved.

---

[252] Burns, 'Friars of the Sack in Valencia', p. 437.
[253] See Ypma, 'L'Acquisition du couvent parisien des Sachets', pp. 107–17.

Pope Boniface VIII, noting the illegitimacy of the earlier royal donation and its episcopal confirmation, authorised the friars to stay, 'by special grace and apostolic authority'.[254] Only three years later, in February 1299, did the Austin Friars finally dispose of their original house at Chardonnet. Other lay patrons also ran into difficulty: at Lamballe in Brittany, the duke, who just took the house he had founded for the order and gave it to the Austin Friars, incurred excommunication, from which he was released by John XXII in 1317.[255]

As at Verdun, some of the friars' buildings may have lain empty for quite a while: in Tournai, the friars are last mentioned in the house in 1282 but the first reference to their successors, the Augustinian Hermit Friars, dates only to 1319. There is a similar gap in Liège, from the early 1290s to 1331, though both cases may of course signal the discontinuity of the sources.[256] In London in 1305 the friars had royal permission to give away their chapel in the former synagogue, apparently a sign of the end of the community, but in 1310 their houses were among those suggested as convenient prisons for the Templars, who had until then been detained in the Tower: presumably the final fate of the buildings had not yet been determined.[257] The Millau house was given to the Clares by John XXII in 1327, but seems to have been empty for a long time before this date. In Hyères in 1328, the empty house was, rather appropriately, given by the same pope to the beguines of Roubaud whose community had been founded by Douceline, sister of Hugh of Digne (*c.* 1250).[258] As such evidence suggests, the final destiny of a house frequently took quite some time to settle: at Tarascon in 1285 where there were just three or four friars remaining, the pope assigned the house to the Dominicans once it was empty; however, ten years later Boniface VIII granted it to the Knights Hospitaller of St John of Jerusalem.[259] Again, in Valencia in 1286 the Dominicans had successfully petitioned the pope to be allowed to take over the house, which had dropped to only two or three friars, either immediately or at their deaths, but in the end the house passed to the Magdalene nuns of the city, who likewise had to wait until the last friars were gone.[260] In Marseilles, the house was first promised to the Hospitallers of St John of Jerusalem in

---

[254] *Vestre religionis*, 13 September 1296 (Alonso 189; Digard 1274; Empoli 43–4).

[255] On the Austin Friars' acquisition of Sack houses, see also above, pp. 111–12.

[256] Elm, 'Ausbreitung', p. 306.

[257] Chettle, 'The Friars of the Sack in England', p. 246 citing *Calendar of Patent Rolls Edward I 1301–7* (London, 1898), p. 316 which grants that the chapel may be assigned 'in fee simple' to 'Robert son of Walter for him and his heirs to find two chaplains to celebrate divine service daily for the soul of Eleanor, sometime queen of England, the king's consort and the souls of himself, his ancestors and all the faithful dead'; see also *Calendar of Close Rolls Edward II 1307–13* (London, 1892), p. 285, for the Templars.

[258] De Fontette, 'Les Mendiants supprimés', p. 213.

[259] *In ordine fratrum*, 7 June 1285 (Prou 84); de Fontette, 'Les Mendiants supprimés', p. 208; *Illa quantum cum*, 21 July 1295 (Digard 1028).

[260] *Ad sacrum fratrum* 23 February 1286 (Prou 353). Burns, 'The Friars of the Sack in Valencia', p. 438.

1285, but friars remained in the house probably until 1320, when John XXII ordered the bishop to sell the now deserted buildings.[261] In at least one case an initial transfer was not definitive. In Strasbourg in 1327 the Premonstratensians gave up the house they had acquired from the Sack Friars just thirty years earlier, to allow a knight, Heinrich of Müllenheim, to build an oratory with five benefices for priests.[262] As in Paris in the 1290s, the terms of these transfers were evidently not clear to all: in Ferrara, in the course of a dispute in 1318, the cathedral chapter argued incorrectly that the Carmelites who had taken over the house of the Sack Friars were illegal residents of the church because the decree of 1274 had established that churches of the friars could not be alienated.[263] Unsurprisingly, the argument was not effective.

In many cases we simply do not know what happened to the friars. In Utrecht, on 14 July 1289 they were clearly planning a move and agreed that, should they change their habit or order, they would continue to pay the rent. A year later, however, on 27 July 1290, when the deans of the chapters of St Martin and St Peter went to inspect the house, they found it empty.[264] There is no record of where the religious had gone. The evidence for buildings is rather better. In the end, perhaps half passed to other regular orders, to the Dominicans, Augustinians or Franciscans and in smaller numbers to various Benedictines, Hospitallers, the Knights of Malta, Templars, regular canons, Carmelites and Clares.[265] A group of four houses in northern Italy (Asti, Milan, Alessandria and Parma) became the core of a new province of the Servites.[266] A very small number passed to the Premonstratensians and as we have seen, one was briefly destined to the Gilbertines. A few, in England at least, seem to have passed entirely to seculars, as at York, where in 1312 Edward II granted their land to Robert de Roston for an annual rent of 8 shillings.[267] The papal Curia gained financially from some of the sales, but as Humbert de Romans had surely hoped before 1274, in the main, the dissolution of the Sack strengthened the other orders of mendicants, at least as far as their property was concerned.

The last friar to survive was long thought to have been Roger de la Ferte at Rouen in 1309, but Burns has shown that at Puigcerdà the friary was still functioning with its own church and a substantial community until at least 1328.[268] The structures of the order also survived the council of 1274: a German

---

[261] *Exhibita nobis dilectorum* 13 November 1285 (Prou 467); see also Boniface VIII, 21 July 1295 (Digard 1028); Amargier, 'Les Frères de la Pénitence de Jésus Christ ou du Sac', pp. 162–3.

[262] Elm, 'Ausbreitung', p. 312.

[263] Samaritani, 'I frati Saccati a san Paolo', p. 47.

[264] Elm, 'Ausbreitung', p. 303.

[265] The list provided in Giacomozzi, *L'ordine della penitenza di Gesù Cristo*, pp. 58–9, requires updating and correction on the basis of the more recent studies listed in the further reading below.

[266] Montagnana, 'Una progettata fondazione a Perugia', pp. 272–3.

[267] *VCH York*, III, p. 296.

[268] Burns, 'The Friars of the Sack in Puigcerdà', p. 219.

prior provincial is still documented in 1279 and 1292, while in 1307 the prior of Lynn, Roger de Flegg, was also vicar general of the order in England.[269] But these were the last hangers on. As an effective force in the Church, the order had long since failed.

Memory of the Sack Friars outlived them by a variety of means: the *Romaunt of the Rose* circulated widely, perpetuating the idea of them as one of the mendicant orders (and not to be trusted).[270] The insertion of constitution 23 of the Council of Lyons in the *Liber sextus,* a key canon-law collection, under Boniface VIII, ensured that later canon lawyers commented on its effect, sometimes naming the friars concerned.[271] Some new religious communities bore the name for a while after transfer: in Cologne, for example, in 1306 the community of Antonites who had taken in the friars and their house were described as 'Friars of the Sack who are now Antonites' (*fratres sacciti qui nunc sunt Anthonii*).[272] The Sack origins of the community had not been forgotten. In the newly Servite houses in Asti and Milan, later documents refer to 'friars of penitence of Jesus Christ who are commonly known as Servites of Holy Mary' (*fratres de penitentia Jesu Christi qui vulgo dicuntur Servi sancte Marie*) or to friars of *Santa Maria del Sacco*, composite names which reflect at least some sense of continuing identification with the original order.[273] Houses of women in central Italy also long continued to be identified with the Sack name: in Foligno in 1347 there was a monastery of 'ladies of the Sack' (*monasterium dominarum de sacchis*) and Trevi in 1385 had a church of San Bartolomeo *delle sacche*, though, as before 1274, such epithets may indicate nothing more formal than shared ideals of humility.[274] More prosaically, place-names also lived on. In Ghent in 1360, city records referred to *Sackbroedersstrate*.[275] In Bordeaux, where the house had been given to the Hospitallers of St John of Jerusalem in 1299, episcopal accounts still referred to the house of the Sack Friars in 1354, 1367 and 1375.[276] In Bologna in 1369, their former church, which had long since passed to the regular canons of San Frediano of Lucca, was known as San Frediano *de sachis*.[277] In Barcelona the name was still used for their former buildings until the turn of the fifteenth century.[278] In Lincoln in 1455 a deed still mentioned 'a stone

---

[269] For the German prior, see Elm, 'Ausbreitung', p. 285n.; for England, Dugdale, *Monasticon Anglicanum*, VI, part 3, p. 1608.

[270] See above, p. 63.

[271] See Elm, 'Ausbreitung', pp. 258–9.

[272] Asen, 'Die Begarden und die Sackbrüder in Köln', p. 179. Elm, 'Ausbreitung', p. 305.

[273] A. Giani, *Annalium sacri ordinis fratrum servorum B. Mariae Virginis*, 3 vols (Lucca 1719–25), I, pp. 90, 164–5; Emery, 'The Friars of the Sack', p. 332n.

[274] Sensi, 'Monachesimo femminile nell'Italia centrale (sec. XV)', argues that these were continuations of a second order of the Sack. See above, p. 191.

[275] Elm, 'Ausbreitung', p. 273 and Simons, *Bedelordekloosters*, p. 90.

[276] De Fontette, 'Les Mendiants supprimés', p. 205.

[277] Giacomozzi, *L'ordine della penitenza di Gesù Cristo*, p. 43.

[278] Jaspert, *Stift und Stadt*, p. 108n.

wall lately belonging to the friars lately called Sekfriars'.[279] In Avignon in 1541 the site of their abandoned convent was referred to as 'St Fenouillet church' (*eglize saint Fenouilhet*), marking the evolution of the early name used for the friars themselves into the name of a saint.[280] Lands in Canterbury were still referred to in a royal grant as formerly belonging to the Sack Friars as late as October 1544.[281]

Names can be very persistent, but how long they carried any association with the order they originally described it is now impossible to say. Numerous misidentifications and misconceptions were soon attached, encouraged by the short-lived nature of the institution. As we have seen, failure opened them up to accusations of heretical leanings, or Joachism. More neutral, but equally inaccurate, was the account of the Augustinian chronicler, Jordan of Quedlinberg, writing before 1357, who stated that the *Ordo fratrum penitentie Iesu Christi* or *Sacciti*, following the rule of Augustine, joined the Austin Friars in 1256.[282] Antonino Pierozzi, archbishop of Florence (1446–59), who had perhaps read Quedlinberg, also described them as one of the groups of hermits who joined the Austin Friars in 1256. It was to be a long-lived mistake. More recent historians have understandably confused them with the Friars of Penance and with other penitent groups of tertiaries associated with the Dominicans, or the tertiary branch of the Franciscan order approved by Nicholas IV in 1289.[283] In fact they remained quite separate, but such associations do reflect one reality of this order. The Friars of the Sack were an expression of the spirituality of penance and renunciation potently combined with evangelism so characteristic of vast numbers of men and women in the thirteenth-century Latin Church. They did not survive long enough for this to change.

---

[279] *VCH Lincoln*, II, p. 225.

[280] Amargier, 'Les Frères de la Pénitence de Jésus Christ ou du Sac', p. 163n.

[281] Chettle, 'The Friars of the Sack in England', p. 249, citing *Letters and Papers, Foreign and Domestic of the Reign of Henry VIII*, ed. J. Gairdner, R. H. Brodie, XIX, part 2 (London, 1905), no. 527 (15).

[282] Jordani de Saxonia (Quedlinburg), *Liber vitasfratrum*, book 1 chapter 14. On the author, see above, pp. 87, 161.

[283] In *Supra montem catholice*, 18 August 1289 (Langlois 1263). See G. G. Meersseman, *Ordo fraternitatis. Confraternite e pietà dei laici nel medioevo*, 3 vols, Italia sacra 24–6 (Rome, 1977), I, p. 440.

CHAPTER TWO

The Friars of Blessed Mary of Areno, or Pied Friars

The last of the orders to be considered here is also the smallest and the least well documented. The Friars of Blessed Mary, or Pied Friars (*fratres de pica*), had their beginnings as a penitential fraternity at some point in mid-thirteenth-century Marseilles. There is no evidence for a particular founder or group of founders and exactly when the order took shape is now a matter of debate. Most recently, Walter Simons has argued that it was created at the point when they acquired a mendicant identity in 1257–8, as first documented in papal and episcopal letters from those years.[1] Richard Emery and Franco dal Pino had previously proposed that the movement originated some time *before* the first papal letter concerning their rule, issued in 1257.[2] This view should perhaps be preferred on the grounds that it was necessary for any new group of religious to achieve organisational weight before acquiring episcopal or papal approval, but there is now no way of knowing how long this process took.

The parallels with the Sack Friars are worth noting: like them, their precise origins are obscure and in *Piis propositis*, issued in September 1257, Alexander IV instructed Benoît d'Alignan, the bishop of Marseilles who had been involved with the Sack Friars, to assign them an approved rule. Predictably they adopted the rule of Augustine, approved by Bishop Benoît in January 1258 and by Pope Clement IV in 1266.[3] They were also already distinguished by a particular devotion to Mary. The papal letter names them 'friars of the blessed Mary of Areno... commonly called servants of Holy Mary, Mother of Christ' (*fratres beate Marie de Areno... qui vulgariter nuncupantur Servi sancte Marie matris Christi*). In 1259 the bishop and cathedral chapter of Marseilles granted Friar Hugh, 'minister of the order of the Virgin Mary, mother of Christ', a church or chapel at Areno, on land belonging to the city, together with a garden and vineyards.[4] By 1263 a nephew of the cathedral provost was a novice in the

---

[1] Simons, *Stad en apostolaat* (as above, p. 185 n. 59), p. 60 and n. 35.

[2] R. W. Emery, 'The Friars of the Blessed Mary and the Pied Friars', *Speculum* 24 (1949), pp. 228–38, 229, and dal Pino, *I frati Servi* (as above, p. 2 n. 4), I, p. 672.

[3] Potthast 17013; M. Félibien, *Histoire de la ville de Paris* (Paris, 1725), I, pp. 374–5. *Piis propositis* (dated either 26 or 27 September 1257) was included in *Litteras domini pape*, issued by Bishop Benoît, 4 January 1258, which was in turn incorporated in *Cum a nobis* of Clement IV, 13 May 1266. See dal Pino, *I frati Servi*, I, p. 672n.

[4] Emery, 'The Friars of the Blessed Mary', p. 229.

order.[5] Such evidence has led Édouard Baratier to conjecture that the cathedral chapter wished to have 'their own mendicants', and to interpret the approval of the order as direct competition for the activities of Bishop Benoît, who had a Sack Friar as his chaplain.[6] There is, however, no evidence to confirm this hypothesis and in 1260 Benoît certainly assigned the Pied Friars alms alongside the Sack Friars and the other mendicants in Marseilles.[7]

In 1263 the friars in Marseilles built a new oratory inside the walls, near Porte-Galle, but kept the Areno chapel, from which they had acquired the epithet *de Areno*, also used when some of the friars reached Paris and London.[8] The names were very varied, with or without reference to the Areno chapel, suggesting a lack of institutional clarity typical of the early stages of a new religious movement. In the papal text, as we have seen, they were called 'friars of the blessed Mary of Areno ... commonly called servants of holy Mary, Mother of Christ', a title leading some historians to confuse them with the Florentine Servites or Servants of Mary (*Servi*). In Limoges, where they arrived in 1260, they were known as brothers or friars of Blessed Mary (*fratres Beate Marie*) in Cahors, Narbonne and Cambridge, as friars of Our Lady (*Domine Nostre*).[9] In Paris they were variously called *blancs manteaux* (white mantles), Friars of Blessed Mary, Mother of Jesus Christ, Brothers of the Order of Our Lady, Servants of Holy Mary (*servi sancte Marie*) or Friars of the Order of Blessed Mary of Vauvert (*vallis viridis*), a name also used for the friars in Solothurn and Viterbo, amongst others.[10] Walter Simons has proposed that the official names changed over the course of the thirteenth century from the original *fratres Servi beate Marie matris Christi*, which was close to that of the Servites, through *fratres beate Marie [de Areno]*, which was uncomfortably similar to the title used by the Carmelites, to *fratres beate Marie matris Christi*.[11] The sources are insufficient to admit any certainty, but similarity to the titles used by the Carmelites, Servites and other thirteenth-century religious with particular devotion to Mary surely led to confusion at the time and undoubtedly makes tracing their activities now particularly difficult for historians.[12]

---

[5] Ibid.

[6] E. Baratier, 'Le Mouvement mendiant à Marseille', in *Les Mendiants en Pays d'Oc au 13e siècle*, Cahiers de Fanjeaux 8 (1976), pp. 177–91, 185.

[7] Dal Pino, *I frati Servi*, I, p. 673.

[8] Simons, *Stad en apostolaat*, p. 61n; Emery, 'The Friars of the Blessed Mary', p. 229, and Emery, *The Friars in Medieval France* (as above, p. 106 n. 18), p. 39n. For London, see *Calendar of the Charter Rolls* (London, 1906), II, p. 89.

[9] De Fontette, 'Les Mendiants supprimés', pp. 193–216, 215–16.

[10] Emery, 'The Friars of the Blessed Mary', p. 229. See *In ordine fratrum* 7 June 1285 (Prou 82).

[11] Simons, *Stad en apostolaat*, pp. 61–62. See also Simons, *Bedelordekloosters* (as above, p. 185 n. 43), p. 121. Dal Pino, *I frati Servi*, I, p. 675, proposes that Clement IV planned the union of the Servites and Pied Friars.

[12] The title *Servorum be[ate Marie]* was used on an extant seal of the prior of the Paris house dated 1268, described in D. d'Arcq, *Collection des sceaux* (Paris, 1863–8), III, no. 9820; see Emery, 'The Friars of

For contemporaries, the key identifying feature was the habit: the nickname Pied Friars derived from the magpie combination of white habit and black scapular.[13] In Bruges they were named *agherste bonten* ('magpie coloured').[14] The name *blancs manteaux* used in Paris, however, implies that the use of white was more prominent for the Pied Friars than for other orders wearing black and white (perhaps in particular the Cistercians, who, like the Carmelites, were also sometimes described as 'pied' brothers).[15] Nothing is known of their constitutions or pastoral activities and very little about their administrative structures. Presumably they adopted the main features of the mendicant (and Augustinian) way of life. Like the Franciscans they used the title minister general for their superior – a Friar Hugh throughout the 1260s and until 1272 at least.[16] In 1269 in Toulouse, however, there is a reference to a prior provincial and the title 'prior' was adopted for the superior of each house.[17] Neither term was ever used by the Franciscans, whose preferred terminology was provincial minister and 'guardian'.

More information is available about the spread of the order than about its spiritual or religious life. At the peak there were at least seventeen houses.[18] Several of these were in the Midi: Cahors (before 1273), Limoges (1260), Narbonne, where a will of 1263 cites them among the orders of the town, and Toulouse, where Alphonse of Poitiers ordered his seneschal to make donations to the order in 1267 and again in 1268.[19] The Toulouse house was isolated from the main settlement, caught between the Château Narbonnais and a dyke built by Simon de Montfort. In 1270, a request for the construction of a bridge across the dyke was approved in principle by the council of Alphonse, for which part of the Jewish cemetery would be used, on condition that there would be no harm to the town.[20] Alphonse was an important patron, as he was for the other friars: in 1267 he gave 40 *solidi* in alms to the house in Paris and in 1268 he approved the establishment of the

the Blessed Mary', p. 229, and, on confusions with the Carmelites, pp. 234–6.

[13] The evidence for the black scapular comes from a single reference in 1289, Little, 'Aumônes', p. 183; Emery, 'The Friars of the Blessed Mary', p. 235.

[14] In German the friars are known as *Pickbrüder*.

[15] Some seventeenth- and eighteenth-century historians suggested the habit changed or was entirely white or black, but the name would seem to contradict this. See A. Franchi, 'Beata Maria Madre di Cristo, Frati o Servi della', in *DIP* I (Rome, 1973), cols 1143–5, 1145.

[16] Simons, *Stad en apostolaat*, p. 24 n. conveniently lists the several references from Marseilles to 'fratri Hugone ministro religionis et ordinis sancte Marie matris Christi' (4 March 1260), 'frater Hugo minister generalis fratrum religionis seu ordinis' (28 March 1263) and 'frater Hugo humilis minister licet indignus ordinis' (14 May 1269). Hugh was also active in Cambrai in 1272: 'frater Hugo minister generalis ordinis servorum beate Marie matris Christi', cited in Emery 'The Friars of the Blessed Mary', p. 231; Dal Pino *I frati Servi*, I, p. 678.

[17] De Fontette, 'Les Mendiants supprimés', p. 215.

[18] Emery, 'The Friars of the Blessed Mary', p. 238, names fourteen, to which must be added Valencia, Bruges and Cahors. Others may yet be traced.

[19] De Fontette, 'Les Mendiants supprimés', pp. 214–15.

[20] Dossat, 'Opposition des anciens ordres' (as above, p. 25 n. 4), p. 266.

friars outside the walls of La Rochelle.[21] In 1269 he gave them wood for the construction of their convent.[22] On the other side of the Pyrenees there were also houses at Valencia (1272) and at Lleida, this last documented only when it was closed down in the 1290s.[23]

In the north, Alphonse's elder brother Louis IX supported the friars' settlement in Paris, paying compensation to the neighbouring Templars for the loss of revenues due to them on the land where the friars were to build. In 1258, Amaury de la Roche, the master of the Temple, then agreed to them having a cemetery, chapel or small church and convent, as long as the bishop consented, approval which was forthcoming only in 1263, followed in 1264 by the agreement of the parish clergy and others with interests in the area.[24] The king later bequeathed them 20 *livres* in his will.[25] The friars had settled in Cambrai by 1272, when the minister general and diffinitors of their general chapter made an agreement with the canons of St-Victor over administration of the sacraments. Two years later they had reached Bruges.[26] In 1267, Henry III of England granted to the 'prior and brethren of St Mary's *de Areno*' that, if they could acquire any place in his realm in which to live and serve God, they and their successors might keep it in perpetuity.[27] By this date there were probably already three friaries in his lands: Norwich, Cambridge and Westminster, but the evidence is again fragmentary.[28] In Norwich, the earliest English house, a document from 1253 refers to the prior and brothers of a fraternity of St Mary, St Nicholas and All Saints, living in the church of St Martin in the *Baile*, but there were also *fratres de pica* in Conisford *c.* 1256 and a house of the Friars of Blessed Mary on a site south of St Julian's churchyard in 1274–5. The first reference seems too early for the order this far north, and whether these were separate houses or the same community transferring to different sites is not clear. A better attested case is Westminster, where a knight, William Arnaud, founded a friary in 1267 on land acquired from the abbot of Westminster.[29] Three years later the king allowed them to enclose

---

21 Berger, *Layettes du tresor des chartes* (as above, p. 183 n. 43), IV, p. 213. A reference to alms in 1264–5 (cited by Emery, 'The Friars of the Blessed Mary', p. 229) seems in practice to be to the Carthusians: 'Fratribus de Valle Viridi, de ordine de Chartrouse, lx s. tur. per fratrem Petrum quondam subpriorum Sancti Bernardi'.

22 Emery, 'The Friars of the Blessed Mary', pp. 229, 231.

23 *Ex parte dilectorum*, 17 October 1296 (Digard 1408).

24 Félibien, *Histoire de la ville de Paris*, I, p. 374.

25 Berger, *Layettes du tresor des chartes*, IV, pp. 419–21, 420.

26 Simons, *Stad en apostolaat*, p. 24n.: 'conventus fratrum ordinis matris Christi apud Cameracum' (22 January 1272); on the agreement with the canons of St-Victor see dal Pino, *I frati Servi*, I, p. 678; Emery, 'The Friars of the Blessed Mary', p. 231. On Bruges, see Simons, *Bedelordekloosters*, pp. 120–2.

27 13 October 1267. *Calendar of Patent Rolls Henry III 1266–72*, p. 122.

28 See Knowles and Hadcock, *Medieval Religious Houses* (as above, p. 38 n. 3), p. 249, and the brief entries in Dugdale, *Monasticon Anglicanum* (as above, p. 184 n. 51), p. 1611.

29 See *VCH London*, I, p. 516. *Calendar of the Charter Rolls 1257–1300* (London, 1906), II, p. 89, and *Calendar of Inquisitions Miscellaneous (Chancery)*, II (London, 1916), p. 70.

a plot of land contiguous to their church of St Margaret in the parish of the Holy Innocents, on which to build.[30] In 1273, Walter de Croxton, proctor of the order in England, bought a site in Cambridge and later the *Liber memorandorum* of Barnwell Priory (*c.* 1300) refers to their presence in the parish of All Saints.[31] Finally, by January 1274 there may have been a community in Basel, when according to the *Annales Basilienses*, at the time of the arrival of Rudolf, king of the Romans, there were forty-two Dominicans, thirty-six Franciscans, twelve Sack Friars and eight Brothers of the Blessed Virgin (*fratribus beate virginis*), who just may have been Pied Friars.[32]

Very little can now be said about the buildings of the friars, except that where they can be located they were often near or outside the walls of towns. In Paris the friary was on land adjoining the city walls themselves. In Limoges in 1263 they acquired the former Dominican house near Pont St Martial, so it seems reasonable to assume that they shared contemporary views on the requirements for their convents.[33] They also acquired the same sort of status as men of integrity in the wider community shared by other mendicants and regular religious: in 1269 a list of witnesses to a peace agreement in Toulouse between the residents of the town and its suburbs refers to two friars of the order.[34] Like the Sack Friars, the little evidence available for the houses of the Pied Friars suggests that it was 'business as usual' in the years leading up to the Council of Lyons. In 1272 they benefited from the will of Jaime of Aragon, alongside the Sack Friars and other religious.[35] New houses were being founded and others planned. On the other hand, like the other smaller orders, they may have faced particular difficulties. Rutebeuf compared their plight to the Sack and Carmelite friars:

> Li Barré, li Sachier, li Frere de la Pie
> Conment troveront il en cest siecle lor vie?
> Il sont trop tart venu, car il est ja complie:
> Se li pains est donnez, ne s'i atendent mie.[36]

Like the Carmelites and the Sack Friars, they would struggle to survive because they arrived too late on the scene. And as we have seen, like the Sack

---

[30] 25 July 1270, *Calendar of Patent Rolls Henry III 1266–72*, p. 447.
[31] *VCH Cambridge and the Isle of Ely*, ed. L. F. Salzman, II (London, 1948), p. 287. Emery, 'The Friars of the Blessed Mary', p. 233, citing J. Clark, *Liber memorandorum ecclesie de Bernewelle* (Cambridge, 1907), p. 218.
[32] 'Annales Basileenses', ed P. Jaffé, *MGH* XVII (Hannover, 1861), cols 195–6.
[33] 'Majus chronicon Lemovicense', in *Receuil des historiens des Gaules et de la France*, XXI (Paris, 1855, repr. 1968), p. 769.
[34] C. Devic and J. Vaissète, *Histoire generale de Languedoc*, VIII, 1 (1879), pp. 245, 426.
[35] *Thesaurus novus anecdotorum*, ed. E. Martene and U. Durand (Paris, 1717), I, col. 1144.
[36] Rutebeuf, 'La Vie du monde', *Oeuvres complètes*, I, p. 406: 'The Carmelites, Sack and Pied Friars/ How will they find their livelihood in this world?/ They have come too late, because it is now compline [the end of the day]./ If the bread has been given out, let them not expect any.'

Friars, they fell foul of the ruling of Lyons 1274 disbanding mendicant orders founded after 1215. There is now no way of knowing whether any members of the order attended the council or fought for the survival of their order. Evidence for the fate of the friars and their houses after 1274 is very similar to that for the Sack Friars and often better than the information about their earlier activities. Three houses can only be documented after the council, but must have existed earlier: Solothurn in the diocese of Lausanne, Zierikzee in the diocese of Utrecht and Viterbo in central Italy.[37] In 1285 Philip III of France remembered them in his will.[38] In 1289 the English king, Edward I (1272–1307), gave alms to the friars in Paris and in 1292 and 1300 the friars in Westminster received royal alms alongside the Dominicans, Franciscans, Augustinians, Carmelites, Crutched and Sack Friars.[39] Hugh of York, the last friar in Westminster, died in 1317, when the land reverted to the Crown.[40] In Cambridge in 1279, judging by the size of royal alms, there were some twenty *fratres de pica* in the town: they began building in the parish of All Saints near the castle as late as 1290. A prior, William de Fakenham, and his confrater Thomas were still there in 1319.[41] William's almond-shaped seal showed the Virgin Mary and child, seated on a panelled throne, with a kneeling friar in a niche below. Unlike the Sack Friars, whose extant seals are very varied, the iconography of William's seal is close to that of the prior of Paris in 1268 and also of Hugh, minister general of the Pied Friars in 1272, whose seals also showed the Virgin and child seated over a praying figure.[42] As Franco dal Pino has noted, that was in turn very similar to the seal of the prior general of the Servites, as extant from 1289.[43] It was also, however, similar to that of other friars.[44]

Elsewhere disposal of houses was fairly rapid, though there is as yet no evidence for the immediate abandonment of convents identified for some of the Sack Friars. In 1285 Honorius IV instructed that the Pied Friars' house in Solothurn be sold to the Dominicans and in the following year the same friars also acquired Zierikzee and Valencia.[45] In Viterbo in 1291 the house was sold

---

[37] *In ordine fratrum*, 7 June 1285, for Solothurn (Prou 82); *Ad sacrum fratrum*, 23 February 1286, for Zierikzee (Prou 353); *Exhibita nobis vestra*, 20 June 1291, for Viterbo (Langlois 5345). Emery, 'The Friars of the Blessed Mary', pp. 231–2.

[38] Emery, 'The Friars of the Blessed Mary', p. 229.

[39] Ibid., p. 232; Little, 'Aumônes', p. 183.

[40] *VCH London*, I, p. 516 and *Calendar of Inquisitions Miscellaneous (Chancery)*, II (London, 1916), p. 70.

[41] *VCH Cambridge*, II, p. 287.

[42] See above, p. 74n.

[43] Dal Pino, *I frati Servi*, I, p. 678.

[44] See, for example, d'Arcq, *Collection des sceaux*, III, no. 9761, seal of the Franciscan Guardian of Angoulême (1297).

[45] *In ordine fratrum*, 7 June 1285 (Prou 82) and *Ad sacrum fratrum* 23 February 1286 (Prou 353, two bulls); Emery, 'The Friars of the Blessed Mary', p. 231.

to the Benedictines of Sassovivo with the permission of Nicholas IV.[46] In 1296 Boniface VIII authorised the sale of the convent in Lleida, described as *quasi desertus*, though it still had five friars, to the Premonstratensians of Belpuig in the diocese of Urgell. In practice the house passed to the Mercedarians in 1319: presumably the five friars had not been prepared to move.[47] In Paris in 1297 the house had just the prior and three brothers when the Williamites acquired it from Boniface VIII for the use of their students.[48] In Marseilles in 1308 there was still one elderly friar left when Clement V authorised the Premonstratensians at Huveaune to occupy their buildings at Porte-Galle. The newcomers had been forced to abandon their remote site on the coast after a pirate raid and because it lacked drinking water in summer and was too far from the town for convenience.[49] Elsewhere buildings were evidently pulled down: in London stones from the church were later used for the construction of a tower.[50]

By the third decade of the fourteenth century, the last of the Pied Friars or Friars of the Blessed Mary had disappeared. The English Benedictine historian Thomas Walsingham (†*c.* 1422) later referred to a cemetery in London which had once belonged to 'freres Pyes' and the name *blancs manteaux* continued to be used for their former house in Paris as late as the seventeenth century.[51] In general, however, this brief experiment in the mendicant life focused on devotion to Mary left very little trace.[52]

[46] *Exhibita nobis vestra*, 20 June 1291 (Langlois 5345); Emery, 'The Friars of the Blessed Mary', p. 232.

[47] *Ex parte dilectorum*, 17 October 1296 (Digard 1408); Emery, 'The Friars of the Blessed Mary', p. 232.

[48] *Quia ex apostolici*, 18 July 1297 (Digard 1992); Emery, 'The Friars of the Blessed Mary', p. 229.

[49] *Religionis vestre meretur*, 8 February 1308 (*Regestum Clementis papae V*, 8 vols (in 7) (Rome 1885–8), III, no. 2434); de Fontette, 'Les Mendiants supprimés', p. 214.

[50] Emery, 'The Friars of the Blessed Mary', p. 232.

[51] Ibid.; Elm, *Beiträge zur Geschichte des Wilhelmitenordens* (as above, p. 76 n. 19), p. 69.

[52] Emery, 'The Friars of the Blessed Mary', p. 230.

Success and Failure in the Late-Medieval Church

All four of the orders examined in this volume experienced the trauma of Lyons 1274. Two survived, two died. Parallels between the Sack experience and that of the much less well-documented Pied Friars demonstrate that closure was haphazard but inexorable. The letter of Otto, rector of the Friars of the Sack, shows just how devastating that end could be. Once Curia and council had decided, the friars were unable to reverse the decision. Filippo Benizi, the superior of the Florentine Servites, hurried to the Curia; the Williamites also secured a letter in their support from a cardinal, Jacopo Savelli, and once pope, as Honorius IV, he reconfirmed their status.[1] The leaders of the Pied and Sack Friars seem not to have taken this route. There are various possible explanations for this, ranging from the supposition that the two largest mendicant orders and the secular clergy had decided that the line had to be drawn somewhere and were in a position to enforce their will, to the more pious assumption that these friars were simply too holy and humble to encompass contesting a decree of the Church. Or perhaps the various commentators who emphasised the strain on lay resources were right, at least in part – there really were just too many mendicants, victims of their own success.

Comparison with the case of the Austin and Carmelite friars is telling. The latter were considered by some contemporaries to be just as vulnerable as the Sack and Pied Friars, were numerically smaller than the former and, unlike them, as yet unengaged in the world of the universities. Although they warded off disaster at the council itself, only slowly did a campaign to overturn the decision gather pace. This was multi-faceted, but focused on a change of identity (the new, simpler habit), a shift of emphasis (to the world of learning) and vocal campaigning by their leaders. But the petition of the prior general, Pierre de Millau, to the English king was sent only in the 1280s. In the years immediately following 1274 there seems to have been a hiatus. Perhaps the death of the pope led them to believe no further action would be taken (as Salimbene of Parma implied when writing about the Austin Friars). Perhaps the Carmelites thought their 'evident utility' would speak for itself and only gradually realised the need for action, combined with the necessity to explain their early history, long pre-dating the council of 1215.

---

[1]   20 April 1286 (Prou 435–41); de Fontette, 'Les Mendiants supprimés', p. 196.

There is less evidence for a campaign on behalf of the Austin Friars, though they too faced difficulties, as demonstrated by the letter of the archbishop of Salzburg concerning the need to support them. The creation of a united order was certainly on the agenda in the late thirteenth century, but only in the 1280s did this agenda begin to take clear shape, triggered perhaps by the re-election of Clemente da Osimo as prior general and the re-appointment of a cardinal-protector for the friars. Still later did the need to explain (and embellish) their early history become evident. But in this both the Augustinian and Carmelite friars were fortunate: their origins were sufficiently long before the council of 1274 that they could justify their existence through age. As the *Annals of Dunstable* put it:

> In that same council, the order of the Friars of the Sack was rejected . . . and many other orders which were newly spreading and did not have property were similarly prohibited, so that many of [their members] flew together to other orders. The order of the friars of St Augustine and the order of the friars of Carmel were approved by the Council, *because of their antiquity.*[2]

Proving this antiquity was not an easy undertaking and the versions of their pasts produced by both Carmelite and Austin Friars were to be challenged by contemporaries. As Rutebeuf observed, those 'who came late' were particularly vulnerable. As so often in the Latin Middle Ages, long tradition and custom were the arguments which could and did win, making the difference between failure and success.

[2]   'Annals of Dunstable', ed. R. Pauli, *MGH SS* XXVII (Hannover, 1885), p. 512 (my italics).

FURTHER READING

The Carmelites

Periodicals and series. There are several periodicals dedicated to the Carmelites and their history. Since 1909, *Analecta Ordinis Carmelitarum* has published the official documents of the order, including historical records such as the constitutions of 1281 ('Constitutiones capituli Londinensis anni 1281', ed. L. Saggi, *AOC* 15 (1950), pp. 203–45) and 1294 ('Constitutiones capituli Burdigalensis anni 1294', ed. L. Saggi, *AOC* 18 (1953), pp. 123–85). *Carmelus* (1954–), published by the Institutum Carmelitanum in Rome, has articles on various aspects of Carmelite devotion and history, including whole volumes dedicated, for example, to the Immaculate Conception (volume 2), or the houses for women (volume 10). *Ephemerides Carmeliticae* (1947–81), originally published by the theology faculty of the Discalced Carmelites in Rome, concentrates particularly on Carmelite spirituality and was renamed *Teresianum Ephemerides Carmeliticae* (1982–). Other journals include the *Études carmelitaines, historiques et critiques* (1911–) published by the French province of the order, whilst the *Analecta ordinis Carmelitarum discalceatorum* (Rome, 1926–52) was mainly concerned with the internal affairs of the modern order. Articles found in these journals are not normally mentioned in the notes or below, but *Carmelus* in particular has works on many of the topics listed. A useful series of occasional studies is *Textus et studia historica Carmelitana*, published by the Institutum Carmelitanum in Rome since 1954, which includes, for example, as volume IV, T. Motta Navarro, *Tertii Carmelitici saecularis ordinis historico-iuridica evolutio* (Rome, 1960).

    General works. Andrew Jotischky has published two valuable studies: *The Perfection of Solitude. Hermits and Monks in the Crusader States* (University Park, Pa, 1995) and, in particular, *The Carmelites and Antiquity. Mendicants and Their Pasts in the Middle Ages* (Oxford, 2002), which includes a brief but excellent account of the order in chapter one. Other useful studies in English include J. Smet, *The Carmelites: A History of the Brothers of Our Lady of Mount Carmel*, vol. 1, which covers *c.* 1200 to the Council of Trent (Barrington, Illinois, and Rome, 1975) and J. Smet, *Cloistered Carmel* (Rome, 1986). See also *The Land of Carmel. Essays in Honor of Joachim Smet*, O.Carm, ed. P. Chandler and K. J. Egan (Rome, 1991), and E. Friedman, *The Latin Hermits of Mount Carmel. A Study in Carmelite Origins* (Rome, 1979). V. Mosca, *Alberto Patriarca di Gerusalemme. Tempo – Vita – Opera* (Rome, 1996) is a detailed study of Albert's career with transcriptions and

233

reprints of pertinent documents. J. Webster, *Carmel in Medieval Catalonia* (Leiden, 1999) also provides more general insights. Relations of all the orders discussed here with the papacy are traced in F. A. dal Pino, 'Papato e ordini mendicanti-apostolici "minori" nel duecento', *Il papato duecentesco e gli ordini mendicanti*, Atti del xxv convegno internazionale. Assisi 1998 (Spoleto, 1998), pp. 107–59.

Primary sources. *Medieval Carmelite Heritage. Early Reflections on the Nature of the Order*, ed. A. Staring (Rome, 1989), has editions of key texts for the early history of the order. *Bullarium Carmelitanum*, ed. E. Monsignani and J. A. Ximénez, 4 vols (Rome 1715–68), is the standard edition of papal bulls. *Monumenta historica Carmelitana*, ed. B. Zimmerman, I (Lérins, 1907), published in fascicules from 1905 to 1907, includes constitutions from the thirteenth century, ordered and corrected in 1324 together with accounts of them by Sibertus de Beka and Trisse; it also has acts of the general chapters 1327–62 and information on the priors general and university masters of the order. The *Libri ordinis*, or *Acta capitulorum generalium ordinis fratrum B. V. Mariae de Monte Carmelo*, were edited by G. Wessels, 2 vols (Rome, 1912, 1934). Volume I covers 1318 to 1593. The constitutions of 1357 are also in *The Carmelite Constitutions of 1357*, ed. P. F. Robinson (Rome, 1992). C. de Villiers, *Bibliotheca Carmelitana* (Rome, 1752, reprinted 1927), lists works by Carmelites. The provincial chapter constitutions for England are lost, but the Italian ones have been published as follows: Lombardy, *AOC* 3 (from 1328), Tuscia, *Rivista storica carmelitana* (1930) (from 1375). The Rule is most easily accessible in *The Rule of St Albert: Latin Text Edited with an Introduction and English Translation*, by H. Clarke and B. Edwards (Aylesford, 1973); see also C. Cicconetti, *La regola del Carmelo: origine, natura, significato* (Rome, 1973). Various narrative sources have been edited and/or translated, for example: Nicholas of Narbonne, *The Flaming Arrow*, trans. B. Edwards (Durham, 1985); P. Chandler, 'Felipe Ribot's *Liber de institutione primorum monachorum*: A Critical Edition', Ph.D. thesis (Toronto, 1991); *The Life of St Peter Thomas by Philippe de Mézières*, ed. J. Smet (Rome, 1954). See also the *Fasciculi Zizaniorum magistri Johannis Wyclif cum tritico; Ascribed to Thomas Netter of Walden*, ed. W. Waddington Shirley, Rerum Britannicarum medii aevi scriptores, V (London, 1858) and *De visione sancti Simonis Stock*, ed. B. Xiberta, Bibliotheca sacri scapularis, I (Rome, 1950).

Regional and local studies. For Britain see *Carmel in Britain, Essays on the English Carmelite Province*, 2 vols, ed. P. Fitzgerald-Lombard (Rome, 1992) and a third volume edited by R. Copsey (Rome, 2004). Earlier studies include L. C. Sheppard, *The English Carmelites* (London, 1943). The sections on ecclesiastical institutions in the volumes of the *Victoria County History of England* are useful on individual houses as is D. Knowles and R. N. Hadcock, *Medieval Religious Houses. England and Wales* (2nd edn, London, 1971). J. Röhrkasten has published a series of articles on the London mendicants which include the Carmelites: 'Londoners and the London Mendicants in the Late Middle Ages', *Journal of Ecclesiastical History* 47 (1996), pp. 446–77; 'Mendicants in the Metropolis: The Londoners and the Development of the London Friaries', in *Thirteenth Century England*, VI, Proceedings of the Durham Conference 1995, ed. M. Prestwick, R. H. Britnell and R. Frame (Woodbridge, 1997), pp. 61–75; 'The Origin and Early Development of the London Mendicant Houses', in *The Church in the Medieval Town*, ed. T. R. Slater and G. Rosser (Aldershot, 1998), pp. 76–99; 'Local Ties and International Connections of the London Mendicants', in *Mendicants, Military Orders, and Regionalism in Medieval Europe*, ed. J. Sarnowsky (Aldershot, 1999), pp. 145–83; and 'Mendikantische Armut in der Praxis – das Beispiel London', in *Proposito paupertatis. Studien zum Armutsverständnis bei den mittelalterlichen Bettelorden*, ed. G. Melville and A. Kehnel (Münster, 2001), pp. 135–67. A book-length study is forthcoming. Ireland is specifically covered in various articles, including M. Kavanagh, 'The White Friars and the White Castle of Leighlin', *Carloviana: Journal of the Old Carlow Society* 43 (1996, for 1995), pp. 24–6, and D. Mac Íomhair, 'The Carmelites in Ardee', *Journal of the County Louth Archaeological and Historical Society* 20:3 for 1983 (1984), pp. 180–9 (for the Middle Ages see pp. 180–1). For France see in particular R. W. Emery, *The Friars in Medieval France. A Catalogue of French Mendicant Convents 1200–1550* (New York and London, 1962); H. Martin, *Les Ordres mendiants en Bretagne (vers 1230 – vers 1530)* (Paris, 1975); P. Volti, *Les Couvents des ordres mendiants et leur environnement à la fin du Moyen Âge* (Paris, 2003). Local studies include J.-A. Dérens, 'Les Ordres mendiants à Montpellier: religieux de la ville nouvelle ou religieux du consolat', *Annales du Midi* 107 (1995), pp. 277–98; S. Lesur, 'Le Couvent des Grands Carmes de Toulouse au XIIIᵉ siècle', *Les Mendiants en Pays d'Oc au XIIIe siècle*, Cahiers de Fanjeaux 8 (1973), pp. 79–100; H. Tribout Morembert, 'De les Carmes à Metz', *Annuaire de la Société d'histoire et d'archéologie de la Lorraine* 72 (1972), pp. 47–68. Other national or regional studies include Walter Simons, *Stad en apostolaat: de vestigung van de bedelorden in het graafschap Vlaanderen (ca. 1225 – ca. 1350)* (Brussels, 1987); W. Simons, *Bedelordekloosters in het graafschap Vlaanderen. Chronologie en topografie van de bedelordenverspreiding vóór 1350* (Bruges, 1987), which is a catalogue of all mendicant houses in Flanders before 1350; H. Lansink, *Studie en onderwijs in de Nederduitse provincie van de karmelieten gedurende de middeleeuwen* (Nijmegen, 1967); D. F. Huot, 'Die Karmeliter in der Schweiz', *Helvetia Sacra*, VI (Bern, 1974), pp. 1125–75, 1239–43; B. Velasco Bayón, *Historia del Carmelo español*, 3 vols (Rome, 1990–3); J. Webster, *Carmel in Medieval Catalonia* (Leiden, 1999), which includes very useful transcripts of documents, lists of priors and lectors, students, friars, royal chaplains and so on, and J. Webster, 'The Barcelona Carmelite Archives before 1348', *Analecta Sacra Tarraconensia* 65 (1992), pp. 5–10.

Liturgy and music. J. Boyce has written a series of important studies, several of which are in *Carmelus*, but see also 'The Medieval Carmelite Office Tradition', *Acta musicologica* 62 (May–Dec 1990), pp. 129–51; 'The Office of the Three Marys in the Carmelite Liturgy, after the Manuscripts Mainz, Dom- und Diozesanmuseum, Codex E and Florence, Carmine, Ms. o', *Journal of the Plainsong and Mediaeval Music Society* 12 (1989), pp. 1–38; 'Die Mainzer Karmeliterchorbucher und die liturgische Tradition des Karmeliterordens', *Archiv für mittelrheinischekirchengeschichte* 39 (1987), pp. 267–303; and '*Cantica carmelitana*: The Chants of the Carmelite Office', Ph.D. thesis (New York University, 1984), 2 vols. A useful study of the distinctive nature of the Carmelite liturgy and feasts is provided by M. Rickert, *The Reconstructed Carmelite Missal* (London, 1952), while C. Dondi, *The Liturgy of the Canons Regular of the Holy Sepulchre of Jerusalem. A Study and a Catalogue of the Manuscript Sources* (Turnhout, 2004), provides new information on the sources for Carmelite practice. See also P. Kallenberg, *Fontes liturgiae Carmelitanae* (Rome, 1962) for a table comparing the Roman, Dominican and Carmelite calendars.

Education, learning, history and disputes. Beyond the important contributions of Andrew Jotischky (see above) see K. W. Humphreys, *The Library of the Carmelites at Florence at the End of the Fourteenth Century* (Amsterdam, 1964); F.-B. Lickteig, *The German Carmelites at the Medieval Universities* (Rome, 1981); B. Flood, 'The Carmelite Friars in Medieval English Universities and Society 1299–1430', *Recherches de théologie ancienne et médiévale* 55 (1988), pp. 154–83, and B. Xiberta, *De scriptoribus scholasticis saeculi XIV ex ordine Carmelitarum* (Louvain, 1931), who discusses the lives and works of various authors including Gerardo da Bologna, Robert Walsingham, Guiu Terreni, Sibertus de Beka, John Baconthorpe, Michele Aiguani of Bologna, Francis Bacon and Francesc Martí. See also B. Bughetti, 'Statutum concordiae inter quatuor ordines mendicantes annis 1435, 1458 et 1475 sancitum', *Archivum Franciscanum historicum* 25 (1932), pp. 241–56, and G. G. Meersseman, 'Concordia inter quatuor ordines mendicantes', *Archivum fratrum praedicatorum* 4 (1934), pp. 75–97. Surviving medieval catalogues and lists of the books of the Carmelites in England are given in *The Friars' Libraries*, ed. K. W. Humphreys, Corpus of British Medieval Library Catalogues, I (London, 1990).

Carmelite saints. The standard list is *Santi del Carmelo*, ed. L. Saggi (Rome, 1972); on Simon Stock see now also R. Copsey, 'Simon Stock and the Scapular Vision', *Journal of Ecclesiastical History* 50 (1999), pp. 652–83, reprinted in *Carmel in Britain*, III, pp. 75–112.

Carmelite spirituality. K. Egan, 'The Spirituality of the Carmelites', in *Christian Spirituality. High Middle Ages and Reformation*, ed. J. Raitt (London, 1987), pp. 50–62; V. Edden, 'The Mantle of Elijah: Carmelite Spirituality in England in the Fourteenth Century', in *The Medieval Mystical*

Tradition: England, Ireland and Wales, ed. M. Glasscoe (Cambridge, 1999), pp. 67–83; V. Edden, 'Marian Devotion in a Carmelite Sermon Collection of the Late Middle Ages', *Mediaeval Studies* 57 (1995), pp. 102–29 (which discusses Oxford, Bodleian Library, MS Auct. F. inf.1.3, possibly written by a Carmelite scribe for the Worcester house); and N. Morgan, 'The Coronation of the Virgin by the Trinity and Other Texts and Images of the Glorification of Mary in Fifteenth-Century England', in *England in the Fifteenth Century: Proceedings of the 1992 Harlaxton Symposium*, ed. N. Rogers (Stamford, 1994), pp. 223–41.

Carmelite buildings. There have been numerous studies and excavations; see for example A. W. Clapham, 'The Architectural Remains of the Mendicant Orders in Wales', *The Archaeological Journal* 34 (1927), pp. 88–104, 101–4; B. Harbottle, 'Excavations at the Carmelite Friary, Newcastle upon Tyne, 1965 and 1967', *Archaeologia Aeliana: Miscellaneous Tracts Relating to Antiquity* 46 (1968), pp. 163–223; R. M. J. Isserling, 'The Carmelite Friary at Maldon: Excavations 1990–91', *Essex Archaeology and History* 30 (1999), pp. 44–143; *Three Scottish Carmelite Friaries: Aberdeen, Linlithgow and Perth 1980–86*, ed. J. A. Stones (Edinburgh, 1989); A. Randla, 'The Mendicant Orders and Their Architecture in Scotland', in *Mendicants, Military Orders, and Regionalism in Medieval Europe*, ed. J. Sarnowsky (Aldershot, 1999), pp. 243–81, who surveys the foundations of the Carmelites, Franciscans and Dominicans; C. Woodfield, 'Coventry, Whitefriars', in 'Medieval Britain in 1966: part 2, Post Conquest', ed. D. M. Wilson and D. G. Hurst in *Medieval Archaeology* 11 (1967), pp. 278–9; S. Lesur, 'Recherches sur l'église du couvent des Grands Carmes de Toulouse', in *La Naissance et l'essor du gothique méridional au XIIIe siècle*, ed. M.-H. Vicaire, Cahiers de Fanjeaux 9 (1974), pp. 273–88; E. Deighton, 'The Carmelite Friary at Sandwich', in *Archaeologia Cantiana: Being Contributions to the History and Archaeology of Kent* 114 for 1994 (1995), pp. 317–27. The Esslingen am Neckar friary excavations have been published on the web (December, 2005): http://home.bawue.de/~wmwerner/essling/english/index.html

Art and patronage. See the brief summary by D. Howard, 'Carmelite Order', *Dictionary of Art* (London and New York, 1996), V, pp. 777–9; C. Gardner von Teuffel, 'Masaccio and the Pisa Altarpiece: A New Approach', *Jahrbuch der Berliner Museen* 19 (1977), pp. 23–68; J. Cannon, 'The Creation, Meaning, and Audience of the Early Sienese Polyptych: Evidence from the Friars', in *Italian Altarpieces 1250–1550: Function and Design*, ed. E. Borsook and F. Superbi Gioffredi (Oxford, 1994), pp. 41–79; M. Holmes, *Fra Filippo Lippi, the Carmelite Painter* (Yale, 1999); M. Israëls, 'Sassetta's Arte della Lana Altarpiece and the Cult of Corpus Domini in Siena', *The Burlington Magazine* 143 (2001), pp. 532–43; and M. Israëls, 'Altars on the Street. The Wool Guild, the Carmelites and the Feast of Corpus Domini in Siena, 1356–1456', in *Ritual in Renaissance Siena. Comparative Disciplinary Approaches*, ed. P. Jackson, F. Nevola, Special issue of *Renaissance Studies* (forthcoming 2006). There is also a volume of studies dedicated to the Brancacci chapel: *The Brancacci Chapel: A Symposium on Form, Function and Setting*, ed. N. A. Eckstein (Florence and Olschki, forthcoming).

The Observant movement. See L. Saggi, *La congregazione mantovana dei Carmelitani sino alla morte del beato Battista Spagnoli (1516)* (Rome, 1954); P. W. Janssen, *Les Origins de la réforme des Carmes en France au XVIIe siècle* (The Hague, 1969), which includes material on the abuses of the late Middle Ages; O. Steggink, *La reforma del Carmelo español* (Avila, 1993), mostly deals with the later period, but has information on the fourteenth and fifteenth centuries in chapter one. See also J. Smet, 'Pre-Tridentine Reform in the Carmelite Order', in *Reformbemühungen und Observanzbestrebungen im spätmittelalterlichen Ordenswesen*, ed. K. Elm (Berlin, 1989), pp. 293–323; J. Guehenneuc, 'Duchesse et carmálite, Françoise d'Amboise, une femme courageuse et loyale', *Bulletin de la Société archéologique et historique de Nantes et de la Loire-Atlantique* 121 (1985), pp. 33–48; and B. Zimmerman, 'Les Réformes dans l'ordre de Notre-Dame du Mont-Carmel', *Études carmelitaines* 19 (1934), pp. 178–88.

The Austin Friars

For studies encompassing all the friars, see also the section on Carmelites above.

Periodicals and series. *Analecta Augustiniana*, published in Rome since 1905, has always included numerous historical articles and editions of key documents (indices to the articles in the early volumes were published in 1981 and 1983). Originally issued in Latin and including news for the modern order, since 1962 it has been published in the languages of the contributors (mostly Italian) and is exclusively historical. *Augustiniana. Tijdschrift voor de studie van Sint Augustinus en de Augustijnenorde. Revue pour l'étude de saint Augustin et de l'ordre des Augustins* has been published by the Institutum Historicum Augustinianum in Louvain, Belgium, since 1951. *Revista agustiniana*, published in Madrid since 1960, and *Ciudad de Dios*, published by the monastery of the Escorial (Madrid) since 1887, are mainly concerned with spirituality and theology but both have occasional historical articles. *Augustinianum* on the other hand focuses on Augustine and the early Church. Items found in these journals are not normally mentioned below, but *Analecta Augustiniana* and *Augustiniana* in particular have works on many of the subjects listed. *Cassiciacum. Studies in St Augustine and the Augustinian Order (American Series)* also includes numerous volumes on the history of the friars. A website now provides electronic versions in Italian of many of the texts listed below: http://web.tiscali.it/ghirardacci

Primary sources. The best edition of the Rule is L. Verheijen, *La Règle de saint Augustin, i, Tradition manuscrite; ii, Recherches historiques* (Paris, 1967), but see also the more recent articles and updated bibliography provided by the same author in *Augustiniana* 21 (1971) to 36 (1986). The records of general chapters from 1281 to 1497 are in 'Antiquiores quae extant definitiones capitulorum generalium ordinis', ed. P. Esteban, *AA* 2–8 (1907–20). The standard edition of the early constitutions is *Las primitivas constituciones de los Agustinos (Ratisbonenses del año 1290)*, ed. I. Arámburu Cendoya (Valladolid, 1966), which also includes Thomas de Strasbourg's *Additiones*. Papal correspondence concerning the order was originally catalogued in *Bullarium ordinis eremitarum sancti Augustini*, ed. L. Empoli (Rome, 1628), and L. Torelli, *Secoli Agostiniani ovvero historia generale del sagro ordine eremitano*, 8 vols (Bologna 1659–86). B. van Luijk produced a new edition for the early years: *Bullarium ordinis eremitarum sancti Augustini. Periodus formationis (1187–1256)* (Würzburg, 1964), also published in *Augustiniana* 12–14 (1962–4). A convenient regest of all bulls after 1256 is provided by *Bullarium ordinis sancti Augustini regesta*, ed. C. Alonso, of which the first four volumes cover the period down to the Council of Trent (Rome, 1997–9). The extant registers of the priors general are being published in *Fontes historiae ordinis sancti Augustini prima series* (Rome, 1976–); the *Series altera* covers the personal and other letters of priors general starting from Giles of Viterbo, 1494–1517 (Rome 1990–).

Modern sources for saints of the order include *Il processo di canonizzazione di Fra Giovanni Bono (1251–1253/54), fondatore dell'Ordine degli eremiti*, ed. M. Mattei (Rome, 2002) (which contains an Italian translation of the text of the process, some of the key bulls and two later lives) and *Il processo per la canonizzazione di San Nicola da Tolentino*, ed. N. Occhioni (Rome, 1984). The texts on Agostino Novello are in *Acta sanctorum*, May, IV (Paris, 1866), pp. 614–26. The historical work of Jordan of Saxony (Quedlinberg) is available as Jordanus de Saxonia, *Liber vitasfratrum*, ed. R. Arbesmann and W. Hümpfner (New York, 1943), and in English as *The Life of the Brethren*, trans. G. Deigl (Villanova, Pa, 1993). The history of the first English house is documented in *The Cartulary of the Augustinian Friars of Clare*, ed. C. Harper-Bill (Woodbridge, 1991). Sources on the friars in Ireland are to be found in 'Irish Material in the Augustinian Archives, Rome 1354–1624', ed. F. X. Martin and A. de Meijer, *Archivium Hibernicum* 19 (1956), pp. 61–134. Innumerable other sources are edited in the volumes of *Analecta Augustiniana*.

Secondary sources. The fullest account of the order in English remains D. Gutiérrez, *The Augustinians in the Middle Ages 1256–1356*, trans. A. J. Ennis, 1 volume in 2 parts (Villanova, Pa, 1984), originally published as *Los Agustinos en la edad media* (Rome, 1977, 1980), which also includes substantial bibliographies.

Early orders predating the union of 1256. The fundamental works are those of Kaspar Elm published in the 1960s: 'Neue Beiträge zur Geschichte des Augustiner-Eremitenordens. Ein Forschungsbericht', *Archiv für Kulturgeschichte* 42 (1960), pp. 357–87; *Beiträge zur Geschichte des Wilhelmitenordens*, Münstersche Forschungen 14 (Cologne-Graz, 1962); 'Italienische Eremitengemeinschaften des 12. und 13. Jahrhunderts. Studien zur Vorgeschichte des Augustiner-Eremitenordens', in *L'eremitismo in occidente nei secoli xi e xii*. Atti della seconda settimana internazionale di studio, Mendola 1962 (Milan, 1965), pp. 491–559, reprinted in *Vitasfratrum. Beiträge zur Geschichte der Eremiten- und Mendikantenorden des zwölften und dreizehnten Jahrhunderts. Festgabe vom 65. Geburtstag*, ed. D. Berg, Saxonia Franciscana 5 (Berlin, 1994); 'Der Wilhemitenorden. Eine geistliche Gemeinschaft zwischen Eremitenleben, Mönchtum und Mendikantenarmut', ibid., pp. 55–66; and 'Zisterzienser und Wilhelmiten. Ein Beitrag zur Wirkungsgeschichte der Zisterzienserkonstitutionen', *Cîteaux. Commentarii Cistercienses* 15 (1964), pp. 97–124, 177–202, 273–81. On the early hermitages around Siena, see O. Redon, 'L'eremo, la città e la foresta', in *Lecceto e gli eremi agostiniani in terra di Siena* (Siena, 1990), pp. 9–43 also in French as 'Les Éremites des forêts Siennoises (xiiie – début xive siècle)', *Revue Mabillon* 50 (1990), pp. 213–40. The most recent study of the Augustinians in the Marche, the home of Nicola da Tolentino, is *Gli Agostiniani nelle Marche. Architettura, arte, spiritualità*, ed. F. Mariano (Milan, 2004), with extensive bibliography of earlier works on the region. A detailed account of the early German houses is provided in volume one of A. Kunzelmann, *Geschichte der deutschen Augustiner-Eremiten*, Cassiciacum 26, 7 vols (Würzburg 1969–76). See also F. Roth, 'Cardinal Richard Annibaldi. First Protector of the Augustinian Order (1243–76)', *Augustiniana* 2 (1952), pp. 26–60, 108–49, 230–47; 3 (1953), pp. 21–34, 283–313; 4 (1954), pp. 5–24. The most recent study is C. Andenna, '*Non est haec vita apostolica, sed confusio babylonica*. L'invenzione di un ordine nel secolo xiii', in *Regulae –consuetudines – statuta. Studi sulle fonti normative degli ordini religiosi nei secoli centrali del medioevo*, ed. C. Andenna and G. Melville, Vita Regularis. Abhandlungen (Münster, 2005), pp. 569–632.

Regional studies. On the English friars the first substantial survey was provided by the Jesuit historian Aubrey Gwynn, *The English Austin Friars in the Time of Wyclif* (Oxford, 1940), followed by Francis Roth, *English Austin Friars 1249–1538*, 2 vols (New York, vol. I 1966, vol II 1961); volume two is a vast calendar of sources. Both Roth's volumes also appeared as instalments in *Augustiniana* 8–17 (1958–67). On the friars in France see the section on Carmelites, 'Regional and local studies' above. On the Italian hermit friars see *Gli Agostiniani a Venezia e la chiesa di Sto Stefano* (Venice, 1997) and numerous articles in *AA*. The German provinces are surveyed in A. Kunzelmann, *Geschichte der deutschen Augustiner-Eremiten*, Cassiciacum 26,

7 vols (Würzburg 1969–76). Local studies include K. Elm, 'Die Augustiner-Eremiten in Westfalen', in *Das monastische Westfalen – Klöster und Stifte 800–1800* (Münster, 1982), pp. 167–76, reprinted in Elm, *Mittelalterliches Ordensleben in Westfalen und am Niederrhein* (Paderborn, 1989), and C. Andenna, '*De introitu fratrum ad civitates*: una fondazione dell'*ordo fratrum eremitarum* a Regensburg', *Studia monastica. Beiträge zum klösterlichen Leben im Mittelalter* (Münster, 2004), pp. 125–50. For the Austrian houses see F. Rennhofer, 'Augustinerklöster in Oesterreich', *Augustiniana* 6 (1956), pp. 491–536 and Rennhofer, *Die Augustiner-Eremiten in Wien, Ein Beitrag zur Kulturgeschichte Wiens*, Cassiciacum 13 (Würzburg, 1956). Cassiciacum also has volumes on Prague and Würzburg. On the area of modern-day Switzerland see P. Zimmer *et al.*, 'Die Augustiner-Eremiten in der Schweiz', *Helvetia sacra*, IV, 6, ed. P. Braun (Basel, 2003), pp. 21–182, and D. Bellettati *et al.*, 'Die Augustinerinnen in der Schweiz', ibid., pp. 185–275. For Spain, B. Estrada Robles, *Los Agustinos ermitaños en España hasta el siglo xix* (Madrid, 1988), provides a summary catalogue of the houses and outline history. See also the various articles in *Conventos agustinos: Madrid, 20–24 de octubre de 1997: Actas del 10 congreso internacional de historia de la orden de San Agustín*, ed. R. Lazcano, Studia Augustiniana historica 11–12 (Rome, 1998). *Revista agustiniana* 35, nos 106–8 (1994), was dedicated to the history of the order on its 750th anniversary (1244–1994) and includes a few articles on houses founded in the Middle Ages.

A detailed account of **the building of an Augustinian church** is provided by *La chiesa e il convento di Santo Spirito a Firenze*, **ed.** C. Acidini Luchinat (Florence, 1996). For the excavations at Leicester, see *The Austin Friars, Leicester*, ed. J. E. Mellor and T. Pearce, CBA Research Report 35 (London, 1981).

Spirituality. See A. Zumkeller, 'The Spirituality of the Augustinians', in *Christian Spirituality, High Middle Ages and Reformation*, ed. J. Raitt (London, 1987) 63–74.

The structure of education and the learning of the Austin Friars has been a major area of research: see D. Gutiérrez, 'Los estudios en la orden agustiniana desde la edad media hasta la contemporánea', *AA* 33 (1970), pp. 75–149, and the various writings of E. Ypma, in particular, *La Formation des professeurs chez les ermites de saint Augustin* (Paris, 1956). A recent study of the audience for one of the most successful works by an Augustinian friar is C. F. Briggs, *Giles of Rome's* De regimine principum: *Reading and Writing Politics at Court and University c. 1275 – c. 1525* (Cambridge, 1999). The fragmentary medieval and early modern catalogues of the libraries of the Austin Friars in England are edited in *The Friars' Libraries*, ed. K. W. Humphreys, Corpus of British Medieval Library Catalogues, I (London, 1990).

Criticisms of William of Saint-Amour. See M.-M. Dufeil, *Guillaume de Saint-Amour et la polémique universitaire parisienne 1250–1259* (Paris, 1972).

On **historiograpny and conflicts** which arose from it see K. Walsh, *The 'Liber de vita evangelica' of Geoffrey Hardeby, A Study in the Mendicant Controversies of the Fourteenth Century* (Rome, 1973); Walsh, *A Fourteenth-Century Scholar and Primate. Richard FitzRalph in Oxford, Avignon and Armagh* (Oxford, 1981); K. Elm, 'Augustinus canonicus – Augustinus eremita. A Quattrocento Cause Célèbre', in *Christianity and the Renaissance. Image and Religious Imagination in the Quattrocento*, ed. T. Verdon, J. Henderson (Syracuse, 1990), pp. 83–107, and E. Saak, *High Way to Heaven. The Augustinian Platform between Reform and Reformation 1292–1524* (Leiden, 2002).

Art. See the fundamental work of J. and P. Courcelle, *Iconographie de saint Augustin*, 5 vols (Paris, 1965–91); *Augustine in Iconography, History and Legend*, ed. J. C. Schnaubelt, F. Van Fleteren (New York, 1999); *Arte e spiritualità negli ordini mendicanti. Gli Agostiniani e il Cappellone di San Nicola a Tolentino* (Rome, 1992); and *Arte e spiritualità nell'ordine agostiniano e il convento di San Nicola a Tolentino* (Rome, 1994); an excellent case study is provided by L. Bourdua, '*De origine et progressu ordinis fratrum heremitarum*: Guariento and the Eremitani in Padua', *Papers of the British School at Rome* 66 (1998), pp. 177–92. See also *Hermits and History: Art and the Augustinian Order in Late Medieval and Early Renaissance Italy*, ed. L. Bourdua and A. Dunlop (forthcoming, Ashgate, 2006).

Observants. See the works of K. Walsh: 'The Observant Congregations of the Augustinian Friars in Italy', unpublished D.Phil. thesis (Oxford, 1972); 'The Observance: Sources for a History of the Observant Reform Movement in the Order of Augustinian Friars in the Fourteenth and Fifteenth centuries', *Rivista di storia della chiesa in Italia* 31 (1977), pp. 40–67; 'Papal Policy and Local Reform: a) The Beginnings of the Augustinian Observance in Tuscany; b) *Congregatio Ilicetana*: the Augustinian Observant Movement in Tuscany and the Humanist Ideal', *Römische historische Mitteilungen* 21 (1979), pp. 35–57; 22 (1980), pp. 105–45; 'The Augustinian Observance in Siena in the age of Santa Caterina and San Bernardino', in *Atti del simposio internazionale Cateriniano-Bernardiniano*, ed. D. Maffei and P. Nardi (Siena, 1982), pp. 939–50; also B. Szabò-Bechstein, 'Die sieneser Urkunden der Staatsbibliothek preussischer Kulturbesitz, Berlin (12.–18.Jh.): die Fonds S. Leonardo al Lago, S. Salvatore di Lecceto, S. Maria del Carmine und Piccolomini', in *Quellen und Forschungen aus italienischen Archiven und Bibliotheken* (1976), pp. 156–99; A. Kunzelmann, *Die sächsische-thüringische Provinz und die sächsische Reformkongregation bis zum Untergang der beiden* (Würzburg, 1974) = vol. 5 of his *Geschichte der deutsche Augustiner-Eremiten*; L. Alvarez Gutierrez, *El movimento 'observante' agustiniano en España y su culminación en tiempo de los reyes católicos* (Rome, 1978), based on the author's doctoral thesis at the Universidad Complutense, Madrid (which also includes material on the early history of the order in the peninsula); A. Zumkeller 'Der

Liber de vita monastica des Conradus de Zenn O.E.S.A. (†1460) und die Spiritualität der spätmittelalterlichen "observantia regularis"', *Revista agustiniana* 33 (1992), pp. 921–38; F. X. Martin, 'The Irish Augustinian Reform of the Fifteenth Century', in *Medieval Studies Presented to Aubrey Gwynn S.J.*, ed. J. Watt *et al.* (Dublin, 1961), pp. 230–64; K. Elm, 'Verfall und Erneuerung des Ordenswesens im Spätmittelalter', in *Untersuchungen zu Kloster und Stift*, ed J. Fleckenstein (Göttingen, 1980), pp. 188–238 and *Reformbemühungen und Observanzbestrebungen im spätmittelalterlichen Ordenswesen*, ed. K. Elm (Berlin, 1989).

The Sack Friars

In 1894, A. G. Little, a noted historian of the mendicant orders, wrote that the history of the Sack Friars 'has attracted, as it deserves, little attention' ('The Friars of the Sack', *English Historical Review* 9 (1894), pp. 121–7). Despite his disparaging assessment, there has been a gradual accumulation of studies over the past century tending to contradict Little's pessimism. Already in the early 1900s there were a few local studies, such as L. Feliu, 'El monestir de frares de Penitència de Jesucrist de Barcelona (1260–1293)', *Analecta sacra Tarraconensia* 10 (1934), pp. 45–59, then in mid-century Richard W. Emery produced three articles which fundamentally changed the level of information available about the order: 'The Friars of the Sack', *Speculum* 18 (1943), pp. 323–34; 'The Second Council of Lyons and the Mendicant Orders', *Catholic Historical Review* 39 (1953–4), pp. 257–71; and 'A Note on the Friars of the Sack', *Speculum* 35 (1960), pp. 591–5.

A more recent **outline** of the order's history and of its expansion in the Empire is provided by K. Elm, 'Ausbreitung, Wirksamkeit und Ende der provençalischen Sackbrüder (Fratres de Poenitentia Jesu Christi) in Deutschland und den Niederlanden. Ein Beitrag zur kurialen und konziliaren Ordenspolitik des 13. Jahrhunderts', in *Francia. Forschungen zur westeuropäischen Geschichte* 1 (1973), pp. 257–324 (completed in 1970), reprinted in K. Elm, *Vitasfratrum*, ed. D. Berg (Berlin, 1994), pp. 67–118. R. I. Burns provides a swift but comprehensive survey in 'Penitenza di Gesu Cristo, Frati della', *DIP* VI (Rome, 1980), cols 1398–1403. Important details for the early history of the order are also to be found in P.-A. Amargier, 'Les Frères de la Pénitence de Jésus Christ ou du Sac', *Provence historique* 15 (1965), pp. 158–67. G. M. Giacomozzi published a general study, 'L'ordine della penitenza di Gesu Cristo, contributo alla storia della spiritualità del secolo xiii', *Studi storici dell'ordine dei Servi di Maria* 8 (1957–8), pp. 3–60, which was reprinted together with a study of the constitutions (see below) as a single volume, *L'ordine della penitenza di Gesù Cristo, contributo alla storia della spiritualità del secolo XIII: excerpta ex dissertatione ad lauream in Facultate historiae ecclesiasticae Pontificiae Universitatis Gregorianae* (Vicenza, 1962).

Primary sources. The constitutions of the order are transcribed in G. M. Giacomozzi, 'Le "Constitutiones fratrum de poenitentia Jhesu Christi"', *Studi storici dell'ordine dei Servi di Maria* 10 (1960), pp. 42–99, reprinted in Giacomozzi, *L'ordine della penitenza*, as above; The only other extensive text produced by the order, a Provençal *exempla* collection, was originally published by J. T. Welter, 'Un receuil d'exempla du XIII⁰ siècle', *Études franciscaines* 30 (1913), pp. 646–65; 31 (1914), pp. 194–213, 312–20. This collection has since been the subject of close study by I. Rava-Cordier, 'La Proximité comme élément de persuasion: les références géographiques, sociales et culturelles dans les *exempla* d'un Sachet provençal au XIII⁰ siècle', in *La Prédication en Pays d'Oc (XIIe – début XVe siècle)*, Cahiers de Fanjeaux 32 (1997), pp. 225–48, who reports that she is preparing an edition. The letter of the last rector general *c.* 1274 is published in A. G. Rigg, 'The Lament of the Friars of the Sack', *Speculum* 55 (1980), pp. 84–90.

Regional and local studies. On the German friars see Elm (as above) and J. Asen, 'Die Begarden und die Sackbrüder in Köln', *Annalen des historischen Vereins für den Niederrhein* 115 (1929), pp. 167–79, 179; for Flanders see the works of Walter Simons listed above in the section on Carmelites, 'Regional and local studies'. R. I. Burns is preparing a comprehensive study of the Friars of the Sack in the Crown of Catalonia-Aragon, and in the meantime has produced a series of useful studies: 'The Friars of the Sack in Valencia', *Speculum* 36 (1961), pp. 435–8, summarised and updated in Burns, *The Crusader Kingdom of Valencia*, 2 vols (Cambridge, Mass., 1967), I, pp. 207–9; 'The Friars of the Sack in Puigcerdà. A Lost Chapter of 13ᵗʰ-Century Religious History', *Anuario de Estudios Medievales* 18 (1988), pp. 217–27; 'The Friars of the Sack in Barcelona: Financial and Pastoral Profile', *Anuario de Estudios Medievales* 28 (1998), pp. 419–35; see also L. Simon, 'The Friars of the Sack in Majorca', *Journal of Medieval History* 18 (1992), pp. 279–92, and N. Jaspert, *Stift und Stadt. Das Heiliggrabpriorat von Santa Anna und das Regularkanonikerstift Santa Eulalia del Camp im mittelalterlichen Barcelona (1145–1423)* (Berlin, 1996). For France, see M. de Fontette, 'Les Mendiants supprimés au 2ᶜ concile de Lyon 1274: Frères Sachets et Frères Pies', in *Les Mendiants en Pays d'Oc au 13e siècle*, Cahiers de Fanjeaux 8 (1973), pp. 193–216. The specific case of Paris is studied in E. Ypma, 'L'Acquisition du couvent parisien des Sachets par les Augustins', *Augustiniana* 9 (1959), pp. 105–17. On Italy, see A. Samaritani, 'I frati Saccati a san Paolo di Ferrara (1260 *ca.* – 1295 *ca.*)', *Carmelus* 31 (1984), pp. 40–64; D.-M. Montagna, 'Una progettata fondazione a Perugia dei frati della Penitenza di Gesù Cristo (1273–1274)', *Studi storici dell'ordine dei Servi di Maria* 24 (1974), pp. 272–3; B. van Luijk, *Gli eremiti neri nel dugento con particolare riguardo al territorio pisano e toscano* (Pisa, 1968). For England, see H. F. Chettle, 'The Friars of the Sack in England', *Downside Review* 63 (1945), pp. 239–57.

Pied Friars

The fundamental work remains Richard W. Emery, 'The Friars of the Blessed Mary and the Pied Friars', *Speculum* 24 (1949), pp. 228–38, but F. A. dal Pino, *I frati Servi di Sta Maria: dalle origini all'approvazione (1233 ca. – 1304)*, 2 vols (Louvain, 1972), I, pp. 672–80, provides a useful outline. There is a brief summary and convenient list of primary sources in A. Franchi, 'Beata Maria Madre di Cristo, Frati o Servi della', in *DIP* I (Rome, 1973), cols 1143–5. Information on individual houses is available in the work of de Fontette, Elm, Knowles and Simons, as listed above.

INDEX

29–32, 47, 50–1; and Sack Friars 198–9, 201–2, 207, 213, 219–20

patronage, royal: and Augustinians 106–7, 134, 141; and Carmelites 25–6, 29–30, 47, 50–1; and Pied Friars 226–7; and Sack Friars 183–4, 199–201, 209–10, 214

Paul, Jerome (Augustinian) 164

Pavia, Carmelites 21, 40

peacemaking and diplomacy, mendicant role 29, 79, 129, 195–6

Peckham, John (Archbishop of Canterbury) 27

penance, and Sack Friars 177, 178, 179, 212, 223

Pere d'Albarada (Augustinian) 196

Pere III of Aragon 26, 31

Pere III of Valencia 200

Peter Comestor, *Historia scholastica* 195

Peter of Corbie 23n.

Peter Damian 71

Peter the Lombard, *Sentences* 43, 60 150, 157, 195, 198

Peter of Tewkesbury (Franciscan provincial) 183, 208

Petrus, Simone (Carmelite) 61

Philip of Brünn (Augustinian) 125

Philip IV of France 93, 141, 149, 150, 219

Phillip III of France and Navarre 26, 212, 214, 229

Pied Friars 224–30; buildings 228; and Council of Lyons (1274) 2, 20, 91, 208, 212, 229, 231; geographical spread 226, 227–8; habit 226; and lay penitential movements 224; and learning 3; names 225; origins 3, 4, 224; and poverty 2; rule 224; transfer of houses 229–30; urban settlement 228

Pierozzi, Antonino (bishop of Florence) 223

Pierre de Millau (Carmelite prior general) 20, 42, 53, 231

Pierre de Narbonne (Sack prior) 213

Piers the Plowman's Crede 64, 144

Pirn, Dietrich Ladtner von (architect) 115

Pisa, Council (1411) 51, 164

Pius II, Pope 64, 135

plays, religious 33, 146–7

Poggi, Giovanni Battista (Augustinian) 166

Poland: and Augustinian nuns 138; and Augustinians 100, 105; and Carmelites 30

Ponç de Gualba (bishop of Barcelona) 110

Portugal: and Augustinian nuns 138; and Augustinians 99, 106

poverty: and Augustinians 88, 122–3, 154–5, 156, 163, 166; and Brettini 82, 187; and Carmelites 14, 35, 41, 50, 55, 67; Franciscan 154–5, 165, 209; and Pied Friars 2; and Sack Friars 177, 178–9, 187–8, 207, 212

Prague: Augustinian nuns 136; Augustinians 105, 133, 157; Carmelites 25, 44

preaching: Augustinian 88, 90, 92–3, 110–11, 118, 140–1; Bonite 80; Carmelite 17, 30, 41, 42, 44–6, 49; of crusade 92–3, 142; and education 42; and mendicant orders 17–18, 87; Sack Friars 180, 194, 196–8, 204

Premonstratensians (White Canons) 21, 102, 221, 230

priors: Augustinian 98, 123, 150; Pied Friars 226; Sack Friars 192; *see also* priors general; priors provincial

priors general: Augustinian 92–3, 96–7, 103, 139, 140, 150, 164–70; Bonite 80–1; Carmelite 12, 17, 19, 20, 22–3, 43, 44–5; Williamite 77

priors provincial: Augustinian 95, 96, 98, 102–3, 104, 130; Carmelite 12, 22–3, 27, 28, 30, 41, 47, 50–1, 54, 58, 61–3, 66; Pied Friars 226; Sack Friars 178, 194, 207

processions 31–2, 141, 146, 203–4

proctors: Augustinian 97, 123; Carmelite 15, 19, 21, 22, 45; Sack Friars 181

profession: age at 47, 67, 121, 137, 155; and Augustinians 84, 122, 127, 137; and Bonites 80; and Carmelites 23, 41, 42, 46, 67

Proles, Andreas (Augustinian) 166–7, 168

property, communal 88, 154; Augustinian 94, 111–12, 114, 118, 140, 142–3; Brettini 82, 187; Carmelite 14, 15, 31; Sack Friars 187, 207–8, 215–17

property, personal: and Augustinians